Brilliant Guides

What you need to know and how to do it

When you're working on your computer and come up against a problem that you're unsure how to solve, or want to accomplish something in an application that you aren't sure how to do, where do you look?? Manuals and traditional training guides are usually too big and unwieldy and are intended to be used as an end-to-end training resource, making it hard to get to the info you need right away without having to wade through pages of background information that you just don't need at that moment – and helplines are rarely that helpful!

Brilliant guides have been developed to allow you to find the info you need easily and without fuss and guide you through the task using a highly visual, step-by-step approach – providing exactly what you need to know when you need it!!

Brilliant guides provide the quick easy-to-access information that you need, using a detailed index and troubleshooting guide to help you find exactly what you need to know, and then presenting each task on one or two pages. Numbered steps then guide you through each task or problem, using numerous screenshots to illustrate each step. Added features include "See Also…" boxes that point you to related tasks and information in the book, whilst "Did you know?…" sections alert you to relevant expert tips, tricks and advice to further expand your skills and knowledge.

In addition to covering all major office applications, and related computing subjects, the *Brilliant* series also contains titles that will help you in every aspect of your working life, such as writing the perfect CV, answering the toughest interview questions and moving on in your career.

Brilliant guides are the light at the end of the tunnel when you are faced with any minor or major task!

Acknowledgments

Perspection, Inc.

Brilliant Microsoft® Access 2013 has been created by the professional trainers and writers at Perspection, Inc. to the standards you've come to expect from Que publishing. Together, we are pleased to present this training book.

Perspection, Inc. is a software training company committed to providing information and training to help people use software more effectively in order to communicate, make decisions, and solve problems. Perspection writes and produces software training books, and develops multimedia and web-based training. Since 1991, we have written more than 130 computer books, with several bestsellers to our credit, and sold over 5 million books.

This book incorporates Perspection's training expertise to ensure that you'll receive the maximum return on your time. You'll focus on the tasks and skills that increase productivity while working at your own pace and convenience.

We invite you to visit the Perspection web site at:

www.perspection.com

Acknowledgments

The task of creating any book requires the talents of many hard-working people pulling together to meet impossible deadlines and untold stresses. We'd like to thank the outstanding team responsible for making this book possible: the writer, Steve Johnson; the production editor, James Teyler; the editor and proofreader, Beth Teyler; and the indexer, Katherine Stimson.

At Que publishing, we'd like to thank Greg Wiegand and Loretta Yates for the opportunity to undertake this project, Cindy Teeters for administrative support, and Lori Lyons for your production expertise and support.

Perspection

About the Author

Steve Johnson has written more than 80 books on a variety of computer software, including Adobe Edge Animate, Adobe Photoshop CS6, Adobe Dreamweaver CS6, Adobe InDesign CS6, Adobe Illustrator CS6, Adobe Flash Professional CS5, Microsoft Windows 8, Microsoft Office 2013 and 2010, Microsoft Office 2008 for the Macintosh, and Apple OS X Mountain Lion. In 1991, after working for Apple Computer and Microsoft, Steve founded Perspection, Inc., which writes and produces software training. When he is not staying up late writing, he enjoys coaching baseball, playing golf, gardening, and spending time with his wife, Holly, and three children, JP, Brett, and Hannah. Steve and his family live in Northern California, but can also be found visiting family all over the western United States.

a

Contents

C

Introduction

Welcome to *Brilliant Microsoft® Access 2013*, a visual quick reference book that shows you how to work efficiently with Microsoft Access. This book provides complete coverage of basic to advanced Access skills.

How This Book Works

You don't have to read this book in any particular order. We've designed the book so that you can jump in, get the information you need, and jump out. However, the book does follow a logical progression from simple tasks to more complex ones. Each task is presented on no more than two facing pages, which lets you focus on a single task without having to turn the page. To find the information that you need, just look up the task in the table of contents or index, and turn to the page listed. Read the task introduction, follow the step-by-step instructions in the left column along with screen illustrations in the right column, and you're done.

What's New

If you're searching for what's new in Access 2013, just look for the icon: **New!**. The new icon appears in the table of contents and throughout this book so you can quickly and easily identify a new or improved feature in Access 2013. A complete description of each new feature appears in the New Features guide in the back of this book.

Keyboard Shortcuts

Most menu commands have a keyboard equivalent, such as Ctrl+P, as a quicker alternative to using the mouse. A complete list of keyboard shortcuts is available on the web at *www.perspection.com*.

How You'll Learn

How This Book Works

What's New

Keyboard Shortcuts

Step-by-Step Instructions

Real World Examples

Workshops

Microsoft Office Specialist

Get More on the Web

Step-by-Step Instructions

This book provides concise step-by-step instructions that show you "how" to accomplish a task. Each set of instructions includes illustrations that directly correspond to the easy-to-read steps. Also included in the text are time-savers, tables, and sidebars to help you work more efficiently or to teach you more in-depth information. A "Did You Know?" provides tips and techniques to help you work smarter, while a "See Also" leads you to other parts of the book containing related information about the task.

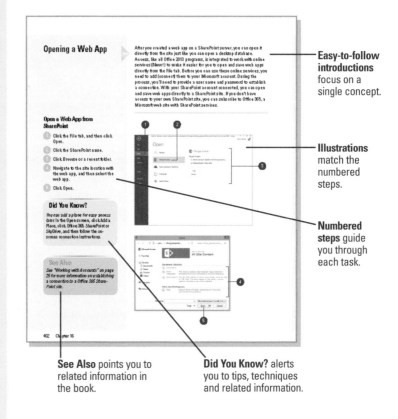

Easy-to-follow introductions focus on a single concept.

Illustrations match the numbered steps.

Numbered steps guide you through each task.

See Also points you to related information in the book.

Did You Know? alerts you to tips, techniques and related information.

Real World Examples

This book uses real world examples files to give you a context in which to use the task. By using the example files, you won't waste time looking for or creating sample files. You get a start file and a result file, so you can compare your work. Not every topic needs an example file, such as changing options, so we provide a complete list of the example files used through out the book. The example files that you need for project tasks along with a complete file list are available on the web at *www.perspection.com*.

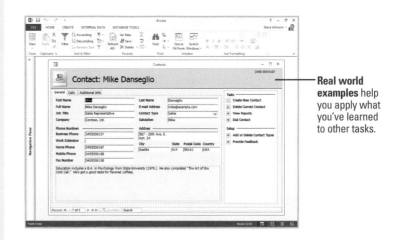

Real world examples help you apply what you've learned to other tasks.

Workshops

This book shows you how to put together the individual step-by-step tasks into in-depth projects with the Workshops. You start each project with a sample file, work through the steps, and then compare your results with a project results file at the end. The Workshop projects and associated files are available on the web at *www.perspection.com*.

Workshops

Introduction

The Workshops are all about being creative and thinking outside of the box. These workshops will help your right-brain soar, while making your left-brain happy, by explaining why things work the way they do. Exploring possibilities is great fun; however, always stay grounded with knowledge of how things work.

Getting and Using the Project Files

Each project in the Workshops includes a start file to help you get started with the project, and a final file to provide you with the results of the project so you can see how well you accomplished the task.

Before you can use the project files, you need to download them from the Web. You can access the files at www.perspection.com in the software downloads area. After you download the files from the Web, uncompress the files into a folder on your hard drive to which you have easy access from Microsoft Access 2013.

Project 1: Creating a Web App

Skills and Tools: Create a Web App on a SharePoint site

A web app in Access provides a browser-based database app that uses SQL Azure or SQL Server. A web app resides on a SharePoint server, such as Office 365 site, a subscription-based Microsoft SharePoint site, unlike a desktop database, which resides on your local system. A web app can be viewed, used and shared on the web. You can use a template to create a web app, or you can create a custom one from scratch. Each template provides a complete out-of-the-box database with predefined fields, tables, queries, reports, and forms, which you can customize. When you create a web app database, you need to assign a name and web server location. To add a location for easy access, you can click Accounts on the File tab. As you work on the app, Access automatically saves it to the server periodically.

The Project

In this project, you'll learn how to create a web app on an Office 365 SharePoint site, add tables, enter data, customize the layout, and use on the web.

1

The **Workshops** walks you through in-depth projects to help you put Microsoft Access to work.

Microsoft Office Specialist

This book prepares you for the Microsoft Office Specialist (MOS) exam for Microsoft Access 2013. Each MOS certification exam has a set of objectives, which are organized into broader skill sets. To prepare for the MOS certification exam, you should review and perform each task identified with a MOS objective to confirm that you can meet the requirements for the exam. Information about the MOS program is available in the back of this book. The MOS objectives and the specific pages that cover them are available on the web at *www.perspection.com*.

Microsoft Office Specialist

About the MOS Program

The Microsoft Office Specialist (MOS) certification is the globally recognized standard for validating expertise with the Microsoft Office suite of business productivity programs. Earning an MOS certificate acknowledges you have the expertise to work with Microsoft Office programs. To earn the MOS certification, you must pass a certification exam for the Microsoft Office desktop applications of Microsoft Word, Excel, PowerPoint, Outlook, Access, OneNote, SharePoint, or Office 365. (The availability of Microsoft Office Specialist certification exams varies by program, program version, and language. Visit www.microsoft.com and search on MOS or Microsoft Office Specialist for exam availability and more information about the program.) The Microsoft Office Specialist program is the only Microsoft-approved program in the world for certifying proficiency with Microsoft Office programs.

What Does This Logo Mean?

It means this book has been approved by the Microsoft Office Specialist program to be certified courseware for learning Microsoft Access 2013 and preparing for the certification exam. This book will prepare you for the Microsoft Office Specialist exam for Microsoft Access 2013. Each certification level, either Core or Expert, has a set of objectives, which are organized into broader skill sets. Content that pertains to a Microsoft Office Specialist objective is identified with the following objective number and the specific pages throughout this book:

 AC13S-1.1
AC13S-2.2

451

Get More on the Web

In addition to the information in this book, you can also get more information on the web to help you get up to speed faster with Access 2013. Some of the information includes:

Transition Helpers

◆ **Only New Features.** Download and print the new feature tasks as a quick and easy guide.

Productivity Tools

◆ **Keyboard Shortcuts.** Download a list of keyboard shortcuts to learn faster ways to get the job done.

More Content

◆ **Photographs.** Download photographs and other graphics to use in your Office documents.

◆ **More Content.** Download new content developed after publication. For example, you can download a chapter on SharePoint server and Office 365.

You can access these additional resources on the web at *www.perspection.com*.

Keyboard Shortcuts

Microsoft Access 2013

If a command on the ribbon or a menu includes a keyboard reference, known as a **keyboard shortcut**, in a ScreenTip or next to the command name, you can perform the action by pressing and holding the first key, and then pressing the second key to perform the command quickly. In some cases, a keyboard shortcut uses three keys. Simply press and hold the first two keys, and then press the third key. For keyboard shortcuts in which you press one key immediately followed by another key, the keys to press are separated by a comma (,). Keyboard shortcuts provide an alternative to using the mouse and make it easy to perform repetitive commands.

Finding a Keyboard Shortcut

To help you find the keyboard shortcut you're looking for, the shortcuts are organized in categories and listed with page numbers.

Access App, 2
Desktop Database, 2
Design, Layout or Datasheet views, 8
Editing, 6
Help, 5
Navigating Records, 7

Navigation Pane, 4
Office, 9
Print Preview, 9
Ribbon 5
Text and Data, 8
Windows Operations, 10

Function Keys

Alt+Function, 11
Function, 10
Ctrl+Function, 11
Ctrl+Alt+Function, 12

Alt+Shift+Function, 12
Shift+Function, 10
Ctrl+Shift+Function, 11

If you're searching for new keyboard shortcuts in Microsoft Access 2013, just look for the letter: N. The N appears in the Keyboard Shortcuts table so you can quickly and easily identify new or changed shortcuts.

1

Additional content is available on the web. You can download keyboard shortcuts.

Getting Started with Access

Introduction

Microsoft Access 2013 is a database program that allows you to:

◆ Store an almost limitless amount of information.

◆ Organize information in a way that makes sense for how you work.

◆ Retrieve information based on selection criteria you specify.

◆ Create forms that make it easier to enter information.

◆ Generate meaningful and insightful reports that can combine data, text, graphics, and other objects.

◆ Create web apps that allow users to enter and work with data on the web from a browser.

Access helps you start working with databases right away by providing template database applications you can use to store your own personal or business data. Access also offers a few samples that aid you in creating common business databases. These sample databases may give you some ideas for designing your own database for storing types of data not covered by the existing databases.

When you are working with an existing database, however, you don't need to worry about the complexities of database design. You just need to know how to move around the database you are using. The tasks that you are likely to perform with an existing database include entering and viewing data or subsets of data, creating and printing reports, and working efficiently with all the windows in front of you.

What You'll Do

Understand How Databases Store Data

Start Access

Use the Ribbon

Choose Commands

Work with the Ribbon and Toolbars

Choose Dialog Box Options

Use the Status Bar

Create and Open a Database

Convert an Existing Database

View the Access Window

Arrange Windows

Use Task and Window Panes

Get Help While You Work

Save a Database

Save a Database with Different Formats

Work with Accounts

Work with Online Storage

Close a Database and Exit Access

Understanding How Databases Store Data

Storing Data on a Computer

Some lists can serve a much more useful purpose when stored on a computer. For example, the names, addresses, and phone numbers you jot down on cards or in a paper address book are only used when you have the paper list in your hand. Suppose you currently store names and addresses on cards. All the information about a particular person is stored in one place.

If you store that list on a computer, however, you can do much more with it than just refer to it. For example, you can generate lists of your most important phone numbers to put next to every phone in the house, you can print mailing labels for greeting cards, you can create lists of this month's birthdays, and so on.

There are a number of ways to store lists on a computer. For example, you can store a list in a Microsoft Word table or on a Microsoft Excel spreadsheet.

If you place this information in a Word table or on an Excel spreadsheet, you are faced with a problem; you end up repeating some of the information. Consider what happens if a family moves or a last name is changed. You have to ensure that information is updated everywhere it's stored. For a small list that might not matter, but for a large list with information that requires constant updating (such as an address list), it is a huge task to keep data up-to-date in this way.

Storing Data in a Database

If, on the other hand, you save address information in an Access desktop database, you can ensure that each piece of information is entered only once.

An Access desktop database consists of objects, such as tables, forms, queries, reports, macros, and modules.

- A **table** is a collection of related information about a topic, such as names and addresses. A table consists of fields and records. A field stores each piece of information in a table, such as first name, last name, or address. A record is a collection of all the fields for one person.

- A **form** provides an easy way to view and enter information into a database. Typically, forms display one record at a time.

- A **query** is a method to find information in a database. The information you find with a query is based on conditions you specify.

- **Reports** are documents that summarize information from the database.

- A **macro** saves you time by automating a series of actions into one action.

- **Modules** are programs you create in a programming language called Visual Basic for Applications (VBA), which extend the functionality of a database.

Desktop Database

Database objects

A database table with fields and records

Starting Access

The two quickest ways to start Microsoft Access are to select it on the Start screen (Win 8) (**New!**) or on the Start menu (Win 7). Access lets you work the way you like and start programs with a click of a button. When you start Access, a program window opens, displaying the Start screen (**New!**) where you can create or open a document in order to quickly get started.

Start Access

1 Start Windows, if necessary, and then use the method for your Windows version.

- ◆ **Windows 8**. Display the Start screen; click or tap the **Start** button on the Charm bar.

- ◆ **Windows 7**. Click **Start** on the taskbar, point to **All Programs** (which changes to Back), and then point to **Microsoft Office**.

2 Click **Access 2013**.

If Office asks you to activate the program, follow the instructions enter an account or product key. to complete the process.

TIMESAVER *To change the accounts, click the File tab, click Account, and then click the Switch Account link.*

Did You Know?

You can create a program shortcut from the Start menu to the desktop. Right-click the Microsoft Access 2013 program on the Start menu or screen. For Win 8, click the Pin To Taskbar button on the App bar. For Win 7, point to Send To, and then click Desktop (Create Shortcut).

You can start Access and open a document from an Explorer window. Double-clicking any Access file icon in an Explorer window opens that file and Access.

Start screen   User name (account)

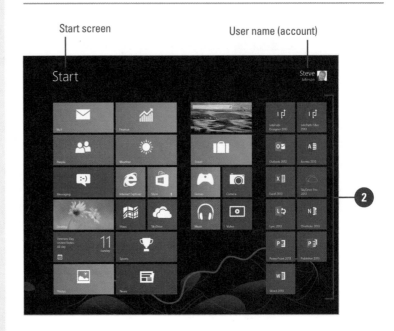

Access 2013 System Requirements

Hardware/Software	Minimum (Recommended)
Computer Processor	1 gigahertz (Ghz) or faster x86 (32 bit) or x64 (64 bit) processor with SSE2
Operating System	Windows 7, Windows 8, Windows Server 2008 R2, or Windows Server 2012
Available RAM	1 GB (32 bit), 2 GB (64 bit)
Hard Drive	3 GB of available space
Monitor Resolution	1024 x 576
Video Card	Graphics hardware acceleration requires a DirectX10 graphics card
Browser	Microsoft IE 8, 9, or 10; Firefox 10.x or later; Apple Safari 5; or Google Chrome 17.x
.NET version	3.5, 4.0, or 4.5

Get Started with Access

1. Start Access.

   The Start screen opens, displaying templates and recently opened databases.

2. Open an existing database or create a new one.

   ◆ **Open recent Access file.** Click the file you want from the Recent list.

   ◆ **Open an Access file.** Click **Open Other Files**, and then use the Open screen to select a file.

   ◆ **Create a blank database or web app.** Click **Blank desktop database** or **Custom web app**.

   ◆ **Create a database or web app from a template.** Click the template you want.

   To find a template, click a suggested search (**New!**) or enter a search, and then select a category (**New!**).

   The icon for the web app includes a globe, while a desktop database doesn't.

3. For a new database, specify a name and save location (local or online), and then click **Create**.

4. If a Getting Stared window opens, view videos and other information to help you get started using a template. When you're done, click the **Close** button in the window.

5. If a security warning appears, click **Enable Content**.

6. To close the database, click the **Close** button in the database window or click the **File** tab, and then click **Close**.

Open recent Access files on the Start screen

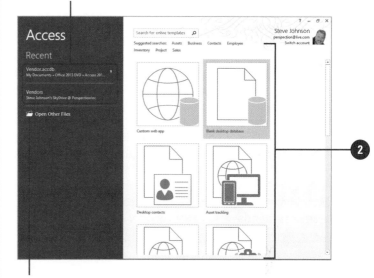

Click to open an Access file from the Open screen

Using the Ribbon

The **Ribbon** is a results oriented way of working in Access 2013. The Ribbon is located at the top of the document window and is comprised of **tabs** that are organized by task or objects. The controls on each tab are organized into **groups**, or subtasks. The controls, or **command buttons**, in each group execute a command, or display a menu of commands or a drop-down gallery. Controls in each group provide a visual way to quickly make document changes. The File tab displays Backstage view, where you can access file-related commands.

If you prefer using the keyboard instead of the mouse to access commands on the Ribbon, Access provides easy to use shortcuts. Simply press and release the ⎇ or F10 key to display **KeyTips** over each feature in the current view, and then continue to press the letter shown in the KeyTip until you press the one that you want to use. To cancel an action and hide the KeyTips, press and release the ⎇ or F10 key again. If you prefer using the keyboard shortcuts found in previous versions of Access, such as Ctrl+P (for Print), all the keyboard shortcuts and keyboard accelerators work exactly the same in Access 2013.

Tabs

Access provides three types of tabs on the Ribbon. The first type is called a **standard** tab—such as File, Home, Create External Data, and Database Tools—that you see whenever you start Access. The second type is called a **contextual** tab—such as Form Design Tools, Report Layout Tools, or Table Tools—that appears only when they are needed based on the type of task you are doing. Access recognizes what you're doing and provides the right set of tabs and tools to use when you need them. The third type is called a **program** tab that replaces the standard set of tabs when you switch to certain views or modes.

Live Preview

When you point to a gallery option on the Ribbon, Access displays a **live preview** of the option change so that you can see what your change will look like before selecting it. The Paste Options button also displays a live preview for pasted content.

Display Options

If you want more display screen, you can collapse the Ribbon or pin the Ribbon back in place as you need it. To collapse the Ribbon, click the Collapse the Ribbon button (Ctrl+F1) or double-click the current tab. To auto display the Ribbon when it's collapsed, click a tab. The Ribbon remains collapsed until you pin it in place). To pin the Ribbon in place, click the Pin the Ribbon button (Ctrl+F1) or double-click a tab.

Key Tip   Standard tabs   Contextual tab   Collapse/Pin the Ribbon

Choosing Commands

Access commands are organized in groups on the Ribbon, File tab, Quick Access Toolbar, and Mini-Toolbar. Commands are available as buttons or options on the Ribbon, or as menus on button or option arrows or the File tab. The Quick Access Toolbar and Mini-Toolbar display frequently used buttons that you may be already familiar with from previous versions of Access, while the File tab on the Ribbon displays file related menu commands; to exit the File tab, click the Back button (**New!**). In addition to the File tab, you can also open a **shortcut menu** with a group of related commands by right-clicking a program element.

Choose a Menu Command Using the File Tab

1. Click the **File** tab on the Ribbon.

2. Click the command you want.

   TIMESAVER *You can use a shortcut key to choose a command. Press and hold down the first key and then press the second key. For example, press and hold the Ctrl key and then press S (or Ctrl+S) to select the Save command.*

3. To return to the program window, click the **Back** button (**New!**).

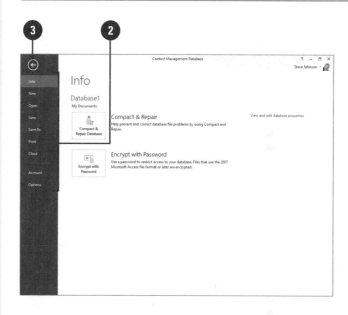

Choose a Command from a Shortcut Menu

1. Right-click an object (text or graphic element).

   TIMESAVER *Press Shift+F10 to display the shortcut menu for a selected command.*

2. Click a command on the shortcut menu. If the command is followed by an arrow, point to the command to see a list of related options, and then click the option you want.

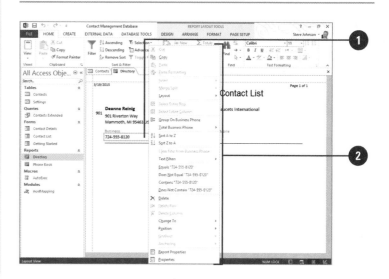

Working with the Ribbon and Toolbars

Access includes its most common commands, such as Save and Undo, on the **Quick Access Toolbar**. Click a toolbar button to choose a command. If you are not sure what a toolbar button does, point to it to display a ScreenTip. When Access starts, the Quick Access Toolbar appears at the top of the window, unless you've changed your settings. You can customize the Quick Access Toolbar or Ribbon by adding command buttons or groups to it. You can also move the toolbar below or above the Ribbon so it's right where you need it. In addition to the Quick Access Toolbar, Access also displays the Mini-Toolbar when you point to selected text. The **Mini-Toolbar** appears above the selected text and provides quick access to formatting tools.

Choose a Command Using a Toolbar or Ribbon

◆ **Get command help**. If you're not sure what a button does, point to it to display a ScreenTip. If the ScreenTip includes *Press F1 for more help*, press F1.

◆ **Choose a command**. Click the button, or button arrow, and then click a command or option.

ScreenTip   Dialog Box Launcher

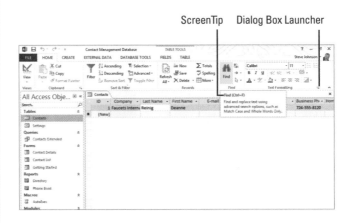

Add or Remove Items from the Quick Access Toolbar

◆ **Add or remove a common button**. Click the **Customize Quick Access Toolbar list arrow**, and then click a button name (checked item appears on the toolbar).

◆ **Add a Ribbon button or group**. Right-click the button or group name on the Ribbon, and then click **Add to Quick Access Toolbar**.

◆ **Remove a button or group**. Right-click the button or group name on the Quick Access Toolbar, and then click **Remove from Quick Access Toolbar**.

Customize Quick Access   Click to add or remove
Toolbar list arrow   frequently used buttons

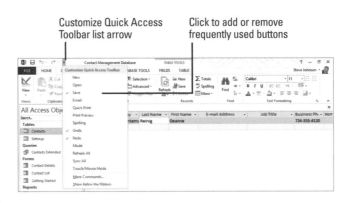

Right-click to add a button or group

Customize the Ribbon or Quick Access Toolbar

1 Click the **File** tab, and then click **Options**.

2 Click the **Customize Ribbon** or **Quick Access Toolbar**.

3 Click the **Choose commands from** list arrow, and then click **All Commands** or a specific Ribbon.

4 Click the list arrow (right column), and then select the tabs or toolbar you want to change.

5 For the Ribbon, click **New Tab** to create a new tab, or click **New Group** to create a new group on the selected tab (right column), or click **Rename** to change the name.

6 To import or export a customized Ribbon or Quick Access Toolbar, click the **Import/Export** list arrow, select a command, and then select an import file or create an export file.

7 Click the command you want to add (left column) or remove (right column), and then click **Add** or **Remove**.

  ◆ To insert a separator line between buttons in the Quick Access Toolbar, click **<Separator>**, and then click **Add**.

8 Click the **Move Up** and **Move Down** arrow buttons to arrange the order.

9 To reset the Ribbon or Quick Access Toolbar, click the **Reset** list arrow, and then select a reset option.

10 Click **OK**.

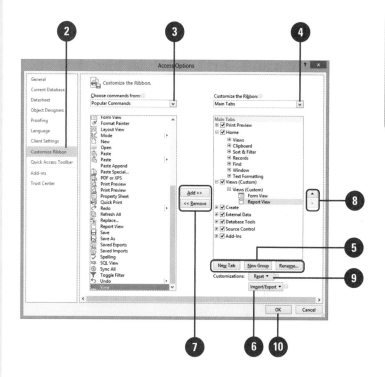

For Your Information

Moving Toolbars and the Ribbon

You can move the Quick Access Toolbar to another location. Click the Customize Quick Access Toolbar list arrow, and then click Show Below The Ribbon or Show Above The Ribbon. You can collapse the Ribbon. Click the Collapse The Ribbon button (Ctrl+F1) on the right side of the Ribbon (to the left of the Help button). Click the Pin The Ribbon button (Ctrl+F1) on the right side of the Ribbon to expand it. When the Ribbon is collapsed, you can click a tab to auto expand it. When you click an option or in the program window, the Ribbon collapses again. Just like an auto-hide option.

Changing ScreenTips

You can turn off or change ScreenTips. Click the File tab, click Options, click General, click the ScreenTip Style list arrow, click Don't Show Feature Descriptions In ScreenTips or Don't Show ScreenTips, and then click OK.

Choosing Dialog Box Options

A **dialog box** is a window that opens when you click a Dialog Box Launcher. **Dialog Box Launchers** are small icons that appear at the bottom corner of some groups. When you point to a Dialog Box Launcher, a ScreenTip with a thumbnail of the dialog box appears to show you which dialog box opens. A dialog box allows you to supply more information before the program carries out the command you selected. After you enter information or make selections in a dialog box, click the OK button to complete the command. Click the Cancel button to close the dialog box without issuing the command. In many dialog boxes, you can also click an Apply button to apply your changes without closing the dialog box. Rather than clicking to move around a dialog box, you can press the Tab key to move from one box or button to the next. You can also use Shift+Tab to move backward, or Ctrl+Tab and Ctrl+Shift+Tab to move between dialog box tabs.

Choose Dialog Box Options

All dialog boxes contain the same types of options, including the following:

◆ **Tabs**. Each tab groups a related set of options. Click a tab to display its options.

◆ **Option buttons**. Click an option button to select it. You can usually only select one.

◆ **Up and down arrows**. Click the up or down arrow to increase or decrease the number, or type a number in the box.

◆ **Check box**. Click the box to turn on or off the option. A checked box means the option is selected; a cleared box means it's not.

◆ **List box**. Click the list arrow to display a list of options, and then click the option you want.

◆ **Text box**. Click in the box and type the requested information.

◆ **Button**. Click a button to perform a specific action or command. A button name followed by an ellipsis (...) opens a dialog box.

◆ **Preview box**. Many dialog boxes show an image that reflects the options you select.

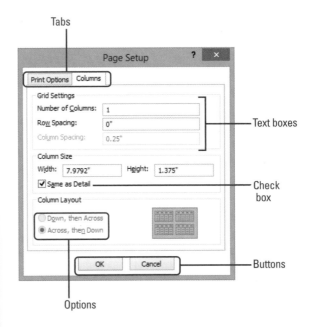

Using the Status Bar

The **Status bar** appears across the bottom of your screen and displays document information—such as cell mode, Office theme name, and current display zoom percentage—and some Office program controls, such as view shortcut buttons, zoom slider, and Fit To Window button. With the click of the mouse, you can quickly customize exactly what you see on the Status bar. In addition to displaying information, the Status bar also allows you to check the on/off status of certain features, such as Filtered, Extended Selection, View Shortcuts, Caps Lock, Num Lock, Scroll Lock, and much more. You can click an item on the Status bar to open or enable a command.

Add or Remove Items from the Status Bar

◆ **Add Item**. Right-click the Status bar, and then click an unchecked item.

You can click an item on the Status bar to open or enable a command.

◆ **Remove Item**. Right-click the Status bar, and then click a checked item.

Did You Know?

You can show or hide the Status bar for the current database. Click the File tab, click Options, click Current Database in the left pane, select or clear the Display Status Bar check box, and then click OK.

You can show or hide the Status bar for all databases. Click the File tab, click Options, click Client Settings in the left pane, select or clear the Status Bar check box, and then click OK.

Right-click the Status bar   Status information

Creating a Database

There are two types of databases: desktop or web app (**New!**). A desktop database provides a traditional database, while a web app provides a browser-based database app that uses SQL Server and Access services. A desktop database resides on your local system, while a web app resides on a SharePoint server or Office 365 site (**New!**). You can use a template to create a database, or you can create a custom database from scratch. The Access database templates help you create databases suited to your specific needs. Each template provides a complete out-of-the-box database with predefined fields, tables, queries, reports, and forms. If you can't find the template you want, additional templates are available online at Office.com. If you need a custom database, you create a blank database, and then you can create the tables, forms, and reports that make up the inner parts of the database. When you create a desktop database, you need to assign a name and location. You can save an Access database in the .mdb format (for Access 2000 or 2002-2003) or .accdb format (for Access 2007-2013).

Create a Blank Desktop Database

1. Start Access, or click the **File** tab and then click **New**.

   The Start or New screen opens, displaying templates and recently opened databases.

2. Click **Blank desktop database**.

3. Type in a name for the desktop database.

4. Click the **Browse** button, click the **Save in** list arrow, select a save location, select an Access database format, and then click **OK**.

5. Click **Create**.

6. To close the database, click the **Close** button in the database window or click the **File** tab, and then click **Close**.

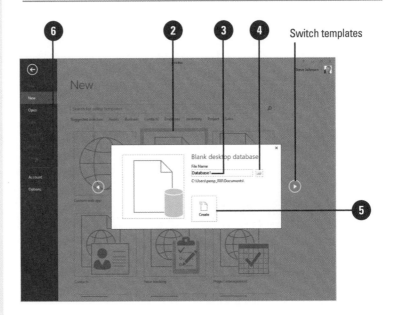

Switch templates

See Also

See "Creating a Web App" on page 400 for more information on creating a web app database in Access.

Create a Database Using a Template

1. Start Access, or click the **File** tab and then click **New**.

   The Start or New screen opens, displaying templates and recently opened databases.

2. Click a suggested search (**New!**) or enter a search, and then select a category (**New!**).

3. Click the template you want.

   The icon for the web app includes a globe, while a desktop database doesn't.

4. Type in a name for the desktop database.

5. Click the **Browse** button, click the **Save in** list arrow, select a save location, select an Access database format, and then click **OK**.

6. Click **Create**.

7. If a security warning appears, click **Enable Content**.

8. To close the database, click the **Close** button in the database window or click the **File** tab, and then click **Close**.

Did You Know?

You can open Access with the last used database. Click the File tab, click Options, click Client Settings in the left pane, select the Open Last Used Database When Access Starts check box, and then click OK.

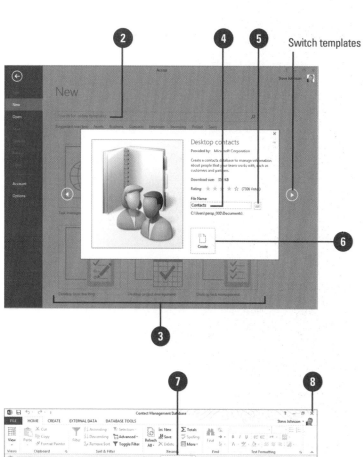

Switch templates

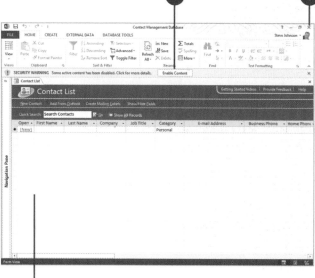

Desktop database template

Opening a Database

You can open an existing Access file from the Start screen (**New!**) when the Access program starts or Open screen by using the File tab. On the Open screen, you can choose a recently used Access file, locate and select the file on your computer, SkyDrive, or SharePoint. SkyDrive (**New!**) is a cloud-based online personal storage system, which requires a Microsoft account to access, while SharePoint server (**New!**) is a cloud-based online organizational storage and management system. The Start and Open screens allow you to pin recently used Access files or folders (**New!**) that you want to remain accessible regardless of recent use. The Pin icon to the right of the file name on the File tab makes it easy to pin or unpin as needed.

Open a Database

1. Click the **File** tab, and then click **Open**.

2. Click **Computer**.

3. Click **Browse** or a recent folder.

4. If you want to open a specific file type, click the **Files of type** list arrow, and then click a file type.

5. Navigate to the folder location with the file you want to open, and then select the database file.

6. Click **Open**.

   ◆ To open a database in exclusive mode, click the **Open** button arrow, and then click **Open Exclusive**. This disables sharing and allows you to perform many database management functions.

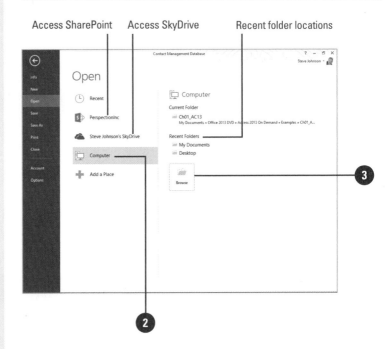

Access SharePoint   Access SkyDrive   Recent folder locations

Did You Know?

You can change the default file location of the Open dialog box. Click the File tab, click Options, click General in the left pane, enter a new location in the Default Database Folder box, and then click OK.

Open a Recently Opened Database

1. Click the **File** tab, and then click **Open**.

   TIMESAVER *In the Start screen (**New!**), click a recent database file.*

2. Click **Recent** (**New!**).

3. To pin or unpin an Access file, point to a file (displays the pin):

   ◆ **Pin an Access file.** Click the **Pin** icon on the Recent list.

   ◆ **Unpin an Access file.** Click the **Unpin** icon to display a pin on the Recent list.

4. Click the database you want to open.

   A database appears with an Access icon, while a web app appears with a globe icon.

Did You Know?

You can change the number of recently opened files that appear on the Start or Open screen. Click the File tab, click Options, click Client Settings in the left pane, change the Show This Number of Recent Databases box, and then click OK.

You can change the number of unpinned folders. Click the File tab, click Options, click Client Settings in the left pane, change the Show This Number Of Unpinned Recent Folders box, and then click OK.

You can show or hide the Backstage. Click the File tab, click Options, click Client Settings in the left pane, select or clear the Don't Show The Backstage When Opening or Saving Files check box, and then click OK.

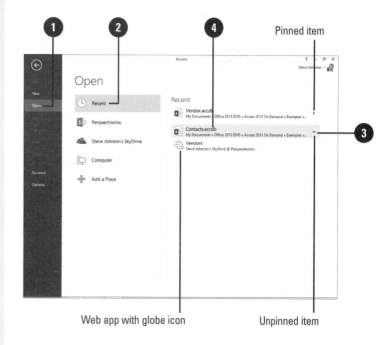

Web app with globe icon   Unpinned item

Open recent Access files on the Start screen

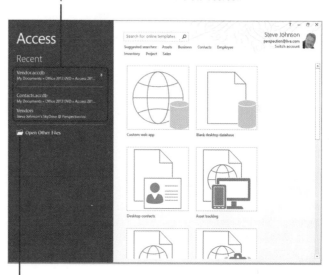

Click to open an Access file from the Open screen

Converting an Existing Database

When you open a database from Access 2000 or 2002-2003 with the .mdb file extension, Access 2013 goes into a compatibility mode where it disables features that cannot be displayed. The database stays in the original file format until you convert it to the Access 2007-2013 file format. You can convert an older database into the Access 2007-2013 file format by saving it with the .accdb file extension.

Convert a Access 2000 or 2002 - 2003 Database to Access 2013

1 Open the Access 2000 or 2002-2003 database (.mdb) you want to convert to the Access 2013 file format.

2 Click the **File** tab, and then click **Save As**.

3 Click **Save Database As**.

4 Click **Access Database (*.accdb)**.

5 Click **Save As**. If necessary, click **Yes** to close any open tables.

6 Navigate to the folder location where you want to save the file, and then click **Save**.

Access converts the file to the Access 2013 format. Access exits compatibility mode, which is only turned on when a previous version is in use.

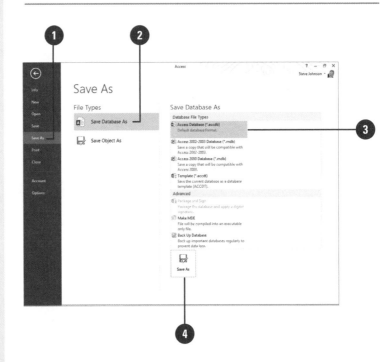

Did You Know?

You can display extensions in the Save As and Open screens and Recent list. Changing the Windows option using the Control Panel (Folder icon) also changes Access. In the Folder Options dialog box on the View tab, clear the Hide Extensions For Known File Types check box. In Windows 8, open the Desktop, open File Explorer, click the View tab, select the File Name Extensions check box

Viewing the Access Window

When you open a database, the Access program window opens and displays an improved tab-based user interface known as the Ribbon, the Navigation pane and one or more tabbed documents for the database. The Navigation pane displays objects—such as tables, queries, forms, reports, macros, and modules—that make up the database. The tabbed documents are the open objects in the database. Typically, you have a main tab—previously known as a switchboard—that acts like a home page, where you perform tasks and get started with the database.

Parts of the Access Window

◆ The **database title bar** displays the name of the open database and the database version.

◆ The **Ribbon** contains tabs that represent groups of related commands.

◆ The **Quick Access Toolbar** displays the most needed buttons that you can click to carry out commands.

◆ The **Navigation pane** displays data base objects, which replaces the Database window from earlier versions of Access.

◆ The **tabbed documents** displays tables, queries, forms, reports, and macros.

◆ The **View selector** displays view buttons.

◆ The **Status bar** displays information about the items you click or the actions you take.

Quick Access Toolbar

Ribbon   Database title bar   Tabbed document

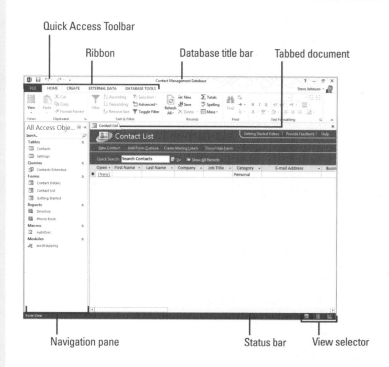

Navigation pane   Status bar   View selector

Did You Know?

You can customize Access startup. Click the File tab, click Options, click Current Database in the left pane, set the options you want under Applications Options, and then click OK. Close and open the database to see the new startup.

Arranging Windows

When you want to work with information in a database, or move or copy information between databases or programs, it's easier to move windows out of the way or display several windows at once. You can use the sizing button on the title bar or the pointer to resize and move windows around for easier viewing. You can also arrange two or more windows, from within Access or from different programs, on the screen at the same time.

Resize and Move a Window

All windows contain the same sizing buttons and mouse functionality:

◆ **Restore Down button**. Click to reduce a maximized window to a reduced size.

◆ **Maximize button**. Click to make a window fill the entire screen.

◆ **Minimize button**. Click to shrink a window to a taskbar button. To restore the window to its previous size, click the taskbar button.

◆ **Close button**. Click to shut a window.

◆ **Mouse pointer**. Position the pointer over the edge of a window (changes to a two-headed arrow), and drag to resize a window.

All windows contain a title bar which you can use to quickly move a window using the mouse:

◆ **Mouse pointer**. Position the pointer over the title bar of the window you want to move, and then Drag the window to a new location.

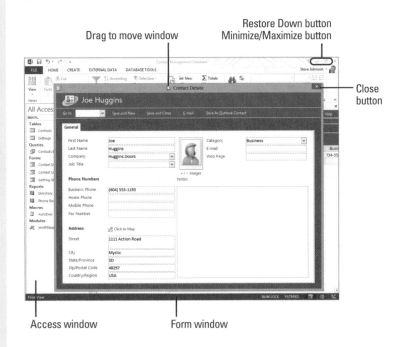

Drag to move window

Restore Down button
Minimize/Maximize button

Close button

Access window   Form window

Using Task and Window Panes

Task panes are separate windows that appear when you need them, such as Field List, or when you click a Dialog Box Launcher icon, such as Clipboard. A task pane displays various options that relate to the current task. **Window panes** are sections of a window, such as the Navigation pane. If you need a larger work area, you can use the Close button in the upper-right corner of the pane to close a pane, move a border edge to resize a pane, or use the Shutter Bar Open/Close button to minimize a window pane.

Work with Task and Window Panes

◆ **Open a Task Pane**. It appears when you need it or when you click a Dialog Box Launcher icon.

◆ **Close a Task or Window Pane**. Click the Close button in the upper-right corner of the pane.

◆ **Resize a Task Pane or Window Pane**. Point to the pane border edge until the pointer changes to double arrows, then drag the edge to resize it.

◆ **Minimize and Maximize a Window Pane**. Click the Shutter Bar Open/Close button (double arrows) in the upper right corner of the Window pane.

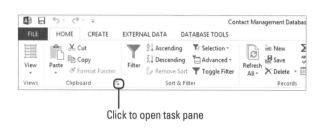

Click to open task pane

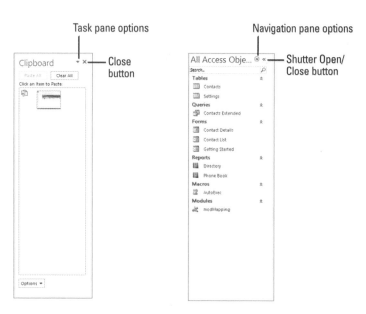

Task pane options

Navigation pane options

Close button

Shutter Open/ Close button

Getting Help While You Work

At some time, everyone has a question or two about the program they are using. The Office Help Viewer provides the answers and resources you need, including feature help, articles, tips, templates, training, and downloads. By connecting to Office.com on the Microsoft web site, you not only have access to standard product help information, but you also have access to updated information over the web without leaving the Help Viewer. The web browser-like Help Viewer allows you to browse a catalog of topics to locate information (**New!**), use popular searches (**New!**), or enter your own phrases to search for information. When you use any of these help options, a list of possible answers is shown to you with the most likely answer or most frequently-used at the top of the list.

Use the Help Viewer to Get Answers

1. Click the **Help** button on the Ribbon.

    TIMESAVER *Press F1.*

2. Locate the Help topic you want.

    ◆ **Popular searches.** Click a popular search (**New!**).

    ◆ **Help topic.** Click a topic tile on the home page (**New!**).

3. Read the topic, and then click any links to get Help information.

4. Click the **Back**, **Forward**, and **Home** buttons on the toolbar to move around in the Help Viewer.

5. If you want to print the topic, click the **Print** button on the toolbar.

6. To keep the Help Viewer window (not maximized) on top or behind, click to toggle the **Keep Help On Top** button (pin pushed in) and **Don't Keep Help On Top** button (pin not pushed in) on the toolbar.

    TIMESAVER *Press Ctrl+T to toggle Help On Top (**New!**).*

7. When you're done, click the **Close** button.

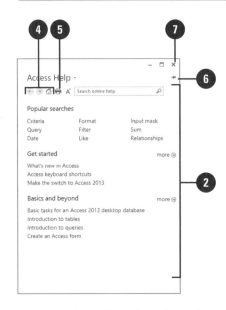

Click to change the topic font size

Topic

Search for Help

1. Click the **Help** button on the Ribbon.

2. To use a popular search, click one of the popular searches (**New!**).

3. Type one or more keywords in the Search For box, and then click the **Search** button to display results.

   ◆ **Prev or Next.** Scroll to the bottom, and then click **Prev** or **Next** to view more results.

4. Click a topic.

5. Read the topic, and then click any links to get information on related topics or definitions.

6. When you're done, click the **Close** button.

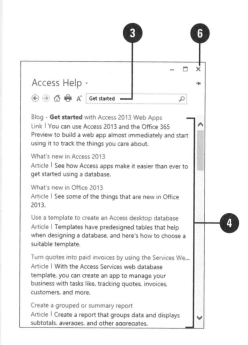

Use Local or Online Help

1. Click the **Help** button on the Ribbon.

2. Click the **Help** list arrow at the top of the Help Viewer.

3. Click the option where you want to get help information:

   ◆ **Help from Office.com** to get product help from this computer and the internet (online).

   ◆ **Help from your computer** to get product help from this computer only (offline).

4. When you're done, click the **Close** button.

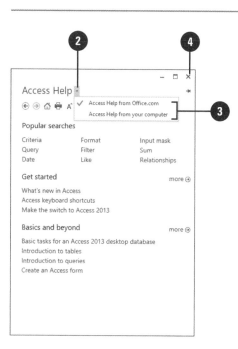

Saving a Database

When you create an Access database, save it as a file on your computer so you can work with it later. When you want to save a copy of a database or change the database file format, use the Save As command. When you want to save the currently open database in the same format, use the Save button on the Quick Access Toolbar. When you save a document, Access 2013 saves 2000 or 2002-2003 files (.mdb) in their older format and 2013 files in a new format (.accdb). Access 2000 or 2002-2003 databases stays in their original file format until you convert it to the 2007-2013 file format.

Save a Database for Access 2013

1. Click the **File** tab, and then click **Save As**.

    TIMESAVER *Press Ctrl+S to save an existing file or open the Save As screen to save a new file.*

2. Click **Save Database As**.

3. Click **Access Database (*.accdb)**.

4. Click **Save As**. If necessary, click **Yes** to close any open tables.

5. Navigate to the folder location where you want to save the file.

6. Type a file name.

7. Click **Save**.

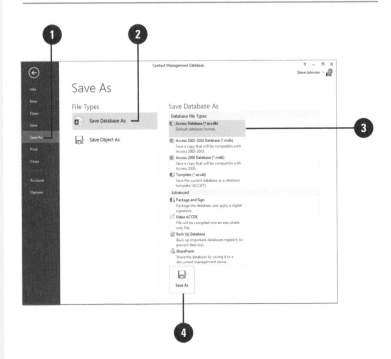

Did You Know?

You can delete or rename a file in a dialog box. In the Open or Save As dialog box, right-click the file, and then click Delete or Rename.

You can move or copy a file quickly in a dialog box. In the Open or Save As dialog box, right-click the file you want to move or copy, click Cut or Copy, open the folder where you want to paste the file, right-click a blank area, and then click Paste.

Access 2013 File Extensions

File Extension	Description
.accdb	The Access 2007-2013 file format, replaces .mdb
.accde	File format used in "execute only" mode. You can only run VBA code, not modify it. This replaces .mde
.accdt	File format for Access Database templates
.accdr	File format used to open a database in runtime mode. By changing the file extension, from .accdb to .accdr you can create a locked database file. You can change the file extension back to .accdb to restore full functionality.

Save an Access 2000 or 2002 - 2003 Database in the Same Version

1. Open the Access 2000 or 2002-2003 database you want to continue to save in the same format.

   The database opens.

2. Click the **Save** button on the Quick Access Toolbar.

Set Save Options

1. Click the **File** tab, and then click **Options**.

2. In the left pane, click **General**.

3. Set the save options you want:

   ◆ **Default File Format For Blank Database.** Click the list arrow, and then click the default format you want.

   You need to close and reopen the current database for the option to take effect.

   ◆ **Default Database Folder.** Specify the complete path to the folder location where you want to save your document.

4. Click **OK**.

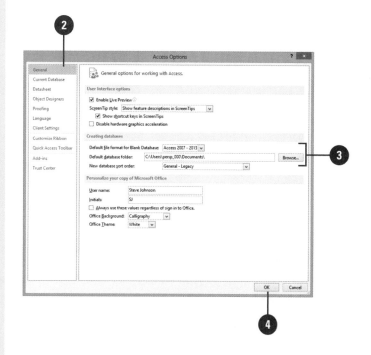

Saving a Database with Different Formats

Access 2013 allows you to save your database in previous Access file format versions. For example, you might want to save a database in an earlier 2000 or 2002-2003 version in case the people you work with have not upgraded to Office 2013. If you save a database to 2000 or 2002-2003 version (.mdb), some new features including attachments, multivalued fields, offline data and links to external data, are not supported by the new file format (.accdb). You can also use the Start screen to create a new database with different formats. In the window, you can use the Browse button (Folder icon) to select another format.

Save a Database with Different Formats

1. Click the **File** tab, and then click **Save As**.

2. Click **Save Database As**.

3. Click the format you want to use:
   - ◆ **Access 2002-2003 Database (*.mdb).**
   - ◆ **Access 2000 Database (*.mdb).**
   - ◆ **Template (*.accdt).**
   - ◆ **SharePoint.**

4. Click **Save As**. If necessary, click **Yes** to close any open tables. If a warning appears, click **OK**.

5. Navigate to the folder location where you want to save the file.

6. Type a file name.

7. Click **Save**.

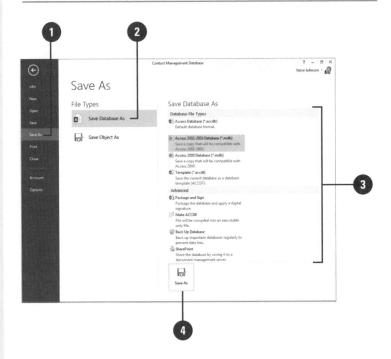

See Also

See "Creating a PDF Document" on page 318 or "Creating an XPS Document" on page 319 for information on using and saving a file with different formats.

Working with Accounts

When you set up Access 2013 or Office 2013, it requests a Microsoft account to work with online services, such as SkyDrive or SharePoint. You can add, switch, or modify accounts or sign out entirely. You can also use to other online services (**New!**), such as Flickr and YouTube for images and video, and Facebook, Linkedin, and Twitter for sharing. Before you can use the services, you need to add them to Access, which requires an established account with a user name and password.

Work with Online Accounts

1. Click the **File** tab, and then click **Account** (**New!**).

   TIMESAVER *Click the User Account list arrow, and then click an account option.*

2. Click any of the following links:

   ◆ **Change photo.** Click to open your account profile.

   ◆ **About me.** Click to open your account profile.

   ◆ **Sign out.** Click to sign out of your account.

   ◆ **Switch Account.** Click to switch or add accounts.

3. Click the **Back** button to exit the File tab.

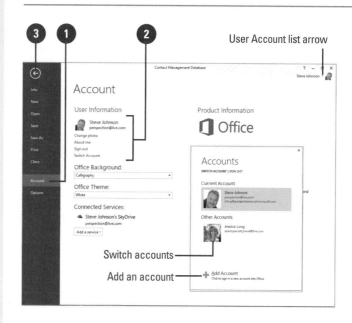

Add Online Services

1. Click the **File** tab, and then click **Account** (**New!**).

2. Click **Add a service** (**New!**), point to a service type (options vary):

   ◆ **Images & Videos**, and then click **Flickr** or **YouTube**.

   ◆ **Storage**, and then click **Office 365 SharePoint** or **SkyDrive**.

   ◆ **Sharing**, and then click **Facebook**, **LinkedIn**, or **Twitter**.

3. Follow the on-screen instructions to add the service.

4. Click the **Back** button to exit the File tab.

Working with Online Storage

Access 2013 is integrated to work with online storage services (**New!**) to make it easier to save and open databases on other devices and share them with others. With a Microsoft or SharePoint account, you can open and save databases directly to a SkyDrive (**New!**), a personal cloud-based online storage system, or Office 365 SharePoint (**New!**), a customized Microsoft web site with SharePoint services. With your databases on a SkyDrive or SharePoint site, you can do a lot of things. You can sync the files from the SkyDrive or SharePoint site to other desktops or devices, such as a tablet or mobile phone for easy access from anywhere. You can view or edit databases online from the desktop Access program or browser-based Access Web App (for SharePoint). You can share a database with other people using e-mail or social networks (**New!**) and even work on the same database at the same time with more than one person (**New!**).

Save a Database to SharePoint Online Storage

1 Click the **File** tab, and then click **Save As**.

2 Click **Save Database As**.

3 Click **SharePoint**.

4 Click **Save As**. If necessary, click **Yes** to close any open tables. If a warning appears, click **OK**.

5 Navigate to the folder location on the SharePoint server where you want to save the file.

◆ To find out the SharePoint URL, sign in to the SharePoint site using your web browser. Select the URL from the Address bar, and then copy it. You can paste it into the Address bar in the Save As dialog box.

6 Type a file name.

7 Click **Save**.

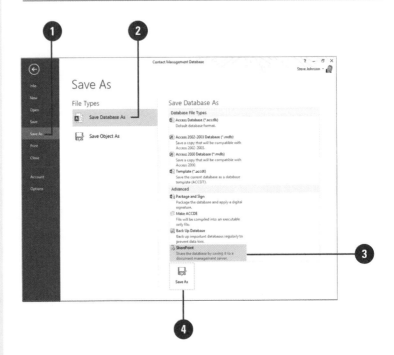

Open and Save a Database to SkyDrive or SharePoint Online Storage

1. Click the **File** tab, and then click **Open**.

2. To add a shortcut place for easy access later, click **Add a Place**, click **Office 365 SharePoint** or **SkyDrive**, and then follow the on-screen connection instructions.

3. Click the SkyDrive or SharePoint name.

4. Click **Browse** or a recent folder.

5. Navigate to the location where you want to open the file, and then select the database file.

6. Click **Open**.

7. Make the changes you want to the file.

8. Click the **Save** button on the Quick Access Toolbar or click the **File** tab, and then click **Save**.

See Also

See "Working with Accounts" on page 25 for more information on establishing a connection between online storage and your Microsoft account for use with Access and other Office 2013 programs.

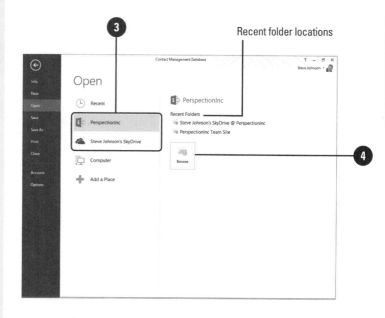

Recent folder locations

Add a Place

Closing a Database and Exiting Access

After you finish working in a database, you can close it. You close a database by using the Close command on the File tab, which keeps the Access program window open. Since each database opens in its own program window, you don't need an Exit command (**New!**), so you exit Access by using the Close button on the program window. If you made any changes to the structure of the database—for example, if you changed the size of any rows or columns in a table—Access prompts you to save your changes. Any changes you make to the data in a table are saved automatically as you make them.

Close a Database

1 Click the **File** tab, and then click **Close**.

TIMESAVER Press Ctrl+W.

2 If you have made changes to the open file since last saving them, a dialog box opens, asking if you want to save changes. Click **Save** to save any changes, or click **Don't Save** to ignore your changes.

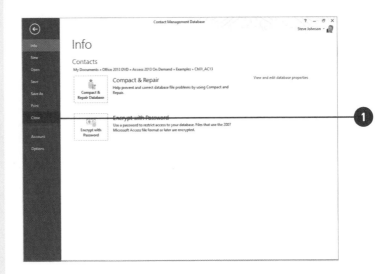

Exit Access

1 Click the **Close** button on the Access program window.

TIMESAVER To create an Exit button, add the Exit command to the Quick Access Toolbar.

2 If you have made changes to the open file since last saving them, a dialog box opens asking if you want to save changes. Click **Save** to save any changes, or click **Don't Save** to ignore your changes.

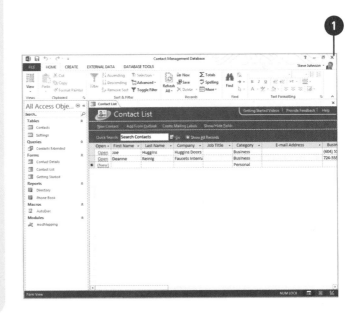

Touring Access Databases

Introduction

Microsoft Access helps you get started working with databases right away by providing sample database applications that you can use to store your own personal or business data. Access also offers a set of database wizards that aid you in creating common business databases. You can study these sample databases and wizards to get ideas for the databases you might want to design for other types of data that aren't covered by the existing samples and wizards.

When you are working with an existing database, however, you don't need to worry about the complexities of database design. You just need to know how to get around the database you are using. The tasks you are likely to perform with an existing database include entering and viewing data or subsets of data, creating and printing reports, and working efficiently with all the windows in front of you.

What You'll Do

Open a Sample Database

Warnings About Macros and Add-ins

Use a Switchboard

Change Database Display Options

View Database Objects

Work with Database Objects

Group and Hide Database Objects

Tour a Table

Tour a Form

Enter Data

Tour a Query

Tour a Report

Switch Views

Opening a Sample Database

Access provides a sample database application called Northwind Traders—a database and project version—for you to explore. The Northwind Traders contains sample data and database objects for a specialty foods company. If you have specialized database needs, you can study the structure of the sample database, and then use them as models for your own.

Open a Sample Database

1. Start Access, or click the **File** tab and then click **New**.

   The Start or New Screen opens, displaying templates and recently opened databases.

2. In the Search box, type *sample*, and then click the **Search** button or press Enter.

3. Click **Desktop Northwind**.

4. If you want to change the save location, click the **Browse** button, click the **Save in** list arrow, select the location where you want to save the new database, select an Access database format, and then click **OK**.

5. Click **Create** to download and create the sample file.

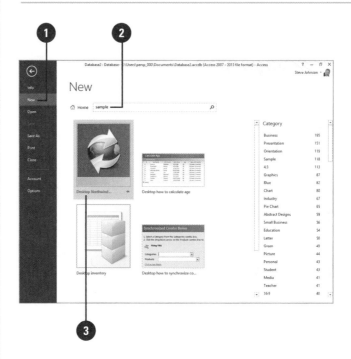

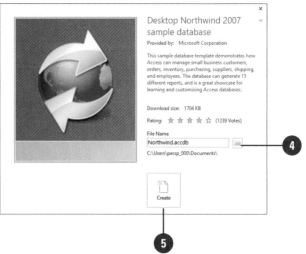

Did You Know?

You can switch to the Database window. You can press F11 to switch to the Navigation pane from a switchboard or any other window.

See Also

See "Warnings About Macros and Add-Ins" on page 31 for information on security alerts that appear when you open a database.

Warnings About Macros and Add-Ins

When you open a database, you might be prompted with a security alert on the Message bar below the Ribbon. Databases can include potentially unsafe functions using additional programming code called macros, which can contain viruses. You can protect your computer from viruses by running up-to-date antivirus software and setting your macro security level to high for maximum protection or medium for less protection. When you set the macro security level to high, some database functionality, such as wizards, is disabled. If macro security is set to medium, database users will be prompted to enable macros. Prompts also might appear to block potentially unsafe functions.

Enable Macros When You Open a Database

1. Open a database with macros.

2. To enable the content and always trust the database, click **Enable Content** on the Message bar.

   When you enable content, the database is ready to use.

   If you want to enable content and trust the database for this session, continue.

3. Click the link on the Message bar (or click the **File** tab, and click **Info**), click the **Enable Content** button, and then click **Advanced Options**.

4. If you trust the content, click the **Enable external content** or **Trust all documents from this session** option (if available) to open it. If you don't trust it, click the **Help protect me from unknown content (recommended)** option to block and disable the macros.

4. Click **OK**.

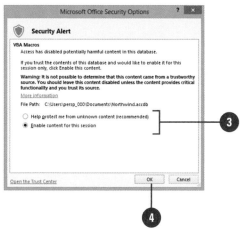

See Also

See "Setting Macro Security Options" on page 348 for information on setting security alerts that appear when you open a database.

Using a Switchboard

The sample database that comes with Access employs a switchboard. A **switchboard** is a customized window that makes many features of a specific database available at the click of a button. The Address Book switchboard, for example, offers immediate access to printing mailing labels, merging addresses with a Word document, or locating an address quickly. Often, switchboard options open forms that allow you to view or enter data, reports that allow you to see summaries of data, or queries that allow you to view subsets of data.

Open and Use a Switchboard

1 Open the database. If the database contains a switchboard, it usually appears automatically when the database is opened.

2 If necessary, click the open the Navigation pane, and then double-click the switchboard you want to view.

3 Read the descriptions on the switchboard to find the task you need to perform.

4 Click the button that corresponds to the task you want to perform.

Access opens or starts whatever database object will help you perform that task.

5 When you're done, click the **Close** button on the window for the database object.

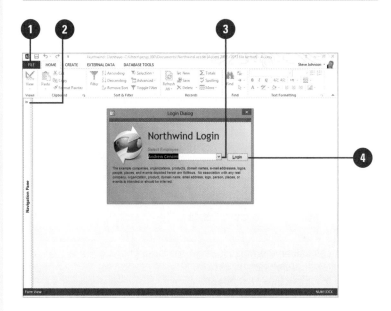

Did You Know?

You can still manage switchboards. The Switchboard Manager button is no longer on the Database Tools tab, however, the button is still available in Access. You can add the button to the Quick Access Toolbar in Access Options. You can find the button is under Commands Not in the Ribbon.

Changing Database Display Options

Access Options allows you to personalize what appears in the Access window. You can customize the way Access appears when you work on the currently opened database. You can specify a title and select an icon to create a database application, and select the form—for a regular or web app database—you want to display on startup. To customize the way you work with database objects, you can choose to display them as tabbed documents for easy access or overlapping windows for a custom interface. You can also display Layout view, which allows you to make design changes while you browse a form or report.

Change Current Database Display Options

1. Open the database you want to customize.

2. Click the **File** tab, and then click **Options**.

3. In the left pane, click **Current Database**.

4. Enter a database application title and then click **Browse** to select an application icon (optional).

5. Click the **Display Form** list arrow and **Web Display Form** list arrow, and then select the form object you want to display on startup.

6. Select or clear any of the check boxes to change the display options you want.

   - **Display Status Bar.** Set to display the Status bar. (Default on).

   - **Document Window Options.** Click the Overlapping windows or Tabbed documents option to hide or show tabs.

   - **Enable Layout View for this database.** (Default on).

   - **Enable design changes for tables in Datasheet view for this database.** (Default on).

7. Click **OK**.

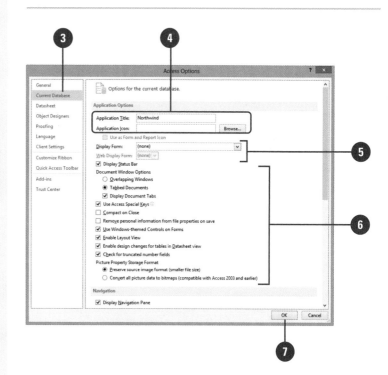

Viewing Database Objects

When you open an existing database, the first thing you usually see is the Database window. Access databases can contain seven database object types, which you use to build a database application. The table on the facing page identifies the database objects that you use when creating a database. To work with database objects, you need to open the Navigation pane, which replaces the Database window used in earlier versions of Access, and can also replace switchboards using custom categories. The Navigation pane divides database objects into categories and includes a file tab at the top, which you can use to set or change the object categories. The categories appear on the Navigation pane as bars, which you can expand or close.

View Database Objects in the Navigation Pane

1. Open the database you want to use.

    If no special startup options are specified, the Database window opens automatically.

2. To open or close the Navigation pane, click the **Shutter Bar Open/Close button**.

    TIMESAVER *Press F11 to open and close the Navigation pane.*

3. To expand or close a group, click the up or down arrows.

Did You Know?

You can switch between Datasheet and Design view. For many of the tasks you do in Access, you will switch back and forth between Design and Datasheet view. In Design view, you format and set controls for queries, reports, forms, or tables that you are creating from scratch or modifying from an original design. In Datasheet view, you observe the result of the modifications you have made in Design view. To switch between the two, click the View button on the Home tab, and then select the appropriate view.

View a List of Database Objects

1. Open the database whose objects you want to view.

2. Click the **Navigation pane file** tab.

   The upper section of the file tab displays categories and the lower section displays groups.

   ◆ **Navigate To Category.** Displays the predefined and custom categories for the open database.

   ◆ **Filter By Group.** Displays the predefined and custom groups for the selected category. Groups change as you select different categories.

   The title of the file tab changes as you select categories and groups.

3. Click a category, and/or then click a filter group.

Did You Know?

You can display and use a Search box to find objects. Right-click a blank area in the Navigation pane at the bottom, and then click Search Box to display it. Type part or all of the object name. As you type, the Navigation pane hides any groups that do not contain objects with a match. When you're done, click the Search button. Delete the text or click the Clear Search String button to restore any hidden groups.

You can prevent the Navigation pane from appearing by default. Click the File tab, click Options, click Current Database in the left pane, clear the Display Navigation Pane check box, and then click OK.

Database Objects

Object	Description
Tables	Grids that store related information, such as a customer list. A table consists of fields and records. A field stores each piece of information in a table, such as a name or address. A record is a collection of all the fields for one person.
Queries	A method to specify search criteria to find information in a database.
Forms	A window that is designed to help you enter information in a database easily and accurately one record at a time.
Reports	Summaries of information from the database that are designed to be readable and accessible.
Pages	Separate HTML files that allow access to a database on the Internet using a web browser; only backwards compatible for Access 2003 databases; not available in Access 2007-2013.
Macros	Stored series of commands to automate them into one action to save time.
Modules	Programs you can write using Microsoft Visual Basic for Applications (VBA), which extend the functionality of a database.

Working with Database Objects

The Navigation pane makes it easy to work with database objects, which help you store and manage your data. You can open, create, hide, group, rename, and delete database objects. If the predefined categories and groups don't meet your needs, you can create custom groups, which can also be used as a switchboard. You can create a simple object or a combination one based on the currently active object. For example, if a table is active and you click the Form button, Access creates a new form based on the active table.

Manage Database Objects

◆ **Open.** Double-click the object to open it for use, or right-click the object, and then click Design View to work with the object's design.

◆ **Create.** Click the Create tab, click the button (Table, Form, Report, Query Wizard, Macro, or Module) with the type of object you want. To create an object based on another, open and display the object before you click a button on the Create tab.

◆ **Delete.** Right-click the object, and then click Delete.

◆ **Rename.** Right-click the object, click Rename, type a new name, and then press Enter.

◆ **Hide** or **Unhide.** Right-click the object, and then click Hide in this Group or click Unhide this Group.

◆ **Import.** Right-click a table, point to Import, select the object type (a database table, text file, or Excel workbook), and then complete the wizard.

◆ **Close.** Click the Close button in the upper-right corner of the object.

Create tab

Right-click an object to perform management operations

Customize the Navigation Pane

① Right-click the menu at the top of the Navigation pane, and then click **Navigation Options**.

② Click a category, and then select or clear the item check boxes in Groups you want to show or hide.

③ To add, delete or rename a custom category, click **Add Item** and type a name, or select a custom category, and click **Rename Item** or **Delete Item**, or use **Up** or **Down** buttons to change order.

④ To create or change a group, click **Add Group** and type a name, or select a group and click **Rename Group** or **Delete Group**, or use **Up** or **Down** buttons to change order.

⑤ Select or clear check boxes to change the options you want.

  ◆ **Show Hidden Objects.** Select to show hidden objects as semi-transparent. (Default off).

  ◆ **Show System Objects**. Select to show system objects, such as system tables. (Default off).

  ◆ **Show Search Bar**. (Default off).

⑥ Click the **Single-click** or **Double-click** option to open objects.

⑦ Click **OK**.

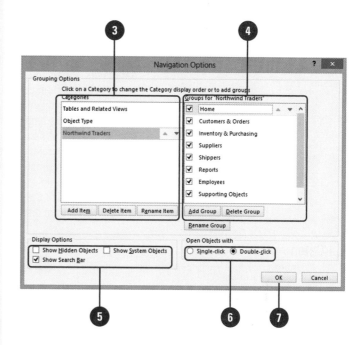

Did You Know?

You can use AutoCorrect to rename objects. When you rename an object, the Name AutoCorrect feature automatically fixes other Access objects that use the object you just renamed. Click the File tab, click Options, click Current Database in the left pane, and then select the Name AutoCorrect options you want.

Grouping and Hiding Database Objects

Objects are organized into groups and groups are organized into categories. You can create custom categories and groups to simplify and organize the objects in the Navigation pane. Categories and groups belong to the current database and cannot be transferred to other databases. When you create a custom category, Access creates a group in the custom category with all the objects called Unassigned Objects, which you can move to other groups. When you first create a custom group, it's empty until you populate it with shortcuts to the related objects. When you add an object to a group, you do not change the object's original location, nor are you creating a new object. Instead, you are simply creating a shortcut to an object that already exists. After you finish adding to a custom group, you can change the group filter to hide the Unassigned Objects group or any other groups you do not want to display. You can also hide objects in a group.

Create a Category and Group

1. Right-click the menu at the top of the Navigation pane, and then click **Navigation Options**.

2. Click **Add Item**, type a name, and then press Enter.

3. Select the custom category to which you want to add a group, click **Add Group**, type a name, and then press Enter.

4. To reorder a category or group in a list, select it, and then click the **Up** or **Down** buttons.

5. Click **OK**.

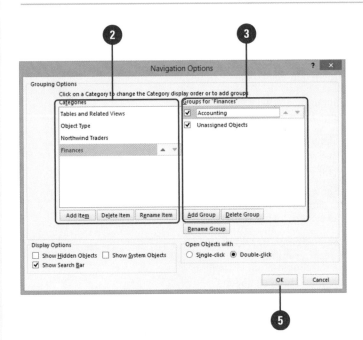

Did You Know?

You can delete or rename a custom group. In the Navigation pane, right-click the custom group you want to delete or rename, and then click Delete or Rename. When you rename a group, type a new name, and then press Enter.

Add Objects to a Custom Group

1 Right-click the object in a custom group you want to add to another custom group, and then point to **Add to group**.

TIMESAVER *You can also drag an object from one custom group to another.*

2 Do either of the following:

◆ **Existing group.** Click the group name you want.

◆ **New group.** Click **New Group**, type a name, and then press Enter.

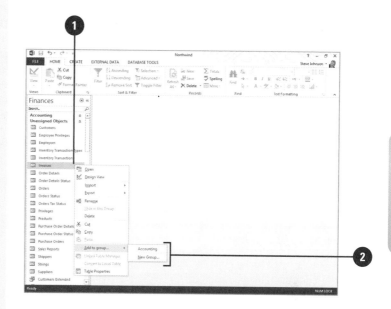

Hide and Unhide Objects

1 To hide an object in a group, right-click the object, and then click **Hide in this Group**.

2 To show hidden objects, right-click the menu at the top of the Navigation pane, click **Navigation Options**, select the **Show Hidden Objects** check box, and then click **OK**.

3 To unhide an object in a group, right-click the object (appears transparent), and then click **Unhide in this Group**.

Did You Know?

You can remove an object from a custom group. In the Navigation pane, display a custom group, right-click the object, and then click Remove.

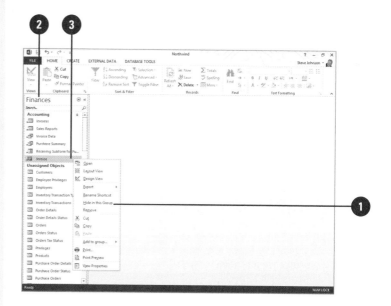

Touring a Table

A database is made up of groups of fields organized into tables. A **field** is a specific category of information, such as a name or a product. Related fields are grouped in tables. All the fields dealing with customers might be grouped in a Customer table, while fields dealing with products might be grouped in a Products table. You usually enter data into fields one entity at a time (one customer at a time, one product at a time, and so on). Access stores all the data for a single entity in a **record**. You can view a table in Datasheet or Design view. Design view allows you to work with your table's fields. Datasheet view shows a grid of fields and records. The fields appear as columns and the records as rows.

Open and View a Table

1. In the Navigation pane, click **Tables** on the Objects bar to expand it.

2. Double-click the table you want to open and view.

   The table opens in Datasheet view.

3. Use the scroll bar to view the table:

   ◆ Drag the horizontal scroll box to scroll through the fields in a table.

   ◆ Drag the vertical scroll box to scroll through the records in a table.

Table   Vertical scroll box

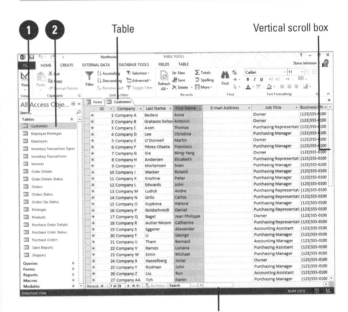

Horizontal scroll box

Did You Know?

You can select and resize a column. Click the column or row selector to select a column or row. Drag the border between the column or row selectors to resize a column or row. Each record has a unique identification number, which appears in the Specific Record box when that record is selected.

Enter a New Record in a Table

1. In the Navigation pane, click **Tables** on the Objects bar, and then double-click the table you want to open and view.

2. Click the **New Record** button.

3. Press Tab to accept the AutoNumber entry.

4. Enter the data for the first field. If you make a typing mistake, press Backspace.

5. Press Tab to move to the next field or Shift+Tab to move to the previous field.

6. When you reach the end of the record, click the **New Record** button or press Tab to go to the next record. Access saves your changes when you move to the next record.

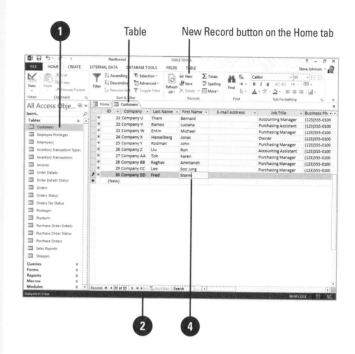

Table   New Record button on the Home tab

Delete a Record from a Table

1. In the Navigation pane, click **Tables** on the Objects bar, and then double-click the table you want to open and view.

2. Click the row selector.

3. Click the **Home** tab.

4. Click the **Delete Record** button arrow, and then click **Delete Record**.

5. Click **Yes** to confirm the deletion.

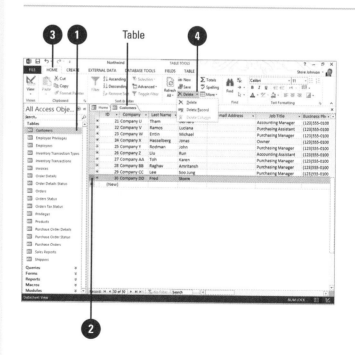

Table

Did You Know?

You can AutoNumber fields. The first field in a table is often an AutoNumber field, which Access uses to assign a unique number to each record. You can't select or change this value.

Touring a Form

Database designers often display data in forms that mimic the paper forms used to record data. Forms facilitate data entry and record viewing. They can also contain buttons that allow you to perform other actions, such as running macros, printing, or creating labels. The options that appear on a form depend on what features the database designer included. A form directs you to enter the correct information and can automatically check your entries for errors. Access places the data you've entered in the form into the proper table or tables. You can open a form in Form view or Design view. Form view allows you to view all the information associated with a record; Design view allows you to modify the form's design.

Enter a New Record in a Form

① In the Navigation pane, click **Forms** on the Objects bar, and then double-click the form you want to open and view.

② Click the **New Record** button.

③ Enter the data for the first field.

④ Press Tab to move to the next field or Shift+Tab to move to the previous field.

⑤ When you have finished entering the data, you can close the form, click the **New Record** button to enter another record, or view a different record.

Form   New Record button on the Home tab

Did You Know?

You can delete a record from a form. Display the record you want to delete, click the Delete Record button on the Home tab, and then click Yes to confirm the deletion.

Entering Data

Normally you enter data into a form, because forms are specifically designed to facilitate data entry. You can, however, enter data into a table or a query. The methods are similar. How you enter data in a field depends on how the database designer created the field. Some fields accept only certain kinds of information, such as numbers or text. Some fields appear as check boxes or groups of option buttons; others appear as text boxes. Some text boxes only allow dates; others only allow certain predefined entries, such as a state or country. When you enter data, you don't have to click a Save button to save the data. Access automatically saves the data as you enter it.

Enter Data into a Field

1. Open the query, table, page, or form into which you want to enter data.

2. Activate the field into which you want to enter data.

   ◆ Click a field to activate it.

   ◆ Press Tab to move to the next field or Shift+Tab to move to the previous field.

3. Enter data in the active field.

   ◆ Click a list arrow, and then click one of the available choices (such as a category).

   ◆ Click a check box or option button.

   ◆ Type text in a box. When you click a box, a blinking insertion point appears, indicating where the text will appear when you type.

   ◆ Enter dates in the required format (such as month/day/year).

Form   Query

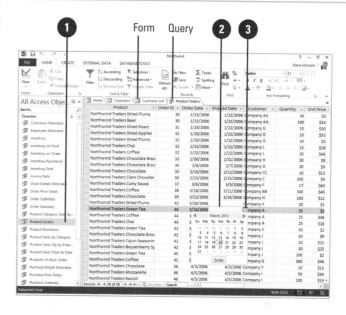

Form in a window

Touring a Query

To locate and retrieve information in a table (or in multiple tables), you create a query. A **query** is simply a question that you ask a database to help you locate specific information. For example, if you want to know which customers placed orders in the last six months, you can create a query to examine the contents of the Order Date field and to find all the records in which the purchase date is less than six months ago. Access retrieves the data that meets the specifications in your query and displays that data in table format. You can sort that information or retrieve just a subset of its contents with still more specific criteria, so that you can focus on exactly the information you need—no more or less.

Open and Run a Query

1. In the Navigation pane, click **Queries** on the Objects bar to expand it.

2. Double-click the query you want to run.

   The query opens in a table called a dynaset. The dynaset displays the records that meet the specifications set forth in the query.

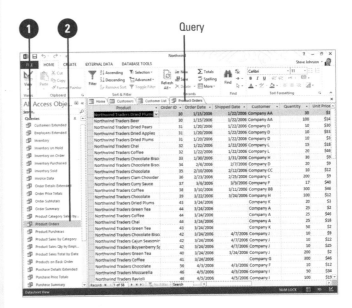

Touring a Report

After you have retrieved and organized only the specific information you want, you can display and print this information as a report. In Access you can create a simple report that displays each record's information, or you can customize a report to include calculations, charts, graphics, and other features to really emphasize the information in the report. You can print a report, a table, a query, or any data in a single step using the Print button, in which case Access automatically prints a single copy of all pages in the report. If you want to print only selected pages or if you want to specify other printing options, use the Print command on the File tab.

View a Report

1. In the Navigation pane, click **Reports** on the Objects bar to expand it.

2. Double-click the report you want to view.

Did You Know?

You can preview a print job. Open the object, click the File tab, click Print, click Print Preview, and then select the view options you want on the Print Preview tab. When you're done, click the Close Print Preview button.

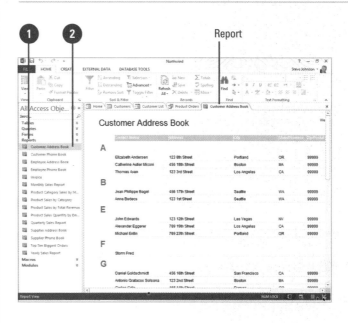

Print Data

1. Open the object you want to print.

2. Click the **File** tab, click **Print**, and then click **Print**.

    ◆ To print without using a dialog box, click **Quick Print**.

3. Click the **Name** list arrow, and then select the printer you want to use.

4. Select the Print Range option for the pages you want to print.

5. Click **OK**.

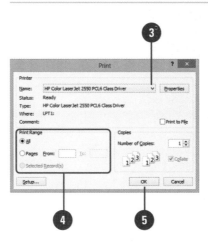

Switching Views

Access provides different views to help you work with and display information. To quickly switch between views—such as Form, Datasheet, Layout, and Design—you can use buttons on the view selector in the lower-right corner of the Program window. Datasheet view is the main view in Access. It lets you focus on entering, modifying, and managing your data. **Design view** lets you create forms and reports. **Layout view** combines Design view and Form or Report view to let you enter data and make basic changes without having to continually change views. In addition to the view selector, you can also use view buttons on the View tab to switch between views. The available views vary depending on the open object.

Switch Between Views

◆ **Use the View Selector.** Open the object you want to view, and then click any of the view buttons on the right-side of the Status bar.

   ◆ Form, Datasheet, Layout, and Design.

◆ **Use the View button.** Open the object you want to view, click the **Home** tab, and then click the **View** button arrow, and then click the view you want:

   ◆ Form, Datasheet, Layout, and Design.

TIMESAVER *The top of the View button displays the icon for the last view selected. You can click the top of the button to quickly display the view for the current object.*

View button

View Selector buttons

View a Query in Design View

1. In the Navigation pane, click **Queries** on the Objects bar.

2. Right-click the query you want to view, and then click **Open**.

3. Click the **Home** or **Design** tab.

4. Click the **View** button arrow, and then click **Design View**.

   TIMESAVER *Click the Design View button on the Status bar.*

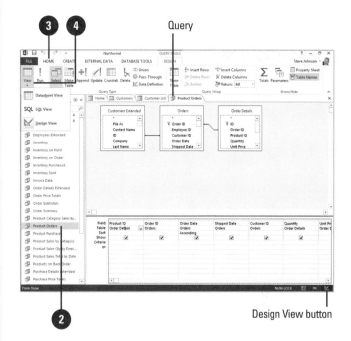

Query

Design View button

Planning and Creating a Custom Database

3

Introduction

The Microsoft Access database wizards make creating databases easy, but you may need to create a database that does not fit any of the predefined template choices. In that situation, you may need to create the database "from scratch."

Creating a database from scratch involves careful planning. You must:

- ◆ Determine the purpose and scope of your data base.
- ◆ Decide what tables your database will contain and what the content of those tables will be.
- ◆ Define how data in one table is related to data in another table.

When you create a database from scratch, you can take advantage of the tools that Access provides. If you don't plan to create a database from scratch but instead plan to use only existing Access databases, you might not need the information in this chapter. Understanding database design concepts, however, will help you better understand how to create effective queries later on.

Creating a Custom Database Template

When you start Access or open a database, you can create a database from an existing template from the Start or New screen. However, if you need a custom template, you can create your own. You can save an entire database as a template, save part of a database as an application part, or save a field or set of fields as a data type template. A database template (.accdt) is a file you can use the create a new database. An application part template (.accdt) are like database templates, however, you can also use them to add elements to an existing database. A data type template (.accft) is a file you can use to create new fields and field combinations. After you create a template file, you can share it with others. When you save a template in the default Access template folder, the database template becomes available on the Start or New screen under the Personal tab (**New!**), and the application part becomes available on the Applications Parts button on the Create tab.

Create a Custom Database Template or Application Part

1. Open the database that you want to create a custom database template or application part.

2. Click the **File** tab and then click **Save As**.

3. Click **Save Database As**.

4. Click **Template (.accdt)**.

5. Click **Save As**.

6. Specify the following in the Create New Template from This Database dialog box:

   ◆ **Name.** Enter a name for the template file. The template file is saved as *name*.accdt.

   ◆ **Description.** Enter text as a description, which appears in the tooltip.

   ◆ **Category.** Select User Templates to have it appear under Application Parts.

   ◆ **Icon.** Select an icon (64 x 32 pixels) to display for the template or application part. Click Browse to select it.

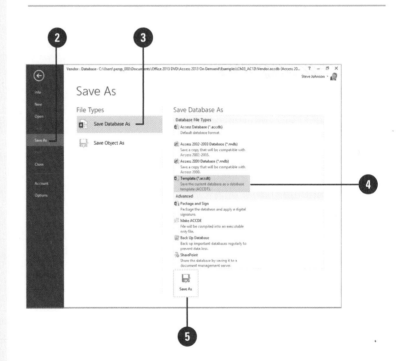

- ◆ **Preview.** Select a larger image to display for the template in the Start and New screen or Backstage view. Click Browse to select it.

- ◆ **Primary Table.** Select a table for use as the primary table for the application part. This table relates the application part to other tables in a database.

IMPORTANT *You need to select the Application Part check box before you can select a value for Primary Table.*

- ◆ **Instantiation Form.** Select a form that opens by default when the template database opens.

- ◆ **Application Part.** Select to save the database as an application part; clear to save the database as a database template.

- ◆ **Include Data in Template.** Select to save the data in the database as part of the template.

7 Click **OK**.

The template file is saved in the default Access templates folder.

- ◆ **Default templates folder.** C:\Users*user name*\AppData\ Roaming\Microsoft\Templates\ Access.

8 Click **OK**.

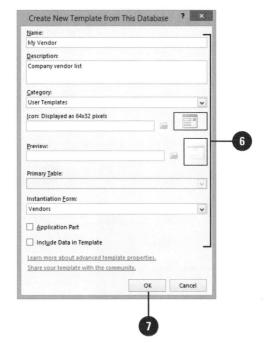

For Your Information

Customizing the Blank Database Template

If you want to customize the Blank Desktop Database template used by Access on the Start or New screen, you can open it like any other database, and then save your changes. You can access the Blank.accdb file from C:\Users*user name*\AppData\Roaming\ Microsoft\Access.

Using a Custom Database Template

Instead of creating a database from scratch, you can also create a new database from an existing one you already have. If you have a database that is close to what you want to create, you can select it from the Start or New screen to create an untitled database with the contents of a database template. When you place a template in the default Access template folder, you can select the database template from the Personal tab (**New!**) in the Start or New screen to create a new database from an existing one.

Create a New Database from a Custom Database Template

1. Start Access or click the **File** tab, and then click **New**.

2. Click **Personal** (**New!**).

   TROUBLE? *If Personal is not available, you need to save a Access template in the default Access templates folder.*

   ◆ **Default templates folder.** C:\Users*user name*\AppData\Roaming\Microsoft\Templates\Access.

3. Click the custom template you want.

4. Type in a name for the desktop database.

5. Click the **Browse** button, click the **Save in** list arrow, select a save location, select an Access database format, and then click **OK**.

6. Click **Create**.

   A new desktop database appears in the Access window.

See Also

See "Creating a Custom Database Template" on page 50 for information on creating a database template.

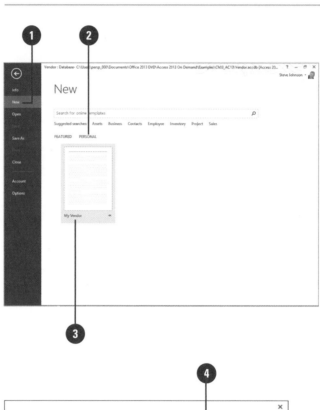

View or Add Templates for Use in Access

1. In the desktop, open the File or Windows Explorer.

2. Navigate to the default Access templates folder

   ◆ **Default templates folder.** C:\Users*user name*\AppData\Roaming\Microsoft\Templates\Access.

   If the Access folder is not there, you can create one.

3. To add a template to Access, copy and paste it in the default Access templates folder.

   ◆ **Office.com.** You can download Access templates directly from Office.com using your web browser.

4. To use the template in Access, click **Personal** in the Start or New screen.

5. Click the custom template you want.

6. Type in a name for the desktop database, specify a save location, and then click **Create**.

   A new desktop database appears in the Access window.

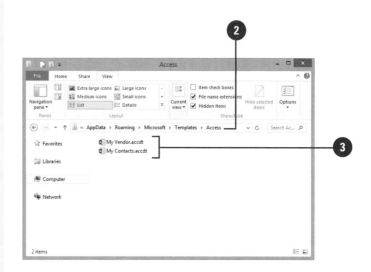

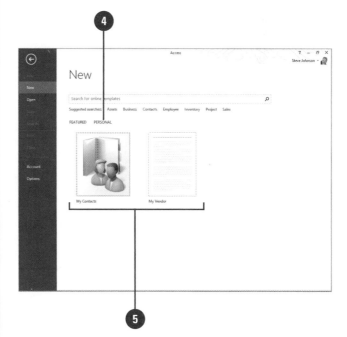

Did You Know?

You can create a new database from a template using File or Windows Explorer. In File or Windows Explorer, navigate to the default Access templates folder, and then double-click the template (.accdt) icon. In the File New Database dialog box, specify a name and save location, and then click OK.

Planning Tables

Although you can always make changes to your database when necessary, a little planning before you begin can save time later on. When you plan a database, consider how you will use the data. What kind of data are you collecting? What kind of data are you entering? How are data values related to one another? Can your data be organized into separate, smaller groups? What kinds of safeguards can you create to ensure that errors do not creep into your data? As you consider these questions, you should apply the answers as you structure your database.

Plan Tables

Tables are one of the fundamental building blocks of a database. Database planning begins with deciding how many and what kinds of tables your database will contain. Consider organizing your database information into several tables—each one containing fields related to a specific topic—rather than one large table containing fields for a large variety of topics. For example, you could create a Customers table that contains only customer information and an Orders table that contains only order information. By focusing each table on a single task, you greatly simplify the structure of those tables and make them easier to modify later on.

Choose Data Types

When you create a table, you must decide what fields to include and the appropriate format for those fields. Access allows you to assign a data type to a field, a format that defines the kind of data the field can accept. Access provides a wide variety of data types, ranging from text and number formats to object-based formats for images, sound,

video clips, and embedded macros. Choosing the correct data type helps you manage your data and reduces the possibility of data-entry errors. To make it easier to create fields, Access provides the Add New Field column in Datasheet view so you can quickly enter a field name. If you already have a defined field in the database that you want to use again, you can drag the existing field from the Field List pane on to the datasheet and Access automatically creates a relationship or guides you through the process. You can also use field templates for creating new fields. A **field template** is a design for a field, complete with a name, data type, length, and predefined properties. You can drag field templates onto the datasheet. Field templates are XSD based so that you can set up standard definitions for shared use. If you create a field for numbers, you can use the Totals row to calculate values using functions such as sum, count, average, maximum, minimum, standard deviation, or variance.

Specify a Primary Key

You should also identify which field or fields are the table's primary keys. Primary keys are those fields whose values uniquely identify each record in the table. A social security number field in a personnel table could be used as a primary key, since each employee has a unique social security number. A table with time-ordered data might have two primary keys—a date field and a time field (hours and minutes), which together uniquely identify an exact moment in time. Although primary keys are not required, using them is one way of removing the possibility of duplicate records existing within your tables.

Creating Tables in a Database

After creating a database file, you need to create the tables that will store the data. There are several ways to create a new table: in Datasheet view, in Design view, with Table Templates, SharePoint Lists, or by importing a table or linking to the data in a table from another Access database. Depending on the method you choose, creating a table can involve one or more of the following:

◆ Specifying the fields for the table

◆ Determining the data type for each field

◆ Determining the field size (for text and number fields only)

◆ Assigning the primary key

◆ Saving and naming the table

Methods for Creating a Table

Type	Method	Description
Datasheet	Table button on the Create tab	When you create a table in Datasheet view, you can start viewing and entering data right away. Access automatically assigns a data type based on the kind of information you entered in the field, and it assigns a default field size for text and number fields. After you close and save the table, Access prompts you to identify a primary key or to allow Access to designate one for you.
Table Template	Table Templates button on the Create tab	When you create a table using table templates, you select the type of table you want. Access provides several table templates, including Contacts, Tasks, Issues, Events, and Assets.
Design	Design View button on the Create tab	In Design view, you must specify the fields, specify the data type for each field, assign the size (for text and number fields), assign the primary key, and save the table yourself.
SharePoint	SharePoint Lists button on the Create tab	When you create a table using data from a SharePoint list, you select the type of table you want. Access provides several table types, including Contacts, Tasks, Issues, Events, Custom,and Existing SharePoint List.
Importing	Access button on the External Data tab	If you want to use data from another Access database in the database you are creating, you can import it. When you import a table, all the field names and data types are retained with the imported data. However, you must name the new table and identify the primary key or have Access create a primary key for you. Also, you may need to change the field size and other properties after importing.
Linking	Access button on the External Data tab	When you link a table, the data is retrieved from a table in another database. Linking a table saves disk space because there is only one table rather than multiple tables with the same data. Linking a table saves time because there is no need to update the same information in more than one table.

Creating a Table by Entering Data

Access allows you to display many of its objects in multiple viewing modes. Datasheet view displays the data in your tables, queries, forms, and reports. Design view displays options for designing your Access objects. You can create a new table in both views. When you create a table in Datasheet view, you enter data and Access creates the table as you type. Access determines the data type of each field based on the data you enter. The Click to Add column shows you where to add a new field. You can also paste data from Microsoft Excel tables into a new database and Access recognizes the data types.

Enter Data to Create a Table

① Click the **Create** tab.

② Click the **Table** button.

③ Enter the data.

Press Tab to move from field to field or click in a cell.

④ To change a field name, click the *Click to Add* field name, type the new name, and then press Enter.

⑤ Click the **Save** button on the Quick Access Toolbar.

⑥ Type a table name.

⑦ Click **OK**.

⑧ To have Access set the primary key, click **Yes**.

⑨ Click the **Close** button in the Table window.

Did You Know?

You can select or resize a column or row like in Excel. To select a column or row in a table, click the Column or Row selector. To resize a column or row, drag the border between the Column or Row selector. You can also click the Home tab, and then click the More button to access commands to resize columns and rows.

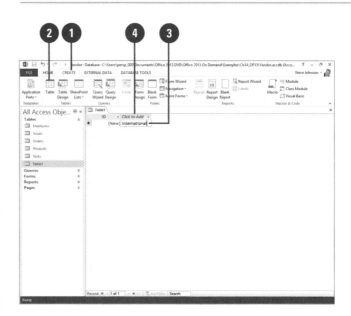

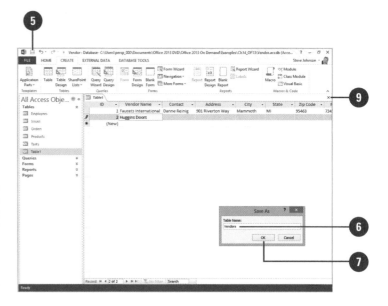

Creating an Application Part Using a Template

An application part template is a predefined portion of a database, such as a table or form, or an entire database application that you can quickly insert and use in a database. Access provides several templates including: Comments, Contacts, Issues, Tasks, Users, and Blank Forms. You can also create your own custom application part template from a database. You can use the Create tab to quickly insert an application part template. When you insert an application part, such as Contacts, you get a table, form, and report, and the option to create a relationship. After you insert an application part, you can add and change fields to meet your own needs, and then name and save it in the database.

Create an Application Part Using a Template

1. Click the **Create** tab.

2. Click the **Application Parts** button.

3. Click a template (**Blank Forms and Quick Starts: Comments, Contacts, Issues, Tasks,** or **Users**) you want.

4. Follow the Create Relationship wizard as prompted to create a simple relationship.

5. Add information and data to the template.

6. When you're done, click the **Close** button in the window.

Did You Know?

You can insert a subdatasheet in a table. In the Datasheet view of a table, click the Home tab, click the More button, point to Subdatasheet, and then click Subdatasheet. Click the Tables tab, click the table, specify the foreign key in the Link Child Fields box and the primary key in the Link Master Fields box, and then click OK.

You can view a subdatasheet. In the Datasheet view of a table, click the plus box next to the record to display the subdatasheet. Click the minus box to hide the subdatasheet.

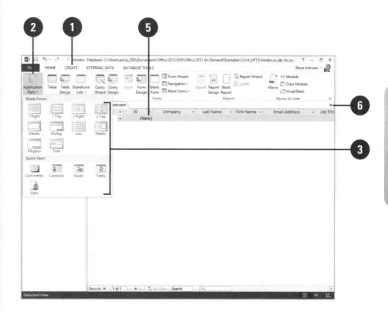

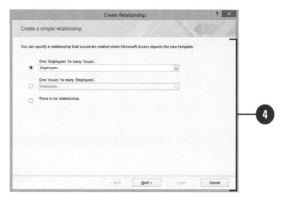

Importing Data into Tables

You can create new tables from other Access databases by importing and linking tables. When you import a table, you copy data from a table in one Access database and place it in a new table in your database. When you link a table, the data stays in its original location, but you can display and access that data from within your database. If data in the original database changes, the changes will appear in your linked database, too. You can also import data from other programs.

Import a Table from a Database

1. Click the **External Data** tab.

2. Click the **Import Access Database** button.

3. Click **Browse**, locate and select the database file that contains the data you want to import, and then click **Open**.

4. Click the import option you want.

5. Click **OK**.

6. Click the tables you want to import. To deselect a table, click the table again.

7. Click **OK**.

8. To save import steps, select the **Save import steps** check box, enter a name and description, and then click **Save Import**.

   Otherwise, click **Close**.

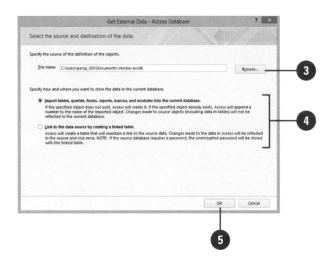

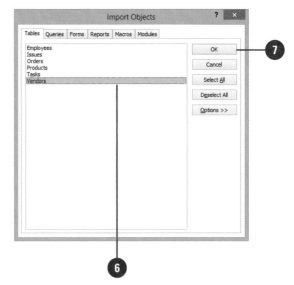

Linking to Data in Tables

You can create new tables from other Access databases by importing and linking tables. When you link a table, the data stays in its original location, but you can display and access that data from within your database. If data in the original database changes, the changes will appear in your linked database, too. After you select the table you want to link during the linking process, you have the option of saving the import steps for use again in the future.

Link to Data from a Database

1. Click the **External Data** tab.

2. Click the **Import Access Database** button.

3. Click **Browse**, locate and select the database file that contains the data you want to import, and then click **Open**.

4. Click the **Link to the data source by creating a linked table** option.

5. Click **OK**.

6. Click the tables you want to import. To deselect a table, click the table again.

7. Click **OK**.

8. To save import steps, select the Save import steps check box, enter a name and description, and then click **Save Import**.

   Otherwise, click **Cancel**.

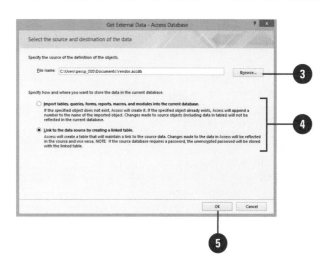

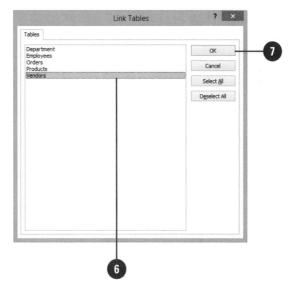

Working with Table Records

A **database** is made up of groups of fields organized into tables. A **field** is a specific category of information, such as a name or a product. Related fields are grouped in tables. You usually enter data into fields one entity at a time (one customer at a time, one product at a time, and so on). Access stores all the data for a single entity in a record. You can view a table in Datasheet or Design view. Design view allows you to work with your table's fields. Datasheet view shows a grid of fields and records. The fields appear as columns and the records as rows. The first field in a table is often an **AutoNumber** field, which Access uses to assign a unique number to each record. You can't select or change this value.

Enter a New Record and Move Around in a Table

1 In the Navigation pane, double-click the table you want to open.

2 Click the **New Record** button.

3 Press Tab to accept the AutoNumber entry.

4 Enter the data. If you make a typing mistake, press Backspace.

5 Press Tab to move to the next field or Shift+Tab to move to the previous field.

6 When you reach the end of the record, click one of the Record buttons:

◆ **First Record** button.

◆ **Previous Record** button.

◆ **Specific Record** box. Enter a record number in the box, and then press Enter.

◆ **Next Record** button.

◆ **Last Record** button.

TIMESAVER *You can also click the Go To button on the Home tab, and then click the same commands.*

Search for Records in a Table

1. In the Navigation pane, double-click the table you want to open.

2. If you want, click in the field where you want to start the search.

3. Click in the Search box.

4. Type the text you want to find in the table.

5. Press Enter to find the first instance of the text.

6. Press Enter again to find the next instance of the text.

7. When you're done, delete the text in the Search box.

See Also

See "Finding and Replacing Text" on page 118 for information on finding records using the Find and Replace dialog box.

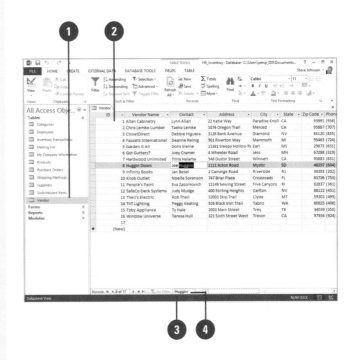

Delete a Record from a Table

1. In the Navigation pane, double-click the table you want to open.

2. Click the row selectors you want.

3. Click the **Home** tab.

4. Click the **Delete** button, and then click **Yes** to confirm.

TIMESAVER Right-click a row selector, and then click Delete Record.

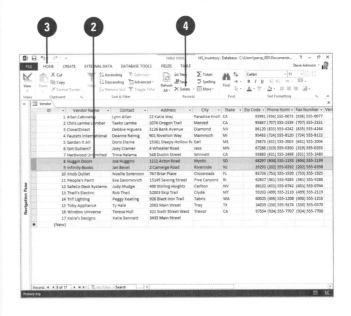

Working with a Table in Design View

Most Access objects are displayed in Design view, which allows you to work with the underlying structure of your tables, queries, forms, and reports. To create a new table in Design view, you define the fields that will comprise the table before you enter any data. In Design view for tables, each row corresponds to a field. You can edit, insert, and delete fields in your database tables in Design view. You insert a field by adding a row, while you delete a field by removing a row. You can also change field order by dragging a row selector to a new position.

Create or Modify a Table in Design View

1. Click the **Create** tab, and then click the **Table Design** button, or select the table you want to modify in the Navigation pane, and then click the **Design View** button.

2. Click in a **Field Name** cell, and then type a modified field name.

3. Click in a **Data Type** cell, click the Data Type list arrow, and then click a data type.

4. Click in a **Description** cell, and then type a description. If the **Property Update Options** button appears, select an option, if necessary.

5. To insert a field, click the row selector below where you want the field, and then click the **Insert Rows** button on the Ribbon.

6. To delete a field, click the row selector for the field you want to delete, and then click the **Delete Rows** button on the Ribbon.

7. Click the **Save** button on the Quick Access Toolbar, and then if necessary, enter a table name and click **OK**.

8. When you're done, click the **Close** button in the Table window.

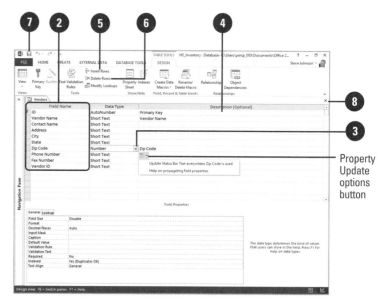

Property Update options button

Specifying a Primary Key in Design View

A primary key is one or more fields in a table that provide a unique identifier for every row. You use the primary key in other tables to refer back to the table with the primary key. In Design view, you can use the Primary Key button to assign or remove the primary key designation for the selected field or fields. When you create a new table in Datasheet view, Access automatically creates a primary key and assigns it the field name "ID" and the data type AutoNumber. When you create a table in Design view, you can specify more than one field as a primary key, known as a composite key, so you are responsible for determining the data type of the primary key. Whatever data type you choose, values for the primary key must be unique for each table record.

Specify a Primary Key

1. In Design view, create a field that will be that table's primary key, and then select an appropriate data type.

   ◆ If you choose the AutoNumber data type, Access assigns a value to the primary key for a new record that is one more than the primary key in the previous record.

   ◆ If you choose any other data type, such as Text, Number, or Date/Time, during data entry, you must enter a unique value in the appropriate format for the primary key of each new record.

2. Click the row selector of that field.

   ◆ To create more than one primary key, press and hold Ctrl, and then click the additional row selector for each field.

3. Click the **Primary Key** button.

4. To remove a primary key, delete any table relationships associated with the primary key, select the row selector for the Primary key, and then click the **Primary Key** button.

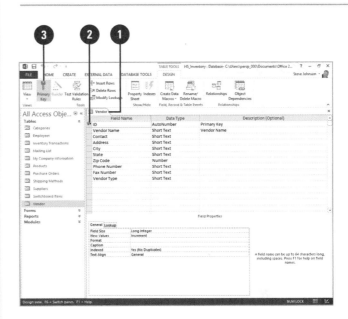

Planning Table Relationships

When you place data into separate tables, you need some way of merging this data together for forms and reports. You can do this by establishing table relationships that indicate how data in one table relates to data in another.

Specifying Common Fields

Data from several different tables is related through the use of common fields. A common field is a field existing in two or more tables, allowing you to match records from one table with records in the other tables. For example, the Customers table and the Orders table might both contain a Customer ID field, which functions as a primary key that identifies a specific customer. Using Customer ID as a common field allows you to generate reports containing information on both the customer and the orders the customer made. When you use a primary key as a common field, it is called a **foreign** key in the second table.

Building Table Relationships

Once you have a way of relating two tables with a common field, your next task is to express the nature of that relationship. There are three types of relationships: one-to-one, one-to-many, and many-to-many.

A table containing customer names and a second table containing customer addresses exist in a one-to-one relationship if each customer is limited to only one address. Similarly, a one-to-many relationship exists between the Customers table and the Orders table because a single customer could place several orders. In a one-to-many relationship like this, the "one" table is called the **primary**

Table Relationships	
Choice	**Description**
One-to-one	Each record in one table is matched to only one record in a second table, and visa versa.
One-to-many	Each record in one table is matched to one or more records in a second table, but each record in the second table is matched to only one record in the first table.
Many-to-many	Each record in one table is matched to multiple records in a second table, and visa versa.

table, and the "many" table is called the **related table**.

Finally, if you allow several customers to be recorded on a single order (as in the case of group purchases), a many-to-many relationship exists between the Customers and Orders tables.

Maintaining Referential Integrity

Table relationships must obey standards of **referential integrity**, a set of rules that control how you can delete or modify data between related tables. Referential integrity protects you from erroneously changing data in a primary table required by a related table. You can apply referential integrity when:

- The common field is the primary table's primary key.

- The related fields have the same format.

- Both tables belong to the same database.

Referential integrity places some limitations on you.

- Before adding a record to a related table, a matching record must already exist in the primary table.

- The value of the primary key in the primary table cannot be changed if matching records exist in a related table.

- A record in the primary table cannot be deleted if matching records exist in a related table.

Access can enforce these rules by cascading any changes across the related tables. For example, Access can automatically copy any changes to the common field across the related tables. Similarly, if a record is deleted in the primary table, Access can automatically delete related records in all other tables.

As you work through these issues of tables, fields, and table relationships, you will create a structure for your database that will be easier to manage and less prone to data-entry error.

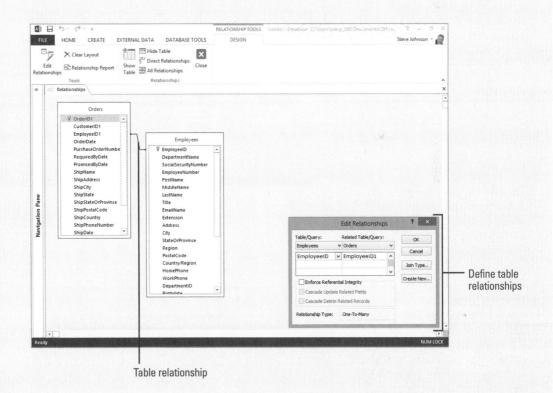

Table relationship

Define table relationships

Defining Table Relationships

Data from several different tables is related through the use of common fields. A common field is a field existing in two or more tables, allowing you to match records from one table with records in the other tables. Once you have a way of relating two tables with a common field, your next task is to express the nature of that relationship. There are three types of relationships: one-to-one, one-to-many, and many-to-many. You can define and manage relationships using buttons on the Database Tools tab. This gives you control over your table relationships and also gives you a quick snapshot of all the relationships in your database. After you define a relationship, you can double-click the connection line to modify or add to the relationship.

Define Table Relationships

1. Click the **Database Tools** tab.

2. Click the **Relationships** button.

   If relationships are already established in your database, they appear in the Relationships window. In this window, you can create additional relationships.

3. If necessary, click the **Show Table** button to display the Show Table dialog box.

4. Click the **Tables** tab.

5. Click the table you want.

6. Click **Add**.

   The table or query you selected appears in the Relationships window. Repeat steps 5 and 6 for each table you want to use in a relationship.

7. Click **Close**.

8. Drag the common field in the first table to the common field in the second table. When you release the mouse button, a line appears between the two tables, signifying that they are related. Also, the Edit Relationships dialog box opens, in which you can confirm or modify the relationship.

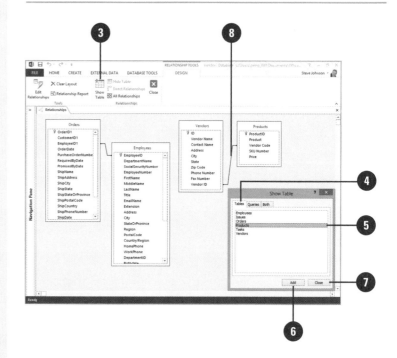

9 Click the **Join Type** button if you want to specify the join type. Click **OK** to return to the Edit Relationships dialog box.

10 Click **Create** to create the relationship.

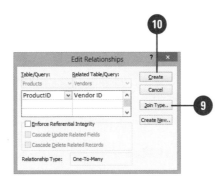

Did You Know?

You can view the relationships you want to see. Click the Design tab under Relationship Tools, click the Show Direct Relationships button to see tables that are directly related to each other. Click the All Relationships button to see all the relationships between all the tables and queries in your database.

You can print the Relationships window. Click the Design tab under Relationship Tools, click the Relationships Report button in the Relationships window you want to print, click the Print button, select the print settings you want, and then click OK.

You can delete a table relationship. In the Relationships window, right-click the line that joins the tables that you no longer want related to one another, and then click Delete. In the message box, click Yes to confirm that you want to permanently delete this relationship. You will not be able to undo this change.

Join Types

Join Types	Description
Include rows only where the joined fields from both tables are equal	Choose this option if you want to see one record in the second table for every record that appears in the first table. The number of records you see in the two tables will be the same.
Include ALL records from "xxx" (the first table) and only those records from "yyy" (the second table) where the joined fields are equal	Choose this option if you want to see all the records in the first table (even if there is no corresponding record in the second table) as well as the records from the second table in which the joined fields are the same in both tables. The number of records you see in the first table might be greater than the number of records in the second table.
Include ALL records from "yyy" (the second table) and only those records from the "xxx" (the first table) where the joined fields are equal	Choose this option if you want to see all the records in the second table (even if there is no corresponding record in the first table) as well as the records from the first table in which the joined fields are the same in both tables. The number of records you see in the second table might be greater than the number of records in the first table.

Creating and Printing a Table Relationship Report

After you create a table relationship, you can create and print a report. In the Relationships window, the Relationship Report button creates a report with the currently displayed relationship and switches to Print Preview, where you can print the report. When you close Print Preview, the report appears in Design view. If you want, you can make changes to the report. To complete the process, you need to save and name the report or close it without saving it. Instead of printing the report, you can also use exporting tools in Print Preview to save the report in another format, including a PDF or XPS document.

Create and Print a Table Relationship Report

1. Click the **Database Tools** tab.

2. Click the **Relationships** button.

   If relationships are already established in your database, they appear in the Relationships window.

3. Do any of the following to display the table relationships you want to use to create a report:

   ◆ **Hide tables.** Click the table you want to hide, and then click the **Hide Table** button.

   ◆ **Add tables.** Click the **Tables** tab, click the table you want, click **Add**, and then click **Close**.

4. Click the **Relationship Report** button.

   The report appears in Print Preview.

5. To print the report, click the **Print** button, specify the settings you want, and then click **OK**.

6. Click the **Close Print Preview** button.

   The relationship report appears in Design view.

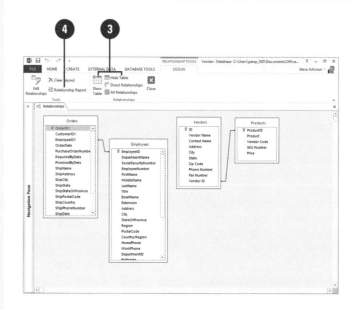

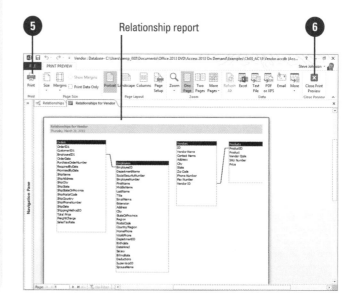

Relationship report

7 Click the **Save** button on the Quick Access Toolbar.

8 Type a name for the relationship report.

9 Click **OK**.

Did You Know?

You can show direct relationships. In the Relationships window, click the Direct Relationships button to display only tables that relate to each other.

You can clear relationships. In the Relationships window, click the Clear Layout button, and then click Yes to remove the layout of the Relationships window.

See Also

See "Creating a PDF Document" on page 318 or "Creating an XPS Document" on page 319 for information on using and saving a file with different formats.

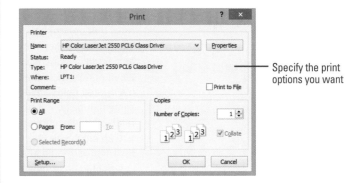

Specify the print options you want

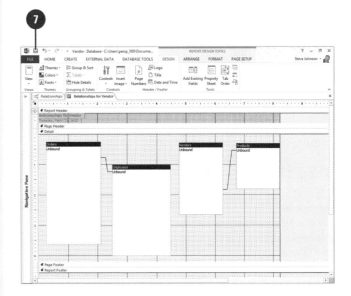

Ensuring Referential Integrity

Table relationships must obey standards of referential integrity, a set of rules that control how you can delete or modify data between related tables. Referential integrity in table relationships keeps users from accidentally deleting or changing related data. You can apply referential integrity when: the common field is the primary table's primary key; the related fields have the same format; or both tables belong to the same database. If a primary table contains a list of employees and related tables contain additional information about those employees, and an employee quits, his record is removed from the primary table. His records should also be removed in all related tables. Access allows you to change or delete related data, but only if these changes are cascaded through the series of related tables. You can do this by selecting the Cascade Update Related Fields and Cascade Delete Related Records check boxes in the Edit Relationships dialog box.

Ensure Referential Integrity

1. Click the **Database Tools** tab.

2. Click the **Relationships** button.

3. Click the join line for the relationship you want to work with.

4. Click the **Edit Relationships** button.

5. Click to select the **Enforce Referential Integrity** check box to ensure that referential integrity always exists between related tables in the database.

6. If you want changes to the primary field of the primary table automatically copied to the related field of the related table, click to select the **Cascade Update Related Fields** check box.

7. If you want Access to delete records in the related tables whenever records in the primary table are deleted, click to select the **Cascade Delete Related Records** check box.

8. Click **OK**.

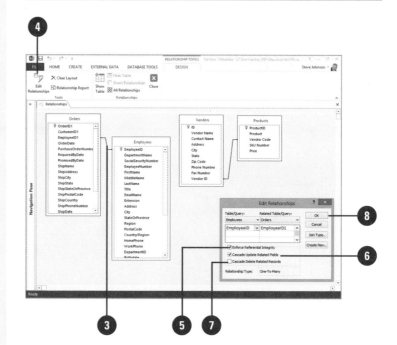

Identifying Object Dependencies

As you develop a database, you create a relationship between objects to share data and provide the information in forms and reports. When you make changes to one object, it might affect another object. For example, if you no longer need a field in a table, instead of deleting it right away and possibly creating problems, you can check object dependencies to make sure that the field you want to delete is not used in another table. Checking for object dependencies helps you save time and avoid mistakes. Access generates dependency information by searching name maps maintained by the Name AutoCorrect feature. If Track Name AutoCorrect Info is turned off on the Current Database pane in the Options dialog box, you cannot view dependency information.

View Dependency Information

1. In the Navigation pane, click the database object in which you want to view dependencies.

2. Click the **Database Tools** tab.

3. Click the **Object Dependencies** button.

4. If prompted, click **OK** to update dependency information. If prompted, click **Yes** to close all objects.

5. Click the **Objects that depend on me** or **Objects that I depend on** option.

   The Object Dependencies task pane shows the list of objects that use the selected object.

6. Click the **Expand** icon (white arrow) next to an object to view dependency information. Click the **Collapse** icon (black arrow) to hide the dependency information.

7. When you're done, click the **Close** button on the task pane.

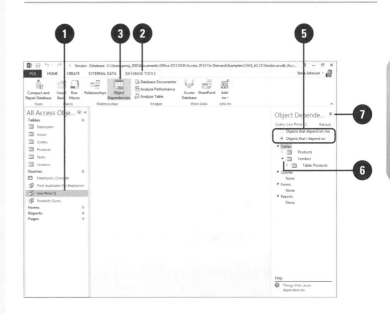

Dependency Information

Object	Dependent	Description
Table	Table or query	A relationship is defined between the objects
Table	Form	Fields in the selected table look up values
Query	Table or query	Query is bound to the table or query
Form	Table or query	Form is bound to the table or query
Form	Form	Form includes the other form as a subform
Report	Table or query	Report is bound to the table or query
Report	Form	Report includes the form as a subform
Report	Report	Report include the other report as a subreport

Modifying Object Dependencies

As you view dependencies for an object in the Object Dependencies task pane and determine you can make changes without effecting other objects, you can open an object in Design view directly from the Object Dependencies task pane and modify it. If you need to look at other objects, you can open more than one from the Object Dependencies task pane. If you are having problems viewing dependency information, you need to turn on the Track Name AutoCorrect Info option on the Current Database pane in Access Options.

Modify Dependency Information

1. In the Navigation pane, click the database object in which you want to view and modify dependencies.

2. Click the **Database Tools** tab.

3. Click the **Object Dependencies** button.

4. Click the **Objects that depend on me** or **Objects that I depend on** option.

   The Object Dependencies task pane shows the list of objects that use the selected object.

5. Click the **Expand** icon (white arrow) next to an object to view dependency information. Click the **Collapse** icon (black arrow) to hide the dependency information.

6. Click the object you want to open in Design view.

7. Modify the object in Design view, and then click the **Close** button in the Design view window.

8. When you're done, click the **Close** button on the task pane.

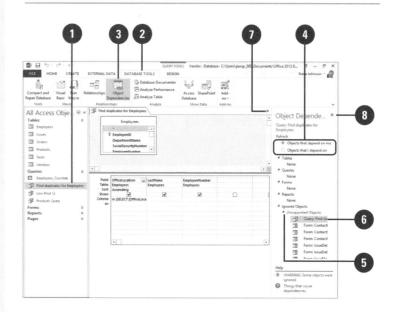

Working with Fields

4

Introduction

An important part of creating your own database is field design. How you design your fields determines how accurately they will be able to store data. Microsoft Access provides flexibility and control in field design. You can design fields so that they allow you to:

- Assign a data type so the field accepts and displays the data in the appropriate format.
- Include input masks that guide users during data entry.
- Specify whether data must be entered into certain fields.
- Include a default value for a field.
- Include validation checks to ensure that correct data is entered.
- Accommodate data whose values are taken from lookup lists.

By taking advantage of these tools during the database design stage, you can save yourself and your database users a lot of trouble later on. By properly designing your fields, you can remove many sources of data-entry error and make your database more simple to manage.

Inserting Fields

To make it easier to create fields, Access provides the *Click to Add* column in Datasheet view so you can quickly add a field. You can also use buttons on the Fields tab under Table Tools for creating new fields. Access uses data type templates to insert fields in a table. A field data type template is a design for a field, complete with a name, data type, length, and predefined properties. You can use one of the predefined data types or create a custom one of your own. The common fields available on the Fields tab include Short Text, Number, Currency, Date & Time, and Yes/No. With the More Fields button, you can access additional fields. If you are working in Design view, you can use the Insert Rows button to create a new field. If you need a field to calculate a value, you can use a calculated field (available on More Fields), which include Text, Number, Currency, Yes/No, and Date/Time.

Insert Fields Using Field Data Type Templates

1. Display the table in Datasheet view.

2. Click the **Fields** tab under Table Tools.

3. Select the field next to where you want to insert a field.

4. To insert fields, use either of the following methods.

   ◆ **Add Common Fields.** In the Add & Delete group, use the field related buttons to insert the type of field you want.

   ◆ **Add Other Fields.** Click the **More Fields** button, and then select the type of field you want to insert.

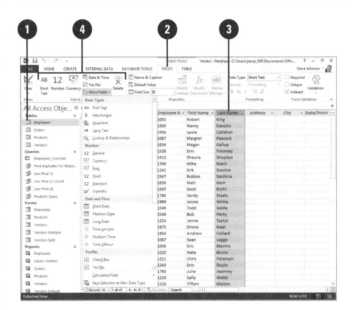

See Also

See "Creating a Field Data Type Template" on page 104 for information on creating a custom field data type template.

Insert a Field in Datasheet View

1. Display the table in Datasheet view.

2. Click the **Fields** tab under Table Tools.

3. Scroll to the right most column.

4. Click the **Click to Add** arrow, and then select the type of field you want to insert.

   A new field column is inserted.

5. Rename the field.

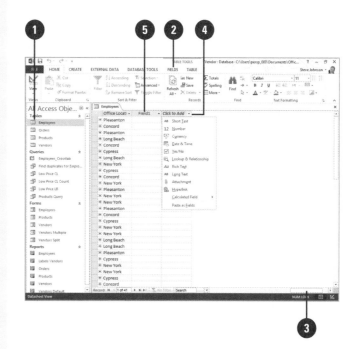

Insert a Field in Design View

1. Display the table in Design view.

2. Click the **Design** tab under Table Tools.

3. Click the row selector for the field that will be below the new field you want to insert.

4. Click the **Insert Rows** button.

   A new blank row appears above the row you selected.

5. Click the Field Name cell for the row you inserted, type the name of the new field.

6. Click the list arrow in the Data Type column, click the data type you want to assign to the field.

7. Click the Description cell, and then type a brief description.

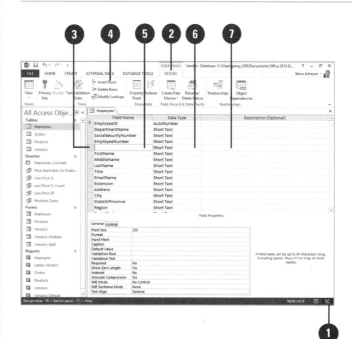

Working with Fields

You can insert, delete, and edit fields in your database tables in Datasheet and Design views. In Datasheet view, each column corresponds to a field. In Design view for tables, each row corresponds to a field. You can add a field by inserting a new column or row that contains the field name, data type, and other properties. You can delete a field by removing a column or row. You can also change field order by re-ordering the columns or rows to better suit your data entry needs.

Delete a Field

1. Display the table in Datasheet or Design view.

2. Click the column header in Datasheet view, or row selector in Design view for the field you want to delete.

3. Click the **Delete** button in Datasheet view or **Delete Rows** button in Design view.

   If any records in the table contain data for this field, a message informs you that deleting this field will also delete any data in the field.

4. Click **Yes** to confirm you want to continue, or click **No** to cancel the deletion.

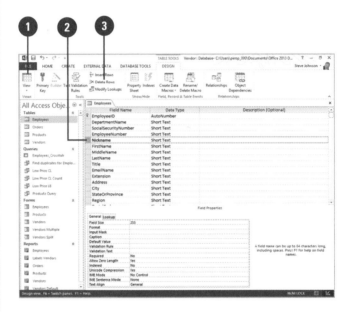

Rename a Field

1. Display the table in Datasheet or Design view.

2. Double-click the column header in Datasheet view, or Field Name cell in Design view for the field you want to rename.

   TIMESAVER *In Datasheet view, you can also click the column header, and then click the Rename button.*

3. Type a new field name, and then press Enter.

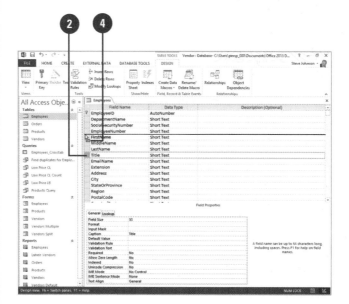

Change the Order of Fields in a Table

1. Display the table in Datasheet or Design view.

2. Click the column header in Datasheet view, or row selector in Design view for the field you want to move.

3. Click the column header or row selector again, and then press and hold the mouse button.

4. Drag the column or row to the new position where you want the field to appear, and then release the mouse button.

Specifying Data Types and Field Properties

Access provides different **data types**— field formats that define the kind of data the field can accept—which cover a wide variety of data. When you choose a data type for a field, Access will accept data entered only in the format specified by the data type. Selecting the appropriate data type makes it easier for users to enter and retrieve information in the database tables. It also acts as a check against incorrect data being entered. For example, a field formatted to accept only numbers removes the possibility that a user will erroneously enter text into the field.

You can change the data type for a field even after you have entered data in it. However, you might need to perform a potentially lengthy process of converting or retyping the field's data when you save the table. If the data type in a field conflicts with a new data type setting, you may lose some or all of the data in the field.

Once you've selected a data type, you can begin to work with field properties. A **field property** is an attribute that defines the field's appearance or behavior in the database. The number of decimal places displayed in a numeric field is an example of a property that defines the field's appearance. A property that forces the user to enter data into a field rather than leave it blank controls that field's behavior. For the Date/Time field, a calendar button automatically appears next to the field to make it easy to find and choose a date. In Design view for tables, Access provides a list of field properties, called the **properties list**, for each data type.

Data Types

Data Type	Description
Short Text or Long Text (**New!**)	Text or combinations of text and numbers, as well as numbers, such as phone numbers. Limited to 255 characters (Short) or 1 GB text (Long, formerly Memo).
Number	Numeric data used in mathematical calculations.
Date/Time	Date and time values for the years 100 through 9999. An automatic calendar for data picking appears next to a date field.
Currency	Currency values and numeric data used in mathematical calculations involving data with one to four decimal places. Values are accurate to 15 digits on the left side of the decimal separator.
AutoNumber	A unique sequential number (incremented by 1) or a random number Access assigns whenever you add a new record to a table. AutoNumber fields can't be changed.
Yes/No	A field containing only one of two values (for example, Yes/No, True/False, On/Off).
OLE Object	An object (such as a Microsoft Excel spreadsheet) linked to or embedded in an Access table.
Hyperlink	A link that, when clicked, takes the user to another file, a location in a file, or a site on the Web.
Attachment	A file attachment icon that allows you to attach a file.
Calculated	An Expression Builder to create an expression to calculate a value.
Lookup Wizard	A wizard that helps you to create a field whose values are chosen from the values in another table, query, or list of values.

Viewing Field Properties

Text Field Properties

Field	Action
Field Size	Specify the maximum number of characters (up to 255) that can be entered in the field.
Format	Specify how the data for the field will appear on the screen.
Input Mask	Specify a format or pattern in which data must be entered.
Caption	Enter a label for the field when used on a form. If you don't enter a caption, Access uses the field name as the label.
Default Value	Specify a value that Access enters automatically.
Validation Rule	Enter an expression that limits the values that can be entered in this field.
Validation Text	Enter an error message that appears when a value prohibited by the validation rule is entered.
Required	Indicate whether data entry is required.
Allow Zero Length	Specify if field allows zero length text strings.
Indexed	Indicate whether Access will keep an index of field values.
Unicode Compression	Indicate whether you want Access to save space if only plain text is entered.

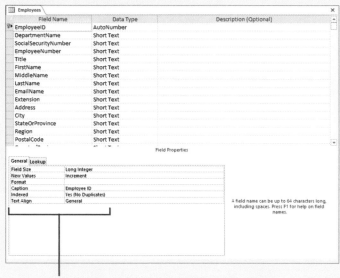

Properties list changes depending on the data type

Changing Field Properties

After you create fields in a table, you can specify properties that define the field's appearance or behavior in Datasheet or Design view. In Datasheet view, you can quickly set the field data type and format. If you want to set more detailed properties, you need to use Design view. In Design view for tables, Access provides a list of field properties for each data type. The properties list changes depending on the data type. Some of the field text properties include Field Size, Format, Input Mask, Caption, Default Value, Validation Rule, Validation Text, Required, Allow Zero Length, and Smart Tags.

Change Field Properties in Datasheet View

1. Display the table in Datasheet view.

2. Click the **Fields** tab under Table Tools.

3. Click the field column header you want to change.

4. Click the **Data Type** list arrow, and then select the field data type you want.

5. If available, click any of the formatting buttons, or click the **Format** list arrow, and then select format.

6. To make this a unique field, select the **Unique** check box.

7. To make this a required field, select the **Required** check box.

8. Click the **Save** button on the Quick Access Toolbar.

9. When you're done, click the **Close** button in the Table window.

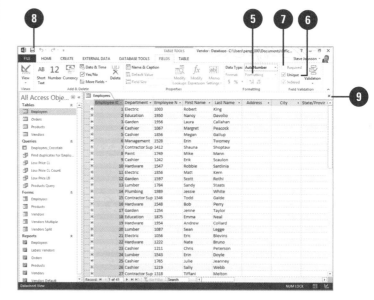

Change Field Properties in Design View

1. Display the table in Design view.

2. Click the field you want to change.

3. Click the field property box you want to change.

4. Type or change the value, or click the list arrow, and then select a value or option.

5. Click the **Save** button on the Quick Access Toolbar.

6. When you're done, click the **Close** button in the Table window.

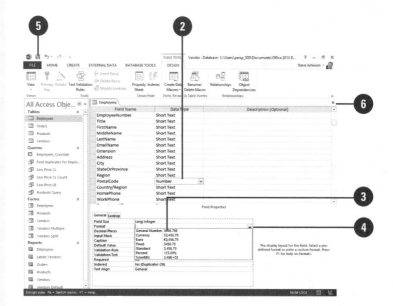

Did You Know?

You can set the number of decimal places. Another way to set the number of decimal places for numeric fields is to specify the number of decimal places in the Decimal Places box in the list of field properties.

You can use different formats for different values. Access allows you to specify different formats for positive, negative, zero, and null values within a single field. Use online Help for more information.

Updating Field Properties

When you make property changes to a field in Table Design view, you can choose to update the corresponding property of controls on forms and reports that are bound to the field. When a bound control inherits a field property change, the Property Update Options button appears in Table Design view, where you can choose the Update command. If a bound control doesn't inherit the field's property change, Access doesn't update the control's property.

Update Field Properties

1. Display the table in Design view.

2. Click the field property box you want to change.

3. Click the **General** or **Lookup** tab, and then change a property.

   If you changed the value of an inherited property, the Property Update Options button appears.

4. Click the **Property Update Options** button, and then click an update command.

5. Select the forms or reports that contain the controls needed to be updated, and then click **Yes**.

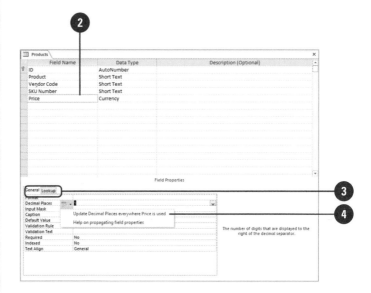

Did You Know?

You can turn off Property Update. Click the File tab, click Options, click Object Designers in the left pane, clear the Show Property Update Options Buttons check box, and then click OK.

Setting Field Size

For Text, Number, and AutoNumber data types, you can use the Field Size property to set the maximum size of data stored in the field. In the case of text data, this property specifies the number of characters allowed (from 0 to 255). Numeric field sizes include Byte, Integer, and Long Integer options for integer values, and Single and Double options for decimals. The difference between these sizes lies in the amount of storage space they use and the range of possible values they cover. If your integers will cover only the range 0 to 255, you should use Byte, but for a larger range you should use Integer or Long Integer.

Specify Field Size

1. Display the table in Design view.

2. Click the text or numeric field in the field list.

3. Click the **Field Size** box in the properties sheet, and then either type the Field Size value (for text fields) or choose the value from the drop-down list (for numeric fields).

Numeric Field Sizes

Field Size	Range	Storage
Byte	Integers from 0 to 255	1 byte
Integer	Integers from -32,768 to 32,767	2 bytes
Long Integer	Integers from -2,147,483,648 to 2,147,483,647	4 bytes
Single	from -3.402823E38 to -1.401298E-45 (negative values) and 1.401298E-45 to 3.402823E38 (positive values)	4 bytes
Double	from -1.797693E308 to -4.940656E-324 (negative values) and 1.797693E308 to 4.940656E324 (positive values)	8 bytes
Replication ID	Values used to establish unique identifiers	16 bytes

Formatting Text Values

A **format** is a property that determines how numbers, dates, times, and text are displayed and printed. Access provides custom formats for dates and times, but you can also create your own formats using formatting symbols. **Formatting symbols** are symbols that Access uses to control how it displays data values. For example, the formatting symbol "<" forces Access to display text characters in lowercase, while the symbol ">" displays those same characters in uppercase. Formatting may also include use of **literals**, which are text strings that are displayed exactly as they appear in format. Formatting only affects the way the data is displayed. It does not affect the data itself.

Format Text Data

1. Display the table in Design view.

2. Click a text field for which you want to set formatting values.

3. Click the **Format** box, and then enter a text format for all data values in the text field.

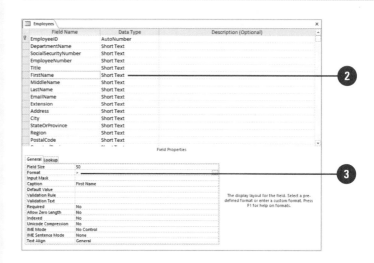

General and Text Formatting Symbols

Symbol	Data	Format	Display
!	321	!	321
<	Today	<	today
>	News	>	NEWS
"ABC"	20	&"lbs."	20lbs.
(space)	16	& "oz."	16 oz.
\	10	&\k	10k
@	5551234	@@@-@@@@	555-1234
&	Mr	&\.	Mr.
*	Hello	&*!	Hello!!!!!!
[*color*]	Alert	[gray]	Alert

Formatting Long Text with Rich Text

With Access, you can format memo or long text using the Rich Text format. You can format text with common formatting options—such as bold, italic, fonts, and colors—or Rich Text specific options—such as numbering, bullets, text highlight and text direction—and store it in the database. The rich text formatting is stored in a compatible HTML-based format. For a field with the Long Text (**New!**) data type, you set the Text Format property to Rich Text, select a field or record in Datasheet view, and then use formatting buttons on the Home tab.

Format Long Text with Rich Text

1. Display the table in Design view.

2. Click a long text field for which you want to set formatting values.

3. Click the **Text Format** box.

4. Click the list arrow in the cell to the right, and then click **Rich Text**.

5. If necessary, click **Yes** to convert the contents of the field to Rich Text.

6. Click the **Datasheet View** button.

7. Select the long text field or record you want to format.

8. Click the **Home** tab.

9. Click any of the formatting buttons: **Bold, Italic, Underline, Highlight Color, Font Color, Font, Font Size, Decrease List Level, Increase List Level, Numbering, Bullets,** or **Text**.

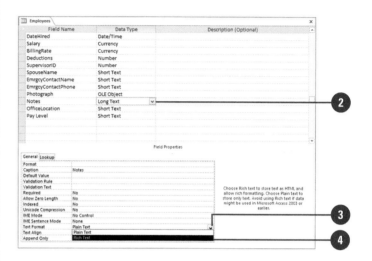

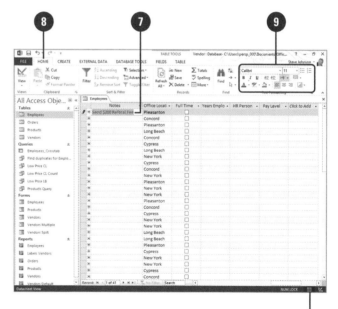

Formatting Date and Time Values

Access provides formatting symbols and predefined formats for date and time values that allow you to display different combinations of the time, date, and day. The predefined formats include a general form, which displays the date and time, as well as short, medium, and long forms of the date and time. To help you find and choose a date, the Date/Time field automatically displays a calendar button.

Specify a Date and Time Format

① Display the table in Datasheet or Design view.

② Click a date and time field.

③ Click the **Format** list arrow on the Fields tab or in the Data Type cell in Design view.

④ Select a format from the predefined list of formats.

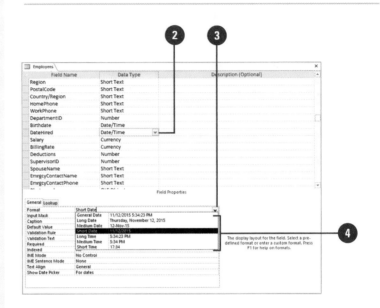

Predefined Date Formats

Format	Display
General Date	1/1/05 12:35:15 PM
Long Date	Saturday, January 1, 2005
Medium Date	01-Jan-05
Short Date	1/1/05
Long Time	12:35:15 PM
Medium Time	12:35 PM
Short Time	12:35

Find and Choose a Date

1. In the Navigation pane, double-click the table you want to open.

2. Select a date field.

   TROUBLE? *If the date field contains an input mask, the date picker doesn't appear.*

3. Click the calendar button.

4. Click the **Next** and **Previous** button to find the month you want, and then click the date you want.

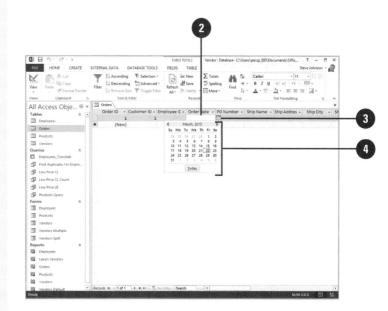

Formatting Number and Currency Values

If a field has a Number or Currency data type, Access provides a list of predefined formats to display the data values in Datasheet or Design view. In Design view, you can also create your own format using formatting symbols applicable to numeric values and currency.

Choose a Predefined Numeric or Currency Format

1. Display the table in Datasheet or Design view.

2. Click a numeric or currency field.

3. Click the **Format** list arrow on the Fields tab or in the Data Type cell in Design view.

4. Select a format from the predefined list of formats, or enter the appropriate formatting symbols.

   TIMESAVER *In Datasheet view, you can also click number and currency buttons.*

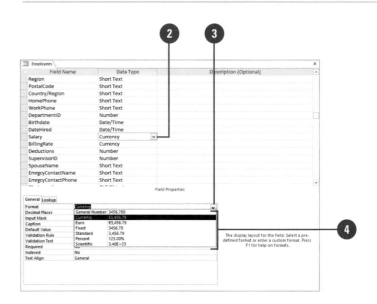

Numeric and Currency Formatting Symbols

Symbol	Data	Format	Display
#	15	#	15
0	20.1	#.00	20.10
.	15	#.	15.
,	92395	#,###	92,395
$	19.3	$#.00	$19.30
%	0.75	#%	75%
E-,E+,e-,e+	625971	#.00E+00	625E+05

Performing a Total Calculation

If you create a field for numbers, you can use the Totals row to calculate values using functions such as sum, count, average, maximum, minimum, standard deviation, or variance. To perform a calculation, select the field you want to use in a table, use the Totals button on the Home tab, select the Total row field, and then select the function you want to use.

Use the Total Row to Perform a Calculation

1. In the Navigation pane, double-click the table you want to open.

2. Click the field with the numbers you want to use in a calculation.

3. Click the **Home** tab.

4. Click the **Totals** button to insert the Totals row at the bottom of the table.

5. Click the Total row field in the column with the numbers you want to use in a calculation.

6. Click the list arrow, and then select the function you want to use.

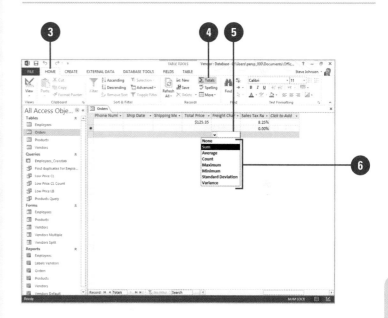

Creating Input Masks

An **input mask** allows you to control what values a database user can enter into a field. Input masks consist of literal characters, such as spaces, dots, parentheses, and placeholders. A **placeholder** is a text character, such as the underline symbol (_), that indicates where the user should insert values. An input mask for a phone number field might appear as follows: (_ _ _) _ _ _ - _ _ _ _ . The parenthesis and dash characters act as literal characters, and the underscore character acts as a placeholder for the phone number values. Access provides several predefined input masks, which cover most situations, but you can create your own customized masks, if necessary. The **Input Mask Wizard** is available only for text and date fields. If you want to create an input mask for numeric fields, you must enter the formatting symbols yourself.

Specify an Input Mask

1. Display the table in Design view.

2. Click a field for which you want to specify an input mask.

3. Click the **Input Mask** box.

4. Click the **Build** button to start the **Input Mask Wizard**.

5. Scroll thru the predefined list to find an input mask form.

6. Type some sample values to see how the input mask affects your sample values.

7. Click **Next** to continue.

Click to modify or add input masks to the predefined list.

8 If you change the input mask, type new formatting codes.

9 If you want to display a different placeholder, click the Placeholder list arrow, and select the placeholder you want to use.

10 Enter values to test the final version of your input mask, and then click **Next** to continue

11 Indicate whether you want to store the input mask symbols along with the data values.

12 Click **Next** to continue, and then click **Finish**.

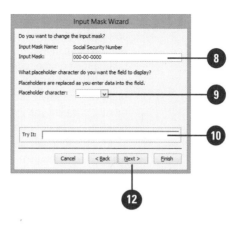

Did You Know?

You can use the Input Mask Wizard. The Input Mask Wizard is available only for text and date fields. If you want to create an input mask for numeric fields, you must enter the formatting symbols yourself.

You can create a password mask. For sensitive data, choose the password input mask from the Input Mask Wizard. Any text the user types will be saved as the text, but displayed as an asterisk (*).

Input Mask Symbols

Symbol	Description
0	Digital 0 to 9 (required)
9	Digital 0 to 9 (optional)
A	Letter or digit (required)
a	Letter or digit (optional)
#	Digit or space
&	Any character or space (required)
C	Any character or space (optional)
L	Letter A-Z (required)
?	Letter A-Z (optional)
>	Make following characters uppercase
<	Make following characters lowercase

Creating Indexed Fields

Just like an index in a book, an index in Access helps you locate and sort information quickly, especially in a very large table. An **index** in Access is an invisible data structure that stores the sort order of a table based on the indexed field or fields. When you sort a large table by an indexed field, Access consults the index and is able to sort the table very quickly. It can be helpful to index fields you frequently search or sort, or fields you join to fields in other tables in queries. If a field contains many different values, rather than many values that are the same, indexing can significantly speed up queries. After indexing a field, you can view and then modify indexes as necessary.

Create a Field Index

1. Display the table in Design view.

2. Click a field you want as an index.

3. Click the **Indexed** box.

4. Click the list arrow, and then select one of the following.

   ◆ **Yes (Duplicates OK)** option if you want to allow multiple records to have the same data in this field.

   ◆ **Yes (No Duplicates)** option if you want to ensure that no two records have the same data in this field.

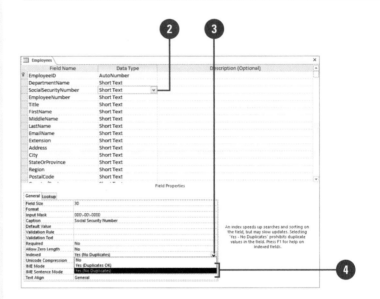

View or Edit Indexes

1. Display the table in Design view.

2. Click the **Indexes** button.

3. Type a name for the index.

4. Select a field to act as an index.

5. Click the list arrow, and then select **Ascending** or **Descending** to indicate the index sort order.

6. Click the **Close** button.

Did You Know?

You can index data types. You don't have to index all data types, and there are some data types you cannot index. For example, you do not need to index the primary key of a table, because it is automatically indexed. You can index a field only if the data type is Text, Number, Currency, or Date/Time. You cannot index a field whose data type is Memo or OLE Object.

You can create a multiple-field index. If you think you'll often search or sort by two or more fields, create a multiple-field index by adding additional fields in the Field Name column for each index name.

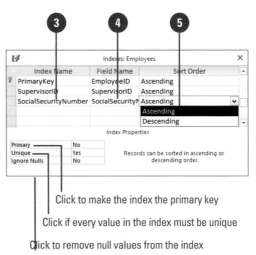

Click to make the index the primary key

Click if every value in the index must be unique

Click to remove null values from the index

Specifying Required Fields and Default Values

Some fields contain essential information. For example, social security numbers are required for employees in order to process payroll and other reports. You set fields like these as **required fields**, which means that Access refuses to accept a record until you enter an acceptable value for that field. You can also set a **default value** for a field, a value Access uses unless a user enters a different one. If a field usually has the same value, such as a city or state if most contacts are local, you could assign that value as the default in order to speed up data entry.

Create a Required Field

① Display the table in Design view.

② Click a field that you want to be a required field.

③ Click the **Required** box.

TIMESAVER *In Datasheet view on the Fields tab, you can also select the Is Required check box.*

④ Click the list arrow, and then click **Yes**.

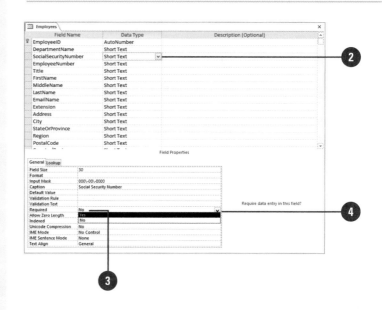

Specify a Default Value

① Display the table in Design view.

② Click a field for which you want to set a default value.

③ Click the **Default Value** box.

④ Enter the default value for the field in the box.

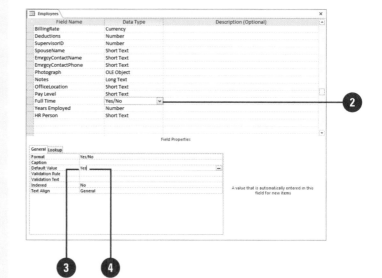

Adding a Caption to a Field

A field **caption** is text displayed alongside a field to better describe its purpose and content. You can add a caption to a field, and later when you create forms and reports that use this field, Access automatically displays the caption you specify. Captions can contain up to 2,048 characters, including spaces. If you don't specify a caption, Access uses the field name as the field caption in any forms or reports you create.

Set the Caption Property

① Display the table in Design view.

② Click a field for which you want to set a caption.

③ Click the **Caption** box.

④ Type text you want to appear as the field's caption.

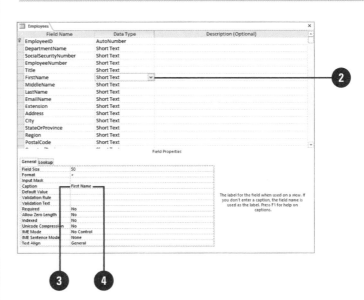

Did You Know?

You can set zero-length strings. Text and Memo data type fields allow you to control whether or not a user can leave a field blank. To ensure that some text is entered, set the Required property to Yes.

Validating Field Values

When you need explicit control over data entered in a field, such as a range of numbers or dates, you can enforce a **validation rule**, which causes Access to test values a user enters in a field. If the value doesn't satisfy the validation rules criteria, Access refuses to enter the value and displays an error message. You can specify the text of the error message yourself. You can use the Expression Builder to create a validation rule by selecting the functions, constants, and operators you need for your rule from a list of options.

Create a Validation Rule

1. Display the table in Design view.

2. Click a field that you intend to validate.

3. Click the **Validation Rule** box, and then click the **Builder** button to open the Expression Builder.

4. Create an expression by clicking the appropriate elements in the Expression Builder dialog box.

5. Click **OK**.

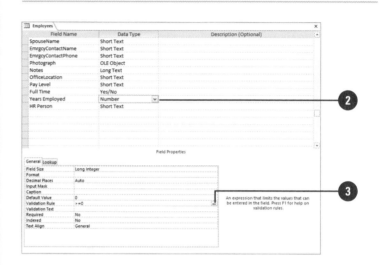

As you select options and type variables, the expression appears in this pane.

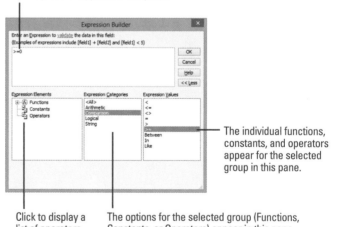

The individual functions, constants, and operators appear for the selected group in this pane.

Click to display a list of operators.

The options for the selected group (Functions, Constants, or Operators) appear in this pane.

Specify Validation Text

1. Display the table in Design view.

2. Click a field.

3. Click the **Validation Text** box.

4. Type the text that Access will display when the user tries to enter incorrect data for the field.

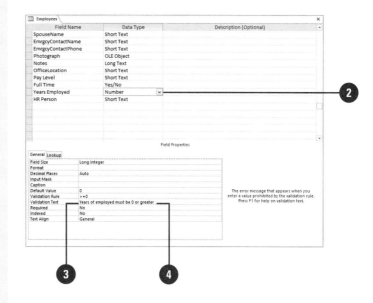

Check Validation Rules

1. Display the table in Design view.

2. Click the **Test Validation Rules** button.

   A validation alert appears, indicating the results of the test or the need to continue the process.

3. If necessary, click **Yes** to continue.

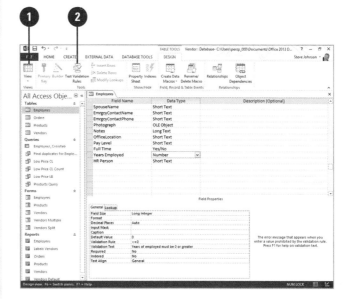

Creating a Lookup Field

The **Lookup Wizard** helps you create a field that displays either of two kinds of lists during data entry: a **Lookup** list that displays values looked up from an existing table or query, or a **Value** list that displays a fixed set of values you enter when you create the field. Because values are limited to a predefined list, using Lookup fields helps you avoid data entry errors in situations where only a limited number of possible values are allowed. The lists are not limited to a single column. You can include additional columns that could include descriptive information for the various choices in the list. However, only a single column, called the **bound column**, contains the data that is extracted from the list and placed into the Lookup field.

Create a Field Based on a Lookup List

1. Display the table in Design view.

2. Click the **Data Type** list arrow, and then click **Lookup Wizard**.

   - You can also open a table in Datasheet view, select a field, click the **Fields** tab under Table Tools, and then click the **Lookup Column** button.

3. Click the **I want the lookup column to look up the values in a table or query** option, and then click **Next** to continue.

4. Select or clear the **Hide key column (recommended)** check box to show or hide the primary key column.

5. Enter the values in the list. Resize the column widths, if necessary. Click **Next** to continue.

6. Choose which column will act as the bound column, and then click **Next** to continue.

7. Enter a label for the Lookup column.

8. Click **Finish**.

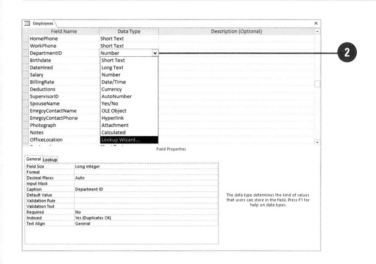

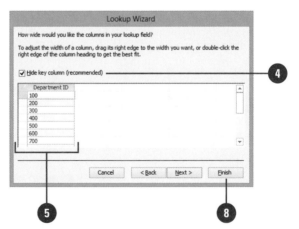

Create a Field Based on a Value List

① Display the table in Design view.

② Click the **Data Type** list arrow, and then click **Lookup Wizard**.

③ Click the **I will type in the values that I want** option, and then click **Next** to continue.

④ Specify the number of columns you want in the Value list.

⑤ Enter the values in the list. If necessary, resize the column widths, and then click **Next** to continue.

⑥ Choose which column will act as the bound column, and then click **Next** to continue.

⑦ Enter a label for the Lookup column.

⑧ Click **Finish**.

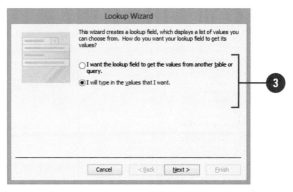

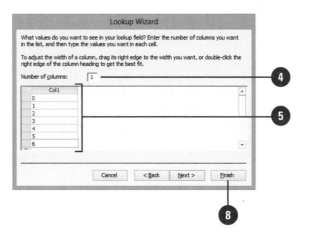

Setting Lookup Properties

If you want to create a Lookup field manually or make changes to the field created by the wizard, you can do so by changing the values in the Lookup properties. These properties allow you to specify the type of drop-down list Access will display, the source of the val-ues in the list, the appearance of the list, and the column that will act as the bound column. You can also indicate whether the user is limited to the choices in the list or can enter other values during data entry.

Specify the type of source for the Lookup data.

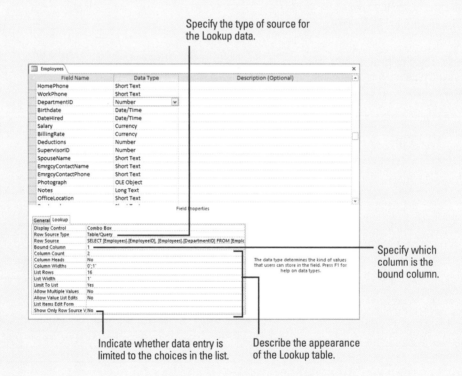

Specify which column is the bound column.

Indicate whether data entry is limited to the choices in the list.

Describe the appearance of the Lookup table.

Creating a Multivalued Field

Sometimes you want to store multiple values in a field. For example, you want to assign a task or responsibility to more than one person. In Access, you can create a multivalued field that lets you select more than one value. When you click a multivalue field, check boxes appear next to each available value. You can select or clear items in the list, and then click OK on the menu. To create a multivalue field, you use the Lookup Wizard, and then select the Allow Multiple Values check box on the last wizard screen. The Lookup Wizard helps you create a field that displays either of two kinds of lists during data entry: a Lookup list that displays values looked up from an existing table or query, or a Value list that displays a fixed set of values you enter when you create the field. Because values are limited to a predefined list, using Lookup fields helps you avoid data entry errors in situations where only a limited number of possible values are allowed.

Create a Multivalued Field

1. Display the table in Design view.

2. Click the **Data Type** list arrow, and then click **Lookup Wizard**.

   ◆ You can also open a table in Datasheet view, select a field, click the **Fields** tab under Table Tools, and then click the **Lookup Column** button.

3. Click the **I want the lookup column to look up the values in a table or query** or **I will type in the values that I want** option, and then click **Next** to continue.

4. Follow the Lookup Wizard instructions depending on how you specified the lookup column values until you get to the final wizard screen.

5. Select the **Allow Multiple Values** check box.

6. Click **Finish**.

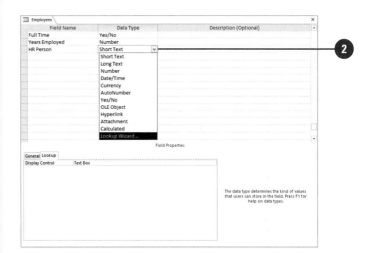

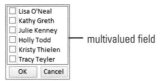

multivalued field

Attaching Files to Field Records

In earlier versions of Access, you needed to use the OLE data type to store images and documents in a database. In Access, you can create a field in a table with the Attachments field and then store multiple files in a single record. You can attach a maximum of two gigabytes of data in a database. Individual files cannot exceed 256 megabytes. After you set the data type to Attachments, you cannot change it. A table with the Attachments field display a paper clip in each record where you can attach files. When you double-click a paper clip, the Attachments dialog opens, where you can add, edit, and manage attachments. Access automatically compresses any attached files in a database to optimize it. You can also view and add attachment files in Forms or Reports view.

Create an Attachment Field

1. Display the table in Datasheet or Design view.

2. Click a blank field name, and then type a field name.

3. Click the **Data Type** list arrow on the Fields tab or in the Data Type cell in Design view.

4. Click **Attachment** from the list.

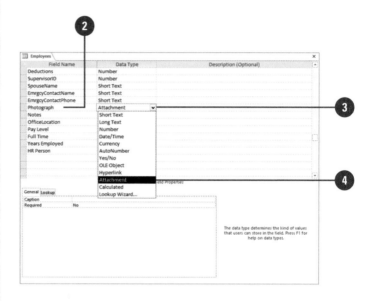

Attachment field

Attach Files in a Record

1 Display the table in Datasheet view.

2 Double-click the record with the paper clip icon where you want to attach a file.

3 Click **Add**.

4 If you want to open a specific file type, click the **Files of type** list arrow, and then select a file type.

5 If the file is located in another folder, click the **Look In** list arrow, and then select the file.

6 Click **Open**.

7 To add more than one file to this record, click **Add**, select the file, and then click **Open**.

8 Click **OK**.

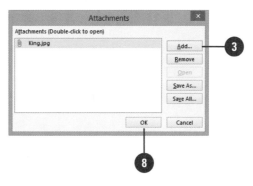

Manage Attachment Files in a Record

1 Display the table in Datasheet view.

2 Double-click the record with the attachments you want to manage.

3 To open an attachment, select it, and then click **Open**.

4 To remove an attachment, select it, and then click **Remove**.

5 To save an attachment, select it, and then click **Save As**. To save all attachments, click **Save All**.

6 Click **OK**.

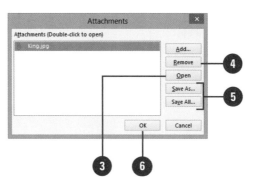

Creating a Field Data Type Template

In addition to creating a database template or application part, you can also save a field as a data type template. You can use an individual or combination of fields as a data type template. For example, you can create a data type template for a Start Date and End Date set of fields. You save a field or set of fields as a data type template file (.accft). After you create a dat type template , you can use it from the More Fields button on the Fields tab.

Create a Custom Field Data Type Template

1. Display the table in Datasheet view with the field(s) you want to save as a data type template.

2. Select the field(s) you want to use.

3. Click the **Fields** tab under Table Tools.

4. Click the **More Fields** button, and then click **Save Selection as New Data Type**.

5. Specify the following in the Create New Data Type from Fields dialog box:

   ◆ **Name.** Enter a name for the data type template. The name appears in the More Fields list.

   ◆ **Description.** Enter text as a description, which appears in the tooltip.

   ◆ **Category.** Select a category in which to list the data type template in the More Fields list.

   ◆ **Instantiation Form.** Select a form that opens by default when the data type template opens.

6. Click **OK**.

   ◆ Default templates folder. C:\Users*user name*\AppData\ Roaming\Microsoft\Templates\ Access.

7. Click **OK**.

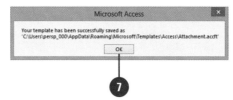

Use a Custom Field Data Type Template

1. Display the table in Datasheet view.

2. Select the field next to where you want to insert a field using a data type template.

3. Click the **Fields** tab under Table Tools.

4. Click the **More Fields** button.

5. Select the custom field from the More Fields menu under the category you specified in the Create New Data Type from Fields dialog box.

Setting Table Properties

In addition to setting field properties, you can also set table properties. Table properties apply to the entire table and to entire records. The Table Properties task pane displays a list of all available properties, which includes DefaultView, ValidationRule, ValidationText, Filter, OrderBy and SubdatasheetExpanded. You can open a table in Design View, and then use the Property Sheet button on the Design tab to open the Table Properties task pane.

Set Table Properties

1. Display the table in Design view.

2. Click the **Design** tab under Table Tools.

3. Click the **Property Sheet** button.

4. Click the box for the property you want to set, and then type a setting for the property.

5. Click the **Close** button on the Property Sheet.

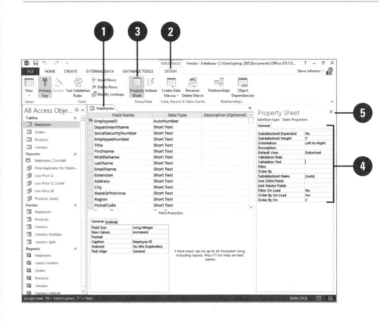

Property	Description
DefaultView	Set default view when you open a table
ValidationRule	Specify an expression that must be true to add or change a record
ValidationText	Enter text that appears when a record fails the ValidationRule
Filter	Specify criteria to display only matching rows
OrderBy	Select fields to specify the default sort order
FilterOnLoad	Apply filter when you open table in Datasheet view
OrderByOnLoad	Apply sort criteria when you open table in Datasheet view
Subdatasheet Expanded	Expand all subdatasheets when you open table open

Common Table Properties

Working with Tables

Introduction

Tables are the storage containers of your data. To help you work effectively with tables, Microsoft Access provides features that assist you not only in entering and editing the data in your tables but also in locating the information you need.

◆ You can locate records based on the text they contain with the Find feature.

◆ You can enter and edit data more accurately with features like AutoCorrect, copy, collect, paste, and language features.

◆ You can display records in either ascending or descending order based on the contents of a specific field.

◆ You can arrange records and columns so your information is listed in the order you want, and adjust the size of your rows and columns to show more or less of the information displayed in any of the fields. You can also view subdatasheets that show groups of data related to the records in your tables.

◆ To focus on certain records in a table, you can apply a filter to change which records are displayed. With a filter, you describe characteristics or contents of the records you want to view.

What You'll Do

Work with Tables

Repair Renaming Errors

Manage Linked Tables

Work with the Clipboard

Edit Text

Enter Data Accurately with AutoCorrect

Find and Replace Text

Check Spelling

Use Custom Dictionaries

Format a Datasheet

Arrange Field Columns

Change the Size of Field Columns

Manage Field Columns

Sort Records

View a Subdatasheet

Filter Out Records

Create Complex Filters Using Forms

Working with Tables

A database is made up of groups of fields organized into tables. As you develop a database, you continually need to work with tables to change, update, and manage information. Instead of creating a new table every time you need one, you can also copy an existing table, and then make changes to it. During the copy and paste process, you can select options to create table a with or without data, or append data into another table. If you want to change a table name, you can quickly change it the same way you rename a file or folder name. If you no longer need a table, you can remove it and its data.

Copy a Table

1. In the Navigation pane, select the table you want to copy.

2. Click the **Home** tab.

3. Click the **Copy** button.

4. Click the **Paste** button.

5. Type a name for the copied table.

6. Click the **Structure Only** or **Structure and Data** option you want.

7. Click **OK**.

Did You Know?

You can delete a table. Select the table you want to delete in the Navigation pane, click the Delete button on the Home tab, and then click Yes to confirm. You can also right-click a table, and then click Delete.

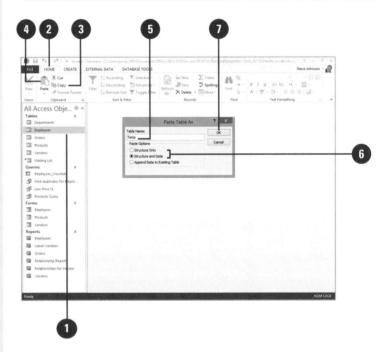

Rename a Table

1. In the Navigation pane, right-click the table you want to rename, and then click **Rename**.

   The table name becomes editable.

2. Type a name to rename the table.

3. Press Enter.

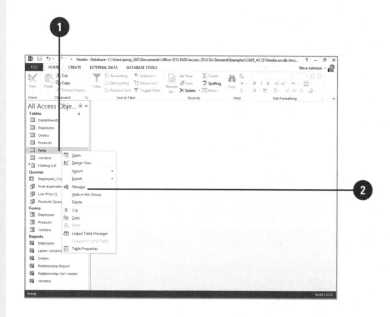

Append Data to Table

1. In the Navigation pane, select the table you want to get data.

2. Click the **Home** tab.

3. Click the **Copy** button.

4. Click the **Paste** button.

5. Type the name of the table to which you want to append data.

6. Click the **Append Data to Existing Table** option.

7. Click **OK**.

8. Click **Yes** to confirm.

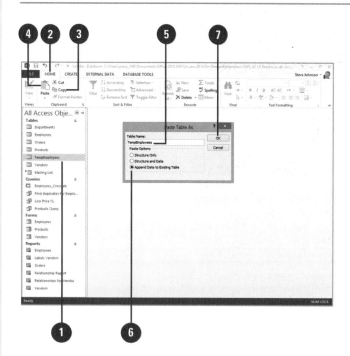

Repairing Renaming Errors

Access can correct errors that commonly occur when you rename forms, reports, tables, queries, text boxes, or other controls in a database. When Access detects a change in the name of one of these objects, it automatically corrects all the other objects that use that name. You can set Access to track renaming without taking action, to apply changes if you rename an object, and to log any changes it makes. Although Name AutoCorrect eliminates errors for database objects that don't employ Visual Basic for Applications (VBA) code, it doesn't repair renaming errors under some circumstances, such as in replicated databases and OBDC linked tables.

Enable and Log Name AutoCorrect

① Click the **File** tab, and then click **Options**.

② In the left pane, click **Current Database**.

③ Select the **Track name AutoCorrect info** check box to allow Access to maintain the information it needs to perform Name AutoCorrect but not take any action.

④ Select the **Perform name AutoCorrect** check box to perform Name AutoCorrect as changes are applied to the database.

⑤ To log name AutoCorrect changes, you need to select all three Name AutoCorrect check boxes: **Track name AutoCorrect info**, **Perform name AutoCorrect**, and **Log name AutoCorrect changes**.

You can view the name changes in a table called AutoCorrect Log.

⑥ Click **OK**.

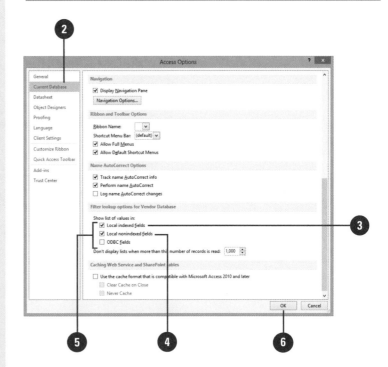

Managing Linked Tables

When you link a table from one Access database to another it's important to keep track of where the source database resides and whether the data in the source table changes. A linked table appears in the Navigation pane with a diamond to the left of the name. The Linked Table Manager allows you to enable and disable the linked tables you want to update. If you need to locate a linked table, the Table Manage displays the complete path to the table so you can find it.

Update Linked Tables

1 Click the **External Data** tab.

2 Click the **Linked Table Manager** button.

◆ You can also right-click the table in the Navigation pane, and then click **Linked Table Manager**.

3 Select or clear the check box next to the table you want to enable or disable.

4 To get a prompt for a new table location, select the **Always prompted for new location** check box.

5 Click **OK**.

6 If you selected the option for a new location prompt, select a file, and then click **Open**.

7 Click **OK** to the successful alert dialog box.

8 Click **Close**.

Did You Know?

You can convert a table to a local table. Right-click the table in the Navigation pane, click Convert to Local Table.

Working with the Clipboard

The Office Clipboard is available from within any Office program and holds information, any or all of which you can paste to a new location. As you cut or copy information, Office collects it in the Office Clipboard. You can use the Office Clipboard task pane to manage the information and use it in Office documents. The Office Clipboard allows you to collect multiple items and paste them quickly. When you paste an item, the Paste Options button appears below it. When you click the button, a menu appears with options to specify how Office pastes the information. The available options differ depending on the content you are pasting.

Paste Items from the Office Clipboard

1. Click the **Home** tab.

2. Click the **Clipboard Dialog Box Launcher**.

3. Click where you want to insert the text.

4. Click any icon on the Clipboard task pane to paste that selection. If there is more than one selection you can paste all the selections at once, by clicking **Paste All**.

5. When you're done, click the **Close** button on the task pane.

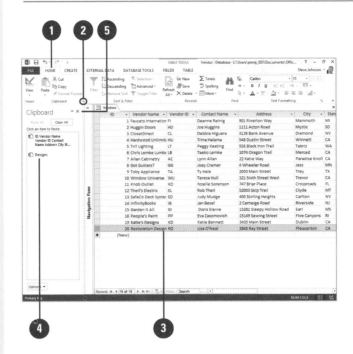

Did You Know?

You can copy and paste a new record. In Datasheet view, select the row selector for the row you want to copy, click the Copy button on the Home tab, select the empty row selector for the new record row, and then click the Paste button.

You can paste information in a different format. Select the object or text, click the Copy button on the Home tab, click to indicate where you want to paste the object, click the Paste button arrow, click Paste Special, click the object type you want, and then click OK.

Delete Items from the Office Clipboard

1. Click the **Home** tab.

2. Click the **Clipboard Dialog Box Launcher**.

3. Click the list arrow of the item you want to paste, and then click **Delete**.

4. To erase all items in the Office Clipboard, click **Clear All**.

5. When you're done, click the **Close** button on the task pane.

Change Clipboard Options

1. Click the **Home** tab.

2. Click the **Clipboard Dialog Box Launcher**.

3. Click **Options**, and then click to select any of the following options:

   ◆ **Show Office Clipboard Automatically.**

   ◆ **Show Office Clipboard When Ctrl+C Pressed Twice.**

   ◆ **Collect Without Showing Office Clipboard.**

   ◆ **Show Office Clipboard Icon On Taskbar.**

   ◆ **Show Status Near Taskbar When Copying.**

4. When you're done, click the **Close** button on the task pane.

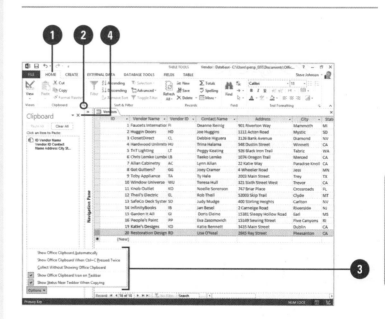

Editing Text

Before you can edit text, you need to highlight, or select, the text you want to modify. You can edit text you enter in a record by selecting the text you want to change and then performing an action. When you want to insert or delete text one character at a time, you point between two characters or words and then click to place the **insertion point**, a vertical cursor that indicates your location in a section of text. When you want to change the entire contents of a table cell, you select the cell. After you select the items you want, you can delete, replace, move (cut), or copy text within Access objects or between different programs. In either case, the steps are the same.

Select and Edit Text and Cell Contents

1 Select the text or cell contents you want to edit.

- ◆ Double-click a word.

- ◆ Drag to select multiple words.

- ◆ Click the border of a table cell to select its entire contents in Datasheet view.

- ◆ Point to the border of a table cell, and then drag to select multiple cells in Datasheet view.

2 Perform one of the following editing commands:

- ◆ To replace text, type your text.

- ◆ To delete text, press the Backspace key or the Delete key.

Did You Know?

You can undo a mistake. If you insert or delete something by mistake, you can click the Undo button on the Quick Access Toolbar to reverse the action.

Insert and Delete Text and Cell Contents

1 Click in the field to place the insertion point where you want to make the change.

◆ To insert text, type your text.

◆ To delete text, press the Backspace key or the Delete key.

Move or Copy Text and Cell Contents

1 Select the text you want to move or copy.

2 Click the **Home** tab.

3 Click the **Cut** or **Copy** button.

4 Click where you want to insert the text.

5 Click the **Paste** button.

◆ To paste the text with another format, click the Home tab, click the **Paste** button arrow, click **Paste Special**, click a format option, and then click **OK**.

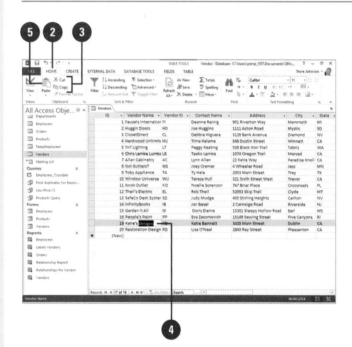

Entering Data Accurately with AutoCorrect

As you enter data in tables, you might occasionally make typing mistakes. For certain errors, Access will correct the errors as soon as you type them and then press the Spacebar or Enter. For example, if you type compnay when you meant to type company, the AutoCorrect feature will correct the error automatically. You can easily customize the preset AutoCorrect options or add errors that you commonly make to the list of AutoCorrect entries.

Set AutoCorrect Options

1. Click the **File** tab, and then click **Options**.

2. In the left pane, click **Proofing**, and then click **AutoCorrect Options**.

3. Select the **Replace text as you type** check box to enable AutoCorrect.

4. Select or clear the **Show AutoCorrect Options buttons** check box to show or hide it.

5. Select the check boxes with the additional options you want:

   ◆ **Correct two initial capital letters so that only the first letter is capitalized.**

   ◆ **Always capitalize the first word in a sentence.**

   ◆ **Capitalize the names of days.**

   ◆ **Correct accidental use of the Caps Lock key.**

6. Click **OK**, and then click **OK** again.

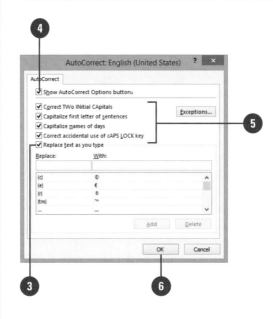

Did You Know?

You can replace text as you type. To correct incorrect capitalization or spelling errors automatically, simply continue to type and AutoCorrect will make the required correction.

Examples of AutoCorrect Changes

Type of Correction	If You Type	AutoCorrect Inserts
Capitalization	cAP LOCK	Cap Lock
Capitalization	TWo INitial CAps	Two Initial Caps
Capitalization	thursday	Thursday
Common typos	can;t	can't
Common typos	windoes	windows

Add or Edit an AutoCorrect Entry

1. Click the **File** tab, and then click **Options**.

2. In the left pane, click **Proofing**, and then click **AutoCorrect Options**.

3. To edit an entry, select the entry you want to change.

4. To add an entry, type a word or phrase that you often mistype or misspell.

5. Type the correct spelling of the word.

6. Click **Add** or **Replace**.

7. Click **OK**, and then click **OK** again.

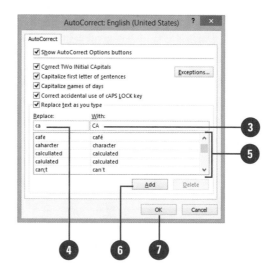

Change Correction as You Type

1. After an AutoCorrect correction, point to the AutoCorrect Options button.

2. Click the **AutoCorrect Options** button.

3. Click any of the following options:

   ◆ **Change Back To**.

   ◆ **Stop Automatically Correcting**.

   ◆ **Control AutoCorrect Options to change the AutoCorrect settings**.

Finding and Replacing Text

To locate one or more records in which you expect to find specific text, you can use the Find feature. In the Find dialog box, you enter the text you want to find, and specify whether Access should search the current field or the entire table, and whether the text you enter should match part of the field or the whole field. You can also indicate whether Access should look for matching capitalization. When Access finds the first record that contains the specified text, it selects that record. You can then move to the next matching record or cancel the search. You can also use the Find and Replace feature to automatically replace specified text with new text. You can review and change each occurrence individually, or replace all occurrences at once.

Search for Text in the Current Field

1. Display the table in Datasheet view.

2. Click the insertion point anywhere in the field (column) where you want to start the search.

3. Click the **Home** tab.

4. Click the **Find** button.

5. Type the text you want to find in either uppercase or lowercase letters.

6. Click the **Look in** list arrow to specify whether Find should search the current field or the entire table.

7. Click the **Match** list arrow, and indicate whether you want the text you typed to match the whole field or part of the field.

8. Click **Find Next** as many times as necessary to view all the records that contain the specified text.

9. When you're done, click the **Close** button.

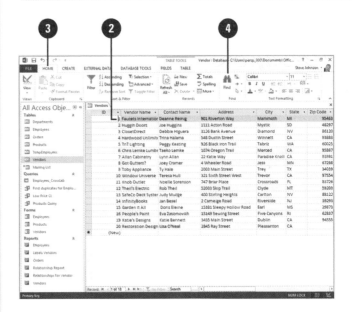

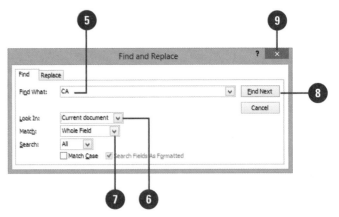

Find and Replace Text

1. Display the table in Datasheet view.

2. Click the insertion point anywhere in the field (column) where you want to start the search.

3. Click the **Home** tab.

4. Click the **Replace** button.

5. Type the text you want to find, and then press Tab.

6. Type the replacement text.

7. Click **Find Next**.

8. Click **Replace** to replace the first occurrence with the replacement text, or click **Replace All** to replace all occurrences with the replacement text, or click **Find Next** to skip to the next occurrence.

9. Click the **Close** button.

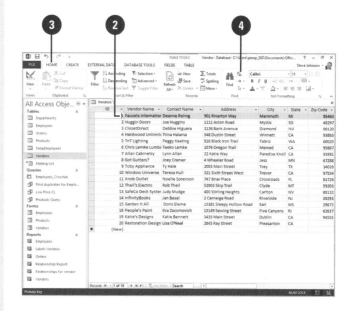

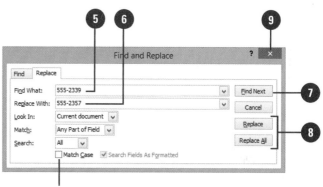

Select the Case check box to search for records matching the case of the text you type.

Did You Know?

You can use wildcards to search for data. When you recall only part of a record data, type an asterisk (*) for two or more unknown characters.

You can go to first, previous, next, or last records. display the table in Datasheet view, click the Home tab, click the Go To button, and then click First, Previous, Next, or Last. You can also click New on the Go To button menu to go to the New record.

For Your Information

Searching for Formatted Text

You might need to find information that has been assigned a specific data format, such as a date format, without entering the information in the specified format. For example, if dates are displayed in the format 05-Jan-13, you can locate that number by typing 1/5/13. Select the Search Fields As Formatted check box to only search for the text as formatted. Be aware that searching this way can be slow.

Checking Spelling

The Spelling feature helps you proofread your data by identifying potentially misspelled words and suggesting possible spellings to use instead. You can correct the spelling, ignore the word, add the word to the dictionary, or create an AutoCorrect entry. Microsoft Office 2013 programs share a common spell checker and dictionary, so you only need to make additions and changes once. In addition, you can control the kinds of spelling errors Access identifies by specifying the spelling options you want in effect. If the text in your database is written in more than one language, you can automatically detect languages or designate the language of selected text so the spelling checker uses the right dictionary.

Check the Spelling in a Table

1. Display the table in Datasheet view.

2. Click the row selector for the record or select the field you want to check. Drag to select additional rows.

3. Click the **Home** tab.

4. Click the **Spelling** button.

   If Access identifies any misspelled words, it opens the Spelling dialog box.

5. Correct or ignore the identified words, as appropriate.

   ◆ Click **Ignore** to ignore the word and retain its spelling. Click **Ignore All** to ignore all instances of the word.

   ◆ Click **Add** to add the word to the dictionary so the spelling checker won't identify it as a misspelled word.

   ◆ Click a word in the Suggestions list, and then click **Change** to spell the word with the selected spelling. Click **Change All** to change all instances of the word to the selected spelling.

   ◆ Click **AutoCorrect** to add the word to the AutoCorrect list.

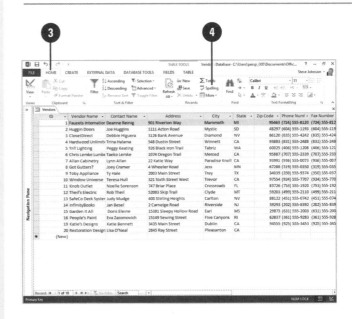

Unrecognized word

Customize Spelling Options

1. In the Spelling dialog box, click **Options**, or click the **File** tab, click **Options**, and then click **Proofing**.

2. Select or clear the Microsoft Office spelling options you want.

   ◆ **Ignore words in UPPERCASE**.

   ◆ **Ignore words that contain numbers**.

   ◆ **Ignore Internet and file addresses**.

   ◆ **Flag repeated words**.

   ◆ **Enforce accented uppercase in French**.

   ◆ **Suggest from main dictionary only**. Select to exclude your custom dictionary.

3. Select or clear the Microsoft Office spelling options you want.

   ◆ **French modes**. Select a mode for the French language: Traditional and new spellings, Traditional spelling, or New spelling.

   ◆ **Spanish modes**. Select a mode for the Spanish language: Tuteo verb forms only, Tuteo and Voseo ver forms, or Voseo verb forms only.

   ◆ **Dictionary language**. Select a language for the dictionary.

4. Click **OK**.

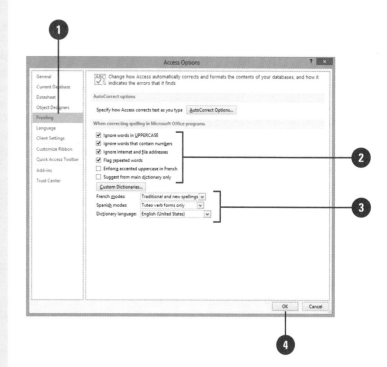

See Also

See "Using Multiple Languages" on page 365 for information on using different languages in Access.

Using Custom Dictionaries

Before you can use a custom dictionary, you need to enable it first. You can enable and manage custom dictionaries by using the Custom Dictionaries dialog box. In the dialog box, you can change the language associated with a custom dictionary, create a new custom dictionary, or add or remove an existing custom dictionary. If you need to manage dictionary content, you can also change the default custom dictionary to which the spelling checker adds words, as well as add, delete, or edit words. All the modifications you make to your custom dictionaries are shared with all your Microsoft Office programs, so you only need to make changes once. If you mistakenly type an obscene or embarrassing word, such as *ass* instead of *ask*, the spelling checker will not catch it because both words are spelled correctly. You can avoid this problem by using an exclusion dictionary. When you use a language for the first time, Office automatically creates an exclusion dictionary. This dictionary forces the spelling checker to flag words you don't want to use.

Use a Custom Dictionary

1. Click the **File** tab, and then click **Options**.

2. In the left pane, click **Proofing**.

3. Click **Custom Dictionaries**.

4. Select the check box next to **CUSTOM.DIC (Default)**.

5. Click the **Dictionary language** list arrow, and then select a language for a dictionary.

6. Click the options you want:

    ◆ Click **Edit Word List** to add, delete, or edit words.

    ◆ Click **Change Default** to select a new default dictionary.

    ◆ Click **New** to create a new dictionary.

    ◆ Click **Add** to insert an existing dictionary.

    ◆ Click **Remove** to delete a dictionary.

7. Click **OK** to close the Custom Dictionaries dialog box.

8. Click **OK**.

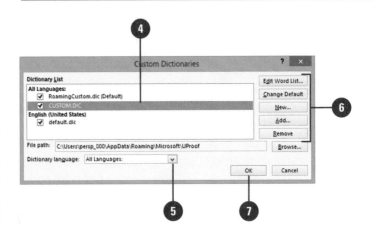

Formatting a Datasheet

If you want to print a datasheet, you can use formatting tools to make it look better than the standard display. You can apply special effects to cells, change the background and gridline color, and modify border and line styles. If you don't want to show the gridlines, you can hide either the horizontal or vertical gridlines, or both. The default display for a datasheet is to display the columns from left to right. If you prefer, you can change the column display to appear from right to left.

Format a Datasheet

1. Display the table in Datasheet view you want to format.

2. Click the **Home** tab.

3. Click the **Text Formatting Dialog Box Launcher**.

4. Click a cell effect option.

5. Select or clear the **Horizontal** or **Vertical** check box to show or hide gridlines.

6. Click the **Background Color**, **Alternate Background Color**, or **Gridline Color** list arrow, and then select a color.

7. Click the **Border and Line Styles** list arrow, and then select the styles you want.

8. Click a display direction option.

9. Click **OK**.

Did You Know?

You can change the formatting in a datasheet using formatting buttons on the Home tab. Open the datasheet you want to format, click the Home tab, click the formatting buttons you want to use, such as Font, Font Style, Font Color, Bold, Italic, or Underline.

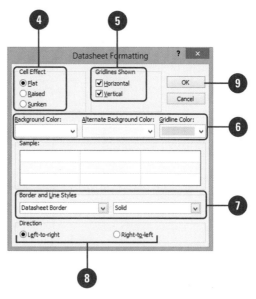

Arranging Field Columns

The order in which field columns appear in the Table window in Datasheet view is initially determined by the order established when you first designed the table. If you want to temporarily rearrange the order of the field columns in a table, you can do so without changing the table design. You can arrange columns in the order you want by selecting and then dragging columns to a new location. You can also hide columns you do not want to view. The **freeze column** feature allows you to "freeze" one or more of the columns on a datasheet so that they are visible regardless of where you scroll.

Move a Field Column

1. In Datasheet view, click the column selector of the column you want to move.

2. Drag the selected column to its new location.

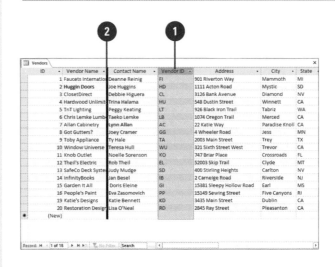

Hide a Field Column

1. In Datasheet view, select the column or columns you want to hide.

2. Click **Home** tab.

3. Click the **More** button, and then click **Hide Fields**.

   TIMESAVER *Right-click the column you want to hide, and then click Hide Fields.*

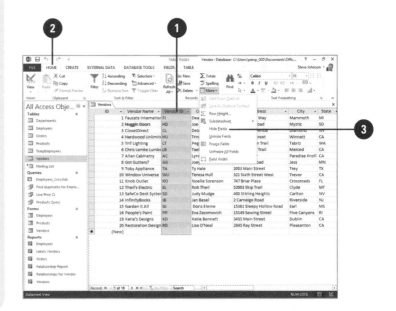

Display a Hidden Column

1. In Datasheet view, click the **Home** tab.

2. Click the **More** button, and then click **Unhide Fields**.

3. Select the names of the columns that you want to show.

4. Click **Close**.

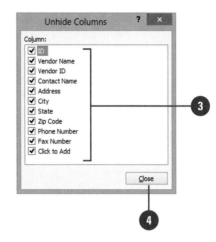

Freeze or Unfreeze Columns

1. In Datasheet view, select the column(s) you want to freeze or unfreeze.

2. Click **Home** tab.

3. Click the **More** button, and then click **Freeze Fields** or **Unfreeze All Fields**.

   TIMESAVER *Right-click a column or the selected columns, and then click Freeze Fields or Unfreeze All Fields.*

Did You Know?

You can format columns in other Access objects. These formatting steps also work for columns in queries, forms, views, or stored procedures.

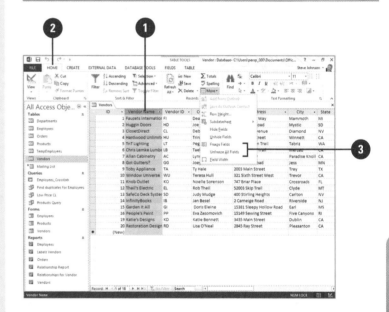

Changing the Size of Field Columns

If some of the text in a field column is hidden because the column is too narrow, you can increase the width of the column. You can also change the height of the rows to provide more space for the text. Unlike changing the field column width, which affects only the selected column or columns, changing the row height affects all the rows in the table. You can adjust the size of columns and rows by using commands or by dragging the borders between columns or rows.

Change Field Column Width

◆ Point to the border between two field selectors, and then drag the border left or right.

◆ Right-click a field selector or select a column and click the **More** button on the Home tab, and then click **Field Width**. Click **Best Fit**, or enter a new width, and then click **OK**.

Drag to resize

Change Row Height

◆ Point to the border between two row selectors, and then drag the border up or down to adjust the height of all the rows in the table.

◆ Right-click a row selector or select a row and click the **More** button on the Home tab, and then click **Row Height**. Enter a new height, and then click **OK**.

Enter row height information

Managing Fields Columns

You can quickly add, remove, and rename field columns from within Datasheet view. If you remove a field column, Access deletes all the data it contains, so delete a field column only if you are sure you no longer require its data. If a field contains a relationship, you must delete the relationship first before you can delete a column. If other database objects contain references to a deleted field, such as a query, Microsoft automatically updates those references.

Insert a Field Column

1. In Datasheet view, right-click the column selector to the right of where you want to add the new column.

   ◆ You can also click the *Click to Add* column, or select a column and then click a field button or **More Fields** button on the Fields tab.

2. Click **Insert Field**.

   The column is inserted with the name Field1, which you can rename.

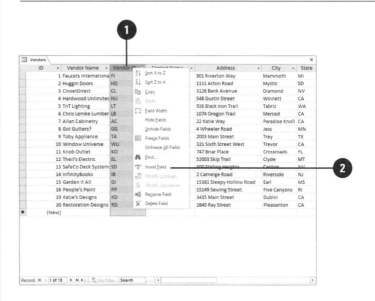

Delete a Field Column

1. In Datasheet view, right-click the column selector(s) for the column(s) you want to delete.

2. Click **Delete Field**.

   ◆ You can also select a column and then click the **Delete** button on the Fields tab.

3. Click **Yes** to confirm the deletion.

Did You Know?

You can rename a field column. In Datasheet view, right-click the selector for the column, click Rename Field, type a name, and then press Enter.

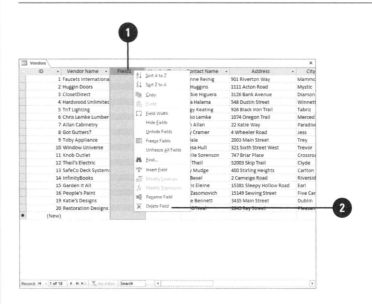

Sorting Records

You can change the order in which records appear in a table, query results, forms, or reports by sorting the records. You can select a field and then sort the records by the values in that field in either ascending or descending order. Ascending order means that records appear in alphabetical order (for text fields), from most recent to later, (for date fields), or from smallest to largest (for numeric fields). In Descending order, the order is reversed. You might also want to sort records by more than one field; this is referred to as a **secondary sort**. For example, in a table containing information about products, you might need to view information about specific prices for each product. You can sort the records first by product and then, in records with the same product, sort the records by price.

Sort Records

1 In the Datasheet view, display the table, query results, form, or report in which you want to sort records.

2 To sort multiple columns, drag the column headers to rearrange them to be adjacent.

3 Click the column selector of the column you want to sort. To select another column, press and hold Shift, and then click the column selector.

4 Click the **Home** tab.

5 Click the **Sort Ascending** button (A to Z), or click the **Sort Descending** button (Z to A).

The list arrow displays an arrow icon indicating the field is sorted. The direction of the arrow indicates the sort direction.

6 To clear all sorts in the current table, click the **Remove Sort** button.

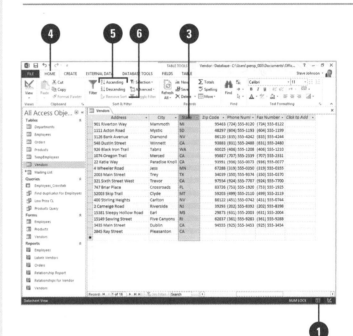

Change the Order of Records Based on Multiple Fields

1. Display the table in Datasheet view.

2. Because multiple fields that you want to sort must be adjacent and in the order of sort priority, rearrange columns if necessary.

3. Click the column selector of the first column you want to sort, and then before you release the mouse button, drag the mouse to the right to select the adjacent columns fields.

4. Click the **Home** tab.

5. Click the **Sort Ascending** button (A to Z), or click the **Sort Descending** button (Z to A).

   The list arrow displays an arrow icon indicating the field is sorted. The direction of the arrow indicates the sort direction.

6. To clear all sorts in the current table, click the **Remove Sort** button.

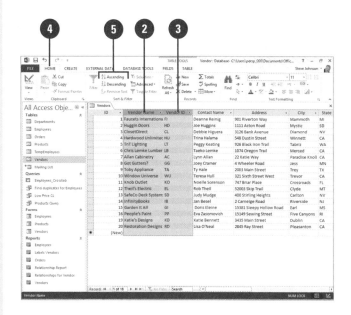

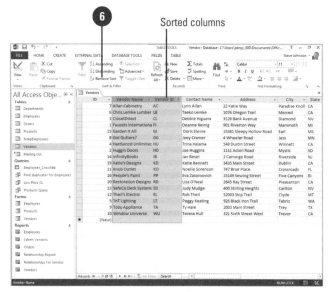

Sorted columns

Did You Know?

You can specify a sort order when designing a table. Changing the order of records displayed in a table is not the same as specifying the sort order when you first design the table. Use the Sort feature when designing a table to display records in the order that you are likely to use most often, and then use the Sort Ascending and Sort Descending buttons to handle the exceptions when you display the table in Datasheet view.

Viewing a Subdatasheet

In a table that has a one-to-many relationship with another table, a given record might have multiple related items. For example, a customer in a Customers table might have many products in a Products table. Access allows you to view the products related to that customer from the Customers table. You can open a **subdatasheet**, a list of the records from the "many" table that relate to a single record from the "one" table in a one-to-one or one-to-many relationship. Subdatasheets help you browse related data in tables, queries, forms, and subform datasheets. For any related tables, Access automatically creates subdatasheets. You can also insert a sub-datasheet in a table or query to view related data.

Insert a Subdatasheet in a Table

1. Display the table or query in Datasheet view.

2. Click the **Home** tab.

3. Click the **More** button, point to **Subdatasheet**, and then click **Subdatasheet**.

4. Click the tab corresponding to the object you want to insert as a subdatasheet.

5. Click a table or query in the list.

6. Select the field you want to use as a foreign key.

7. Select the field you want to use as a primary key.

8. Click **OK**.

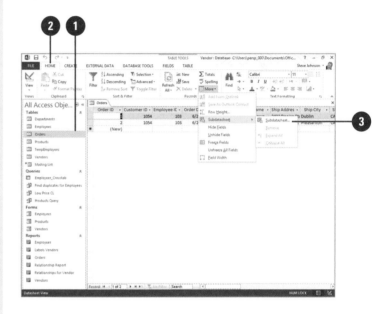

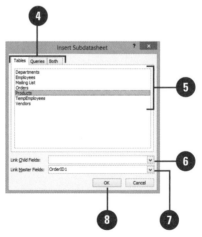

Display or Hide a Subdatasheet

1 In Datasheet view of the table, click the plus sign next to the record for which you want to see related information.

2 To hide the subdatasheet, click the minus sign next to the record whose subdatasheet you want to hide.

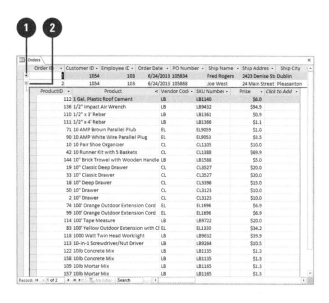

Remove a Subdatasheet

1 Display the table or query in Datasheet view with the subdatasheet you want to remove.

2 Click the **Home** tab.

3 Click the **More** button, point to **Subdatasheet**, and then click **Remove**.

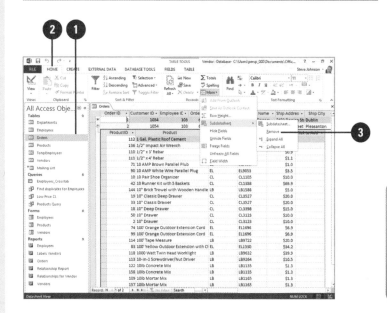

Filtering Out Records

Instead of displaying all the records in a table, you can use a **filter** to display only those records that you want to see. You can display records based on a specific value in one field or on multiple values in multiple fields. You can filter by selecting quick AutoFilter options for the field values on which to base the filter in Datasheet view or by using Filter By Form to help you create more complex filters involving multiple field values. After you apply a filter, Access displays only those records that match your specifications. You can remove a filter to return the datasheet to its original display.

Filter a Table

1. Display the table in Datasheet view.

2. Click the list arrow for the field you want to filter.

3. Select the check boxes with the items that records must match in order to be included in the table.

4. To use built-in filters, point to **<Column Name> Filters**, and then select a filter option, such as Equals, Begins With, or Contains.

5. Repeat steps 2 through 4, as necessary, to filter out more records using additional fields, and then click **OK**, if necessary.

   The list arrow displays an icon indicating the field is filtered. Also, *Filter* appears in the Status bar.

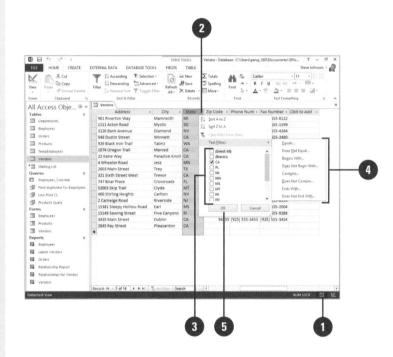

Did You Know?

You can quickly clear a filter from a table. Display the filtered table in Datasheet view, click the Toggle Filter button.

Sorted records

Save a Filter as a Query

1. Display the filtered table in Datasheet view.

2. Click the **Home** tab.

3. Click the **Advanced** button, and then click **Advanced Filter/Sort**.

   The details of the filter appear in Design view.

4. Click the **Save** button on the Quick Access Toolbar.

5. Type the name you want to assign to the query. If you enter the name of an existing query, Access will ask if you want to overwrite the existing query. Be sure to answer "No" if you want to retain the original query, so you can give the new query a different name.

6. Click **OK** to save the filter as a query.

   The query you have just saved appears in the Queries list in the Navigation pane.

7. If necessary, click **OK**.

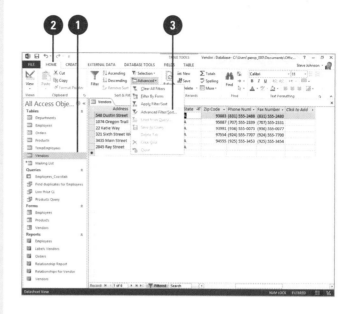

Creating Complex Filters Using Forms

The Filter By Form feature allows you to create a more complex filter. Adding criteria on a particular tab in the form restricts the filter so that records must match all the criteria on the form for the records to be displayed; this is called an AND filter. To expand the filter to include more records, you can create an OR filter by specifying criteria on the subsequent Or tab in the Filter By Form grid. To be displayed, a record needs to match only the criteria specified on the Look For tab or the criteria specified on any one of the Or tabs.

Create an AND or OR Filter

1. Click the **Home** tab.

2. In Datasheet view, click the **Advanced** button, and then click the **Filter By Form**.

3. Click in the empty text box below the field you want to filter.

4. Click the list arrow, and then click the field value by which you want to filter the records.

5. For each field by which you want to filter, click the list arrow, and select the entry for your filter. Each new field in which you make a selection adds additional criteria that a record must match to be included.

6. If you want to establish Or criteria, click the **Or** tab at the bottom of the form to specify the additional criteria for the filter. If not, proceed to step 7.

7. Click the **Toggle Filter** button to turn the filter on or off.

Did You Know?

You can clear previous filters. If necessary, click the Home tab, click the Advanced button, and then click Clear All Filters to clear the previous filter.

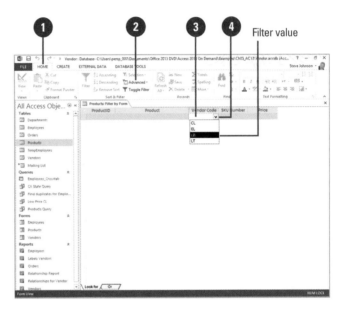

Filter value

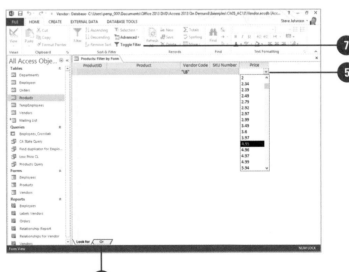

Locating Specific Information Using a Query

6

Introduction

A **query** is a description of the records you want to retrieve from a database. As the name implies, a query helps answer specific questions about the information in your database— for example, "Which customers have placed orders in the last six months?" or "Who sent us greeting cards over the holidays in the last two years?" The description of the records you want to retrieve identifies the names of the fields and the values they should contain; this description is called the **selection criteria**. With a Microsoft Access query you can:

- Focus on only the information you need by displaying only a few fields from a large table.

- Apply functions and other expressions to fields to arrive at calculated results.

- Add, update, or delete records in tables; or create entirely new tables.

- Summarize and group values from one table and display the result in a table.

- Save a query definition that Access will treat as a table for the purpose of creating forms and reports.

- Retrieve information stored in multiple tables, even if the tables are not open.

What You'll Do

Understand Types of Queries

Create and Modify a Query in Design View

Get Information with a Query

Create a Query Using a Wizard

Change the Query Fields

Specify Criteria for a Single or Multiple Fields

Create Queries with Comparison and Logical Operators

Perform Calculations in Queries

Create a Parameter Query

Find Duplicate Fields and Unmatched Records

Create New Tables with a Query

Add Records with a Query

Delete Records with a Query

Update Records with a Query

Summarize Values with a Crosstab Query

Create SQL-Specific Queries

Understanding Types of Queries

Access offers several types of queries that help you retrieve the information you need—select queries, crosstab queries, action queries, and parameter queries.

◆ A select query retrieves and displays records in the Table window in Datasheet view.

◆ A crosstab query displays summarized values (sums, counts, and averages) from one field in a table, and groups them by one set of fields listed down the left side of the datasheet and by another set of fields listed across the top of the datasheet.

◆ An action query performs operations on the records that match your criteria. There are four kinds of action queries that you can perform on one or more tables: delete queries delete matching records; update queries make changes to matching records; append queries add new records to the end of a table; and make-table queries create new tables based on matching records.

◆ A parameter query allows you to prompt for a single piece of information to use as selection criteria in the query. For example, instead of creating separate queries to retrieve customer information for each state in which you do business, you could create a parameter query that prompts the user to enter the name of a state, and then continues to retrieve those specific records from that state.

Creating Queries in Access

As with most database objects you create in Access, there are several ways to create a query. You can create a query from scratch or use a wizard to guide you through the process of creating a query.

With the Query Wizard, Access helps you create a simple query to retrieve the records you want. All queries you create and save are listed under Queries in the Navigation pane. You can then double-click a query to run it and display the results. When you run a select query, the query results show only the selected fields for each record in the table that matches your selection criteria. Of course, once you have completed a query, you can further customize it in Design view. As always, you can begin creating your query in Design view without using the wizard at all. Queries are not limited to a single table. Your queries can encompass multiple tables as long as the database includes a field or fields that relate the tables to each other.

Query Wizard

Creating a Query in Design View

Although a wizard can be a big help when you are first learning to create a query, you do not need to use a wizard. If you prefer, you can create a query without the help of a wizard. Instead of answering questions in a series of dialog boxes, you can start working in Design view right away. As you create a query, you can include more than one table or even another query in Design view. You can use comparison operators, such as >, <, or =, to compare field values to constants and other field values in the Criteria box. You can also use logical operators to create criteria combining several expressions, such as >1 AND <5.

Create a Query in Design View

1. Click the **Create** tab.

2. Click the **Query Design** button.

3. Select the table or query you want to use.

4. Click **Add**.

5. Repeat steps 3 and 4 for additional tables or queries, and then click **Close**.

6. Double-click each field you want to include in the query from the field list.

7. In the Design grid, enter any desired search criteria in the Criteria box.

8. Click the list arrow in the Sort box, and then specify a sort order.

9. Click the **Save** button, type a name for the query, and then click **OK**.

Did You Know?

You can show or hide table names in query properties. Open your query in Design view, and then click the Table Names button on the Design tab under Query Tools. The tables field toggles on and off when you click the Table Names button.

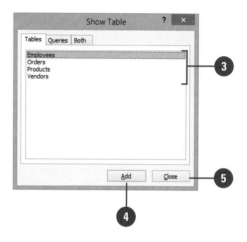

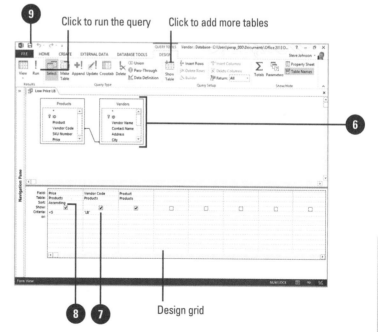

Click to run the query   Click to add more tables

Design grid

Getting Information with a Query

Access saves and lists the queries you create on the Queries bar in the Navigation pane. You can double-click a query to run it and display the results. When you run a query, the query results show only the selected fields for each record in the table that matches your selection criteria. After you run a query, you can close it for use again later.

Run a Query

1 In the Navigation pane, click **Queries** on the Objects bar to display the available queries in the database.

2 Double-click the query you want to run.

TIMESAVER *You can also drag the object or objects onto the Access work area.*

The query opens in a table called a dynaset. The dynaset displays the records that meet the specifications set forth in the query.

3 To close the query, click the **Close** button.

Results of query

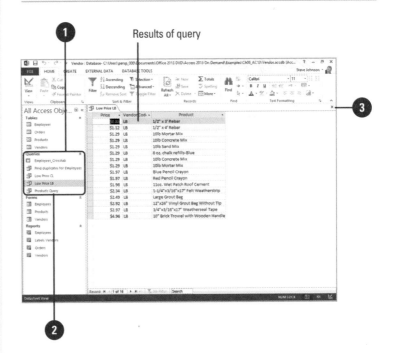

Did You Know?

You can make a query display only records with top or bottom values, or recent or older values. Display the query in Design view, click the Design tab, click the Return list arrow, and then select an option: 5, 25, 100, 5%, 25%, or All.

Modifying a Query in Design View

Once you have completed a query, you can further customize it in Design view. However, you can also create a query in Design view without using the wizard. Queries are not limited to a single table. Your queries can encompass multiple tables as long as the database includes a field or fields that relate the tables to each other. You can create a query using specific criteria and sort the results. If you no longer want to include a table or field, you can remove it from the query. In some cases you might want to hide a field from the query results while keeping it part of the query design for selection design purposes.

Modify a Query in Design View

1. In the Navigation pane, click the **Queries** bar to display the available queries in the database.

2. Click the query you want to modify.

3. Click the **Design View** button.

4. Double-click or drag each field you want to include in the query from the field list.

5. In the Design grid, enter any search criteria in the Criteria box.

6. Click the list arrow in the Sort box, and then specify a sort order.

7. To hide a field, clear the **Show** check box.

8. To delete a field, select the field, and then press Delete.

9. Click the **Save** button on the Quick Access Toolbar.

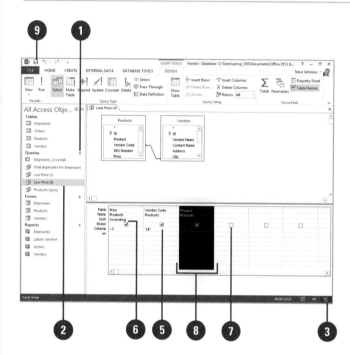

Did You Know?

You can sort the retrieved records. Display the query in Datasheet view, select the field in which you want to sort, and then click the Sort Ascending or Sort Descending button on the Home tab.

You can remove a table. In the query, right-click the table, and then click Remove Table.

Creating a Query Using a Wizard

A query is a simple question you ask a database to help you locate specific information within the database. When you create a query with the **Query Wizard**, you can specify the kind of query you want to create and type of records from a table or existing query you want to retrieve. When you use an existing query to create a new query, the existing one is known as a **subquery**. The Query Wizard guides you through each step; all you do is answer a series of questions, and Access creates a query based on your responses. All queries you create are listed under Queries in the Navigation pane.

Create a Query or Subquery Using the Query Wizard

1. Click the **Create** tab.

2. Click the **Query Wizard** button.

3. Click **Simple Query Wizard**, and then click **OK**.

4. Select a table or existing query.

5. Click to select the fields that you want included in the query.

6. Click **Next** to continue.

7. If you selected numeric or date fields in step 5, indicate whether you want to see detail or summary information.

8. If you choose Summary, click **Summary Options** to specify the calculation for each field, and then click **OK**.

9. Click **Next** to continue.

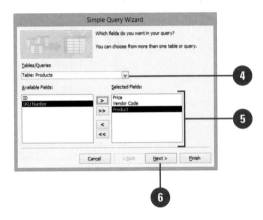

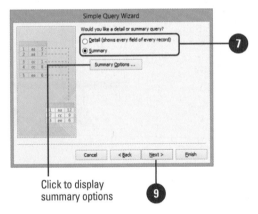

Click to display summary options

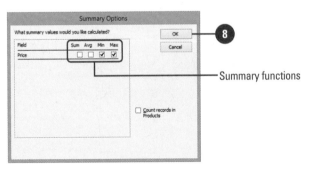

Summary functions

10 In the final wizard dialog box, type the name of the query.

11 Choose whether you want to view the results of the query or modify the query design in Design view.

12 Click **Finish**.

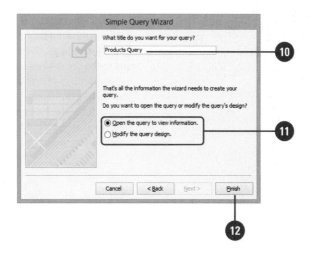

Did You Know?

You can include fields from another source. Click the Tables/Queries list arrow if you want to include a field from another source.

You can create aliases for a table name. An alias makes it easier to work with tables. For example, you can create an alias "e" for a table name Employees, and then refer to the table as "e" throughout the rest of the query. Open the query you want to change in Design view, right-click the table for which you want to create an alias, select Properties, and then enter an alias in the Alias box in the Property Sheet.

Name of query   Results of query

Changing the Query Fields

In Design view, you can add or remove fields in your query design to produce different results. You can also include fields from other tables in your database. In some cases you might want to hide a field from the query results while keeping it part of the query design for selection criteria purposes. When you remove a field from the query design grid, you're only removing it from the query specifications. You're not deleting the field and its data from the underlying table. When you hide a field by clearing the Show check box, the field remains part of the query; it just won't be displayed to the user.

Add a Field to a Query

1. Display the query in Design view.

2. Double-click a field name from the field list to place the field in the next available column in the design grid, or drag a field to a specific column in the design grid.

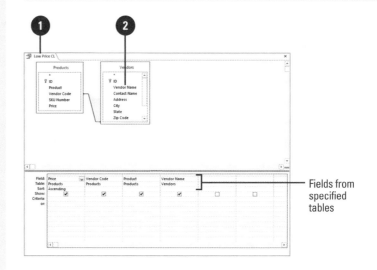

Fields from specified tables

Remove a Field from a Query

1. Display the query in Design view.

2. Select the field you want to remove from the query.

3. Press Delete, or click the **Design** tab under Query Tools, and then click the **Delete Columns** button.

Did You Know?

You can get field properties. Display the query in Design view, select the field you want to view, and then click the Property Sheet button.

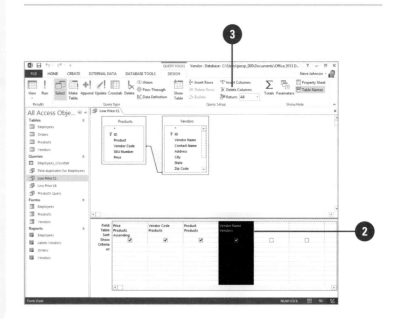

Add a Field from Another Table to a Query

1. Display the query in Design view.

2. Click the **Design** tab under Query Tools.

3. Click the **Show Table** button.

4. Select the table that contains the fields you want to include in the query.

5. Click **Add**.

6. Repeat steps 4 and 5 for each table you want to include.

7. Click **Close**.

8. Double-click or drag the fields you want to include to the design grid.

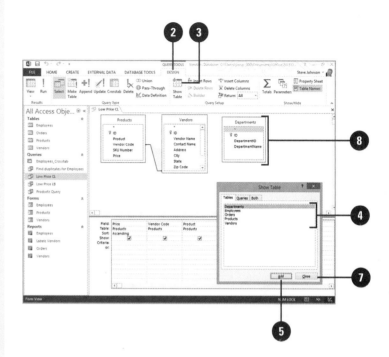

Did You Know?

You can remove a table from the Query design grid. To remove a table, right-click its field list in the top portion of the Query Design View window, and then click Remove Table.

You can change the order of fields in a query. In the design grid, point at the column selector for the column you want to move. (The column selector is the thin gray box at the top of a column.) When the pointer changes to a small black arrow, click to select the column. When the black arrow changes back, use the mouse pointer to drag the selected column to a new position.

Specifying Criteria for a Single Field

For each field you include in a query, you can specify criteria that a record must match to be selected when you run the query. For example, you can create a query to retrieve toys of a certain type, such as infant toys, from a toys database. You do this by entering a criterion's value in the Query Design window. Access allows you to add multiple criteria values for a single field so that the query retrieves records that meet either (or both) of the criteria you specify.

Specify Criteria for a Single Field in a Query

1. Display the query in Design view.

2. Click the **Design** tab under Query Tools.

3. Click the field's Criteria box.

4. Enter a criterion value for the field.

5. If additional values of the field are allowed, enter them into the Or box listed below the Criteria box.

6. Click the **Run** button.

Did You Know?

You can specify text to search for in your selection criteria. When the criterion is a text value, it must be enclosed in quotation marks. Access inserts quotation marks after you type the value and press Tab or Enter.

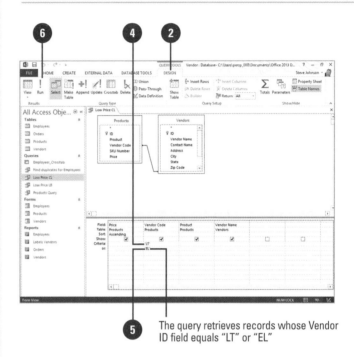

The query retrieves records whose Vendor ID field equals "LT" or "EL"

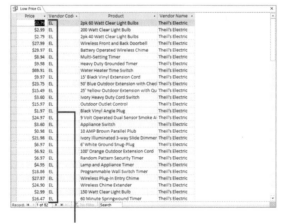

The query retrieves products by vendor LT and EL

Specifying Criteria for Multiple Fields

You can specify several query fields. If the criteria for the fields occupy the same row in the Query Design window, Access retrieves records for which **all** of the criteria are satisfied. For example, if you specify the vendor ID as "LT" (TnT Lighting) and the product price equal to "9.99," only products equal to $9.99 by LT will be retrieved. On the other hand, if the criteria are entered into different rows, Access retrieves records for which **any** of the criteria are satisfied. For example, placing "LT" and "9.99" in different rows will cause Access to retrieve either LT products or products with the price $9.99.

Specify Criteria for Multiple Fields in a Query

1. Display the query in Design view.

2. Click the **Design** tab under Query Tools.

3. Enter the criteria value or values for the first field.

4. Enter a criteria value or values for additional fields.

5. Click the **Run** button.

Did You Know?

You can format a query field. To modify the appearance of a query field, click anywhere within the query field's column, and then click the Property Sheet button. You can then specify the format, caption, input mask, and other features of the query field.

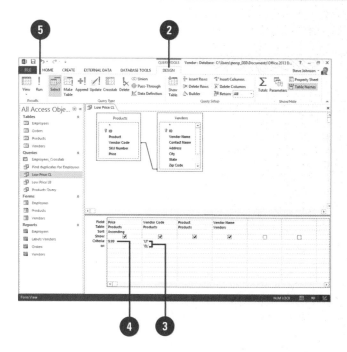

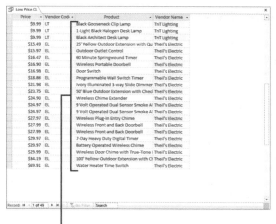

The query retrieves products with a price of $9.99 for LT or any price for EL

Creating Queries with Comparison and Logical Operators

You can use the Expression Builder to create more complicated queries. For example, you can use **comparison operators**, such as >, <, or =, to compare field values to constants and other field values. For example, you can use the greater-than operator (>) to create a query that retrieves records in which more than 1 toy is ordered. You can also use logical operators to create criteria combining several expressions. For example, you can use the AND operator to retrieve records in which the number of toys ordered is greater than 1 AND less than 5. You can also use **logical operators** to negate expressions. For example, you could run a query that retrieves toy records that are NOT infant toys.

Use a Comparison Operator

1. Display the query in Design View.

2. Click the **Design** tab under Query Tools.

3. Click the **Criteria** box for the field.

4. Click the **Builder** button.

5. Click the **Operators** folder.

6. Click **Comparison**, and then choose the comparison operator you want from the list on the right.

7. Enter a value or click a field whose value you want to compare.

8. Click **OK**.

9. Click the **Run** button.

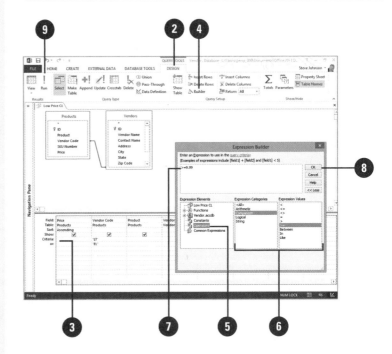

Did You Know?

You can see expression options in Expression Builder as you type. As you type in Expression Builder, you can see your options with IntelliSense. It also displays help for the currently selected expression value.

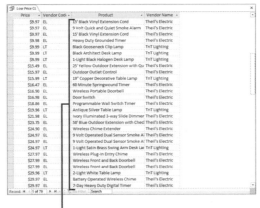

Access retrieves only those records whose price is greater then or equal to $9.99 for LT or any price for EL

Use a Logical Operator

① Display the query in Design view.

② Click the **Design** tab under Query Tools.

③ Click the **Criteria** box for the field.

④ Click the **Builder** button.

⑤ Click the **Operators** folder.

⑥ Click **Logical**, and then choose the logical operator you want from the list on the right.

⑦ Enter any values needed to complete the expression.

⑧ Click **OK**.

⑨ Click the **Run** button.

Did You Know?

You can fine-tune selection criteria. To fine-tune your selection criteria, combine logical and comparison operators in the same expression.

You can compare one field with another. To create an expression that compares one field with another, use the Expression Builder and look within the Tables folder to locate the table and field of interest. Double-click the field name to add it to the expression. The expression should contain the table name and field name in brackets, separated by an exclamation point. For example, to choose records where the value of the OnOrder field in the Orders table is greater than the value of the InStock field, the expression is: *[Orders]![OnOrder]>[Orders]![InStock]*.

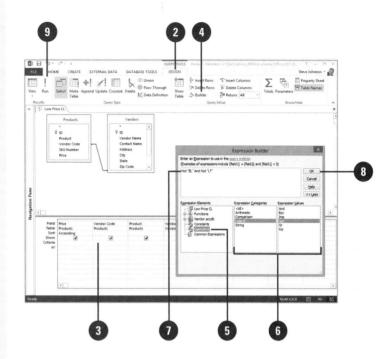

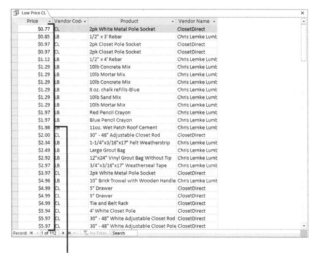

Access retrieves only those records in which the vendor is not EL and LT

Performing Calculations in Queries

In addition to the built-in functions you can use to compare values in a query, you can use the **Expression Builder** to create your own calculations using arithmetic operators. By clicking the operator buttons you want to use and entering constant values as needed, you can use the Expression Builder to include expressions in a query. For example, to determine fees based on a contract amount, you can create an arithmetic expression in your query to compute the results. When you run the query, Access performs the calculations and displays the results. You can also insert functions, such as AVG and Count, to perform other operations. When you insert a function, <<expression>> appears in parentheses, which represents an expression. Select <<expression>> and replace it with a field name, which you can select in Expression Builder. To create subtotals across groups of records, you can create a totals query, which calculates grand totals for column data.

Create a Calculated Field Using Expression Builder

1. Display the query in Design view.

2. Click the **Design** tab under Query Tools.

3. Click to position the insertion point in the Field row of a blank column in the Design grid.

4. Click the **Builder** button.

5. Double-click the field (or fields) you want to use in the calculation, and then build an expression using the operator buttons and elements area.

   ◆ Click the button corresponding to the calculation you want.

   ◆ Click the Operators folder, click the Arithmetic folder, and then click the operator you want.

   ◆ Click the Functions folder, click Built-In Functions, and then click the function you want.

6. Type any other values (constants) you want to include in the expression.

7. Click **OK**.

8. Click the **Run** button.

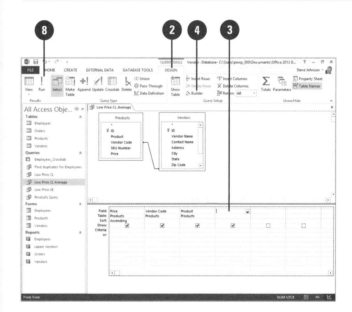

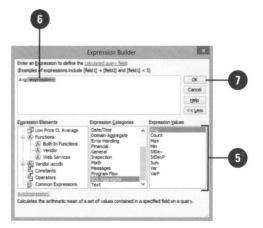

Calculate Grand Totals by Using a Query

① Display the query in Design View.

② Click the **Design** tab under Query Tools.

③ Click the **Totals** button.

The Total box appears in query properties with the *Group By*.

④ Click the **Total** box you want to create a calculated field.

⑤ Click the list arrow, and then click the function you want to use: Sum, Avg, Min, Max, Count, StDev, Var, First, Last, Expression, or Where.

⑥ Click the **Run** button.

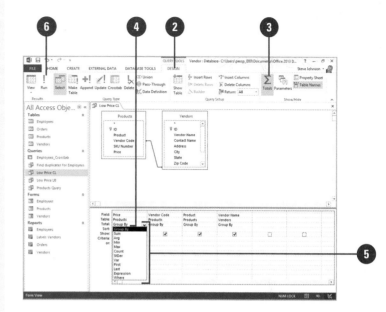

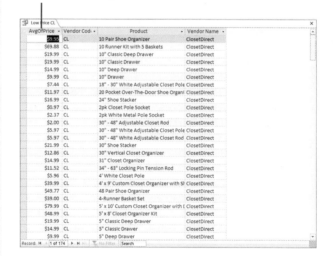

Calculated Average

Did You Know?

You can use aggregate functions in a field. In the Expression Builder under Built-In Functions, you can use an aggregate function, such as Sum, Count, Avg, or Max, to calculate totals. In writing expressions and in programming, you can use SQL aggregate functions (including the four listed here) and domain aggregate functions to determine various statistics.

You can create aliases for column names. An alias makes it easier to work with column names, calculations, and summary values. Open the query you want to change in Design view, right-click the field name in a table which you want to create an alias, select Properties, and then enter an alias in the Alias box in the Property Sheet.

Creating a Parameter Query

When you need to change the criterion value for a query, you either must edit the old query or create a new one. However, if the change involves simply altering a value, you might consider using a parameter query. A **parameter query** prompts the user for the value of a particular query field, rather than having the value built into the query itself. For example, if you want to display the records for particular toy types, a parameter query can prompt you for the type, saving you from creating a separate query for each type.

Create a Parameter Query

1. Display the query in Design view.

2. Click the **Design** tab under Query Tools.

3. Click the **Criteria** box for the field.

4. Enter the text of the prompt surrounded by square brackets; you can enter multiple criteria in a field (use AND), or use different fields.

5. Click the **Run** button.

6. Enter a criteria value in response to the prompt.

7. Click **OK**.

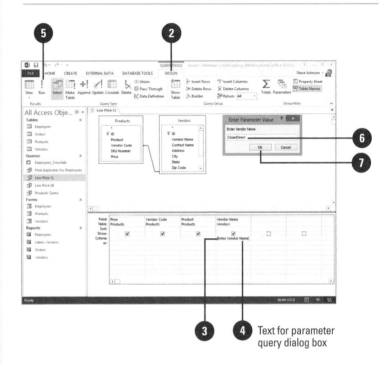

Text for parameter query dialog box

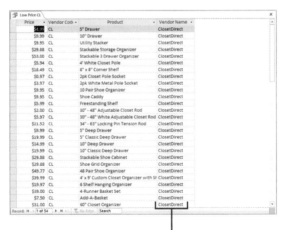

Access retrieves records with ClosetDirect Vendor

Create a Custom Parameter Query

1. Display the query in Design view.

2. Click the **Design** tab under Query Tools.

3. Click the **Parameters** button.

4. In the Parameter box, enter the text of the prompt surrounded by square brackets; you can enter multiple criteria in a field (use AND), or use different fields.

5. In the Data Type box, click the list arrow, and then select a data type.

6. When you're done, click **OK**.

7. Click the **Run** button.

8. Enter a criteria value in response to the prompt, and then click **OK** until you're done.

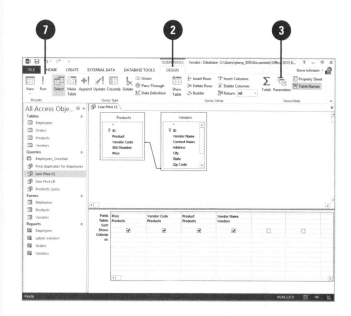

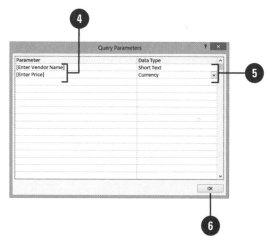

Did You Know?

You can control parameter order and data type. To control the order in which the Enter Parameter Value dialog boxes appears, use the Query Parameters dialog box. To open the Query Parameters dialog box, first open your query in Design view, and then click the Parameters button on the Design tab under Query Tools. The values you enter in the Query Parameters dialog box control the order in which to display the parameters, and the data type to expect for each parameter. When you run your parameter query, Access uses the data types you chose in the Query Parameters dialog box to validate the data that is entered.

Finding Duplicate Fields

In some tables, you need to find records that have duplicate values in particular fields. For example, in a table of employees, you might want to discover which employees work at the same location. You can create a query that retrieves all the records from the Employees table that have duplicate values for the Office Location field. Access provides the Find Duplicate Query Wizard to guide you through each step to help you create the query.

Find Duplicate Records

1. Click the **Create** tab.

2. Click the **Query Wizard** button.

3. Click **Find Duplicates Query Wizard**, and then click **OK**.

4. Choose the table or query that you want to search for duplicate records.

5. Click **Next** to continue.

6. Select the field or fields that might contain duplicate information.

7. Click **Next** to continue.

8. Select any other fields that you want displayed in the query.

9. Click **Next** to continue.

10. Enter a name for the new query.

11. Specify whether you want to view the query results or further modify the query design.

12. Click **Finish**.

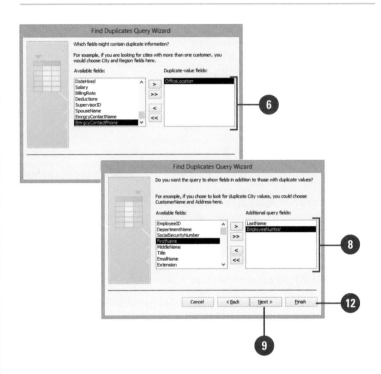

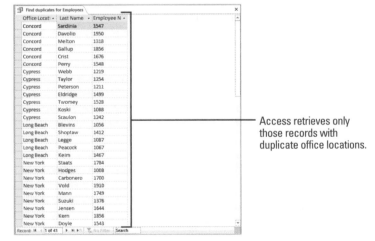

Access retrieves only those records with duplicate office locations.

Finding Unmatched Records

When you have related tables, you might want to find which records in one table have no match in the other table. For example, if you have a table of products and a table of customer orders, you might need to know whether there are products that have no match in the Orders table. In other words, are there some products that no customer has yet purchased? Access provides a query wizard to help you answer questions of this type.

Find Unmatched Records

1. Click the **Create** tab.

2. Click the **Query Wizard** button.

3. Click **Find Unmatched Query Wizard**, and then click **OK**.

4. Choose the table or query whose values you want displayed in the query.

5. Click **Next** to continue.

6. Choose the related table or query.

7. Click **Next** to continue.

8. Specify the field that matches records in the first table to records in the second.

9. Click **Next** to continue.

10. Choose which fields from the first table to display in the query results.

11. Click **Next** to continue.

12. Enter a name for the new query.

13. Specify whether you want to view the query results or further modify the query design.

14. Click **Finish**.

Table displayed in the query results

Related links

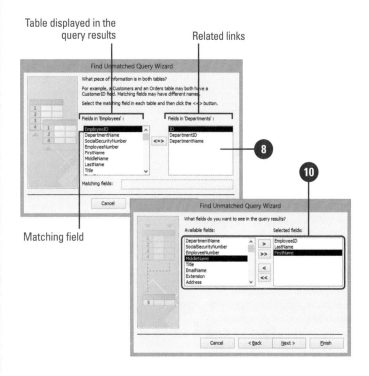

Matching field

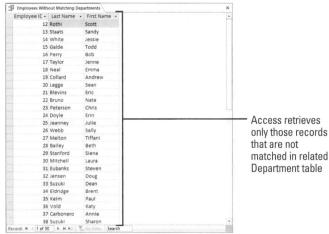

Access retrieves only those records that are not matched in related Department table

Creating New Tables with a Query

The data that appears after you run a query appears in table form and Access allows you to work with those results like tables. However, query results are not tables. If you want to place the results of a query into a separate table, you can use the **make table query**. This query directs Access to save the results of your query to a new table in either the current database or a different database.

Create a New Table with a Query

1. In Query Design view, create a select query, including any combination of fields, calculated fields, or criteria.

2. Click the **Design** tab under Query Tools.

3. Click the **Make Table** button.

4. Type the name of the table you want to create, or click the list arrow, and then select a table from the list if you want to replace the existing one.

5. Click the **Current Database** option if the table is in the currently open database, or click the **Another Database** option and type the name of another database (including the path, if necessary).

6. Click **OK**.

7. Click the **Run** button.

8. Click **Yes** when Access asks if you're sure you want to create the new table.

9. Open the new table to view the records resulting from the query.

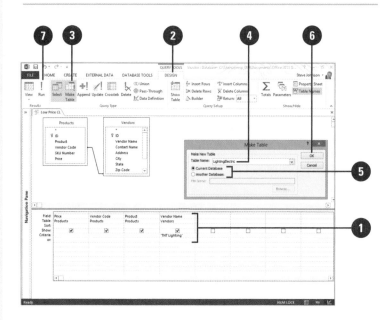

New table

Adding Records with a Query

You can use a query to add records to a table by creating an **append query**. If the fields you've selected have the same name in both tables, Access automatically fills the matching name in the Append To row in the design grid. If the fields in the two tables don't have the same name, enter the names of the fields in the Append To row in the design grid. If the table you are appending records to includes a primary key field, the records you are appending must have the same field or an equivalent field of the same data type. Access won't append any of the records if either duplicate or empty values would appear in the primary key field.

Add Records with a Query

1. In Query Design view, create a select query.

2. Click the **Design** tab under Query Tools.

3. Click the **Append** button.

4. Type the name of the table to which you want to append the records, or click the list arrow, and then choose one.

5. Click the **Current Database** option, or click the **Another Database** option and type the name of another database (including the path, if necessary).

6. Click **OK**.

7. Specify which fields will contain the appended values by entering the field names in the Append To row of the design grid.

8. Click the **Run** button.

9. Click **Yes** when Access asks if you're sure you want to append records to the table.

10. Open the table to view the appended records.

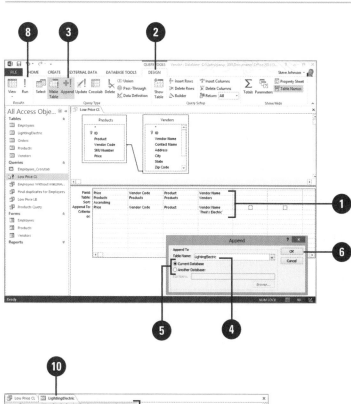

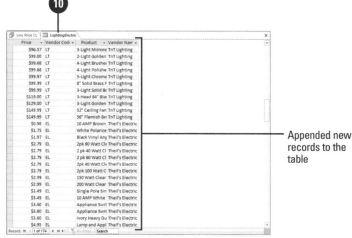

Appended new records to the table

Deleting Records with a Query

If you want to remove records from a table based on a criterion or criteria, you can do so with a **delete query**. The delete query searches the table you specify and removes all records that match your criteria. Because Access permanently deletes these records, use caution before you run a delete query. You can preview the results before you actually run the query. By clicking the Datasheet View button, you can see which records will be deleted before you actually run the query.

Create a Query to Delete Records

1. In Query Design view, create a select query.

2. Click the **Design** tab under Query Tools.

3. Click the **Delete** button.

4. Click the **Datasheet View** button to preview the list of deleted records.

5. If you're satisfied that the appropriate records would be deleted, click the **Design View** button to return to Query Design view.

6. Click the **Run** button.

7. Click **Yes** when Access asks if you're sure you want to delete records from the table.

8. Open the table to view the remaining records.

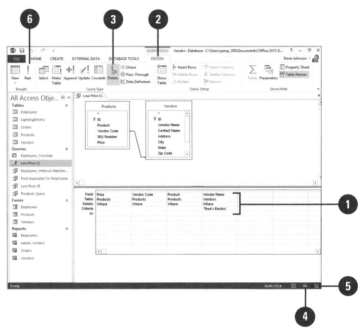

List of deleted records

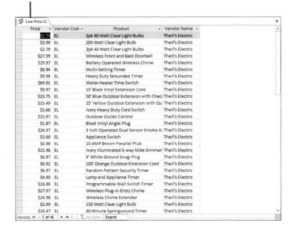

Updating Records with a Query

An **update query** allows you to make changes to a set of records that match your query's criteria. For example, if you want to increase the unit price of board games in a toy product table by $3, you can construct a query that will locate those records and update them to the new value. Make sure you preview the changes to the records before you run the query, because once the records are changed you can't easily change them back.

Create a Query to Update Records

1. Display a new query in Query Design view.

2. Add the fields or fields you intend to update and any fields that you want to use for the selection criteria.

3. Click the **Design** tab under Query Tools.

4. Click the **Update** button.

5. Enter an expression to update the selected field.

6. Enter a criterion, if needed, to indicate which records should be updated.

7. Click the **Datasheet View** button to preview the list of deleted records.

8. If you're satisfied that the appropriate records would be updated, click the **Design View** button to return to Query Design view.

9. Click the **Run** button.

10. Click **Yes** when Access asks if you're sure you want to update the records.

11. Open the table to view the remaining records.

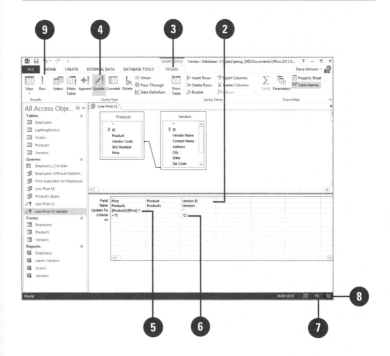

Access decreases the price by $1 for every product by CL over $10

Summarizing Values with a Crosstab Query

A **crosstab query** allows you to summarize the contents of fields that contain numeric values, such as Date fields or Number fields. In this type of query, the results of the summary calculations are shown at the intersection of rows and columns. For example, you can use a crosstab query to calculate the total number of toy products on sale, broken down by toy type. Crosstab queries can also involve other functions such as the average, sum, maximum, minimum, and count. You cannot update crosstab queries. The value in a crosstab query cannot be changed in order to change the source data.

Create a Crosstab Query

1. Click the **Create** tab.

2. Click the **Query Wizard** button.

3. Click **Crosstab Query Wizard**, and then click **OK**.

4. From the list at the top of the dialog box, select the table or query that contains the records you want to retrieve.

5. Click the view option you want: **Tables**, **Queries**, or **Both**.

6. Click **Next** to continue.

7. Double-click the field(s) you want to use in the crosstab query.

8. Click **Next** to continue.

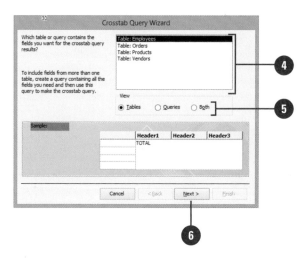

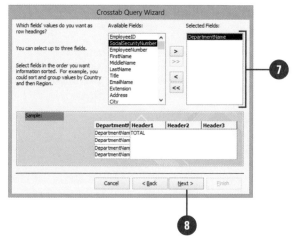

9 Select the field for the columns in the crosstab query.

10 Click **Next** to continue.

11 Click the field whose values you want to be calculated and displayed for each row and column intersection.

12 Click the function you want for the calculation to be performed.

13 Select the **Yes, include row sums** check box if you want to see a total for each row, or clear the check box if you do not want to see a total for each row.

14 Click **Next** to continue.

15 Enter a name for your query.

16 Indicate whether you want to immediately view the query or modify the design.

17 Click **Finish**.

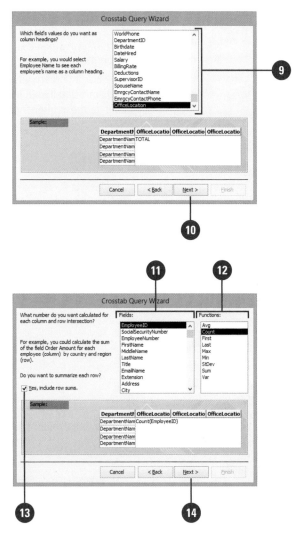

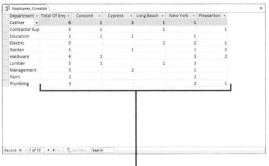

Total broken down by category and whether or not the product is on special

Creating SQL-Specific Queries

SQL (Structured Query Language) is a powerful database language used in querying, updating, and managing relational databases. For each query, Access automatically creates an equivalent SQL statement. If you know SQL, you can edit this statement, or write an entirely new one, to create new, more powerful queries. Access supports three kinds of SQL-specific queries: union, pass-through, and data-definition. Each of these query types fulfills a different need.

Create a SQL-Specific Query

① Click the **Create** tab.

② Click the **Query Design** button.

③ In the Show Table dialog box, click **Close**.

④ Click the **Union**, **Pass-Through**, or **Data Definition** button.

The query switches from Design view to SQL view.

⑤ In SQL view, enter SQL commands to create the query.

◆ **Union example.** Type SELECT, followed by a list of fields from the first table. Type FROM, followed by the name of the first of the tables. If you want, type WHERE followed by criterion. Type UNION, and then press Enter. Use the same format for the second table. Type a semicolon (;) to indicate the end of the query. See the illustration for specifics.

⑥ Click the **Run** button.

⑦ Save and view the query.

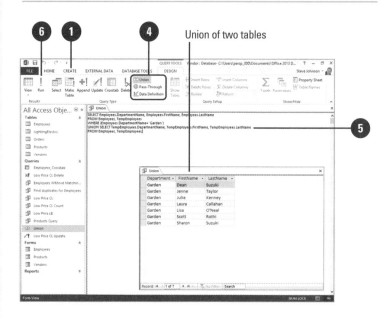

Union of two tables

Did You Know?

You can view a query in SQL. To see what your query looks like in SQL, click the View button arrow on the Home tab and then click SQL View.

Types of SQL-Specific Queries

Type	Definition
Union	A query that combines related fields from multiple tables into one field, thus combining the data from several tables.
Pass-Through	A query that sends SQL commands directly to an SQL database server. This allows you to work with tables on the server instead of linking the tables to your Access database.
Data Definition	A query that creates, deletes, or alters tables, or creates indexes in a database table. For example, the following data-definition query uses the CREATE TABLE statement to create a table.
Subquery	A SELECT statement nested inside a SELECT, SELECT...INTO, INSERT...INTO, DELETE, or UPDATE statement or inside another query.

Simplifying Data Entry with Forms

7

Introduction

Forms allow a database designer to create a user-friendly method of data entry in Microsoft Access. Instead of entering records in the grid of rows and columns in Datasheet view, you can use a form that can represent a paper form. Such a form can minimize data-entry errors because it closely resembles the paper-based form containing the information you want to enter in your table. A form can include fields from multiple tables, so you don't have to switch from one table to another when entering data. You can use one of the form buttons available on the Create tab to quickly create a basic form, blank form, navigation form, split form, datasheet form, tabular form using multiple items, and dialog box form.

If your table contains fields that include graphics, documents, or objects from other programs, you can see the actual objects in Form view. You can open a form in Form, Design, or Layout view. Form view allows you to view all the information associated with a record; Design view allows you to modify the form's design; and Layout view allows you to view information associated with the record and make changes to the form. To make it even easier to enter and maintain data, you can also include instructions and guidance on the form so that a user of the form knows how to complete it. You can add borders and graphics to the form to enhance its appearance.

The Windows operating system offers you several themes. If you have chosen a theme other than the default, Access will apply the chosen theme to views, dialog boxes, and controls. You can prevent form controls from inheriting themes from the operating system by setting an option in the database or project.

161

Creating Forms

As with most objects you create in a database, you have several choices when creating a form on the Create tab.

- The **Form** button creates a simple form that contains all the fields in the selected table or query.

- The **Form Design** button creates a blank form in Design view where you can add the fields you want.

- The **Blank Form** button creates a blank form to which you can add the fields you want.

- The **Form Wizard** button lets you can specify the kind of form you want to create and the wizard guides you through each step of the process.

- The **Navigation** button creates a blank form with vertical or horizontal navigation tabs to which you can add the fields you want.

- The **Multiple Items** command (More Forms button) creates a tabular form that contains all the fields in the selected table or query.

- The **Datasheet** command (More Forms button) creates a datasheet form that contains all the fields in the selected table or query.

- The **Split Form** command (More Forms button) creates a form that contains all the fields and a datasheet from the selected table or query.

- The **Modal Dialog** command (More Forms button) creates a dialog box form that contains the fields you want.

After you create a form, you can further customize it in Layout or Design view. You can use the Field List pane to add existing fields from related or unrelated tables, and then arrange and format them.

Use to create forms

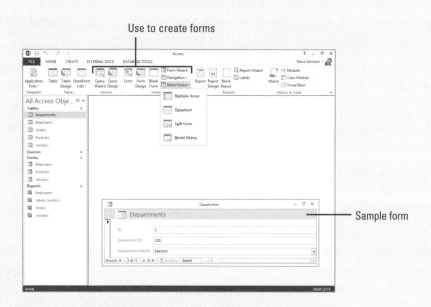

Sample form

Working with Form Controls

Each item on a form, such as a field name, a field value, and the form title, is called a **control**. You can create a from scratch or use a wizard. When you create a form with a wizard, the wizard takes care of arranging and sizing the controls to make a form. You can modify a new or existing form in Design view by:

- Moving and sizing controls.
- Changing control properties.
- Changing the appearance of controls with borders, shading, and text effects such as bold and italics.
- Inserting new controls.
- Organizing controls using groups.

Types of Form Controls

There are three kinds of controls you can use in a form:

- **Bound controls** are data fields from a table or query. A form must contain a bound control for each field that you want on the form. You cannot create a calculation in a bound control.
- **Unbound controls** are controls that contain a label or a text box. Typically, you use unbound controls to identify other controls or areas on the form. You can create a calculation from an unbound control.
- **Calculated controls** are any values calculated in the form, including totals, averages, percentages, etc.

Working with Form Controls

To add an existing field to a form, you open the Field List pane, and then drag a field from the pane—from related or unrelated tables in the database—to where you want it to appear on the form. You can show or hide the Field List pane by using the Add Existing Fields button on the Design tab.

To create a control, you click the control button for the kind of control you want to create and then drag the pointer over the area where you want the control to appear. The control buttons are available on the Design tab in Design view.

In Design view, you see two parts for every control: the control itself and its corresponding label. When you drag a control to position it, its corresponding label moves with it (and visa versa). You cannot separate a label from its control.

If you are unsure of how to create controls, you can click the Use Control Wizards command on the More list for Controls on the Design tab to activate the Control Wizards. With the Control Wizards active, a wizard guides you through the process of creating certain types of controls. For example, if you create a list box control with the Control Wizards active, the wizard opens, providing steps and information to create this type of control. To turn off the Control Wizards, click the Use Control Wizards command again (so that it is no longer indented).

Each type of form control has specific characteristics you can change using Properties. You simply select the control you want to modify, and then click the Property Sheet button on the Design tab under Form Layout Tools or Form Design Tools. In the Property Sheet pane, you can specify the characteristics you want to change.

After you add fields, you can use the Tab Order button on the Design tab under Form Layout Tools or Form Design Tools to change the selection order when you tab through fields in a form.

Creating a Form

To create a simple form, you can use one of the form buttons available on the Create tab. You can create a basic form, blank form, navigation form, split form, datasheet form, tabular form using multiple items, and dialog box form. These buttons quickly arrange the fields from the selected table or query into an attractive form. The new form is based on the active object. For example, if a table is active and you click the Form button, Access creates a new form based on the active table. After you create a form, you can save and name it so that you can use it again.

Create a Form

1. In the Navigation pane, select the table or query you want to use in the form.

2. Click the **Create** tab.

3. Click one of the following form buttons:

   ◆ **Form.** Creates a columnar form displaying a single record.

   ◆ **Form Design.** Creates a blank form in Design view.

   ◆ **Blank Form.** Creates a blank form.

   ◆ **Form Wizard.** Creates a form using a step-by-step wizard.

   ◆ **Navigation.** Creates a form with horizontal and/or vertical tabs.

   ◆ **Multiple Items (More Forms).** Creates a tabular form displaying multiple records.

   ◆ **Datasheet (More Forms).** Creates a form from a table or query.

   ◆ **Split Form (More Forms).** Creates a columnar form and includes the table datasheet.

   ◆ **Modal Dialog (More Forms).** Creates a form with a dialog box, which requires data entry.

4. Click the **Save** button on the Quick Access Toolbar, type a name, and then click **OK**.

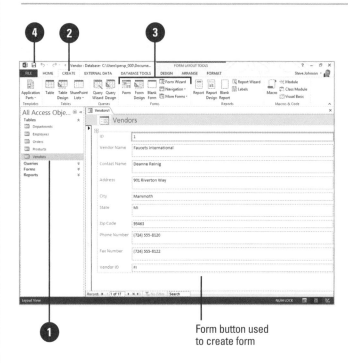

Form button used to create form

Creating a Blank Form

If you plan to use only a few fields in a form, the Blank Form tool makes it easy to quickly drag-and-drop fields from any table in the database. You can use the Blank Form button on the Create tab to quickly create a blank form in Layout view. When you create a blank form, the Field List opens, where you can drag the fields you want onto the blank form. After you add fields in Layout view, you can switch to Design view, and add controls. In Design and Layout views, you can add pictures, titles, pages numbers, date and time, and format the appearance of the form.

Create a Blank Form

① Click the **Create** tab.

② Click the **Blank Form** button.

The form appears in Layout view along with the Field List.

③ To show or hide the Field List, click the **Add Existing Fields** button on the Design tab under Form Layout Tools.

④ Drag fields from the Field List onto the blank form where you want to place them to create a form.

◆ To display all available tables, click **Show all tables** in the Field List.

◆ To show only fields in the current record source, click the link at the top of the Field List.

⑤ Click the **Save** button on the Quick Access Toolbar, type a name, and then click **OK**.

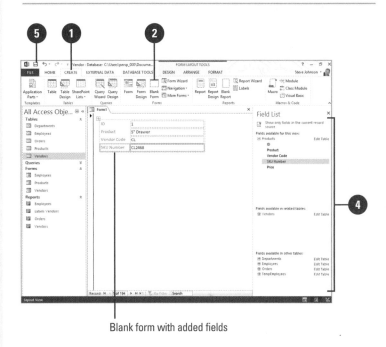
Blank form with added fields

Creating a Form Using the Form Wizard

If you need a more custom form, you can use the Form wizard to select the information you want to include from a variety of places. The Form wizard takes you step by step through the form creation process. During the process, you select the data source (tables or queries, and then specific fields), determine the arrangement of information on the form (Columar, Tabular, Datasheet, or Justified), specify a form name, and whether to open the form or modify the form's design.

Create a Custom Form Using the Form Wizard

1. Click the **Create** tab.

2. Click the **Form Wizard** button.

3. Click the list arrow for choosing a table or query on which to base the form, and then click the name of the table or query you want.

4. Specify the fields that you want included in the form by double-clicking the fields, or clicking the Arrow buttons.

   ◆ **Single Arrow.** Move the selected field from one side to the other.

   ◆ **Double Arrow.** Moves all fields from one side to the other.

5. Click **Next** to continue.

6. Determine the arrangement and position of the information on the form:

   ◆ **Columar.** Creates a form with columns.

   ◆ **Tabular.** Creates a form of rows and columns, a table that contains cells.

   ◆ **Datasheet.** Create a form like Datasheet view.

   ◆ **Justified.** Creates a form from right to left, margin to margin.

7. Click **Next** to continue.

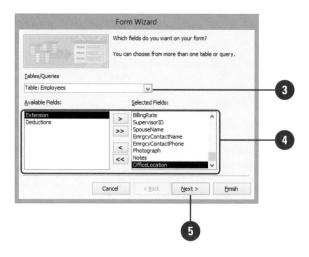

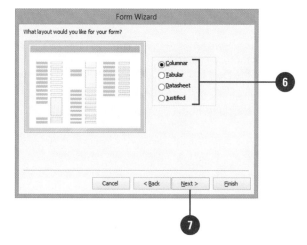

8 Enter a name for your form.

9 Select the option to open the form or display it in Design view.

10 Click **Finish**.

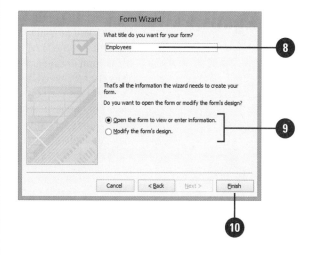

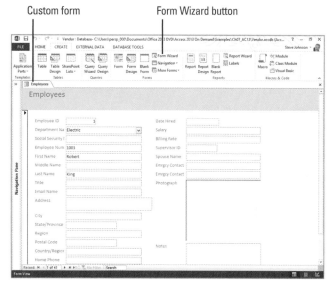

Custom form

Form Wizard button

Creating a Navigation Form

If you want a form with navigation buttons to make it easy to move around, you can quickly create a form with a built-in navigation layout. You can use the Navigation button on the Create tab to quickly create a blank form in Layout view with one of the following layouts: Horizontal Tabs (1 or 2 Levels), Vertical Tabs (Left or Right), or Horizontal Tabs and Vertical Tabs (Left or Right). When you create a navigation form, the Field List opens, where you can drag the fields you want onto the blank form. After you add fields in Layout view, you can switch to Design view, and add controls. In Design and Layout views, you can add pictures, titles, pages numbers, date and time, and format the appearance of the form.

Create a Navigation Form

1. Click the **Create** tab.

2. Click the **Navigation** button, and then select the type of navigation form you want.

   ◆ **Horizontal Tabs.**

   ◆ **Vertical Tabs, Left.**

   ◆ **Vertical Tabs, Right.**

   ◆ **Horizontal Tabs, 2 Levels.**

   ◆ **Horizontal Tabs and Vertical Tabs, Left.**

   ◆ **Horizontal Tabs and Vertical Tabs, Right.**

   The form appears in Layout view along with the Field List.

3. To show or hide the Field List, click the **Add Existing Fields** button on the Design tab under Form Layout Tools.

4. Drag fields from the Field List onto the blank form where you want to place them to create a form.

   ◆ To display all available tables, click **Show all tables** in the Field List.

   ◆ To show only fields in the current record source, click the link at the top of the Field List.

5. Click the **Save** button on the Quick Access Toolbar, type a name, and then click **OK**.

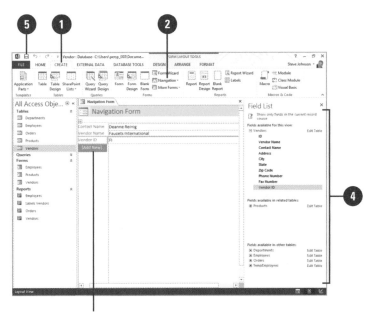

Navigation form with added fields

Creating a Multiple Items Form

When you create a form using the Form button on the Create tab, Access creates a form that display a single record at a time. If you need to display multiple records in a form, you can use the More Forms button on the Create tab to select the Multiple Items command to quickly create a tabular form using the selected table or query in the Navigation pane. A multiple items form shows multiple records in a datasheet, with one record per row. The data on the form appears in rows and columns.

Create a Multiple Items Form

1. In the Navigation pane, select the table or query you want to use in the form.

2. Click the **Create** tab.

3. Click the **More Forms**, and then click **Multiple Items**.

   The form appears in Layout view with fields from the selected table or query.

4. To show or hide the Field List, click the **Add Existing Fields** button on the Design tab under Form Layout Tools.

5. To add fields to the form, drag fields from the Field List.

   ◆ To display all available tables, click **Show all tables** in the Field List.

   ◆ To show only fields in the current record source, click the link at the top of the Field List.

6. Click the **Save** button on the Quick Access Toolbar, type a name, and then click **OK**.

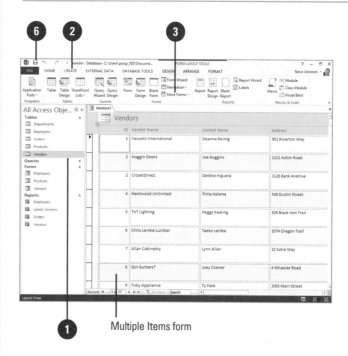

Multiple Items form

Creating a Datasheet Form

Datasheet view is an easy way to scroll through information in a table. Access provides the ability to create a datasheet form, which you can use in the same way as a table. You can use the More Forms button on the Create tab to select the Datasheet command to quickly create a datasheet form using the selected table or query in the Navigation pane.

Create a Datasheet Form

1. In the Navigation pane, select the table or query you want to use in the form.

2. Click the **Create** tab.

3. Click the **More Forms** button, and then click **Datasheet**.

   The form appears in Datasheet view with fields from the selected table or query.

4. To show or hide the Field List, click the **Add Existing Fields** button on the Datasheet tab under Form Tools.

5. To add fields to the form, drag fields from the Field List.

   ◆ To display all available tables, click **Show all tables** in the Field List.

   ◆ To show only fields in the current record source, click the link at the top of the Field List.

6. Click the **Save** button on the Quick Access Toolbar, type a name, and then click **OK**.

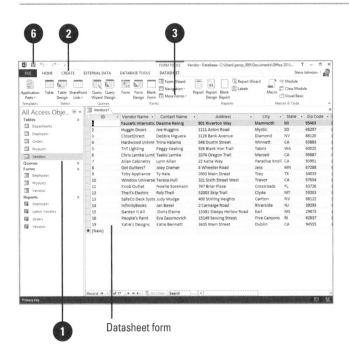

Datasheet form

Creating a Dialog Form

If you need to make sure information is entered in a form, the Modal Dialog tool requires you to close the window before you can move on. You can use the More Forms button on the Create tab to select the Modal Dialog command to quickly create a dialog form in Design view. When you create a dialog form, the Field List opens, where you can drag-and-drop fields from any table in the database onto the form in Design view. After you add fields in Design view, you can add controls, pictures, titles, pages numbers, date and time, and then format the appearance of the form.

Create a Dialog Form

1. Click the **Create** tab.

2. Click the **More Forms** button, and then click **Modal Dialog**.

   The form appears in Design view along with the Field List.

3. To show or hide the Field List, click the **Add Existing Fields** button on the Design tab under Form Design Tools.

4. Drag fields from the Field List onto the blank form where you want to place them to create a form.

   ◆ To display all available tables, click **Show all tables** in the Field List.

   ◆ To show only fields in the current record source, click the link at the top of the Field List.

5. Click the **Save** button on the Quick Access Toolbar, type a name, and then click **OK**.

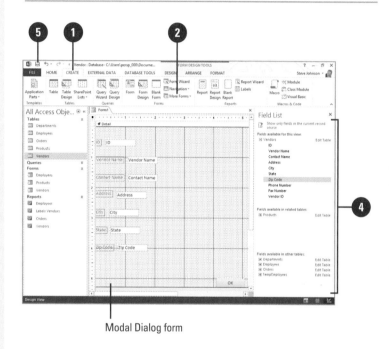

Modal Dialog form

Creating a Split Form

A split form displays Form view and Datasheet view on the same form. The top of the form displays Form view, while the bottom of the form display Datasheet view. The two views in a split form use the same table or query data source and Access keeps them synchronized. You can use the Split Form button on the Create tab to quickly create a split form using the selected table or query in the Navigation pane. When you select a field in one view of a split form, Access selects the same field in the other view. If you already have a form that you want to change to a split form, you can modify form properties to make the conversion.

Create a Split Form

1. In the Navigation pane, select the table or query you want to use in the form.

2. Click the **Create** tab.

3. Click the **More Forms**, and then click **Split Form**.

   The form appears in Layout view with fields from the selected table or query.

4. To show or hide the Field List, click the **Add Existing Fields** button on the Datasheet tab under Form Tools.

5. To add fields to the form, drag fields from the Field List.

   ◆ To display all available tables, click **Show all tables** in the Field List.

   ◆ To show only fields in the current record source, click the link at the top of the Field List.

6. Click the **Save** button on the Quick Access Toolbar, type a name, and then click **OK**.

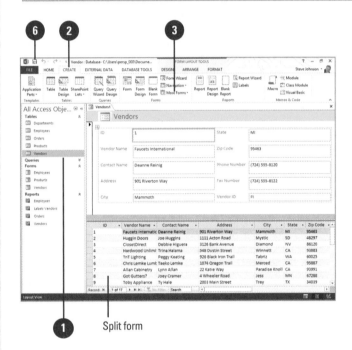

Split form

Create an Existing Form into a Split Form

1. Display the form you want to change into a split form in Design view.

2. Click the **Design** tab under Form Design Tools.

3. Click the **Property Sheet** button.

4. Click the list arrow at the top of the Property Sheet, and then click **Form**.

5. Click the **Format** tab on the Property Sheet.

6. Click the **Default View** list arrow, and then click **Split Form**.

7. Click the **Close** button on the Property Sheet.

8. Click the **Save** button on the Quick Access Toolbar.

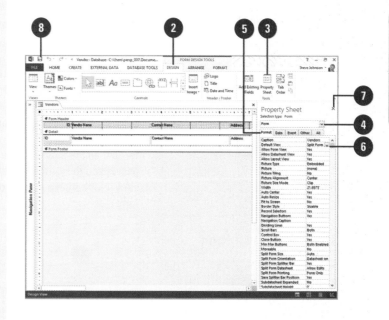

Did You Know?

You can format field contents in Layout view. You can format an input box using buttons on the Home tab. For example you can change the color, alignment, or style.

See Also

See "Working with Table Records" on page 60 for information on entering and editing record data.

Common Split Form Properties

Property	Description
Split Form Orientation (set in Design view)	Select the location of the datasheet: Top, Bottom, Left, or Right.
Split Form Datasheet	Allow or prevent edits on the datasheet.
Split Form Splitter Bar (set in Design view)	Allow or prevent the splitter bar between the form and datasheet to resize.
Save Splitter Bar Position (set in Design view)	Opens the splitter bar in the same position or hides it.
Split Form Size	Specifies the exact height or width of the split form. Type Auto to set size using the splitter bar in Layout view.
Split Form Printing	Define which portion of the form prints: Forms Only or Datasheet Only.

Entering and Editing Data in a Form

Database designers often display data in forms that mimic the paper forms used to record data. Forms facilitate data entry and record viewing. They can also contain buttons that allow you to perform other actions, such as running macros, printing reports, or creating labels. The options that appear on a form depend on what features the database designer included. A form directs you to enter the correct information and can automatically check your entries for errors. Access places the data you've entered in the form into the proper table. You can open a form in Form, Design, or Layout view. Form view allows you to view all the information associated with a record; Design view allows you to modify the form's design; and Layout view allows you to view information associated with the record and make changes to the form.

Enter a New Record in a Form

1. In the Navigation pane, click **Forms** to expand the group.

2. Double-click the form you want to open.

3. Click the **Form View** or **Layout View** button on the Status bar.

4. Click the **New Record** button on the Record bar or Home tab.

    TIMESAVER *Press Ctrl++ (Plus) to create a new record.*

5. Enter the data for the first field.

6. Press Tab to move to the next field or Shift+Tab to move to the previous field.

    When you have finished entering the data, you can close the form, click the New Record button to enter another record, or view a different record.

7. Click the **Save Record** button on the Home tab.

    TIMESAVER *Press Shift+Enter to save record changes.*

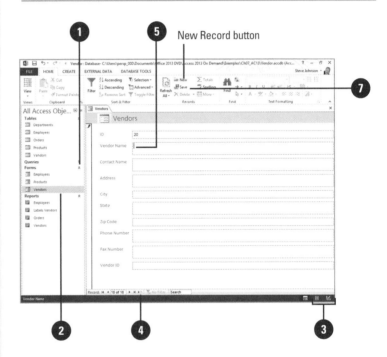

New Record button

Edit a Record in a Form

1. In the Navigation pane, click **Forms** to expand the group.

2. Double-click the form you want to open.

3. Click the **Form View** or **Layout View** button on the Status bar.

4. Click in the field you want to edit to place the insertion point, and then edit the text.

5. Press Tab to move to the next field or Shift+Tab to move to the previous field.

6. Click the **Save Record** button on the Home tab.

   TIMESAVER *Press Shift+Enter to save record changes.*

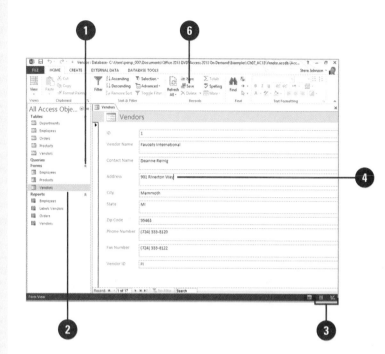

Did You Know?

You can delete a record from a form. In Form view, display the record you want to delete, click the Home tab, click the Delete button arrow, click Delete Record, and then click Yes.

You can refresh a record in a form. In Form view, display the record you want to work with, click the Home tab, click the Refresh All button arrow, click Refresh.

You can change the tab order in a form. Tab order determines the sequence when move between fields using the Tab key. To change the tab order, open the form you want in Design view, click the Design tab, click the Tab Order button, click a section option, drag selected row to a new tab order, and then click OK.

Working with a Form in Layout View

After you create a form, you can fine-tune the design by working in Layout view, where you can view actual form data as a guide while you make common changes. Since you can view actual form data, Layout view is very useful for sizing controls and fields and changing the appearance of the form. You can also enter and edit data like you can in Form view. If you need to add controls or make more detailed changes to a form, you need to switch to Design view where you can work with the structure of a form. If Layout view is not available, you can enable it for the current database by selecting an option in Access Options.

View a Form in Layout View

1. In the Navigation pane, click **Forms** to expand the group.

2. Double-click the form you want to view.

3. Click the **Layout View** button on the Status bar.

◆ You can also click the **View** button on the Home tab, and then click **Layout View** or right-click a form in the Navigation pane, and then click **Layout View**.

Switch Between Views

1. Display the form you to view.

2. Do either of the following:

   ◆ **View Selector Buttons.** Click the **Form View**, **Layout View**, or **Design View** button you want on the Status bar.

   ◆ **View Button.** Click the **Home** tab, click the **View** button arrow, and then click the view you want (**Form View, Layout View**, or **Design View**).

   Views vary depending on the form type. Others include Datasheet and SQL.

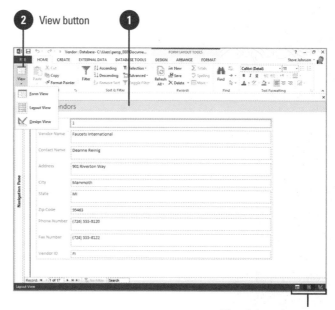

View button

View Selector buttons

Enable Layout View for the Current Database

1. Click the **File** tab, and then click **Options**.

2. In the left pane, click **Current Database**.

3. Select the **Enable Layout View** check box.

4. Click **OK**.

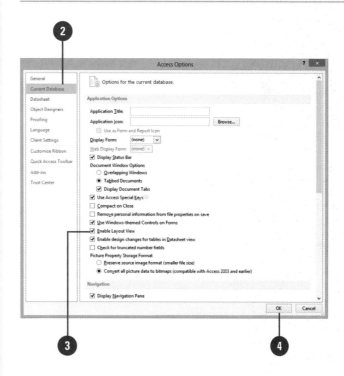

Working with a Form in Design View

Although a wizard can be a big help when you are first learning to create a form, you can create a form without the help of a wizard if you have a good idea of how you want the form to look. Instead of answering questions in a series of dialog boxes, you can start working in Design view right away. Design view is useful for working with the structure and development of a form. You can create, modify, move, and format controls to create the exact form you want. In Design view, form data doesn't appear like it does in Layout view.

Create a Form in Design View

1. Click the **Create** tab.

2. Click the **Form Design** button.

   The form appears in Design view along with the Field List.

3. To add a bound control, click the **Add Existing Fields** button on the Design tab under Form Layout Tools to show the Fields List.

4. Select the field you want to add to the form, and then drag the field to the location in the form where you want the field to appear.

5. Create new controls as needed; use any of the control buttons on the Design tab under Form Design Tools, drag to create the control and then follow the wizard.

6. Select the element, and then move or resize it in the form, as needed.

   ◆ **Move.** Drag the gray square handle or border (orange).

   ◆ **Resize.** Drag a corner or middle border resize handle (orange).

7. Select and format the text in the form, as needed, with options on the **Format** tab under Form Design Tools.

8. Click the **Save** button on the Quick Access Toolbar, type a name, and then click **OK**.

Field add to form

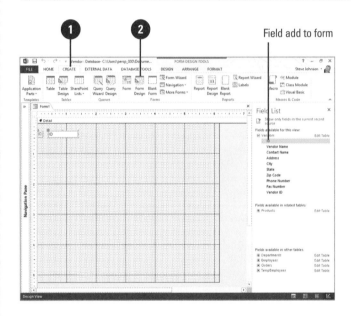

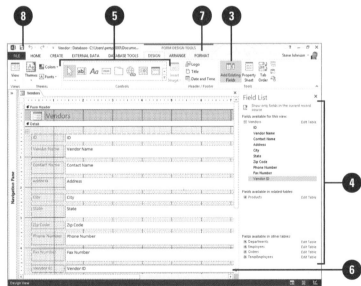

Modify a Form in Design View

1. Display the form you want to change.

2. Click the **Design View** button on the Status bar.

3. Click the **Design** tab under Form Design Tools.

4. To add a bound control, click the **Add Existing Fields** button on the Design tab under Form Layout Tools to show the Fields List.

5. Select the field you want to add to the form, and then drag the field to the location in the form where you want the field to appear.

6. Create new controls as needed; use any of the control buttons on the Design tab under Form Design Tools, drag to create the control and then follow the wizard.

7. Select the element, and then move or resize it in the form as needed.

   ◆ **Move.** Drag the gray square handle or border (orange).

   ◆ **Resize.** Drag a corner or middle border resize handle (orange).

8. Select and format the element in the form, as needed, with options on the Format tab under Form Design Tools.

9. Click the **Save** button on the Quick Access Toolbar.

See Also

See "Modifying a Form" on page 180 for more information on adding and modifying fields and controls.

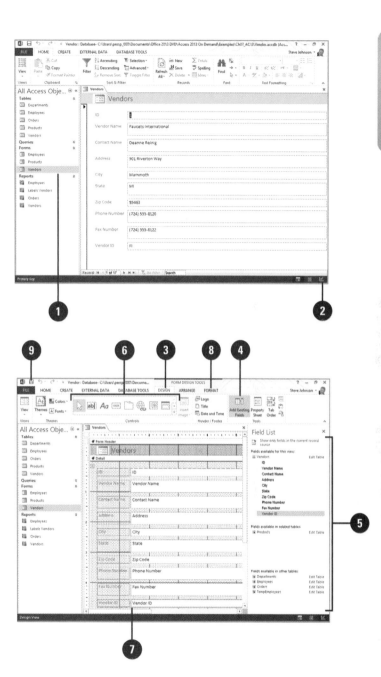

Modifying a Form

Controls can make a form easier to use and improve its appearance. Controls also allow you to display additional information on your forms. To create a control on a form, you click the appropriate control button on the Design tab under Form Design Tools. With the control pointer, drag in the form where you want the control to appear. When you release the mouse for some controls, such as the Combo box or List box, the Control Wizard starts, which steps you through the creation process. You can also edit controls to change text and delete controls that you no longer want.

Add Fields and Controls to a Form

1. Display the form you want to change in Design view.

2. Click the **Design** tab under Form Design Tools.

3. Click the button on the Design tab under Form Design Tools for the type of control you want to create.

4. In the Form window, drag the pointer to draw a box in the location where you want the control to appear.

5. If you want to switch to Layout view, click the **Layout View** button on the Status bar.

6. To display the Field List, click the **Add Existing Fields** button.

7. Select the field you want to add to the form, and then drag the field to the location in the form where you want the field to appear.

8. If a smart tag appears indicating an error, click the **Smart Tag Options** button, and then click an option.

See Also

See "Changing Tab Order" on page 244 for information on the tab order for fields.

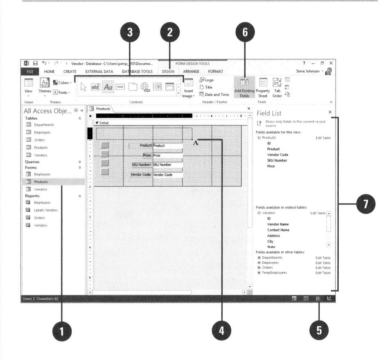

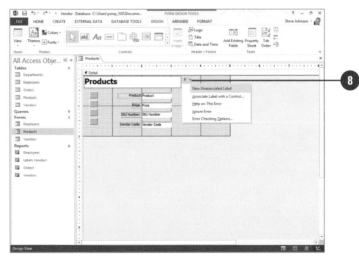

Modify and Format Fields and Controls in a Form

1. Display the form you want to change in Design or Layout view.

2. Click the **Design** tab.

3. Click the **Select** button, click the element(s) you want to edit. You can Ctrl+click or drag to select multiple elements.

   Small boxes, called handles, appear around the control to indicate it is selected.

4. Move or resize an element in the form as needed.

   ◆ **Move.** Drag the gray square handle or border (orange).

   ◆ **Resize.** Drag a corner or middle border resize handle (orange).

5. To arrange elements, select the elements, click the **Arrange** tab, and then use Sizing & Ordering buttons: **Size/Space**, **Align**, **Bring to Front**, or **Send to Back**.

6. To format elements, select the elements, click the **Format** tab, and then use the formatting buttons for Font, Number, Background, or Control Formatting.

7. To remove the selected element(s), press Delete.

8. To edit the contents of an element, click the selected element to place the insertion point, and then use the Backspace or Delete key to remove text or type to insert text.

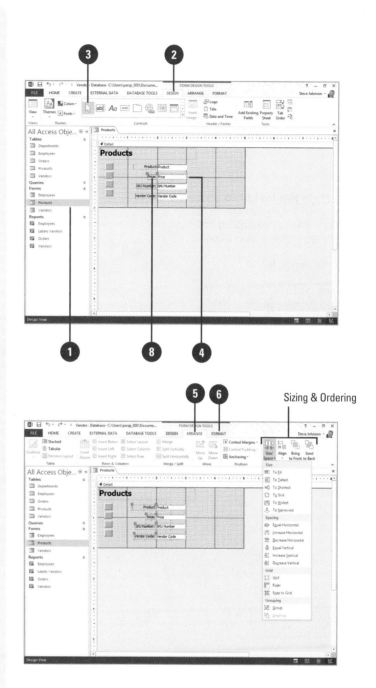

Sizing & Ordering

Adding Existing Fields

After you create a form, you can add fields from related or unrelated tables in the database. To add an existing field to a form, you open the Field List pane, and then drag a field from the pane to where you want it to appear. You can show or hide the Field List pane by using the Add Existing Fields button on the Design tab in Layout or Design view. When you create a new form, the Field List pane automatically opens. In the Field List pane, you can expand or collapse tables to show or hide fields, show all tables or only table fields in the current record source, or edit tables.

Show or Hide the Field List Pane

1. Display the form you want to add fields in Design or Layout view.

2. Click the **Design** tab.

3. To show the Field List pane, click the **Add Existing Fields** button.

4. To expand or collapse a table to show or hide fields, click the Expand icon (Plus) or Collapse icon (Minus).

5. To hide the Field List pane, click the **Add Existing Fields** button or click the **Close** button on the pane.

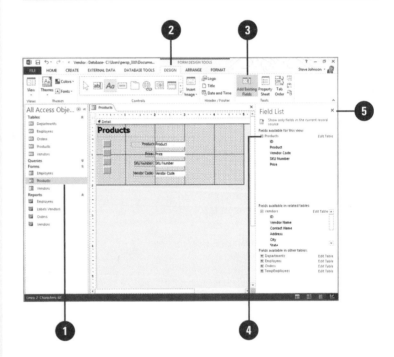

Add Fields from the Field List Pane

1. Display the form you want to add fields in Design or Layout view.

2. Click the **Design** tab.

3. To show the Field List pane, click the **Add Existing Fields** button.

4. Click **Show only fields in the current record source** to display only fields found in the current record or click **Show all tables** to display all tables in the database.

5. To expand or collapse a table to show or hide fields, click the Expand icon (Plus) or Collapse icon (Minus).

6. To add a field to the form, select the field you want, and then drag the field to the location in the form where you want the field to appear.

7. To open and edit a table, click **Edit Table** in the Field List.

   The link is only available when you display all tables.

8. To hide the Field List pane, click the **Add Existing Fields** button or click the **Close** button on the pane.

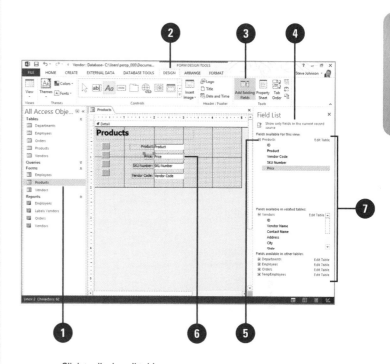

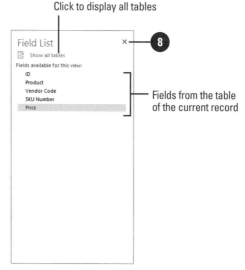

Click to display all tables

Fields from the table of the current record

Adding and Modifying Controls

Controls can make a form easier to use and improve its appearance with text and pictures. Controls also allow you to display information and add functionality on your forms with hyperlinks, navigation, and buttons. To create a control on a form, you click the appropriate control button in the Controls group on the Ribbon. With the control pointer, drag in the form where you want the control to appear. You can also edit controls to change text and delete controls that you no longer want.

Add Controls to a Form

1. Display the form you want to add controls in Design view.

2. Click the **Design** tab under Form Design Tools.

3. Click the button in the Controls group for the type of control you want to create.

4. In the Form window, drag the pointer to draw a box in the location where you want the control to appear.

5. Some controls require additional information or options.

   ◆ **Text or Label.** Click in the control, and then enter text.

   ◆ **Dialog Box.** If a dialog box opens, select the control options you want.

   ◆ **Property Sheet.** Select a tab, and then specify the options you want.

   ◆ **Smart Tab.** If a smart tag appears indicating an error, click the **Smart Tag Options** button, and then click an option.

See Also

See "Using Buttons and Controls" on page 206 for more information on individual buttons and controls.

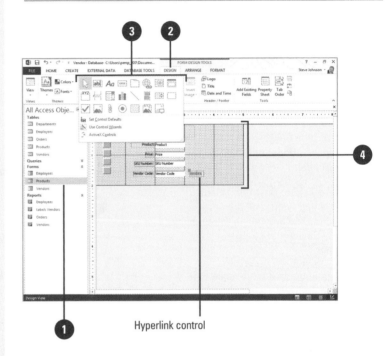

Hyperlink control

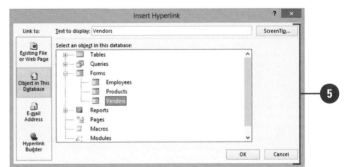

Edit Controls in a Form

1. Display the form you want to edit controls in Design view.

2. Click the **Design** tab under Form Design Tools.

3. Click the **Select** button, and then click the control you want to edit.

   Small boxes, called handles, appear around the control to indicate it is selected. You can use them to resize the control.

4. To remove the selected control(s), press Delete.

5. To edit the contents of a control, click the selected control to place the insertion point, and then use the Backspace or Delete key to remove text or type to insert text.

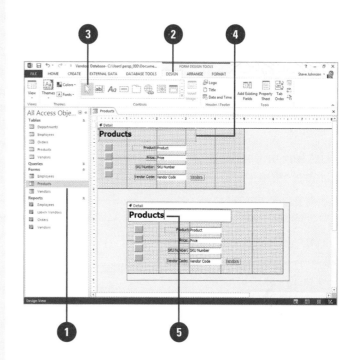

Modify Control Properties

1. Display the form you want to modify control properties in Design view.

2. Click the **Design** tab under Form Design Tools.

3. Click the **Select** button, and then click the control you want to view or change properties.

4. Click the **Property Sheet** button.

   TIMESAVER *Double-click the object or its edge (control, section, or form) to open the object's property sheet.*

5. Enter the property information you want to add or change.

6. Click the **Close** button on the Property Sheet.

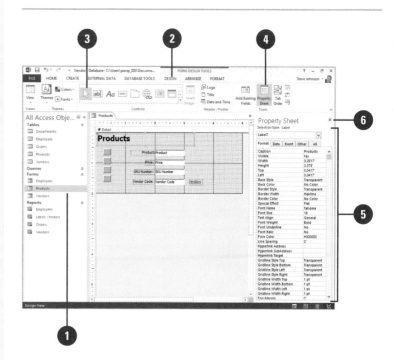

Adding Controls with a Wizard

The **Control Wizards** help you create controls on your form. Although there are many controls you can create, the procedures for creating each control are quite similar, with minor variations depending on the type of control. For example, when you want to include a list of valid options for a field on a form, you can create either a **combo box** or **list box** control. Both controls provide a list from which a user can choose when entering data. The easiest way to create either of these controls is with a Control Wizard, which includes additional sorting options.

Create a List Box or Combo Box Using a Control Wizard

1. Display the form you want to edit controls in Design view.

2. Click the **Design** tab under Form Design Tools.

3. Click the **More** list arrow for Controls, and then click **Use Control Wizards** to highlight it.

4. Click the **Combo Box** or **List Box** button.

5. In the Form window, drag to create a rectangle for the control.

   The control wizard opens, asking you to step through the process.

6. Specify whether you want the control to get its values from a table or query, from what you type in the box, or from what value is selected in the list or combo box. Click **Next** to continue.

7. If applicable, select the table that contains the values you want displayed in the list or combo box. Click **Next** to continue.

8. Select the field that contains the values you want displayed in control. Click **Next** to continue.

9. Select the first sort list arrow, select a field to sort, and then click the **Ascending/Descending** button. If you want, select additional sorts. Click **Next** to continue.

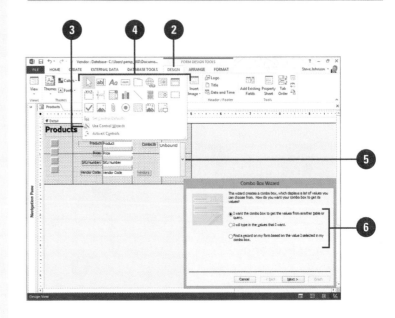

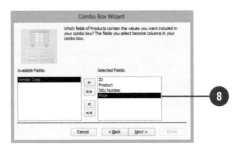

10 Adjust the width of the columns for the list box as necessary. Click **Next** to continue.

11 If necessary, specify which column contains the value that will be stored in the list box control. Click **Next** to continue.

12 Specify whether you want Access to display the column value (for later use to perform a task) or to store the value in a field in a table.

13 If you choose to store the value in a field, specify the field.

14 Click **Next** to continue.

15 Enter a label for the new control, and then click **Finish**.

Did You Know?

You can create a combo or list box with custom values. If you want specific values (rather than values from a table) to populate the list box, click the I Will Type In The Values That I Want option in the wizard's first step, and then enter the values manually when you are prompted by the wizard.

You can create a combo or list box to display a specific record. If you want your list box to retrieve records, click the Find A Record On My Form Based On The Value I Selected In My Combo or List Box option in the wizard's first step. The wizard then prompts you for the field from which the control will receive its values. When the control is added to the form, choosing a specific value causes Access to retrieve the matching record.

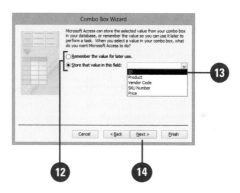

Creating a Subform

Some forms use fields from multiple tables. One of the most common forms involves a one-to-many relationship between two tables. For example, an order form would include a single order date and customer, but the order might involve several different products. Thus there are two tables involved: an orders table with information about the order and a detailed orders table with data about the products purchased. The user should not have to enter the order date for each product. This can be avoided with a **subform**, a form embedded within a **main form**. The user enters the order date and other general information in the main form, and the individual products are listed in the subform. Access then stores the appropriate data in each table without the user being aware that multiple tables are involved.

Create a Subform

1. Display the form you want to add a subform in Design view.

2. Click the **Design** tab under Form Design Tools.

3. Click the **More** list arrow for Controls, and then click **Use Control Wizards** to highlight it.

4. Click the **Subform/subreport** button.

5. Drag to create a frame for the subform.

   The Subform wizard opens, asking you to step through the process.

6. Select the data option you want, and then click **Next** to continue.

7. Click the **Tables/Queries** list arrow, and then select the table that will appear in the main form.

   The table contains general information (the *one* table).

8. Select the fields from the table that will appear in the main form. Make sure you include the common field that links the one table to the many table.

9. On the same wizard screen, click the **Tables/Queries** list arrow, and then select the table that will appear in the subform.

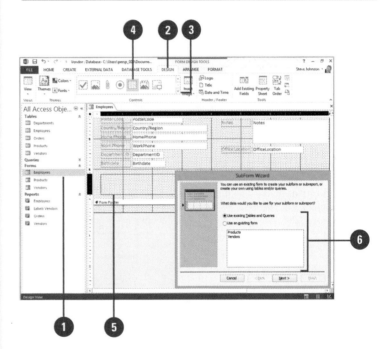

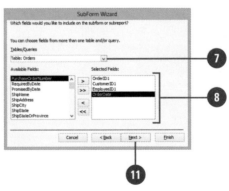

The table contains detailed information (the *many* table).

10 Select the fields from the table that will appear in the subform. Do not include the common field you entered in the previous step, since this will appear in the main form.

11 Click **Next** to continue.

12 Click the option to view the data by the one table.

13 Click **Next** to continue.

14 Specify whether you want the subform to be laid out in tabular or datasheet format. Click **Next** to continue.

15 Specify a style for the form. Click **Next** to continue.

16 Enter a name for the subform.

17 Click **Finish**.

The form and subform are ready for data entry or further editing.

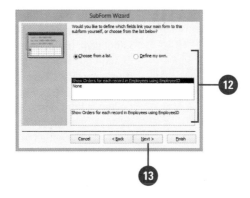

Did You Know?

You can create a form with tables in a one-to-one relationship. If the tables have a one-to-one relationship, use the Form Wizard to create the form, including the common field only once in the field list. The wizard will create a single form, combining the fields from both tables.

You can create a linked form. If you want a linked form instead of a subform (so that the form appears in response to the user clicking a button), click the Linked Forms option when the Form Wizard asks you how you want to view your data.

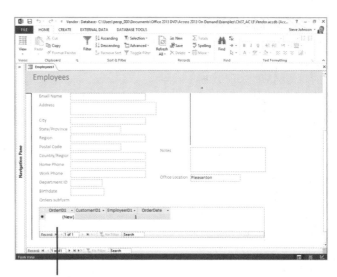

Form with subform

Enhancing a Form

After you create a form and arrange the fields and controls where you want, you can format them. You can change the font or font size, apply a font style (Bold, Italic, Underline, Color, or Background Color), or change the alignment. For numbers, you can apply number formatting (Currency ($), % Percent (%), Comma Number, or Increase or Decrease Decimals). When you create a form or report, you typically want to include a title, logo, and the date and time. You can quickly add them using buttons on the Design tab in Design view or Layout view. These elements are added to the form or report header or footer by default, so they appear on every page. In addition, you can change the color fill or border style (Color, Thickness, and Type) of an element using the Shape Fill and Shape Outline buttons.

Format Elements in a Form

1. Display the form you want to format in Design or Layout view.

2. Click the **Format** tab.

3. Select the element(s) you want to format. You can Ctrl+click or drag to select multiple elements.

4. Use any of the following buttons to format the selected elements:

   ◆ Text. Click a list arrow or button (Bold, Italic, Underline, Color, or Background Color) in the Font group.

      ◆ Text formatting buttons are also available on the Home tab.

   ◆ Number. Click a list arrow or button ($, %, Comma, or Increase or Decrease Decimals) in the Number group.

5. To apply a fill or border style, click the **Shape Fill** button or **Shape Outline** button, and then select a color or option.

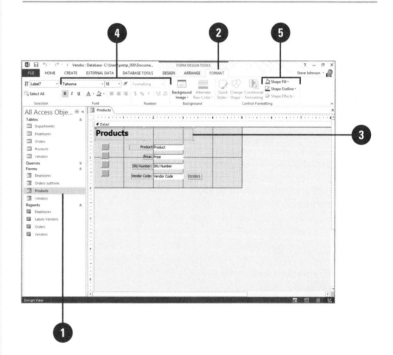

Insert a Title, Logo or Date and Time into a Form Header or Footer

1. Display the form you want to change in Design or Layout view.

2. Click the **Design** tab.

3. Use the following to insert an element in the header or footer:

   ◆ Title. Click the **Title** button, type a type, and then click click a blank area to deselect it.

   ◆ Logo. Click the **Logo** button, select the picture files, and then click **OK**.

   ◆ Date and Time. Click the **Date and Time** button, select or clear the **Include Date** or **Include Time** check boxes, select a data or time format, and then click **OK**.

Did You Know?

You can insert a picture in a form. Open the form you want, click the Design tab, click the Insert Image button, click Browse, select the picture file, click Open, and then drag to create a control to store the picture.

Logo and title   2   3   Header

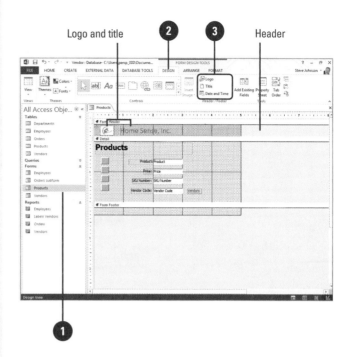

Insert a logo in the header

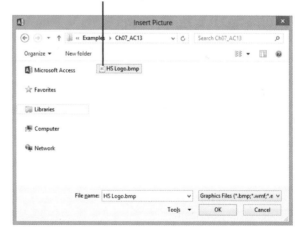

Working with Themes on Forms

A theme consists of theme colors and fonts. You can quickly format an entire form with a professional look by applying a theme. Access comes with themes from Office and you can create your own. To quickly see if you like a theme, point to one on the themes gallery to display a ScreenTip with name, and a live preview of it on the current form. If you like the theme, you can apply it. When you apply a theme, the background, text, graphics, fields, and controls all change to reflect the theme. You can choose from one or more standard themes and use it or customize it with different color or fonts. When you add new content, the document elements change to match the theme ensuring all of your material will look consistent.

Apply a Theme to a Form

1. Display the form you want to change in Design or Layout view.

2. Click the **Design** tab.

3. Click the **Themes** button, and then point to a theme to preview it or select a theme under In this Database, Custom, or Office.

   ◆ **Custom Theme File.** Click **Browse for Themes**, select an Office theme file (.thmx), and then click **Open**.

4. To apply theme colors, click the **Theme Colors** button, and then select a color theme.

5. To apply theme fonts, click the **Theme Fonts** button, and then select a font theme.

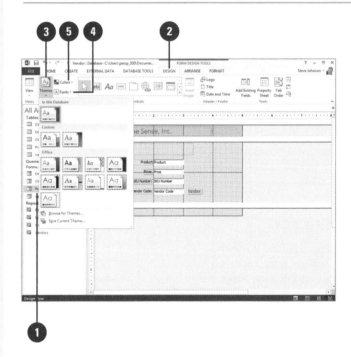

Did You Know?

You can apply a theme to an object. Open the form you want, select an element as desired, click the Themes button on the Design tab, right-click the theme, and then click Apply Theme To All Matching Objects or Apply Theme To This Object Only.

Set Theme Fonts and Colors to Elements in a Form

1. Display the form you want to change in Design or Layout view.

2. Click the **Format** tab.

3. Select the element(s) you want to set theme fonts or colors. You can Ctrl+click or drag to select multiple elements.

4. To set a theme font, click the **Font** list arrow, scroll to the top, select the font name that ends with (Header) or (Detail).

5. To set a theme color, click the **Font Color**, **Background Color**, **Shape Fill**, or **Shape Outline** list arrow, and then select a theme color.

Did You Know?

You can save a custom theme. Open the form or report with the formatting you want to save as a custom theme, click the Design tab, click the Themes button, click Save Current Theme, specify a name and location, and then click Save. The Office Theme file is saved with the .thmx file extension.

You can apply a custom theme from a file. Open the form or report you want to apply a custom theme, click the Design tab, click the Themes button, click Browse for Themes, select the Office Theme file (.thmx), and then click Open.

Theme fonts

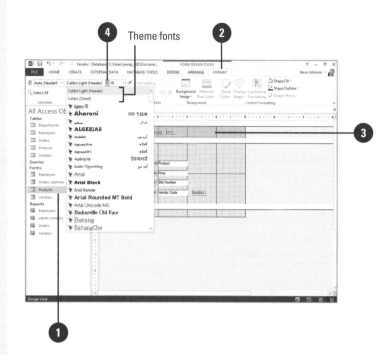

Theme colors   Shape Fill/Outline

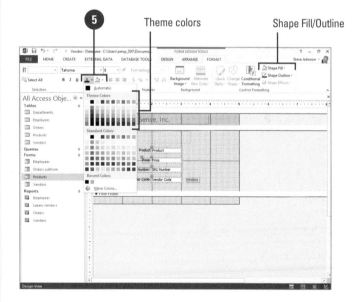

Using Windows Themes on Forms

The Microsoft Windows operating system offers you several themes. If you have chosen a theme other than the default, Access applies the selected theme to views, dialog boxes, and controls. However, you can prevent form controls from taking on themes from the operating system by setting an option on the database or project.

Enable or Disable Windows Themes in Forms

1. Click the **File** tab, and then click **Options**.

2. In the left pane, click **Current Database**.

3. Select or clear the **Use Windows-themed Controls on Forms** check box.

4. Click **OK**.

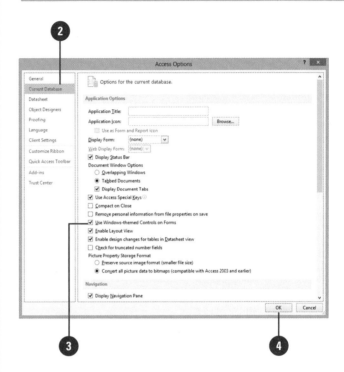

Did You Know?

You can change a Windows visual theme. In Windows 7 or 8, right-click the desktop, click Personalize, and then click a default or custom theme. To change individual elements, click Desktop Background, Window Color, Sounds, or Screen Saver, make the changes you want, and then click Save Changes. When you're done, click the Close button.

Creating Reports to Convey Information

8

Introduction

You can use print commands on the File tab to print a simple list of the records in your table. But if you want to include calculations, graphics, or a customized header or footer, you can create a report. A report is a summary of information in one or more tables. Reports allow you to include enhancements that a simple printout of records in a table would not provide. In many cases a report answers important questions about the contents of your database. For example, a report might tell you how many movies in several different categories (such as drama, comedy, and western) have been rented each month or the amount of catalog sales made to customers in Canada in the last quarter. In addition to providing detailed and summary information that can include calculations, reports also provide these features:

- Attractive formatting to help make your report easier to read and understand.

- Headers and footers that print identifying information at the top and bottom of every page.

- Grouping and sorting that organize your information.

- Graphics to enhance the appearance of a report with clip art, photos, or scanned images.

Exploring Different Ways to Create a Report

As with most objects you create in a database, you have several ways to create a report—by using Report buttons, Report wizard or by creating it from scratch in Design view.

Quick Reports

With the Report button, Access creates a simple report based on the data in the currently selected table or query. You can create a report using a column format.

Report Wizard

With the Report Wizard you can specify the kind of report you want to create, and the Report Wizard guides you through each step of the process. All you do is answer a series of questions about your report, and Access builds a report with your data, using your formatting preferences. Creating a report with the Report Wizard allows you to select the fields you want to include from available tables and queries.

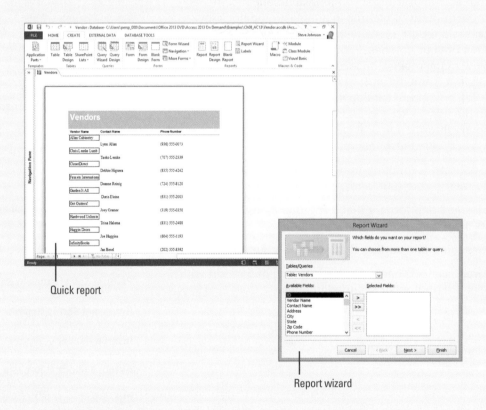

Quick report

Report wizard

Design View

Once you have completed a report, you can further customize it in Design view. As always, you can also begin creating your report in Design view without using a wizard.

When you work with a report in Design view, Access displays not the report data, but rather the individual parts, or controls, that make up the report, including titles, fields whose data appear in the report, labels that clarify the report contents, and objects such as headers and footers.

Previewing a Report

Once you have created your report and finalized its design, you can preview it using two views: Print Preview and Layout Preview. Print Preview displays the report as it will print, in a "what you see is what you get" format. Layout Preview displays a sample of the report as it will print, with just a few rows of data, so you can get a feel for the report's appearance without having to view all the data in the report.

Report in Design view

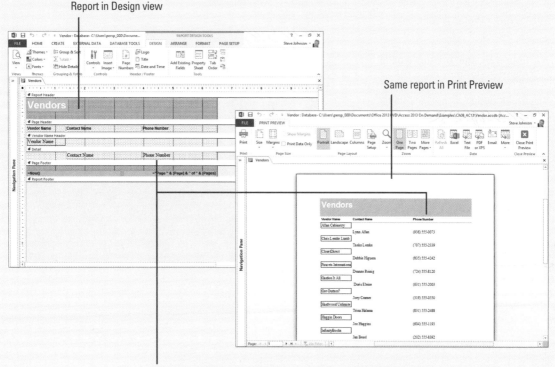

Same report in Print Preview

Objects in Design view correspond to objects in the printed report

Creating a Report

To quickly create a simple report in Access, you can use one of the form buttons available on the Create tab. You can create a basic report, blank report, and labels. These buttons quickly arrange the fields from the selected table or query into an attractive report. The new report is based on the active object. For example, if a table is active and you click the Report button, Access creates a new report based on the active table. After you create a report, you can save and name it so that you can use it again. You can also create a report using the **Report Wizard**, which allows you to select the fields and information you want presented and to choose from available formatting options that determine how the report will look.

Create a Report

1. In the Navigation pane, select the table you want to use in the report.

2. Click the **Create** tab.

3. Click the any of the following form button:

   ◆ **Report.** Creates a columnar report.

   ◆ **Report Design.** Creates a blank report in Design view.

   ◆ **Blank Report.** Creates a blank report.

   ◆ **Labels.** Creates a columnar report of labels.

   Access displays the form in Print Preview, but you can switch to Design view, save, print, or close the report.

4. Click the **Save** button on the Quick Access Toolbar, type a name for your report, and then click **OK**.

Create a Report Using the Report Wizard

1. Click the **Create** tab.

2. Click the **Report Wizard** button.

3. Click the list arrow for choosing a table or query on which to base the form, and then click the name of the table or query you want.

4. Select the fields you want to include, indicating the source of any fields you want to include from other tables or queries. Click **Next** to continue.

5. If necessary, specify any groupings of the records, choosing any or all of the selected fields (up to ten). Click **Next** to continue.

6. Specify the order of records within each group, sorting by up to four fields at a time, and then specify ascending or descending order. Click **Next** to continue.

7. Determine the layout and orientation of your report. Click **Next** to continue.

8. Specify the style of the report, which affects its formatting and final appearance. Click **Next** to continue.

9. In the final wizard dialog box, name your report, and then indicate whether you want to preview the report or display it in Design view. Click **Finish**.

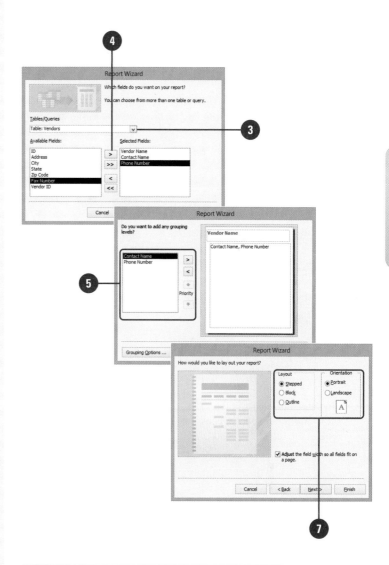

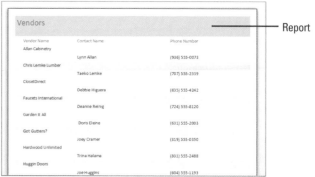

Report

Creating a Blank Report

If you plan to use only a few fields in a report, the Blank Report tool makes it easy to quickly drag-and-drop fields from any table in the database. You can use the Blank Report button on the Create tab to quickly create a blank report in Layout view. When you create a blank report, the Field List opens, where you can drag the fields you want onto the blank report. After you add fields in Layout view, you can switch to Design view, and add controls. In Design and Layout views, you can add pictures, titles, pages numbers, date and time, and format the appearance of the report.

Create a Blank Report

1. Click the **Create** tab.

2. Click the **Blank Report** button.

   The form appears in Layout view along with the Field List.

3. Drag fields from the Field List onto the blank form where you want to place them to create a form.

   - To display all available tables, click **Show all tables** in the Field List.

   - To show only fields in the current record source, click the link at the top of the Field List.

4. Click the **Save** button on the Quick Access Toolbar, type a name, and then click **OK**.

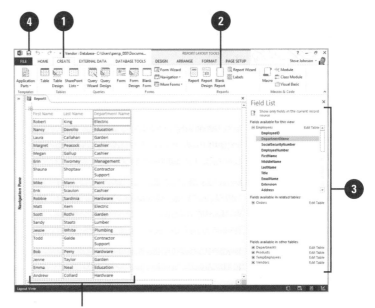

Fields added to a blank report

Did You Know?

You can create a subreport. In the Navigation pane, double-click the report you want to add a subreport, click the Design tab under Report Design Tools, click the Subform/subreport button, drag to create a frame for the subreport, and then follow the wizard instructions.

Creating Mailing Labels

Access provides a **Label Wizard** to help you create mailing labels quickly. The wizard supports a large variety of label brands and sizes. You can also create customized labels for brands and sizes not listed by the wizard, provided you know the dimensions of your labels and label sheets. You can create labels by drawing data from any of your tables or queries. In addition to data values, labels can also include customized text that you specify.

Create Mailing Labels

1. In the Navigation pane, select the table you want to use for mailing labels.

2. Click the **Create** tab.

3. Click the **Labels** button.

4. Select the type of mailing label you're using. Click **Next** to continue.

5. Specify the font style and color for the label text. Click **Next** to continue.

6. Double-click the field names in the Available Fields list to place them on your mailing labels. Type any text that you want to accompany the field values. Click **Next** to continue.

7. If necessary, select a field to sort your labels by. Click **Next** to continue.

8. Enter a name for your mailing labels report, and then choose whether to preview the printout or modify the label design.

9. Click **Finish**.

Click to create your own label size.

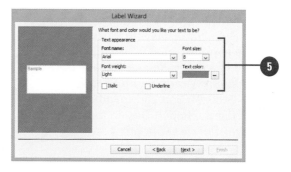

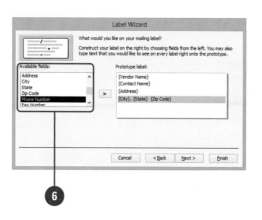

Using Sections in Design View

When Access displays a report or a form in Design view, it divides the report or form into sections, individual parts that control what elements appear and how they are formatted.

Each section has a **selector**, a box to the left of its heading, that you can click to select the section. Any formatting changes you make then affect just that section. Clicking the selector in the upper-left corner selects the entire report or form. To set section properties, double-click the selector, and then change properties, such as Force New Page or Visible, you want on the Property sheet.

Header and footer sections come in pairs. **Headers** in a report display text at the top of each page or at the top of the report. **Footers** appear at the bottom of the page. Headers and footers can also appear at the start and end of records you have grouped together. A group header is useful for displaying a title for a group, while a group footer is useful for summarizing data in a group. You can create a group using the Report Wizard button on the Create tab or the Group & Sort command on the Design tab under the Report Design Tools in Layout or Design view. As with other sec-

tions in a report, you can add controls to headers and footers that include text, expressions, page numbers, and the date and time.

Design View Sections

Section	Description
Report Header	Text that appears at the top of the first page of a report, such as a title, logo, or introduction.
Page Header	Text that appears at the top of each page of a report, such as page numbers or report date.
Group Header	Text that appears before each group of records, such as a vendor name.
Detail	Contains the main body of the report, the fields that display values.
Group Footer	Text that appears at the end of a group of records, such as totals.
Page Footer	Text that appears at the bottom of each page of a report, such as page numbers.
Report Footer	Text that appears at the end of the report, such as report totals or other summary information.

Design view sections

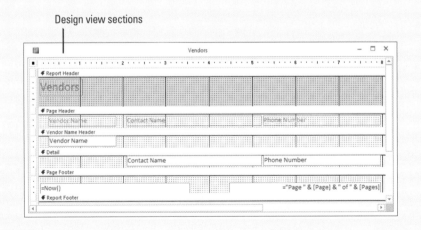

Working with Controls

Each item in a report or form—such as a field name, a field value, and the report title—is represented in Design view by a control. When you create a report or form with a wizard, the wizard arranges and sizes the controls to make the report according to the selections you provided. If you want to modify a report, you can do so in Design view by:

- Creating and deleting controls
- Moving and sizing controls
- Changing control properties
- Formatting the contents and appearance of controls

Types of Report Controls

There are three kinds of controls you can use in a report:

- **Bound controls** are fields of data from the table or query. You cannot create a calculation in a bound control.

- **Unbound controls** are controls that contain a label or a text box. They don't have a source of data (a field or expression). You can create calculations in an unbound control.

- **Calculated controls** are any values calculated in the report, including totals, subtotals, averages, percentages, and so on. They are controls with an expression as the data source.

Each type of control has specific characteristics you can change using the Properties feature. You can modify properties by right-clicking the control you want to modify, and then clicking Properties. In the controls property sheet, you can specify the characteristics you want to change. Although there are commands and buttons you can use to change a specific characteristic, using the Properties button is a fast way to see all of the characteristics for a control and make several changes at once.

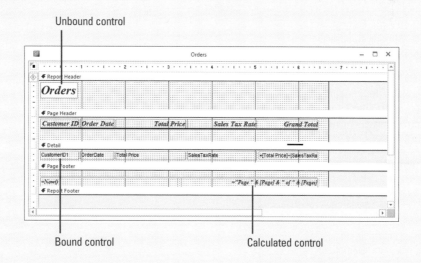

Unbound control

Bound control

Calculated control

Creating and Modifying a Report in Design View

When you create a report from scratch in Design view, three sections appear: Page Header, Detail, and Page Footer. Once you create the report, you need to populate it with data. You can add **bound controls**—fields of data from a table or query—directly from the Field List, or you can add other types of **unbound controls**—text boxes, labels, pictures, buttons, and so on—from the Ribbon. In Design view, you see two parts for every control: the control itself and its corresponding label. When you move a control, its corresponding label moves with it.

Create or Modify a Report in Design View

1. Click the **Create** tab.

2. Do either of the following to create or modify a form:

   ◆ **Create.** Click the **Report Design** button, and then click the **Design View** button.

   ◆ **Modify.** Double-click the report you want to change in the Navigation pane, and then click the **Design View** button.

3. Click the **Design** tab under Report Design Tools.

4. To add a bound control, click the **Add Existing Fields** button on the Design tab under Report Design Tools to show the Fields List.

5. Use the Field List and control buttons on the Ribbon to create or modify a report in Design view.

6. To view or hide headers and footers, right-click the grid, and then click **Report Header/Footer** or **Page Header/Footer**.

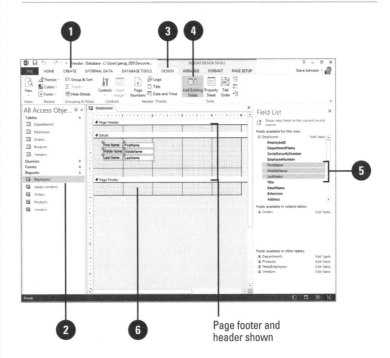

Page footer and header shown

Did You Know?

You can create an unbound report. Create a report without choosing a table or query on which it is based. Such reports are called unbound reports. A dialog box is an example of an unbound report.

Add a Unbound or Bound Control

1. Display the report you want to add controls in Design view.

2. Click the **Design** tab under Report Design Tools.

3. To add a unbounded control, click the **Controls** button, if necessary, click the control button you want to add, such as a text box, and then drag to draw a box in the location where you want the control.

4. To add a bounded control, select the fields you want to include from the Field List; press Shift or Ctrl while you click to select multiple fields. Drag the selected field or fields to the section in which you want the field to appear.

Two boxes appear for each field: one containing the label and one for the field values.

◆ To show the Fields List, click the **Add Existing Fields** button on the Design tab under Report Design Tools.

Did You Know?

You can show or hide the ruler and grid. The ruler and grid provide guides to help you arrange your controls. Click the Arrange tab under Report Design Tools, click the Size/Space button, and then click Ruler or Grid to select it.

You can have controls snap to the grid as you drag for easy alignment. As you drag controls near grid points, they snap to the grid for easy alignment. Click the Arrange tab under Report Design Tools, click the Size/Space button, and then click Snap To Grid to select it.

Controls

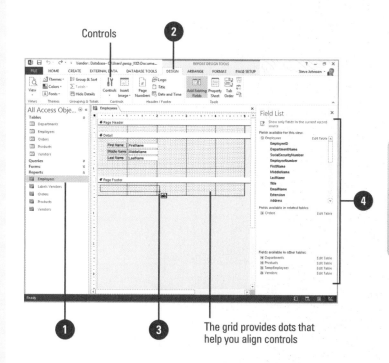

The grid provides dots that help you align controls

Working With Controls

To	Do This
Change control font	Select a control, click the Font list arrow on the Home tab and then click the font name you want, or click the Bold, Italic, or Underline button on the Home tab.
Remove formatting	Select the control, and then click the button that corresponds to the formatting you want to remove.
Change the position of	Select the control, and then click the Align Left, text within a control Center, or Align Right button on the Home tab. If the control is in a header or footer, the control is aligned within the page margins.
Keep labels aligned with controls in the Detail section	When you adjust bound controls in the Detail section, be sure to make the same adjustments in the Header sections so that the headings appear directly over the data.

Using Buttons and Controls

	Buttons and Controls	
Button	**Name**	**Description**
abl	Text Box	This button creates a text box in which the user can enter text (or numbers) for the selected field in the record. Use this control for fields assigned to a text or number data type.
Aa	Label	This button creates a text label. Because the other controls already include a corresponding label, use this button to create labels that are independent of other controls, such as text needed for user instructions or the name of the form or report in a heading.
xxxx	Command Button	This button creates a button that runs a macro or Microsoft Visual Basic function when the user clicks the button in the form or report.
	Combo Box	This button creates a combo box in which the user has the option to enter text or select from a list of options. You can enter your own options in the list, or you can display options stored in another table.
	List Box	This button creates a list box that allows a user to select from a list of options. You can enter your own options in the list, or can have another table provide a list of options.
	Subform/Subreport	This button inserts another form or report within the current form or report at the insertion point.
	Line	This button creates a line that you draw on the form or report.
	Rectangle	This button creates a rectangle or border that you draw on the form or report.
XYZ	Bound Object Frame	This button inserts an OLE object from another source within the same database. Use this button to insert an object that is linked to another source in the database and needs to be updated to reflect recent changes.
XYZ	Option Group	This button creates a box around a group of option buttons. The user is only allowed to make one selection from the buttons enclosed by a group box.
✓	Check Box	This button creates a check box that allows a user to make multiple yes or no selections. Use this control for fields assigned to the yes/no data type.
●	Option Button	This button creates an option button (also known as a radio button) that allows the user to make a single selection from at least two choices. Use this control for fields assigned to the yes/no data type.

Buttons and Controls (continued)

Button	Name	Description
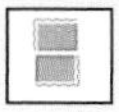	Toggle Button	This button creates a button that allows the user to make a yes or no selection by clicking the toggle button. Use this control for fields assigned to the yes/no data type.
	Tab Control	This button creates a tab in your form. Creating tabs in a form gives your form the appearance of a dialog box in a program so that related controls can appear together on their own tab.
	Chart	This button inserts a chart using the Microsoft Chart OLE program. The program starts a wizard and steps you through the chart creation process.
	Unbound Object Frame	This button inserts an OLE object from another source. Use this button to insert an object that is linked to another program and needs to be updated to reflect recent changes.
	Image	This button inserts a frame, in which you can insert a graphic in your form or report, such as clip art or a logo.
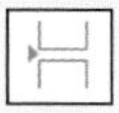	Page Break	This button forces the fields that start at the insertion point to appear on the next screen.
	Insert Hyperlink	This button inserts a hyperlink to an existing file or web page, object in a database, or e-mail address. This button uses the Insert Hyperlink dialog box.
	Attachment	This button inserts an attachment field that allows you to insert an attachment file into a form or report.
	Select	Click this button, and then click the control you want to select. To select multiple controls that are grouped together, click this button, and then drag a rectangle shape around all the controls you want to select.
	Web Browser	This button inserts a layout to display a web page on a form. You can link fields or controls to access the web.
	Navigation	This button inserts a layout for adding navigation in a form to access various forms and reports in a database.
	Control Wizards	Enable this command to use control wizards when they are available, such as List box or Combo box.
	ActiveX	This command inserts an ActiveX control. Use to insert an ActiveX functionality installed on your computer, such as Button Bar, Calendar, or Contact Selector.

Arranging Information

The information in a form or report is arranged according to the arrangement of the sections and controls in Design view. You can modify that arrangement by changing section heights and by moving and resizing controls. When you select a control on a form, sizing handles appear on the sides and at the corners of the control. You can drag the sizing handles to adjust the size of the control. You can also drag inside a selected control to move the control to a new location.

Change the Size of a Control

1. In Design view, click the control you want to resize.

2. Position the pointer over a sizing handle until the pointer shape changes to a two-headed arrow.

3. With the sizing pointer, drag to resize the control.

   For example, to make the control wider, drag the sizing handle on the center- right area of the control further to the right.

Sizing handles indicate control is selected

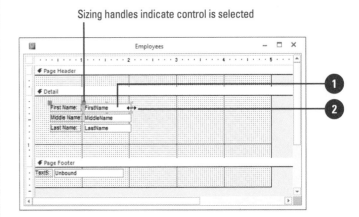

Move a Control

1. Display the report or form in Design view, and then display controls you want to move.

2. Select the control you want to format.

3. To move a control without a label, position the pointer over the large sizing handle in the upper-left corner of the control, and then drag to a new location.

   Only the label or control will move, not both.

4. To move a control, position the pointer over an edge of a control until the pointer changes to a four-headed arrow, and then drag to a new location.

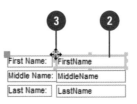

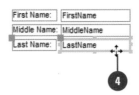

Adjust Page or Section Spacing

1. Display the report or form in Design view whose page or section size you want to change.

2. Position the pointer (which changes to a two-headed arrow) over the bottom of the section whose height you want to change.

3. Drag the border up or down in the appropriate direction to change the spacing. You can drag the border all the way to the previous or next section to hide that section.

Did You Know?

You can change the size in two directions at once. You can change the height and width of a control at the same time by dragging a corner sizing handle.

You can select controls. To select controls that are next to each other, click the Select button on the Design tab, and then drag a rectangle around the controls you want to select. To select controls that are not next to each other, press and hold Shift as you click each control. You can also select a control by clicking the Object list arrow on the Home tab, and then clicking the control you want.

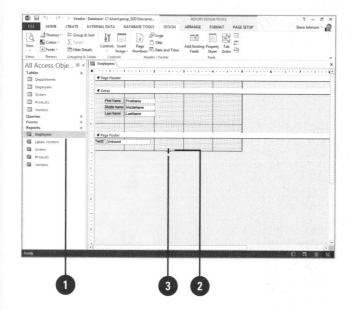

Inserting a Title, Page Numbers, or the Date and Time

When you create a report or form, you typically want to include a title, page number, and the date and time. If Access doesn't include a title, page number, or the date and time in a form or report, you can quickly add them using buttons on the Design tab in Design or Layout view. These elements are added to the report or form header or footer by default, so they appear on every page. After you insert the elements, you can move them around and format them.

Insert a Title into a Report or Form

1. Display the report or form in Design or Layout view you want to insert a picture.

2. Click the **Design** tab in Design or Layout view.

3. Click the **Title** button.

4. Type the title you want.

5. Click a blank area of the report or form to deselect the title.

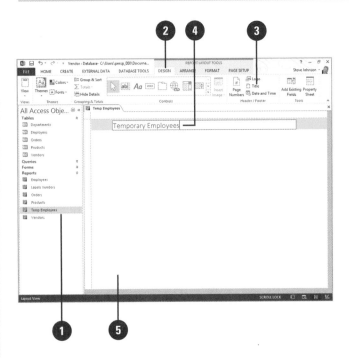

Insert Page Numbers into a Report or Form

1 Display the report or form in Design or Layout view you want to insert a picture.

2 Click the **Design** tab in Design or Layout view.

◆ You cannot insert page numbers on a form in Layout view, only in Design view.

3 Click the **Page Numbers** button.

4 Select a format and position option.

5 Click the **Alignment** list arrow, and then select an alignment option.

6 Select or clear the **Show Number on First Page** check box.

7 Click **OK**.

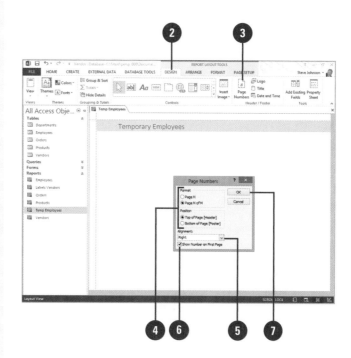

Insert the Date and Time into a Report or Form

1 Display the report or form in Design or Layout view you want to insert a picture.

2 Click the **Design** tab in Design or Layout view.

3 Click the **Date and Time** button.

4 To include the date, select the **Include Date** check box, and then select a date format option.

5 To include the time, select the **Include Time** check box, and then select a time format option.

6 Click **OK**.

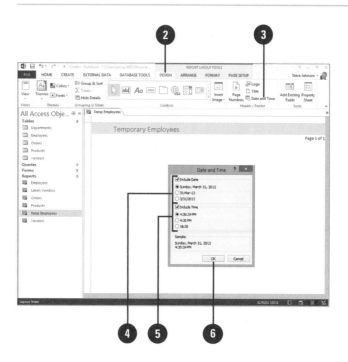

Inserting a Picture as a Logo

If you have pictures, graphics, scanned photographs, art, photos, or artwork from a CD-ROM or other program, you can insert them into a report or form to personalize your Access database. You can use the Logo button on the Design tab in Design or Layout view to quickly insert a picture on your hard disk drive, scanner, digital camera, or Web camera. The picture is inserted into the report or form header by default. You can move the picture to another location by dragging the image or resize it by dragging the edge.

Insert a Picture as a Logo from a File into a Report or Form

1. Display the report or form in Design or Layout view you want to insert a picture.

2. Click the **Design** tab in Design or Layout view.

3. Click the **Logo** button.

4. Click the **Look in** list arrow, and then select the drive and folder that contain the file you want to insert.

5. Click the file you want to insert.

6. Click **OK**.

Inserted logo

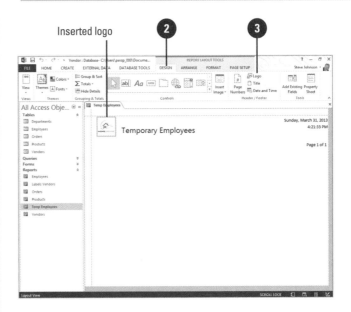

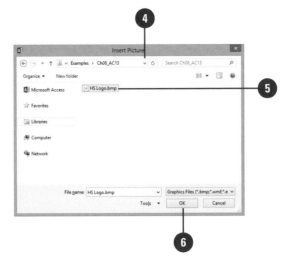

Setting Properties

Every object has **properties**, or settings, that control its appearance and function. A form or report has properties; each section in a form or report has properties, and each control in a section has properties. When you work with a control in a form or report, you can open a property sheet that displays all the settings for that control.

Set Properties

1. In Design view, select the control, section, form, or report whose properties you want to modify.

2. Click the **Design** tab under Form or Report Design Tools.

3. Click the **Property Sheet** button.

4. Click the tab that contains the property you want to modify.

5. Click the property box for the property you want to modify, and then do one of the following.

   ◆ Type the information or expression you want to use.

   ◆ If the property box contains a list arrow, click the arrow and then click a value in the list.

   ◆ If a Builder button appears to the right of the property box, click it to display a builder or a dialog box giving you a choice of builders.

6. Click the **Close** button on the Property Sheet.

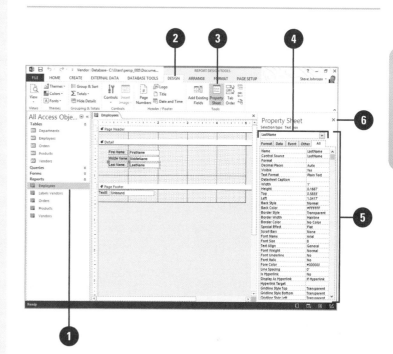

Did You Know?

You can open a subreport in a new window. When you open a report with a subreport, it opens in the subreport control by default. To open a subreport in a new window, open the subreport in Design view, select the subreport, click the Design tab, and then click the Subreport in New Window button.

Performing Calculations in Reports

When you create a report, you might want to include summary information or other calculations. The wizards often include built-in functions, but you can use the **Expression Builder** to create your own by clicking buttons for the arithmetic operators you want to use and including constant values as needed. For example, if you want to determine bonuses based on a percentage of sales, you can create an arithmetic expression to compute the results. When you generate the report, Access will perform the required calculations and display the results in the report. To display the calculations in the appropriate format, you can also use the Properties feature to specify formats for dates, currency, and other numeric data.

Choose Fields to Use in a Calculation

1. In Design view, create a text box control and position it where you want the calculated field to appear, or select an existing unbound control.

2. Click the **Design** tab under Report Design Tools.

3. Click the **Property Sheet** button.

4. Click the **Control Source** property box, which specifies what data appears in a control, and then click the **Expression Builder** button (...).

5. Click the equal sign (=) button, and then enter the values and operators you want to use.

   ◆ Click operator buttons to supply the most common operations.

   ◆ Double-click folders in the left pane to open lists of objects you can use in your expression, including existing fields, constants, operators, and common expressions.

   ◆ Manually type an expression.

6. Click **OK** to insert the calculation.

7. Click the **Close** button on the Property Sheet.

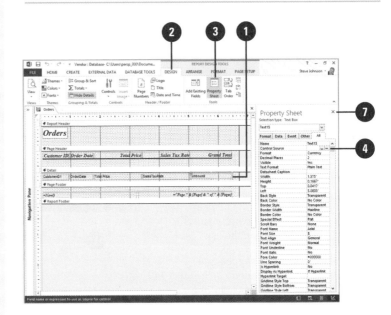

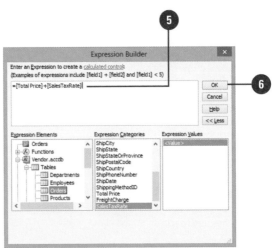

Format Values in a Report

1. In Design view, position the insertion point in the field whose format you want to change.

2. Click the **Design** tab under Report Design Tools.

3. Click the **Property Sheet** button.

4. On either the **All** tab or the **Format** tab of the property sheet, click the Format property box, click the list arrow that appears, and then click the format you want to use.

   The names of the formats appear on the left side of the drop-down list, and examples of the corresponding formats appear on the right side.

5. If you are formatting a number (rather than a date), and you do not want to accept the default, "Auto," click the Decimal Places property box, click the list arrow, and then click the number of decimal places you want.

6. Click the **Close** button on the Property Sheet.

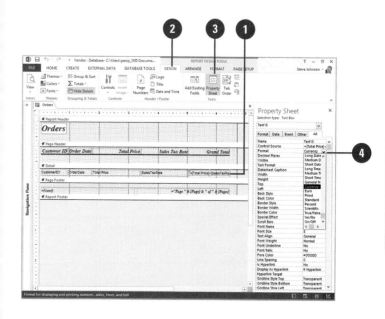

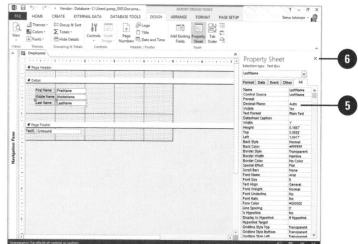

Did You Know?

You can use a builder. Access makes it easy to change many types of settings by providing builders, or tools that simplify tasks. The Expression Builder is just one of many builders in Access. You know a builder is available for a task when you click a property box and a Build button appears.

Grouping and Sorting in Reports

In Layout view, you can use the Group, Sort, and Total pane to create group levels and add totals. The Group, Sort, and Totals pane provides a visual interface to make it easy to understand, use, and navigate. In Layout view, you see group, sort, and total changes right when you make them, so you can quickly decide if you need to make any changes. You can quickly add simple grouping and sorting, or take a little more time to create complex ones. The Totals drop-down list makes it quick and easy to add a sum, average, count, maximum or minimum to report headers or footers.

Create a Group or Sort in a Report

1. Display the report you want to format in Layout view.

2. Click the **Design** tab under Report Layout Tools.

3. Click the **Group & Sort** button.

4. Click **Add a group** or **Add a sort**.

5. Click the **select field** list arrow on the Group on or Sort by bar.

6. Click the field you want to group or sort by.

   The grouping or sorting is applied to the report.

7. To create a more complex grouping or sorting, click the **More** arrow (toggles to Less) on the Group on or Sort by bar, click a list arrow with the criteria you want, and then select options.

8. When you're done, click the **Close** button on the Group, Sorting, and Totals pane.

Did You Know?

You can hide details in a group. To hide the records at the next lower level of grouping, display the report in Layout view, click the Formatting tab, and then click the Hide Details button.

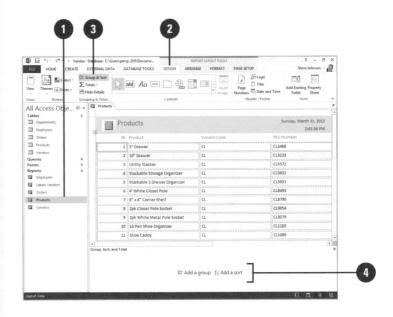

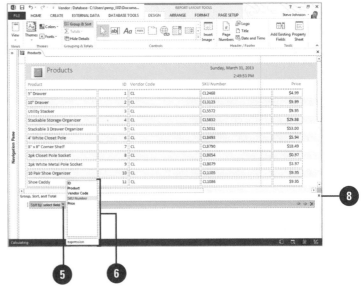

Change or Delete a Group or Sort in a Report

① Display the report you want to format in Layout view.

② Click the **Design** tab under Report Layout Tools.

③ Click the **Group & Sort** button.

④ To change the order of grouping and sorting, click the **Move Up** or **Move Down** button at the end of the Group on or Sort by bar.

⑤ To delete a grouping or sorting, click the **Delete** button at the end of the Group on or Sort by bar.

⑥ When you're done, click the **Close** button on the Group, Sorting, and Totals pane.

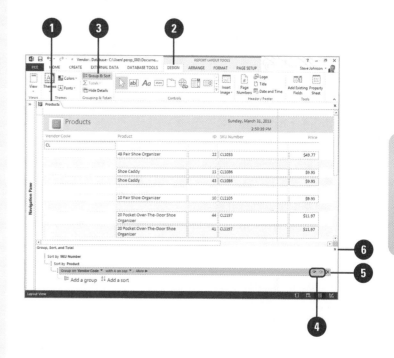

Add a Totals Function for a Group to a Report

① Display the report you want to format in Layout view.

② Click the **Design** tab under Report Layout Tools.

③ Click the field you want to use with a Totals function.

④ Click the **Totals** button, and then select the function you want.

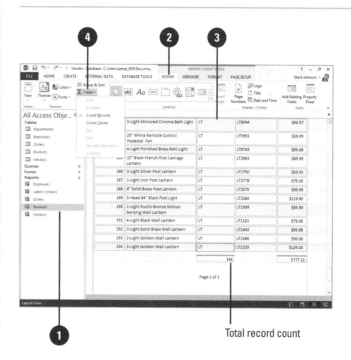

Total record count

Inserting a Header or Footer

Most reports use headers and footers to help you keep track of where you are. A **header** is text printed in the top section of every page within a document. **Footer** text is printed in the bottom section. Commonly used headers and footers contain your name, the document title, the file name, the print date, and page numbers. You can also add a header and footer to a form.

Insert a Header or Footer

1. Display the report in Design view in which you want to insert a header or footer.

2. Click the **Design** tab under Report Design Tools.

3. Click the **Controls** button, and then click the **Text Box** button.

4. Drag a text box control in the header or footer section.

5. Click the **Property Sheet** button.

6. Click the **All** tab, click the **Control Source** property box, which specifies what data appears in a control, and then click the **Expression Builder** button.

7. Double-click the **Common Expressions** folder.

8. Double-click the expression you want to use, such as Page Number, Total Pages, Page N of M, Current Date/Time, and so on.

9. Click **OK** to insert the expression.

10. Click the **Close** button on the Property Sheet.

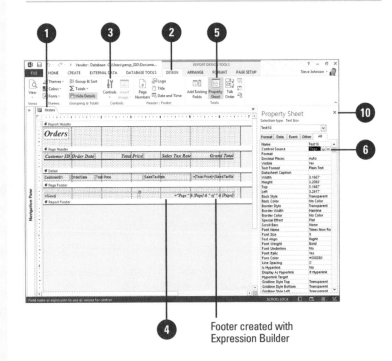

Footer created with Expression Builder

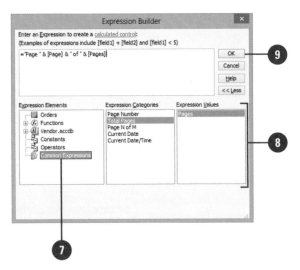

See Also

See "Formatting a Form or Report" on page 232 for information on showing and hiding headers or footers.

Assigning a Shortcut Key to a Control

You can make selecting a control easier in a form or report by assigning it a shortcut key (also known as an **access key**). When you assign an access key to a label or button on a form or report, you can press Alt + an underline character to move the focus to the control. If you have a data access page—a Web page published by an earlier version of Access—you can assign the access key to the control instead of the label attached to the control.

Assign an Access Key to a Control

1. Display the form or report with the label or button you want to assign an access key.

2. Click the **Design** tab under Form or Report Design Tools.

3. Select the label or button.

4. Click the **Property Sheet** button.

5. In the Caption property box, type an ampersand (**&**) immediately before the character you want to use as the access key.

6. Click the **Close** button on the Property Sheet.

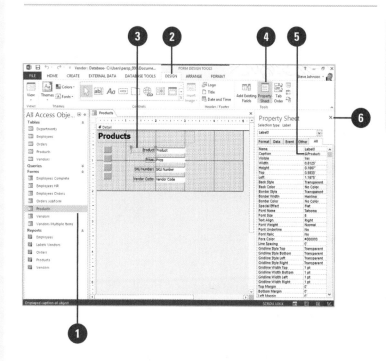

Did You Know?

You can assign an access key to a control on a data access page. In a data access page, select the control in which you want to assign a key, type the character you want in the Access Key property box.

Checking for Errors in Reports and Forms

As you create reports and forms, Access helps you by catching common errors, such as controls being positioned outside the page size, as they happen. Error checking points out errors in a report or form, and provides you with options using a smart tag button for correcting them. When an error occurs, the Error Checking Options button appears, indicating a problem. Click the button to display a list of options to correct or ignore the problem.

Enable Error Checking

1 Click the **File** tab, and then click **Options**.

2 In the left pane, click **Object Designers**.

3 Select the **Enable error checking** check box.

4 To change the color of the error indicator, click the **Error indicator color** list arrow, and then select a color.

5 Select or clear check boxes for the specific errors in which you want to check.

◆ **Check for unassociated label and control.**

◆ **Check for new unassociated labels.**

◆ **Check for keyboard shortcut errors.**

◆ **Check for invalid control properties.**

◆ **Check for common report errors.**

6 Click **OK**.

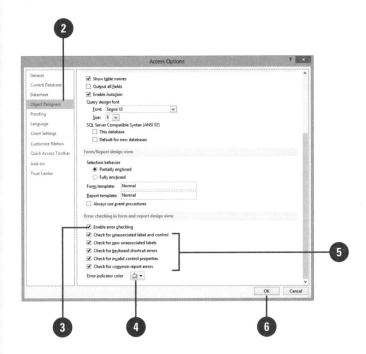

Error Checking Types

Type	Description
Unassociated label and control	A label and a control, such as a text box or list box, are not associated with each other. The Trace Error button appears instead of the Error Checking Options button.
New unassociated labels	A label to a form or report is not associated with any other control.
Keyboard shortcut errors	A control with an invalid shortcut key; either an unassociated label has a shortcut key, or a label or button has a duplicated shortcut key or a space character as its shortcut key.
Invalid control properties	A control with one or more properties is set to an invalid value.

Correct Errors in Reports and Forms

1 When an error indicator (small triangle) appears in a control, select the control.

2 Click the **Error Checking Options** button.

3 Click the option you want (options vary depending on the type of error found). Some of the common options include:

- ◆ **Help on this error.**

- ◆ **Ignore error or dismiss error.**

- ◆ **Error checking options.**

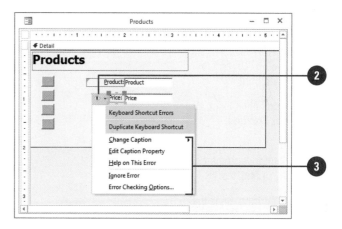

Unassociated label and control

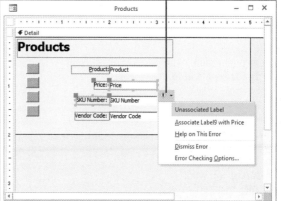

Changing the Page Setup

Once you have created a report or form, you can change the page setup, which includes the margin, paper size and orientation, and grid and column settings. Margins are the blank space between the edge of a page and the text. You can also select the page orientation (portrait or landscape) that best fits the entire document or any section. Portrait orients the page vertically (taller than it is wide), and landscape orients the page horizontally (wider than it is tall). When you shift between the two, the margin settings automatically change.

Change Page Setup Options

1. In the Navigation pane, click the report, form, table, query, or any data you want to change.

   ◆ **For Reports.** Display the report in Design or Layout view, click the **Page Setup** tab, and then continue with Step 3.

2. Click the **File** tab, click **Print**, and then click **Print Preview**.

3. To change margin settings, click the **Margins** button, and then click **Normal**, **Wide**, or **Narrow**.

   ◆ **Set Exact Margins.** Click the **Page Setup** button, specify exact margin settings on the Print Options tab, and then click **OK**.

4. To change paper settings, click the **Size** button, and then select the size you want.

5. To change paper orientation, click the **Portrait** or **Landscape** button.

6. To change column settings, click the **Columns** button, change or select the column and row grid settings, column size, and column layout (**Down, Then Across** or **Across, Then Down**) you want, and then click **OK**.

7. When you're done, click the **Close Print Preview** button.

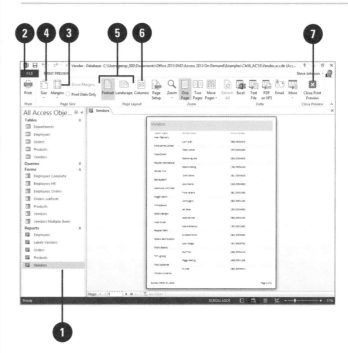

Change Default Print Margins

1. Click the **File** tab, and then click **Options**.

2. In the left pane, click **Client Settings**.

3. Specify the default margin for datasheets, modules, and new forms and reports.

   ◆ **Left Margin.**

   ◆ **Right Margin.**

   ◆ **Top Margin.**

   ◆ **Bottom Margin.**

   You can use values from zero to the width or height of the printed page.

4. Click **OK**.

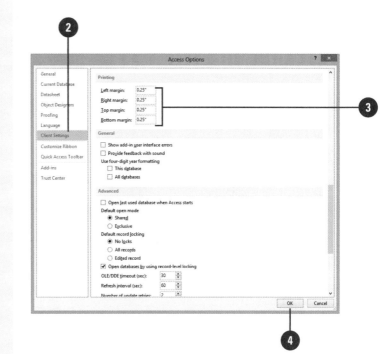

Did You Know?

You can export objects from Print Preview. Access allows you to export data from Print Preview. The available formats include Word RTF, text, PDF or XPS, Snapshot Viewer, HTML Document, XML File, Excel, SharePoint List, and Access Database. The available options vary depending on the objected displayed in Print Preview.

See Also

See "Creating a PDF Document" on page 318 or "Creating an XPS Document" on page 319 for information on using and saving a file with different formats.

Previewing Information

Before printing, you should verify that the data you want to print looks the way you want. You save time, money, and paper by avoiding duplicate printing. Print Preview shows you exactly how your data will look on each printed page. This is especially helpful when you have a multi-page report. Print Preview provides the tools, such as the One Page, Two Pages, Multiple Pages, Previous, and Next buttons, you need to proof the look of each page. Instead of printing the report, you can also use exporting tools in Print Preview to save the report in another format, including a PDF or XPS document.

Preview Data

1. In the Navigation pane, click the report, form, table, query, or any data you want to preview.

2. Click the **File** tab, click **Print**, and then click **Print Preview**.

3. Use the **One Page**, **Two Page**, or **More Pages** buttons to view the data pages the way you want.

4. Use the record navigation buttons (**First**, **Previous**, **Record Selection** box, **Next**, and **Last**) to display pages.

5. To print from the Print Preview window, click the **Print** button, specify the options you want, and then click **OK**.

6. To export objects from Print Preview, use the export buttons.

7. When you're done, click the **Close Print Preview** button.

See Also

See Chapter 11, "Importing and Exporting Information," on page 299 for information on exporting data from Access.

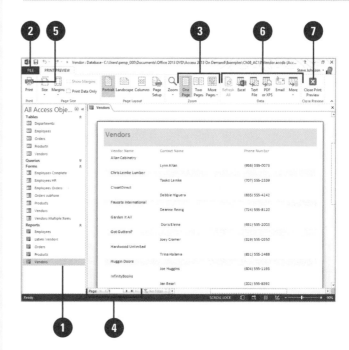

Printing Information

Printing a paper copy is one of the most common ways to share your data from Access. You can print a report, a table, a query, or any data in a single step using the Print button, in which case Access prints a single copy of all pages. If you want to print only selected pages or if you want to specify other printing options, use any of the Print commands on the File tab.

Print Data

① Display the report, form, table, query, or any data you want to format in Design View.

② Click the **File** tab, click **Print**, and then click **Print**.

In Print Preview, click the **Print** button.

TIMESAVER *To print using default settings (without the Print dialog box), click the File tab, click Print, and then click Quick Print.*

③ If necessary, click the **Name** list arrow, and then select the printer you want to use.

④ To adjust page margins, click **Page Setup**, specify the settings you want, and then click **OK**.

⑤ Select the print range you want.

◆ To print all pages, click the **All** option.

◆ To print selected pages, click the **Pages** option, and then type the first page in the From box and the ending page in the To box.

◆ To print selected record, click the **Selected Record(s)** option.

⑥ Click **OK**.

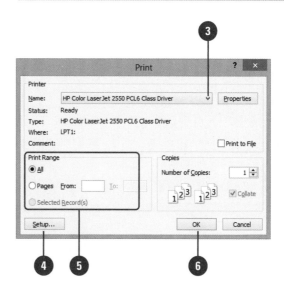

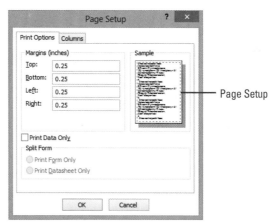

Page Setup

Improving the Appearance of Forms and Reports

Introduction

The objects in a database most "on display" are the forms and reports designed for those individuals responsible for data entry and those who receive reports from the database. For this reason, database designers often give extra attention to the visual appearance and clarity of those objects.

Microsoft Access offers database designers many aids in creating attractive data entry and display objects. The templates that create databases, forms, and reports format those objects attractively, but if you want to go beyond the design provided by a template, Access provides numerous formatting, layout, and style options. You can enhance the appearance of your forms and reports with different fonts and font styles, borders and lines, and judicious use of color. You can also add special effects to certain objects, giving them an embossed or 3-D effect. Access formatting features help you give your customized reports and forms the exact look you want. Although most design changes take place within Design view, you can make color, line, and other formatting changes from within a form or report using Layout view.

You can also insert pictures, charts, and graphs to enhance the appearance of database forms and reports. Access allows you to insert Microsoft Excel charts and objects such as graphs created with other software programs that display data from database tables or queries. When you insert an object, you can edit the inserted information without having to leave Access.

What You'll Do

Apply a Theme to a Form or Report

Create a Custom Theme

Format a Form or Report

Add Lines and Rectangles

Change Line Thickness and Colors

Apply Styles, Shapes, and Effects

Apply the Format Painter

Apply Conditional Formatting

Change Tab Order

Resize and Move Controls

Align, Position, and Group Controls

Change Gridlines

Create a Tabular or Stacked Layout

Change Control Margins and Padding

Change Control Rows and Columns

Share Information Among Documents

Copy and Paste Objects

Insert Objects and Pictures

Insert Excel Charts and Worksheets

Insert and Format a Graph Chart

Move and Resize an Object

Set OLE Options

Applying a Theme to a Form or Report

A theme consists of theme colors and fonts. You can quickly format an entire form or report with a professional look by applying a theme. Access comes with themes from Office and you can create your own. To quickly see if you like a theme, point to one on the themes gallery to display a ScreenTip with name, and a live preview of it on the current form or report. If you like the theme, you can apply it. When you apply a theme, the background, text, graphics, fields, and controls all change to reflect the theme. You can choose from one or more standard themes and use it or customize it with different color or fonts. When you add new content, the form or report objects change to match the theme ensuring all of your material will look consistent.

Apply a Theme to a Form or Report

1. Display the form or report you want to change in Design or Layout view.

2. Click the **Design** tab.

3. Click the **Themes** button, and then point to a theme to preview it or select a theme under In this Database, Custom, or Office.

   ◆ **Custom Theme File.** Click **Browse for Themes**, select an Office theme file (.thmx), and then click **Open**.

4. To apply theme colors, click the **Theme Colors** button, and then select a color theme.

5. To apply theme fonts, click the **Theme Fonts** button, and then select a font theme.

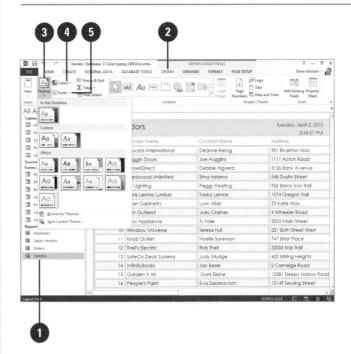

Did You Know?

You can apply a theme to an object. Open the form you want, select an object as desired, click the Themes button on the Design tab, right-click the theme, and then click Apply Theme To All Matching Objects or Apply Theme To This Object Only.

Set Theme Fonts and Colors to Objects in a Form or Report

1. Display the form or report you want to change in Design or Layout view.

2. Click the **Format** tab.

3. Select the object(s) you want to set theme fonts or colors. You can also drag to select multiple objects.

4. To set a theme font, click the **Font** list arrow, scroll to the top, select the font name that ends with (Header) or (Detail).

5. To set a theme color, click the **Font Color**, **Background Color**, **Shape Fill**, or **Shape Outline** list arrow, and then select a theme color.

See Also

See "Creating a Custom Theme" on page 230 for more information on creating a custom theme or custom theme colors and fonts.

Did You Know?

You can select all controls and objects on a form or report. In Design view, display the form or report you want to use, click the Format tab, and then click the Select All button. You can also use the keyboard shortcut, Ctrl+A, to select everything on the page.

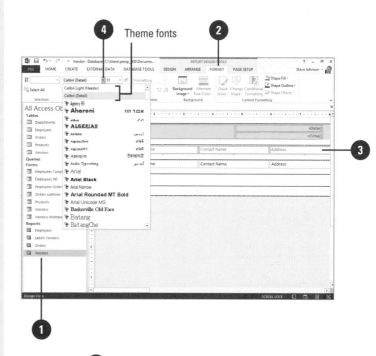

Theme fonts

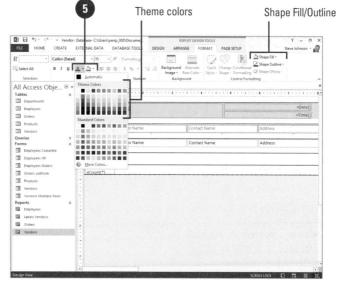

Theme colors   Shape Fill/Outline

Creating a Custom Theme

If you have special needs for specific colors and fonts, such as a company look and feel, you can create your own theme by customizing theme colors and theme fonts, and saving them as a theme file (.thmx), which you can reuse. You can apply the saved theme to other documents. When you save a custom theme, the file is automatically saved in the Document Themes folder and added to the list of custom themes used by Access 2010-2013 and other Office programs. When you no longer need a custom theme, you can delete it. In addition to creating a custom theme, which includes theme colors and fonts, you can also create an individual custom color theme or font theme, which you can select and apply from the Theme Colors or Theme Fonts buttons on the Design tab.

Create a Custom Theme

1. Display the form or report in Design or Layout view.

2. Click the **Design** tab.

3. Create a theme by customizing theme colors and theme fonts.

4. Click the **Themes** button, and then click **Save Current Theme**.

    Office themes are typically stored in the following location:

    Windows 8 or 7. C:/Users /*your name*/AppData/Roaming /Microsoft/Templates/Document Themes

5. Type a name for the theme file.

6. Click **Save**.

Custom theme

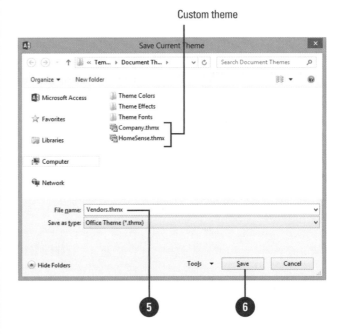

Create a Custom Color Theme

1. Display the form or report in Design or Layout view.

2. Click the **Design** tab.

3. Click the **Theme Colors** button, and then click **Customize Colors**.

4. Click the Theme Colors buttons (Text/Background, Accent, or Hyperlink, etc.) for the colors you want to change.

5. Click a new color, or click **More Colors** to select a color from the **Standard** or **Custom** tab, and then click **OK**.

6. If you don't like your color choices, click the **Reset** button to return all color changes to their original colors.

7. Type a new name for the color theme.

8. Click **Save**.

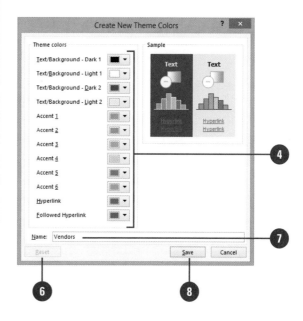

Create a Custom Font Theme

1. Display the form or report in Design or Layout view.

2. Click the **Design** tab.

3. Click the **Theme Fonts** button, and then click **Customize Fonts**.

4. Click the **Heading font** list arrow, and then select a font.

5. Click the **Body font** list arrow, and then select a font.

6. Type a name for the custom theme fonts.

7. Click **Save**.

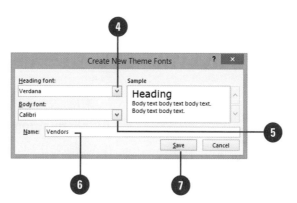

Formatting a Form or Report

After applying a theme, you can always make additional changes to the formatting using buttons on tabs under Report or Form Design Tools. If you don't see the header and footer sections, you can display them to add controls. When you select a control, sizing handles appear around the control, which you can drag to size it. You can also drag inside a selected control to move it to a new location. In Datasheet, and Form View, you can also select text and use the Mini-Toolbar to format the text.

Format a Form or Report Using Formatting Tools

1. Display the form or report you want to format in Design or Layout view.

2. Click the **Format** tab.

3. Select the object(s) you want to format. You can also Ctrl+click or drag to select multiple objects.

4. Use any of the following buttons to format the selected objects:

   ◆ **Text.** Click a list arrow or button (Bold, Italic, Underline, Color, or Background Color) in the Font group.

   ◆ **Number.** Click a list arrow or button ($, %, Comma, or Increase or Decrease Decimals) in the Number group.

5. To apply a fill or border style, click the **Shape Fill** button or **Shape Outline** button, and then select a color or option.

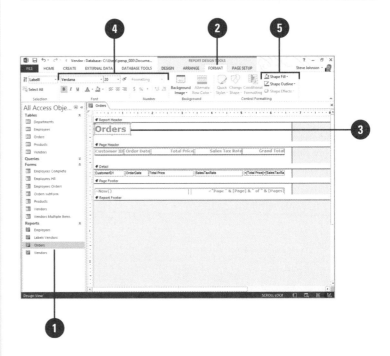

For Your Information

AutoFormatting a Form or Report

In Access 2007, you could use the AutoFormat button to quickly format a form or report with a variety of layouts and styles, or step through the formatting process with the AutoFormat Wizard. The AutoFormat button is no longer on the Design tab (replaced by themes), however, the button is still available in Access if you want to use it. You can add the button to the Quick Access Toolbar in Access Options. You can find the button is under Commands Not in the Ribbon.

Format Text in a Form or Report

1. Display the form or report you want to format in Design or Layout view.

2. Click the **Home** tab.

3. Select the object(s) you want to format. You can also Ctrl+click or drag to select multiple objects.

4. Use any of the available buttons to format the selected objects:

   ◆ **Font.** Click a list arrow or button (Font, Font Size, Bold, Italic, Underline, Color, Text Highlight Color, or Background Color).

   ◆ **Alignment.** Click a button (Align Left, Center, or Right).

   ◆ **Paragraph.** Click a list arrow or button (Bullet, Numbering, Increase or Decrease List level, or Left-to-Right Text Direction).

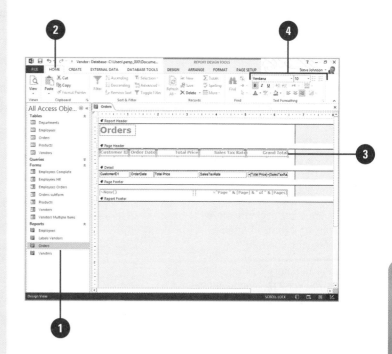

Show and Hide Headers and Footers

1. Display the form or report in Design view.

2. Right-click a blank area of the form or report, and then click the option you want to show or hide the Header/Footer:

   ◆ **Page Header/Footer.** Displays a header and footer for each page.

   ◆ **Form or Report Header/Footer.** Displays a header and footer for the form or report.

3. If necessary, click **Yes** or **No** to delete the header/footer section.

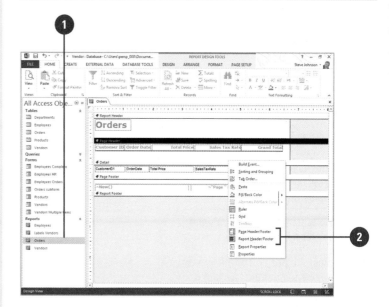

Adding Lines and Rectangles

You can make forms and reports that contain a lot of information easier to read by adding lines between sections or by adding rectangles around groups of controls. Lines and rectangles help organize the information so that reports are easier to read and forms are easier to fill out.

Add a Line to a Form or Report

1. Display the form or report you want to change in Design view.

2. Click the **Design** tab.

3. Click the **Line** button.
   - If necessary, click the **More** list arrow or **Controls** button to display the controls.

4. With the Line pointer, drag a line where you want the line to appear.

5. To adjust the line length or angle, drag a sizing handle left, right, up, or down.

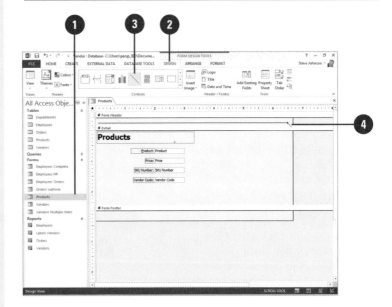

Add a Rectangle to a Form or Report

1. Display the form or report you want to change in Design view.

2. Click the **Design** tab.

3. Click the **Rectangle** button.
   - If necessary, click the **More** list arrow or **Controls** button to display the controls.

4. Drag a rectangle where you want the border to appear.

5. To adjust the position of the line or rectangle, point to the line (not a sizing handle), and then drag the object to a new position.

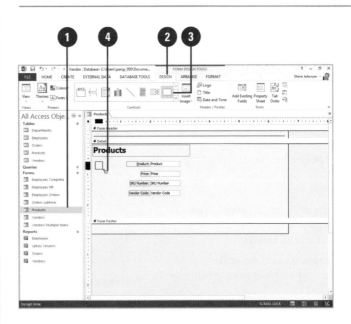

Changing Line or Border Thickness and Style

You can adjust the thickness and style of any line, shape, or field border with the Line Thickness and Line Type buttons. The Line Thickness button provides six different sizes, while the Line Type button provides eight different styles, including dots, dashes, and no style at all. You can modify field border thickness and type from Layout view, but to modify lines or rectangles, you must work in Design view.

Change Line or Border Thickness and Style

1. Display the form or report in Design view or Layout view.

2. Click the **Format** tab.

3. Select the line or border whose line thickness you want to adjust.

4. Click the **Line Thickness** button, and then select the thickness you want.

5. Click the **Line Type** button, and then select the type you want, such as dotted or dashed.

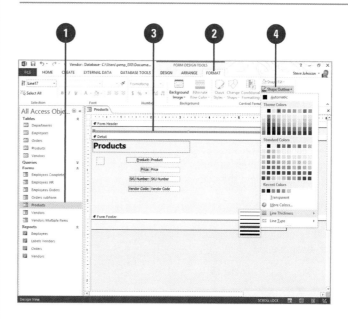

Did You Know?

You can set control defaults. When you create a control, you can set the initial formatting. Create a control, format the control the way you want, click the Design tab under Report or Form Design Tools, and then click Set Control Defaults.

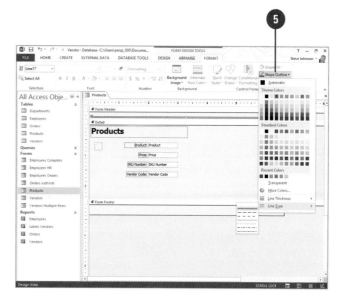

Changing Colors

Choosing appropriate colors for your form or report is an important formatting decision. For example, colors on forms can be used to assist users in correctly filling them out. Also, if you have a color printer available, you can significantly enhance the appearance of a report or form by adding color to lines or text. Other objects you can add color to include rectangles, backgrounds, headers, footers, or detail areas of a report or form.

Change Line or Border Color

1. Display the form or report in Design view or Layout view.

2. Click the **Format** tab.

3. Select the line or border whose color you want to change.

4. Click the **Shape Outline** button arrow, and then select the color you want.

   You can also select Transparent to make the border around a colored object disappear.

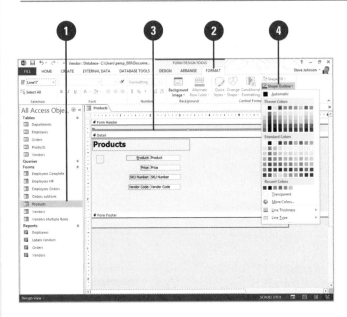

Did You Know?

You can quickly select a repeat color. After you select a color using the color palette on a color button, the color appears in the button. Instead of clicking the button arrow to select the same color, you can simply click the button.

Change Fill Color

1. Display the form or report in Design view or Layout view.

2. Click the **Format** tab.

3. Select the object whose color you want to change.

4. Click the **Shape Outline or Background Color** button arrow, and then select the color you want.

Did You Know?

You can change the background color for alternate rows. In a form or report in Design or Layout view, click the Design tab, click a blank area of the background (under Detail), click the Alternate Row Color button arrow, and then select the color you want.

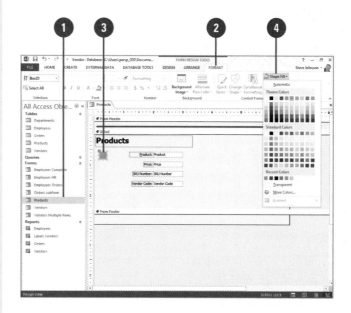

Change Text Color

1. Display the form or report in Design view or Layout view.

2. Click the **Format** tab.

3. Select the text box with the text whose color you want to change.

4. Click the **Font Color** button arrow, and then select the color you want.

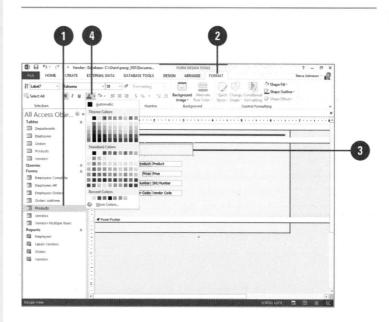

Applying Styles, Shapes, and Effects

If you add a Button control to a form or report, you can enhance its appearance by applying special formatting, such as quick styles, change shapes, and shape effects. If you use other Office programs, you should recognize these shape formatting options. Quick Styles allow you to quickly apply a formatting style based on the current theme colors in the database. Change Shapes allows you to change the shape of a button control. Shape Effects allows you to apply three-dimensional effects, including shadows, glows, soft edges, or bevels.

Apply a Quick Style to a Button Control

1. Display the form or report in Design view.

2. Click the **Format** tab.

3. Select the button control to which you want to apply a quick style.

4. Click the **Quick Styles** button arrow, and then select the style you want to use.

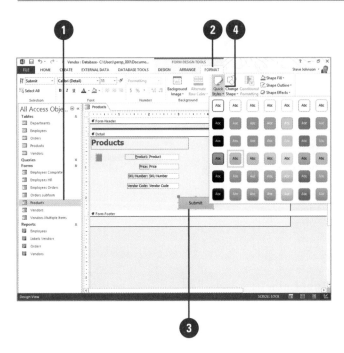

Change the Shape of a Button Control

1. Display the form or report in Design view.

2. Click the **Format** tab.

3. Select the button control you want to change.

4. Click the **Change Shape** button, and then select the shape you want to use.

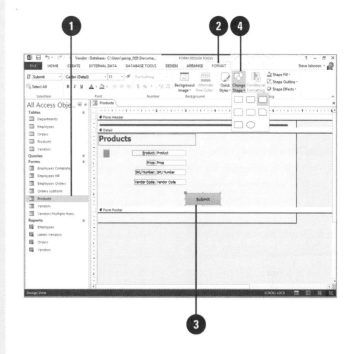

Apply a Shape Effect to a Button Control

1. Display the form or report in Design view.

2. Click the **Format** tab.

3. Select the button control you want to apply a shape effect.

4. Click the **Shape Effects** button, point to **Shadow**, **Glow**, **Soft Edges**, or **Bevel**, and then select the effect you want to use.

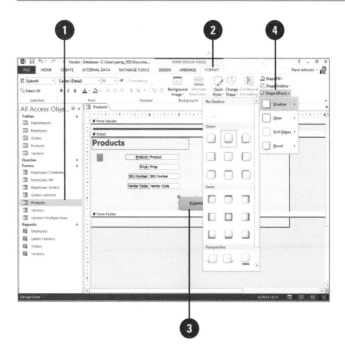

Applying Special Effects

You can apply special effects to one or more controls in a form or report to enhance the appearance of the form or report. For example, you can create three-dimensional effects, including flat (the default effect), raised, sunken, etched, shadowed, and chiseled. Use the effect that seems most appropriate for the tone of the form or report. For example, in a more formal financial report, you might choose the simple flat effect. In a report outlining future technology needs, consider using a high-tech shadowed effect.

Apply a Special Effect to a Control

1. Display the form or report in Design view.

2. Select the control(s) to which you want to apply a special effect.

3. Right-click the selection, point to **Special Effect**, and then select the effect you want to use.

   Note that only the control's line or border is affected. Any text in the control is not affected by applying a special effect.

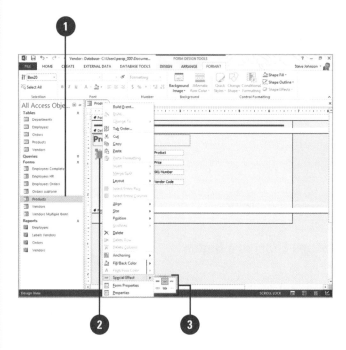

Applying the Format Painter

After formatting an object or control in a form or report, you might want to apply those same formatting changes to other objects and controls. The Format Painter lets you "pick up" the style of one section and apply, or "paint" it to another. To apply a format style to more than one item, double-click the Format Painter button instead of a single-click. The double-click keeps the Format Painter active until you want to press Esc to disable it, so you can apply formatting styles to any text or object you want in your document.

Apply a Format Style Using the Format Painter

1. Display the form or report in Design view or Layout view.

2. Click the **Format** tab.

3. Select the control or object with the style you want to copy.

4. Click the **Format Painter** button.

   If you want to apply the format to more than one item, double-click the Format Painter button.

5. Click the object or control to which you want to apply the format.

6. If you double-clicked the Format Painter button, click another object or control to which you want to apply the format, and then click the **Format Painter** button again or press Esc when you're done to exit.

Did You Know?

You can use the Esc key to cancel format painting. If you change your mind about painting a format, cancel the marquee by pressing Esc.

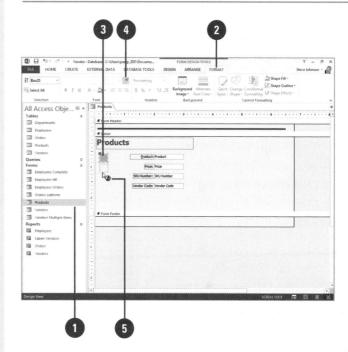

Applying Conditional Formatting

You can make your reports and forms more powerful by setting up conditional formatting. **Conditional formatting** allows you to format a field based on values the user enters. You can display conditional value formatting, such as making negative values appear in red and positive values appear in black or data bar formatting, like those found in Microsoft Excel, where the length of the bar indicates the value. You can incorporate an expression to evaluate values using Expression Builder. The formatting is applied to fields only if the values meet the conditions that you specify. Otherwise, no conditional formatting is applied to the fields.

Create Conditional Formatting for a Field

1. Display the form or report in Design view or Layout view.

2. Click the **Format** tab.

3. Select a field to create conditional formatting.

4. Click the **Conditional Formatting** button.

5. Click **New Rule**.

6. Select the type of rule you want, either check record values or compare record values.

7. Specify the conditional values you want to check record values or the data bars to compare record values.

8. To add an expression, click **Expression Builder** (...), construct the expression, and then click **OK**.

9. Click **OK**.

10. Click **OK**.

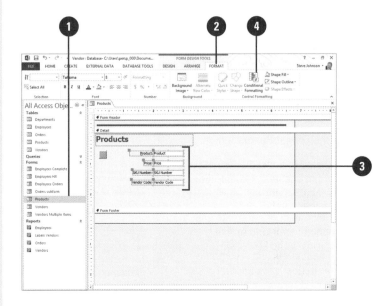

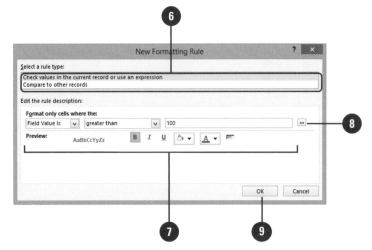

Apply Conditional Formatting to a Field

1. Display the form or report in Design view or Layout view.

2. Click the **Format** tab.

3. Select a field to create conditional formatting.

4. Click the **Conditional Formatting** button.

5. Click the **Show formatting rules for** list arrow, and then select the field with the rules you want to view.

6. Select an existing rule or click **New Rule** to create a new rule.

7. To edit the rule, click **Edit Rule**, make changes, and then click **OK**.

8. To delete the rule, click **Delete Rule**, and then click **Yes**.

9. To change the order that rules are applied, click the **Move Up** or **Move Down** button.

10. Click **Apply** to apply the rule to the selected field or click **OK** to exit.

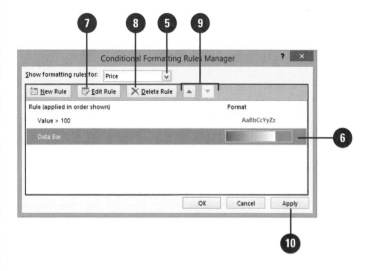

Compare records to create data bar formatting

Changing Tabbing Order

In Design view, the order in which you create controls is the order in which you tab from field to field in Form, Report, or Layout views. As you change a form or report, you typically need to change the tab order too. You can use the Tab Order button on the Design tab in Design or Layout view to change tab order. You can change the tab order for specific sections in a form or report, such as the Page Header, Detail, or Page Footer.

Change Tab Order

1. Display the form or report in Design or Layout view.

2. Click the **Design** tab.

3. Click the **Tab Order** button.

4. To have Access create a top-to-bottom and left-to-right tab order for you, click **Auto Order**, and then skip to Step 8.

5. To create a custom order, click the section you want to change.

6. Click to select a row, or click and drag to select multiple rows.

7. Drag the selected rows to move them to the tab order you want.

8. Click **OK**.

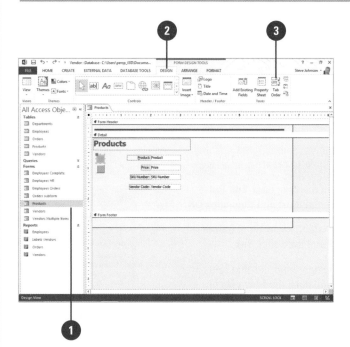

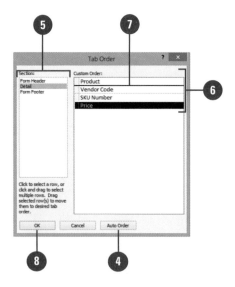

Remove an Object from the Tab Order

1. Display the form or report in Design or Layout view.

2. Click the **Design** tab.

3. Select the field you want to remove from the tab order.

4. Click the **Property Sheet** button.

5. Click the **Other** tab on the Property Sheet pane.

6. Click the property box for Tab Stop click the list arrow, and then click **No**.

7. Click the **Close** button on the Property Sheet.

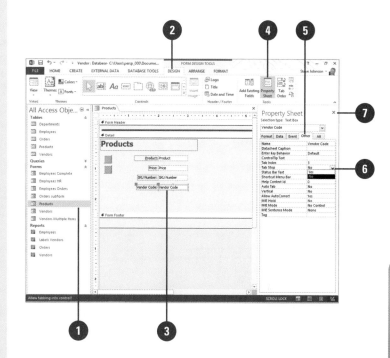

Resizing and Moving Controls

When you select a control, sizing handles appear around the control, which you can drag to size it. You can also drag inside a selected control to move it to a new location. Access also provides tools to resize controls and objects relative to each other and anchor them to a section or another control. When you move or resize an anchored control, the item moves or resizes in conjunction with the movement or resizing of the parent.

Resize or Move a Control

1 Display the form or report in Design view.

2 Select the control(s) you want to format.

> **TROUBLE?** *If you have trouble selecting a control or object, make sure the Select button on the Design tab is highlighted.*

3 To resize one or more controls, position the pointer over a sizing handle, and then drag to a new location.

4 To move one or more controls and a label, position the pointer over an edge of a control until the pointer changes to a four-headed arrow, and then drag to a new location.

To move one or more controls or a labels, position the pointer over the brown square handle until the pointer changes to a four-headed arrow, and then drag to a new location.

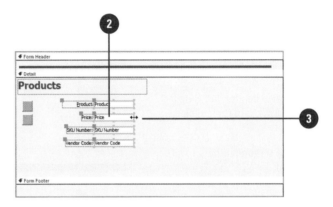

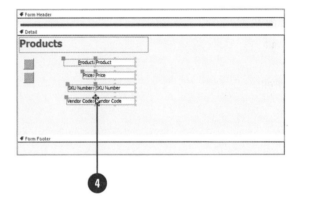

Change the Size of Controls and Objects

1. Display the form or report in Design view.

2. Select the control(s) and object(s) you want to resize.

3. Click the **Arrange** tab.

4. Click the **Align** button, and then select the sizing option you want: **To Fit, To Grid, To Tallest, To Shortest, To Widest,** or **To Narrowest**.

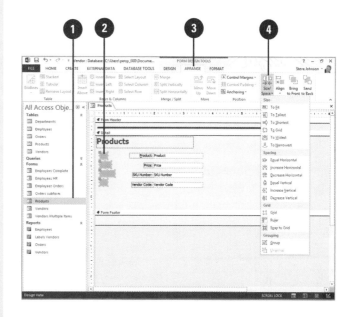

Anchor Controls and Objects

1. Display the form or report in Design view.

2. Select the control(s) and object(s) you want to anchor.

3. Click the **Arrange** tab.

4. Click the **Anchoring** button, and then select the anchoring position you want: **Top Left, Stretch Down, Bottom Left, Stretch Across Top, Stretch Down and Across, Stretch Across Bottom, Top Right, Stretch Down and Right,** or **Bottom Right**.

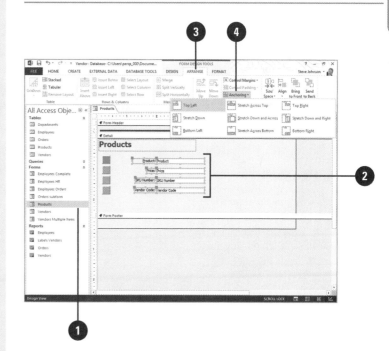

Aligning Controls

Often when you work with multiple controls and objects, they look best when aligned with each other. You can manually align and group controls and objects to create your own layout. In Design and Layout view, the controls and other objects you create align themselves along an invisible grid as you move them. To gain control over the placement of objects, you can turn on and off the Snap to Grid option. When Snap to Grid is turned on, Access aligns the upper-left corner of the control to the grid. If you create a control by dragging, Access aligns all corners of the control to the grid.

Align Controls and Objects to Each Other

1 Display the form or report in Design or Layout view.

2 Select the control(s) and object(s) you want to align.

3 Click the **Arrange** tab.

4 To align controls to each other using the grid, click the **Align** button, and then select **To Grid** (in Design view only) to highlight it.

◆ To disable the command, click the **Align** button, and then select **To Grid** to unhighlight it.

5 Click the **Align** button, and then select the alignment option you want: **Left**, **Right**, **Top**, or **Bottom**.

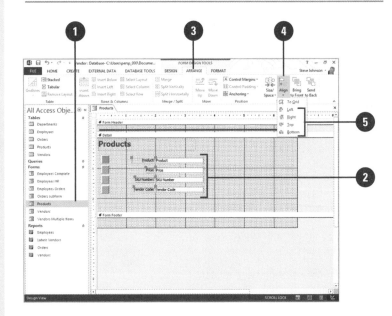

Did You Know?

You can show or hide the ruler. In Design view, click the Arrange tab under Form or Report Design Tools, click the Size/Space button, and then select Ruler to toggle the ruler on and off.

Enable or Disable Snap to Grid

1 Display the form or report in Design or Layout view.

2 Click the **Arrange** tab.

3 To enable the command, click the **Size/Space** button, and then select **Snap to Grid** to highlight it.

4 To disable the command, click the **Size/Space** button, and then select **Snap to Grid** to unhighlight it.

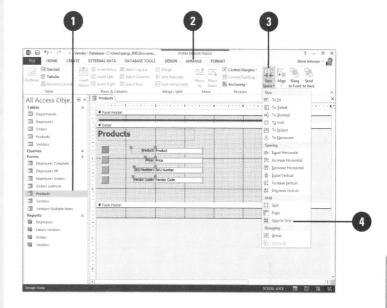

Did You Know?

You can temporarily override the current Snap to Grid setting. Hold down the Ctrl key while you're placing, moving, or resizing a control.

You can show or hide the grid. In Design view, click the Arrange tab under Form or Report Design Tools, click the Size/Space button, and then select Grid to toggle the grid on and off.

You can change the grid dot spacing. In Design view, click the Design tab under Form or Report Design Tools, click the Property Sheet button, click the list arrow at the top of the Property Sheet pane, click Form or Report, click in the Grid X or Grid Y box, and then enter a number in dots per inch. The default is 24.

Positioning Controls

Multiple objects in a form or report appear in a stacking order, like layers of transparencies. Stacking is the placement of objects one on top of another. In other words, the first object that you draw is on the bottom and the last object that you draw is on top. You can change the order of this stack of objects by using Bring to Front or Send to Back, commands on the Arrange tab. You can also change the horizontal and vertical spacing between controls and objects and resize controls and objects relative to each other and group them together.

Change Stacking Order of Objects and Controls

1. Display the form or report in Design or Layout view.

2. Select the control(s) and object(s) you want to align.

3. Click the **Arrange** tab.

4. Click the **Bring to Front** or **Send to Back** button.

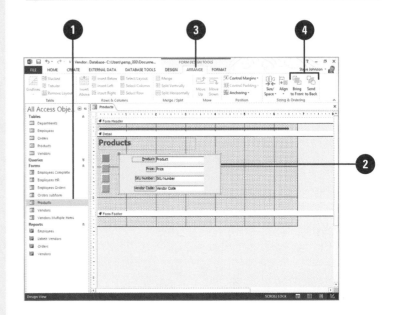

Change Horizontal or Vertical Spacing

1. Display the form or report in Design view.

2. Select the control(s) and object(s) whose spacing you want to change.

3. Click the **Arrange** tab.

4. Click the **Size/Space** button, and then select the spacing option you want: **Equal Horizontal**, **Increase Horizontal**, **Decrease Horizontal**, **Equal Vertical**, **Increase Vertical**, or **Decrease Vertical**.

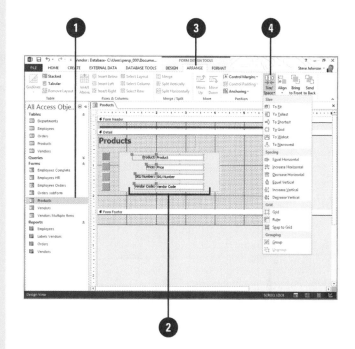

Grouping and Ungrouping Controls

Objects can be grouped and ungrouped in a form or report. Rather than moving several objects one at a time, you can group the objects and move them all together. Grouped objects appear as one object, but each object in the group maintains its individual attributes. You can change an individual object within a group without ungrouping. This is useful when you need to make only a small change to a group, such as changing the color of a single field in the group. Simply select the object within the group, change the object or edit text within the object, and then deselect the object. However, if you need to move an object in a group, you need to first ungroup the objects, move it, and then group the objects together again.

Group or Ungroup Controls and Objects

1. Display the form or report in Design or Layout view.

2. Select the control(s) and object(s) you want to group or an object already in a group you want to ungroup.

3. Click the **Arrange** tab.

4. Click the **Size/Space** button, and then click **Group** or **Ungroup**.

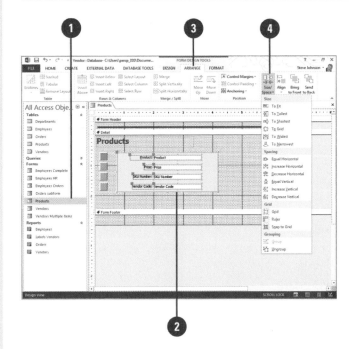

Changing Gridlines

If your controls are located in a control layout, you can add gridlines to provide a visual distinction between the controls. A control layout aligns your controls in a predefined layout, either tabular or stacked, to give your reports and forms a uniform appearance. You can quickly add gridlines to a control layout in a variety of different ways, including Horizontal, Vertical, Cross Hatch, Top, Bottom, and Outline. After you add a gridline, you can change the gridline color, width, and border.

Change Gridlines

1. Display the form or report in Design view or Layout view with the control layout you want to add or change gridlines.

2. Click the **Arrange** tab.

3. Select the control(s) to which you want to apply gridlines.

4. Click the **Gridlines** button, and then select the style you want: **Both, Horizontal, Vertical, Cross Hatch, Top, Bottom, Outline,** or **None**.

5. To change line width, style, or color, click the **Gridlines** button, and then point to the option you want:

   ◆ **Color.** Click to select a gridline color.

   ◆ **Width.** Click to select a gridline thickness.

   ◆ **Border.** Click to select a gridline border style.

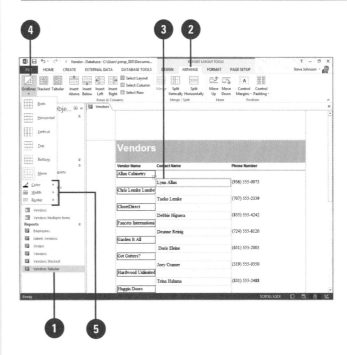

Creating a Tabular or Stacked Layout

Often when you work with multiple controls and objects, they look best when aligned with each other. You can quickly create a predefined tabular and stacked layout, or you can manually align and group controls and objects to create your own layout. The tabular layout arranges controls in rows and columns like a spreadsheet with labels across the top. The stacked layout arranges controls vertically down the page with a label to the left of each control. You can also have more than one layout of each type. If you no longer want a tabular or stacked layout, you can quickly remove it.

Change Form or Report Fields to a Tabular Layout

1. Display the form or report in Design view or Layout view.

2. Select the control(s) you want to change.

3. Click the **Arrange** tab.

4. Click the **Tabular** button.

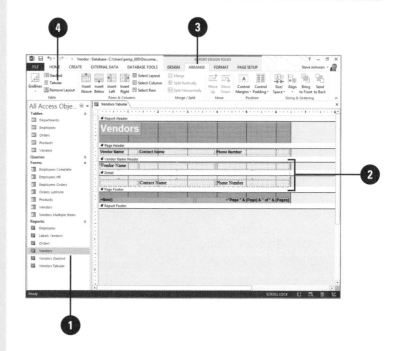

Change Form or Report Fields to a Stacked Layout

1 Display the form or report in Design view or Layout view.

2 Select the control(s) you want to change.

3 Click the **Arrange** tab.

4 Click the **Stacked** button.

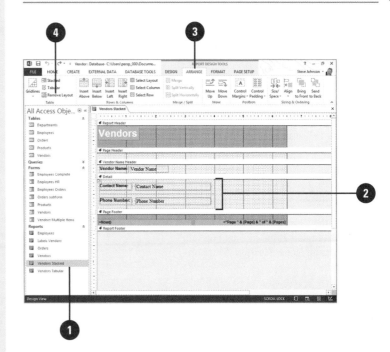

Remove a Tabular or Stacked Layout

1 Display the form or report in Design view or Layout view.

2 Select the control(s) with the tabular or stacked layout you want to remove.

3 Click the **Arrange** tab.

4 Click the **Remove Layout** button.

Changing Control Margins and Padding

In the same way you can adjust margins for a page, you can also adjust margins within a control. If the spacing between controls is to tight or large, you can change the spacing, known as padding, between them. You have three control margins and padding options from which to choose: Narrow, Medium, or Wide. If you no longer want to set control margins or padding, you can set either option to None.

Change Control Margins

1. Display the form or report in Design view or Layout view.

2. Select the control(s) you want to change.

3. Click the **Arrange** tab.

4. Click the **Control Padding** button, and then select the padding option you want: **None**, **Narrow**, **Medium**, or **Wide**.

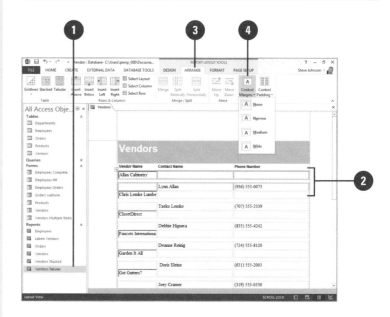

Change Control Padding

1. Display the form or report in Design view or Layout view.

2. Select the control(s) you want to change.

3. Click the **Arrange** tab.

4. Click the **Control Padding** button, and then select the padding option you want: **None**, **Narrow**, **Medium**, or **Wide**.

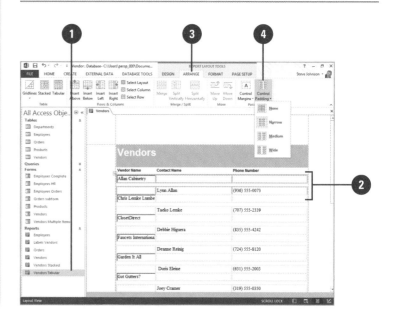

Changing Control Rows and Columns

In the same way you can adjust margins for a page, you can also adjust margins within a control. If the spacing between controls is to tight or large, you can change the spacing, known as padding, between them. You have three control margins and padding options from which to choose: Narrow, Medium, or Wide. If you no longer want to set control margins or padding, you can set either option to None.

Change Control Rows and Columns

1. Display the form or report in Design view or Layout view.

2. Select the control(s) you want to change.

3. Click the **Arrange** tab.

4. To select entire rows or columns, click the **Select Layout**, **Select Column**, or **Select Row** button.

5. To insert rows or columns, click the **Insert Above**, **Insert Below**, **Insert Left**, or **Insert Right** button.

6. To move controls up or down, click the **Move Up** or **Move Down** button.

7. To split a control, click the **Split Vertically** or **Split Horizontally** button.

8. To merge a control, select multiple controls, and then click the **Merge** button.

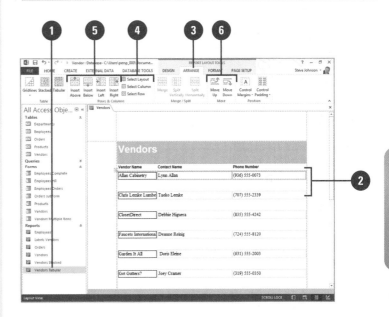

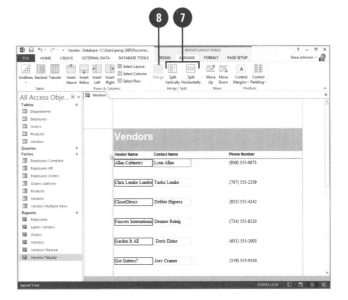

Sharing Information Among Documents

The ability to insert an object created in one program into a document created in another program allows you to create documents that meet a variety of needs. Access can convert data or text from one format to another using a technology known as **object linking and embedding (OLE)**. OLE allows you to move text or data between programs in much the same way as you move them within a program. The table below includes terms that you'll find useful in understanding how you can share objects among documents.

Embedding and Linking

Term	Definition
Source program	The program that created the original object
Source file	The file that contains the original object
Destination program	The program that created the document into which you are inserting the object
Destination file	The file into which you are inserting the object

To better understand how these objects and terms work together, consider this example: If you place an Excel chart in an Access database, Excel is the source program and Access is the destination program. The chart is the source file; the database is the destination file.

There are three ways to share information in Windows programs: pasting, embedding, and linking.

Pasting

You can cut or copy an object from one document and then paste it into another using the Cut, Copy, and Paste buttons on the source and destination program tabs.

Embedding

When you embed an object, you place a copy of the object in the destination file. When you activate the embedded object, the tools from the source program become available in the destination file. For example, if you insert an Excel chart into an Access database, the Excel ribbons and tabs become available, replacing the Access tabs so you can edit the chart if necessary. With embedding, any changes you make to the chart in the database do not affect the original file.

Linking

When you link an object, you insert a representation of the object itself into the destination file. The tools of the source program are available, and when you use them to edit the object you've inserted, you are actually editing the source file. Moreover, any changes you make to the source file are reflected in the destination file.

Copying and Pasting Objects

When you copy or paste an object, Access stores the object in the Clipboard. You can paste the object into the destination file using the Clipboard task pane, Paste button, or Paste Special command, which gives you more control over how the object will appear in the destination file. When you use the Paste button, you are sometimes actually embedding. Because embedding can greatly increase file size, you might want to use Paste Special. You can select a format that requires minimal disk space and paste the object as a simple picture or text.

Paste an Object

1. Select the object in the source program.

2. Click the **Copy** button on the source program's Home tab.

3. Switch to Access and display the area where you want to paste the copied object.

4. Click the **Paste** button on the Home tab and position the object.

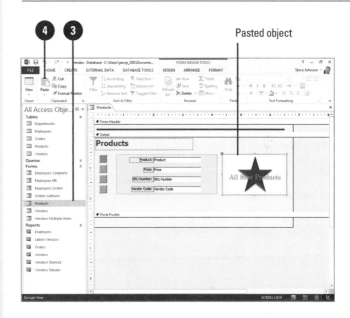

Pasted object

Paste Information in a Specified Format

1. Select the object in the source program.

2. Click the **Copy** button on the source program's Home tab.

3. Switch to Access and display the area where you want to paste the copied object.

4. Click the **Paste** button arrow, and then click **Paste Special.**

5. Click the object type you want.

6. Click **OK**.

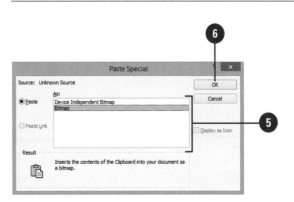

Inserting a New Object

You can create objects from scratch without leaving the Access program. After you drag to create a new unbound object frame control, the Insert Object dialog box appears, and you can select the program in which you want to create the graphic. The programs that appear correspond to the software installed on your computer. For example, if you want to create a picture in Microsoft Paint, a graphics accessory that accompanies the Microsoft Windows operating system, you can choose the Bitmap Image option.

Insert a New Object

1. Display the form or report in Design view.

2. Click the **Design** tab.

3. Click the **Unbound Object Frame** button.

   ◆ If necessary, click the **More** list arrow or **Controls** button to display the controls.

4. Drag a rectangle where you want the picture to the size you want.

5. Click the **Create new** option.

6. Click the program in which you want to create an object.

7. Click **OK**, and then create the new object using the tools that appear in the program you selected.

8. Click outside the window in which you created the unbound object.

   The program you created the object closes, and the new object is inserted in the form or report.

Did You Know?

You can edit the original graphic.
Double-click the graphic object you created to redisplay the program in which you created the object, and then modify the graphic. When you close the program, the modified graphic will be inserted in the form or report.

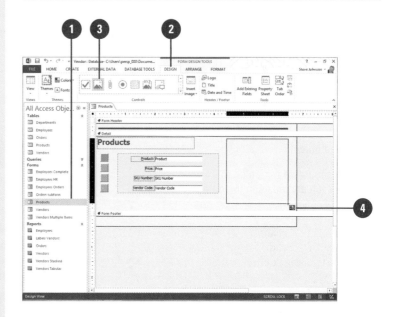

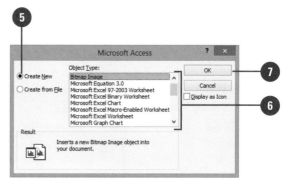

Inserting an Object from a File

There are several ways to embed or link an object from a file. If you want to embed a new object that you create from scratch, you can use the Insert Object command. If you want to insert an existing file, you can also use Insert Object and you can specify whether or not you want to link the object. If your object is already open in the program that created it, you can copy it, and in some cases, paste it into a form or report, automatically embedding it. Finally, you can use the Paste Special command to paste link a copied object—pasting and linking it at the same time.

Insert an Object from a File

1. Display the form or report in Design view.

2. Click the **Design** tab.

3. Click the **Unbounded Object Frame** button, and then drag to create a frame.

4. Click the **Create from file** option, click **Browse**, select the file you want to insert, and then click **OK**.

5. To embed the object, make sure the **Link** check box is clear. To link it, select the **Link** check box.

6. Click **OK**.

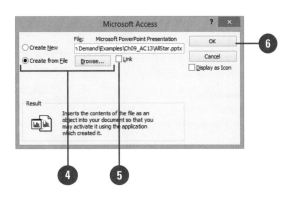

Paste Link an Object

1. In the source program, select the object you want to paste link.

2. Click the **Cut** or **Copy** button on the Home tab in the source program.

3. Switch to your database form or report.

4. Click the **Paste** button arrow, click **Paste Special**, and then click the **Paste Link** option.

5. Click the format you want, and then click **OK**.

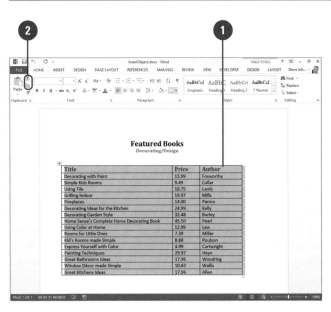

Inserting a Picture

You can insert interesting visuals, such as pictures, into your forms and reports or even fields. For example, in an employee table a field could contain employee photos. Or a field might contain a Word document that is a recent performance review. When you run a report that includes this field, the report will display the contents of the field. In Datasheet view, you can double-click the field to display the field's contents.

Insert a Graphic File

1. Display the form or report in Design view.

2. Click the **Design** tab.

3. Click the **Image** button.

   ◆ If necessary, click the **More** list arrow or **Controls** button to display the controls.

4. Drag a rectangle where you want the picture to appear. Make the rectangle approximately the same size as the picture you will insert.

5. Click the **Look in** list arrow, and then locate the folder containing the picture you want to insert.

6. Click the picture file you want to insert.

7. Click **OK**.

8. If necessary, drag the sizing handles to resize the graphic as needed.

Did You Know?

You can crop parts of a graphic that you want to hide. Press and hold Shift, and then drag a sizing handle over the area you want to crop. To create more space around the graphic, drag the handle away (while holding down Shift) from the center of the graphic.

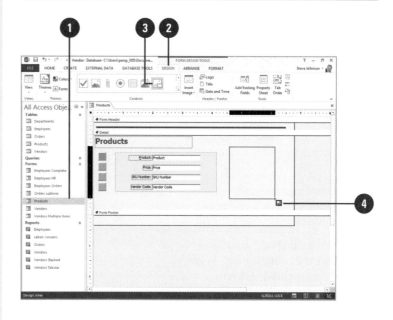

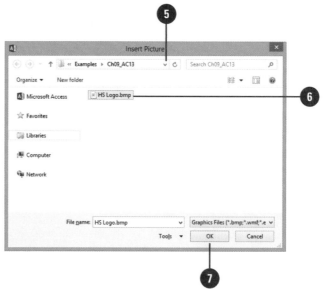

Set Picture Alignment and Size Property Settings

1 Display the form or report in Design view.

2 Click the **Design** tab.

3 Select the picture you want to change.

4 Click the **Property Sheet** button.

5 Click the **Format** tab on the Property Sheet pane.

6 Click the property box for Picture Alignment, click the list arrow, and then click **Top Left**, **Top Right**, **Center**, **Bottom Left**, or **Bottom Right**.

7 Click the property box for Size Mode, click the list arrow, and then click **Clip**, **Stretch**, or **Zoom**.

Clip stays the same regardless of control size. Stretch resizes to match control size. Zoom resizes to match control size with the original aspect ratio.

8 Click the **Close** button on the Property Sheet.

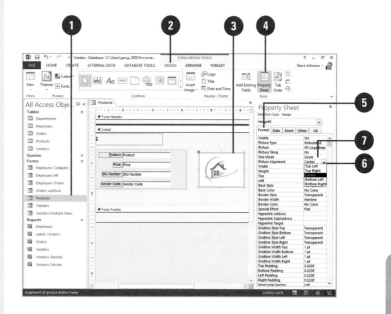

For Your Information

Adding Attachments to a Form or Report

If you have added an attachment field to a table, you can add the attachment control to a form or report. To add the attachment control, display the form or report in Design view, click the Design tab, click the Add Existing Fields button, drag the entire attachment field (the parent and child items: name.FileData, name.FileName, and name.FileType) from the list to your form or report, and then save your changes. After you add the attachment field to your form or report, you can add, edit, remove, and save attachments files directly from the form or report. When you select the attachment field in a form or report, a mini-toolbar appears, where you can use the Back and Forward buttons to scroll through attachments, or use the View Attachments button to open the Attachments dialog box.

Inserting Excel Charts and Worksheets

There are several types of Excel objects that you can insert into your form or report. Two of the most common are worksheets and charts. You can insert a new Excel worksheet and then add data to it, or you can insert an existing Excel worksheet. You can also insert a chart from an Excel workbook.

Insert an Excel Chart

1 In Excel, click the chart you want to insert in the Access report or form.

2 In Excel, click the **Copy** button on the Home tab.

3 Switch to Access and display the form or report on which you want the chart in Design view.

4 Click the **Paste** button on the Home tab.

5 Click outside the chart to deselect it.

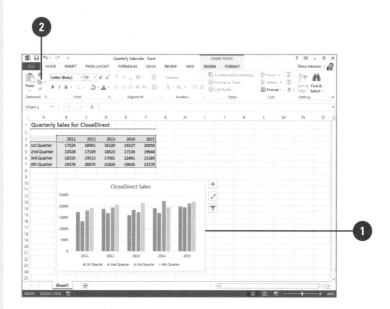

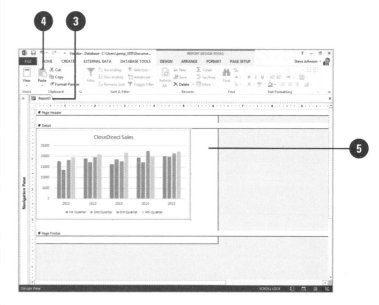

Did You Know?

You can drag and drop to Excel. You can drag objects from Excel right into Design view. Make sure that neither window is maximized and that both the object you want to drag and its destination are visible.

You can edit an inserted Excel worksheet. If you want to modify the worksheet, double-click it, and then use the Excel tools to edit. When you're done, click the Close button, and then click Yes to save changes.

Insert an Excel Worksheet

1. Display the form or report in Design view into which you want to insert the Excel worksheet.

2. Click the **Design** tab.

3. Click the **Unbound Object Frame** button, and then drag to create a frame.

   ◆ If necessary, click the **More** list arrow or **Controls** button to display the controls.

4. Click the **Create from file** option.

5. Click **Browse**, locate and select the worksheet, and then click **OK**.

6. To link back to the original content for updates, select the **Link** check box.

7. Click **OK**.

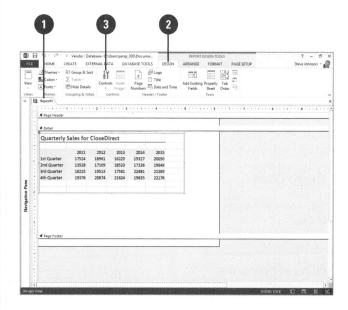

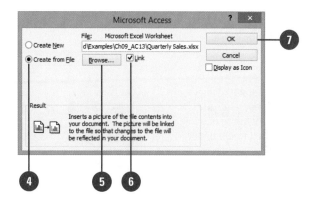

Inserting a Graph Chart

You can create a chart from data in a table or query using the Chart Wizard. The wizard steps you through the process to select the data and chart type. The Graph chart uses two views to display the information that makes up a graph: the datasheet, which is a spreadsheet-like grid of rows and columns that contains your data, and the chart, which is the graphical representation of the data. A datasheet contains cells to hold your data. A cell is the intersection of a row and column. Graph Chart comes with a gallery that lets you change the chart type and then format the chart to get the result that you want. You can also save your customized settings as a format to use when you create other charts.

Create a Graph Chart

1. Display the form or report in Design view.

2. Click the **Design** tab.

3. Click the **Insert Chart** button.

   ◆ If necessary, click the **More** list arrow or **Controls** button to display the controls.

4. Drag the pointer to create a rectangle the size of the chart you want to create.

5. When the wizard appears, click a chart option, and then click the table or query you want to use for the chart. Click **Next** to continue.

6. Click a field, and then click the **Add** button for each field you want to chart. Click **Next** to continue.

7. Click the chart type you want. Click **Next** to continue.

8. Make any layout modifications that are desired. Click **Next** to continue.

9. If you want the chart to change from record to record, select the fields that link the document and the chart. Click **Next** to continue.

10. Enter a chart name, click the No option if you do not want to display the legend, and then click **Finish**.

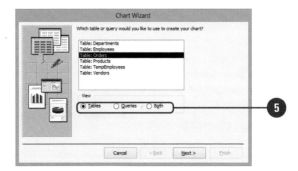

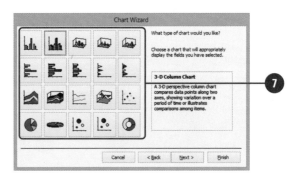

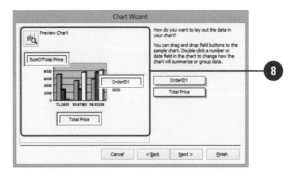

Change a Chart Type

1. In Design view, double-click the chart on your form or report.

2. Click the **Chart Type** button list arrow.

3. Click the button for the chart type you want.

4. To exit back into Access, click the **Close** button, and then click **Yes** to update the chart.

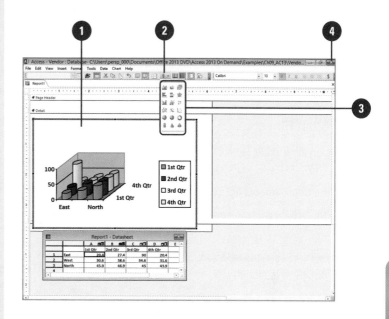

Save Chart Settings as a Custom Chart Type

1. In Design view, double-click the chart on your form or report.

2. Click the **Chart** menu, and then click **Chart Type**.

3. Click the **Custom Types** tab.

4. Click the **User-defined** option.

5. Click **Add**.

6. Type a name and description for the chart, and then click **OK**.

7. Click **OK**.

8. To exit back into Access, click the **Close** button, and then click **Yes** to update the chart.

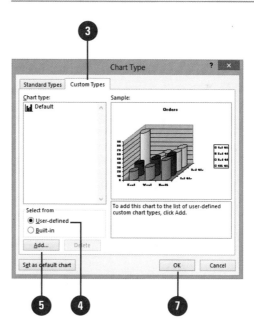

Formatting Chart Objects

Chart objects are the individual objects that make up a chart, such as an axis, the legend, or a data series. The **plot area** is the bordered area where the data are plotted. The **chart area** is the area between the plot area and the Microsoft Graph object selection box. To suit your needs, you can format chart objects and individual objects that make up a chart, such as an axis, legend, or data series.

Select a Chart Object

1. In Design view, double-click the chart on your form or report.

2. Click the **Chart Objects** list arrow.

3. Click the chart object you want to select.

    When a chart object is selected, selection handles appear.

4. To exit back into Access, click the **Close** button, and then click **Yes** to update the chart.

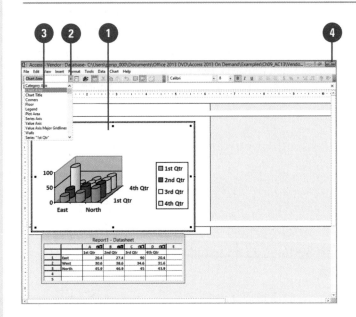

Format a Chart Object

1. In Design view, double-click the chart on your form or report.

2. Double-click the chart object you want to format, such as an axis, legend, or data series.

3. Click the tab corresponding to the options you want to change. Tabs differ depending on the chart object.

4. Select the options to apply.

5. Click **OK**.

6. To exit back into Access, click the **Close** button, and then click **Yes** to update the chart.

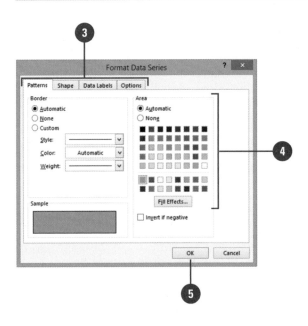

Customize a Chart

1. In Design view, double-click the chart on your form or report.

2. If necessary, select the chart object.

3. Click the **Chart** menu, and then click **Chart Options**.

4. Click the tab (**Titles, Axes, Gridlines, Legend, Data Labels,** or **Data Table**) corresponding to the chart object you want to customize.

5. Make your changes.

6. Click **OK**.

7. To exit back into Access, click the **Close** button, and then click **Yes** to update the chart.

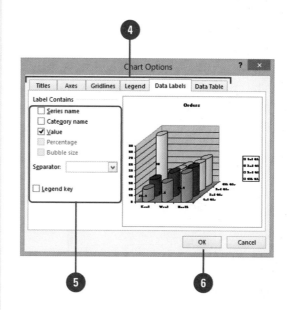

Change the View of a 3-D Chart

1. In Design view, double-click the chart on your form or report.

2. Select the 3-D chart you want to change.

3. Click the **Chart** menu, and then click **3-D View**.

4. Click the left or right rotation button.

5. Click the up or down elevation button.

6. Click **OK**.

7. To exit back into Access, click the **Close** button, and then click **Yes** to update the chart.

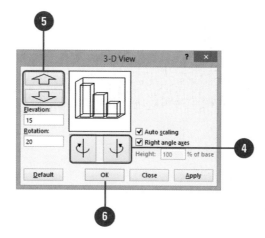

Moving and Resizing an Object

After you insert a graphic object, you can resize or move it with its selection **handles**, the little squares that appear on the edges of the object when you click the object to select it. If you need to select more than one object, you can drag a selection rectangle around the objects, or press and hold down the Shift key, and then click each object to select it.

Move an Object

1 In Design view, select an object you want to move.

2 Select the object(s) you want to move, position the mouse pointer over the object, and then when the mouse pointer changes to a hand, drag it to move the outline of the object to a new location.

Do not click a handle or else you will resize the object.

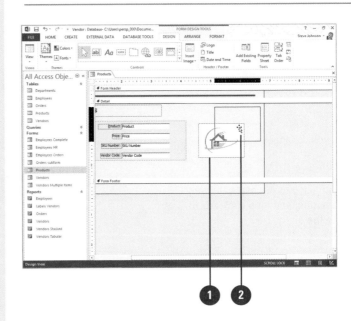

Resize an Object

1 In Design view, select the object you want to resize.

2 Select the object(s) you want to resize, and then position the mouse pointer over one of the handles.

3 When the pointer changes to a two-headed arrow, drag the handle until the object is the size you want.

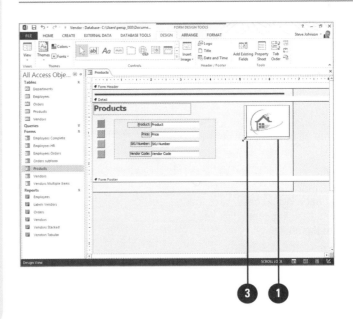

Setting OLE Options

When you insert an OLE object, also known as a DDE (Dynamic Data Exchange) object, into a database, you are creating a link to another program. When you open a database with a linked object, Access checks the link to make sure it's working properly. If the linked object is not located in the linked location, Access keeps trying to re-establish the link until the specified timeout period in Access Options. If you don't want other programs to use Access as an OLE object, you can ignore requests from other programs. When linked information changes, you can enable or disable the option to refresh the data.

Set OLE Options

1. Click the **File** tab, and then click **Options**.

2. In the left pane, click **Client Settings**.

3. Select or clear check boxes for the following OLE options:

   ◆ **OLE/DDE timeout (sec).** Specify the interval after which Access retries a failed OLE or DDE attempt. The default value is 30. You can set a range from zero to 300.

   ◆ **Ignore DDE requests.** Access ignores DDE requests from other applications.

   ◆ **Enable DDE refresh.** Enables Access to update DDE links at the interval specified in the Refresh interval (sec) box.

4. Click **OK**.

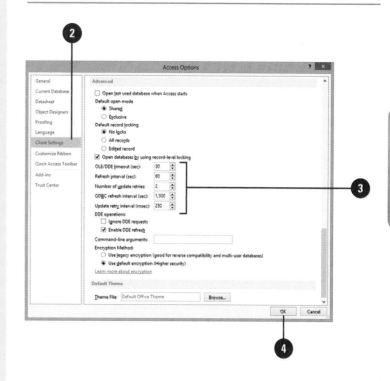

Connecting to Information on the Web

Introduction

The Internet and the web have become an integral part of computing today. By providing quick and easy communication and data sharing to users around the world, the Internet has made it possible for data to have a global, rather than simply local, application. Microsoft Access provides support for the web in different ways:

◆ By allowing database tables, queries, forms, and reports to contain links to objects on the web.

◆ With tools to navigate the web from within the database.

◆ With tools to display web pages on a form from within the database.

◆ With the ability to import and export tables, queries, forms, and reports as HTML documents.

Each of these features makes it easier for you to work with data from the web in your database and makes your data available to the outside world.

If you have access to a Microsoft SharePoint server or the subscription-based Microsoft Office 365 SharePoint site (www.office365.com), you can share information from Access with other people using the web site. For example, you can create a table or import data from SharePoint site and export data to a SharePoint site. If you don't have access to the Internet, you can work with SharePoint data locally on your computer and then synchronize the data back with the online SharePoint site when a connection is available. You can also publish an Access database to a SharePoint site in a similar way that you save a database on your hard disk.

What You'll Do

Integrate Access and the Internet

Create a Hyperlink Field

Insert a Hyperlink to a File or Web Page

Build a Hyperlink with Expressions

Link to an Object in a Database

Insert a Hyperlink with an E-mail Address

Navigate Hyperlinks

Work with Hyperlinks

Insert a Web Browser Control

Export Database Objects to HTML

Import or Link to an HTML File

Create a Table Using SharePoint

Import or Link to SharePoint Data

Export Data to SharePoint

Move Data to SharePoint

Work with SharePoint Data Offline

Publish a Database to SharePoint

Integrating Access and the Internet

One of the chief uses of computers today lies in accessing the **Internet**, a structure of millions of interconnected computers that allows users to communicate and to share data with one another. In its early years, the Internet was limited to a small community of university and government organizations. This was due, in part, to the sometimes difficult commands needed to navigate the Internet.

However, the introduction of the World Wide Web in the early 1990s led to an explosion in Internet use by businesses and the general public. The web made Internet navigation easy by replacing arcade commands with a simple point-and-click interface within an application called a **web browser**. The web made data accessible to a wider audience than ever before. Companies could create web sites containing product information, stock reports, and information about the company's structure and goals. Later innovations allowed businesses to accept and process orders online and to enter those orders into databases containing inventory and customer information.

Because of the importance of these developments, Microsoft has worked to integrate Access more tightly with the Internet and the web. You can now navigate the web from inside Access. Access databases can contain links to Internet resources, and you can save tables, forms, and reports as web documents. These features make it possible for you to manage Access data locally and across the globe.

Creating Hypertext Links

The web is a giant structure of documents connected together through hypertext links. **Hypertext links**, or **hyperlinks**, are elements on a web page that you can activate, usually with a click of your mouse, to retrieve another web document, which is called the **target** of the link. For example, a document about the national park system might contain a hypertext link whose target is a page devoted to Yosemite National Park. The great advantage of hypertext is that you don't have to know where or how the target is stored. You need only to click the hyperlink to retrieve the tar-

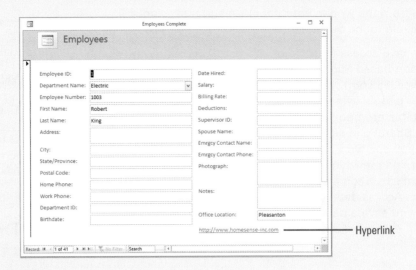

Hyperlink

get. A target is identified by its **Uniform Resource Locator (URL)**, an address that uniquely identifies the location of the target on the Internet.

Access incorporates hypertext in two ways. First, through **hypertext fields**, fields in tables that contain hyperlinks, you can view and click a link and retrieve the link's target. Second, Access allows you to insert hyperlinks as elements within forms and reports. A footnote on a form, for example, could be a link to a Word document.

The targets of these links need not be pages on the web. You can also direct the links to target other files on a hard disk drive, to an object within the current database, or to a different database altogether.

Creating Web Pages

Web pages are created in a special language called **HTML (Hypertext Markup Language)**, a cross-platform language which any operating system, including Microsoft Windows, Macintosh, and UNIX, can use to access a web page. The cross-platform nature of HTML is one reason for the popularity of the web.

Static Web Pages

Access allows you to export reports, forms, and tables to HTML format. Once you export these database objects, you can publish them as web pages for others to view. These web pages are **static web pages** because their content is unchanged until you export the database object again. You have some control over the appearance of the web page through the use of **HTML templates**, files that consist of HTML commands describing the page's layout. The templates can be used to insert company logos, graphics, and other elements. However, Access does not supply the templates for you, and you must have some working knowledge of HTML to create your own.

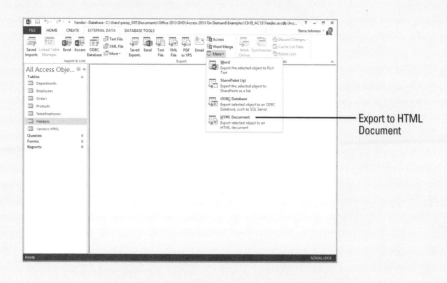

Export to HTML Document

Creating a Hyperlink Field

The Hyperlink data type allows you to create a Hyperlink field, a field that can store hyperlinks. The hyperlink can be a path to a file on your hard disk drive or network, or it can be a link to a page on the web. When you click a Hyperlink field, Access jumps to the target specified by the link. For example, if you have a Clients table, and most of your clients have their own web pages, you might want to create a Hyperlink field that contains links to each client web page.

Create a Hyperlink Field in a Table

1. Display the table in Design view.

2. Create a new field in which you want to store a hyperlink.

3. Click the **Data Type** list arrow, and then click **Hyperlink**.

4. Click the **Save** button on the Quick Access Toolbar to save the changes to the table.

See Also

See "Viewing Field Properties" on page 79 and "Changing Field Properties" on page 80 for more information on working with data types.

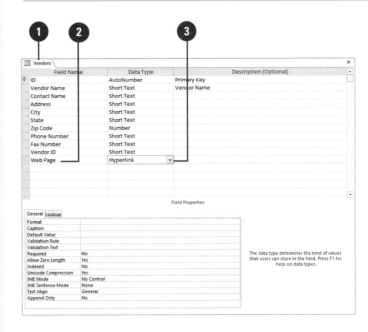

Inserting a Hyperlink to a File or Web Page

Use the Insert Hyperlink button to create a hyperlink within a Hyperlink field or as hypertext within a form or report. A hyperlink consists of the text that the user sees that describes the link, the URL of the link's target, and a ScreenTip that appears whenever the pointer passes over the link. If you have created a Hyperlink field for client web pages, you can use this method to add a URL for each client's web page.

Insert a Hyperlink to a File or Web Page

1. Within a Hyperlink field or while editing a form or report in Design view, click the **Design** tab.

2. Click the **Insert Hyperlink** button.

    ◆ If necessary, click the **More** list arrow or **Controls** button to display the controls.

3. Click **Existing File or Web Page** on the Link to bar.

4. Enter the hyperlink text.

5. Specify the linked document by either:

    ◆ Entering the file name or URL of the linked document

    ◆ Choosing the linked document from the Recent Files, Browsed Pages, or Inserted Links list

6. Click **ScreenTip** to create a ScreenTip that will be displayed whenever the mouse pointer moves over the hyperlink.

7. Click **OK**.

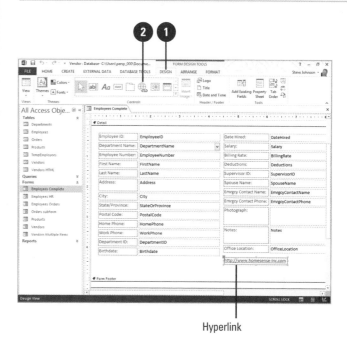

Hyperlink

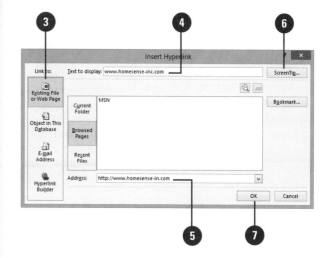

Building a Hyperlink with Expressions

You can use the Hyperlink builder to create a relative hyperlink and control how the link opens when you follow it. Hyperlink builder allows you to specify a base, path, and parameters options. For example, you can create a link to a search engine, such as Google or Bing, and specify search parameters. You can use the Browse the Web button to display and copy the URL for use in the Insert Hyperlink dialog box, which also automatically parses out any paths and parameters. If you want to change the URL based on the data in the form, you can replace URL components with expressions from Expression Builder.

Insert a Hyperlink with Hyperlink Builder

1. Within a Hyperlink field or while editing a form or report in Design view, click the **Design** tab.

2. Click the **Insert Hyperlink** button.

   ◆ If necessary, click the **More** list arrow or **Controls** button to display the controls.

3. Click **Hyperlink Builder** on the Link to bar.

4. Click the **Browse the Web** button.

   Your default web browser opens.

5. Navigate to the URL you want, including the results page with the parameters you want.

6. Select the complete URL in the Address bar, copy (Ctrl+C) it, and then close the browser.

7. Click in the Address box in the Insert Hyperlink dialog box, and then paste (Ctrl+X) the URL.

8. Press Tab.

   The Address box clears and separates the URL into the appropriate boxes: Base URL, Paths, and Parameters. The complete URL is displayed in a box at the bottom.

9. Click **OK**.

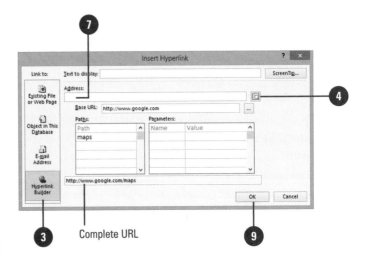

Complete URL

For Your Information

Understanding Web Addresses and URLs

Every web page has a **uniform resource locator** (URL), a web address in a form your browser program can decipher. Like postal addresses and e-mail addresses, each URL contains specific parts that identify where a web page is located. For example, the URL for Perspection's web page is http://www.perspection.com where "http://" shows the address is on the web and "www.perspection.com" shows the computer that stores the web page. As you browse various pages, the URL includes their folders and file names.

Use Expression Builder with Hyperlink Builder

1. Within a Hyperlink field or while editing a form or report in Design view, click the **Design** tab.

2. Click the **Insert Hyperlink** button.

   ◆ If necessary, click the **More** list arrow or **Controls** button to display the controls.

3. Click **Hyperlink Builder** on the Link to bar.

4. Specify an address or use the **Browse the Web** button, and then press Tab to create a base, paths, and parameters.

   See the previous page for details.

5. Click the path or parameter you want to replace, and then click the **Expression Builder** button (...).

6. In the elements list, find the control you want to use, and then double-click it to add it to the expression.

7. Manually enter or select any other operators and expression elements you want to complete the expression.

8. Click **OK**.

9. Click **OK**.

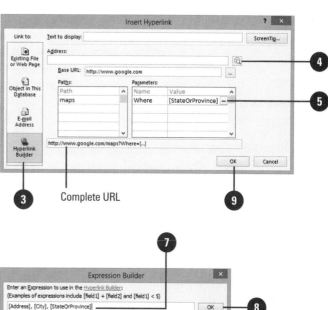

Complete URL

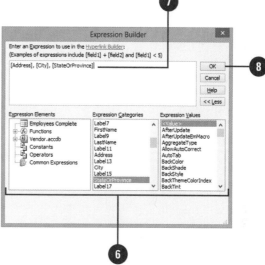

Linking to an Object in a Database

You can create hyperlinks that target forms, tables, and reports within the current database. You can also link to objects in other databases by specifying the database's file name and selecting the form, table, or report you want to target. You will have immediate access to those objects by clicking the hyperlink you insert.

Insert a Hyperlink to an Object in the Database

1. Within a Hyperlink field or while editing a form or report in Design view, click the **Design** tab.

2. Click the **Insert Hyperlink** button.

   ◆ If necessary, click the **More** list arrow or **Controls** button to display the controls.

3. Click **Object in This Database** on the Link to bar.

4. Enter the hyperlink text.

5. Select the database object.

6. Click **OK**.

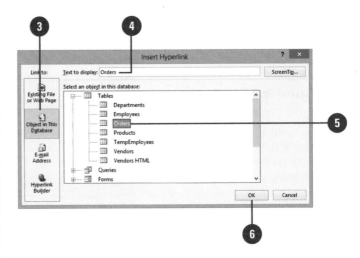

Insert a Hyperlink to an Object in Another Database

1. Within a Hyperlink field or while editing a form or report in Design view, click the **Design** tab.

2. Click the **Insert Hyperlink** button.

   ◆ If necessary, click the **More** list arrow or **Controls** button to display the controls.

3. Click **Existing File or Web Page** on the Link to bar.

4. Enter the hyperlink text.

5. Enter the database file name or click **Browse** to locate and select a database file name.

6. Click **Bookmark**.

7. Select the database object.

8. Click **OK**.

9. Click **OK**.

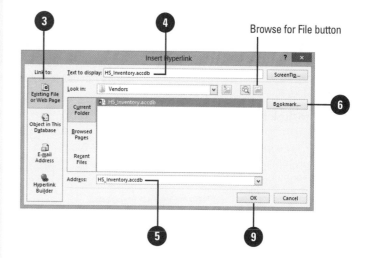

Browse for File button

Creating a Hyperlink to an E-mail Address

You can use the Insert Hyperlink button to create a hyperlink with an e-mail address. When you click the hyperlink with an e-mail address, Access starts Outlook and creates a new message with the e-mail address you specified in the hyperlink. In the Insert Hyperlink dialog box, Access adds *mailto:* in front of the e-mail address, which commands Access to open your mail program.

Insert a Hyperlink to an E-mail Address

1. Within a Hyperlink field or while editing a form or report in Design view, click the **Design** tab.

2. Click the **Insert Hyperlink** button.

   ◆ If necessary, click the **More** list arrow or **Controls** button to display the controls.

3. Click **E-mail Address** on the Link to bar.

4. Enter the e-mail address, or select an recently used e-mail address.

5. Enter a subject for use in the e-mail.

6. Enter the text you want to display for the e-mail address in a form or report.

7. Click **ScreenTip** to create a ScreenTip that will be displayed whenever the mouse pointer moves over the hyperlink.

8. Click **OK**.

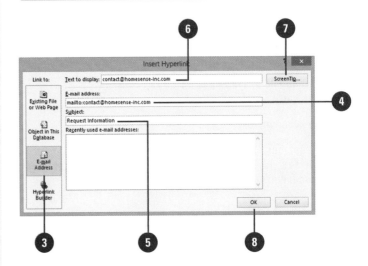

Navigating Hyperlinks

When you have added a hyperlink to a form, report, or table, you can activate the link by clicking it with the mouse in Form, Report, or Datasheet view. As the pointer moves over the hyperlink, the pointer changes to a hand, which indicates the presence of the link. If you have supplied a ScreenTip when you created the link, the tip appears, giving additional information about the link.

Navigate a Hyperlink

1. Open a table, form, or report containing a hyperlink.

2. Move the pointer over the hyperlink so that the pointer shape changes to a hand.

3. Click the hyperlink.

Depending on the type of hyperlink, the screen

- Jumps to a new location within the same or another database.

- Jumps to a location on an intranet or Internet web site.

- Opens a new file and the program in which it was created.

- Opens Outlook and displays a new e-mail message.

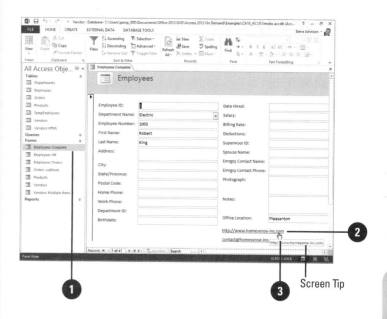

Screen Tip

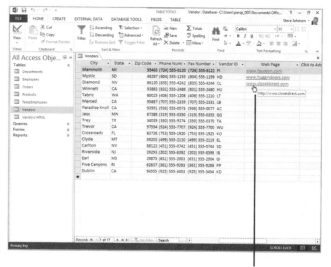

Hyperlink field

Working with Hyperlinks

Hyperlinks connect you to web pages, files, and information in other databases or documents. Rather than duplicating the important information stored in other places, you can create hyperlinks to the relevant material. If a hyperlink becomes outdated or unnecessary, you can easily edit or remove it. If you're not sure where a hyperlink leads too, you can open a hyperlink in an existing browser window or a new one.

Edit a Hyperlink

1. Display the form or report with the hyperlink in Design view.

2. Right-click the hyperlink you want to edit, point to **Hyperlink**, and then click **Edit Hyperlink**.

3. If you want, change the display text, if available.

4. If you want, click **ScreenTip**, edit the custom text, and then click **OK**.

5. If necessary, change the destination.

6. Click **OK**.

Did You Know?

You can copy a hyperlink. Display the form or report with the hyperlink in Design view, right-click the hyperlink you want to copy, point to Hyperlink, and then click Copy Hyperlink. The hyperlink is copied to the Clipboard where you can paste it where you want.

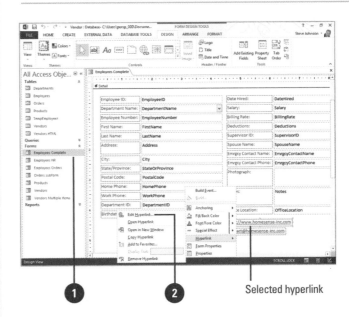

Selected hyperlink

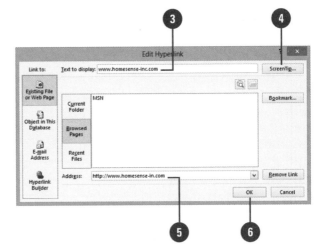

Remove a Hyperlink

1. Display the form or report with the hyperlink in Design view.

2. Right-click the hyperlink you want to edit, point to **Hyperlink**, and then click **Remove Hyperlink**.

   ◆ In the Edit Hyperlink dialog box, you can also click **Remove Link**.

   The hyperlink is removed from the object. The object and the text is not deleted.

3. If necessary, delete the text or object.

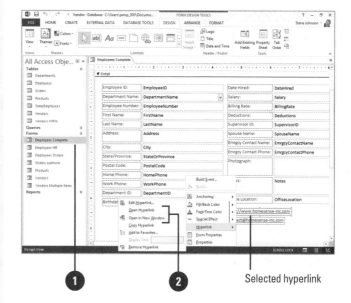

Selected hyperlink

Open a Hyperlink

1. Display the form or report with the hyperlink in Design view.

2. Right-click the hyperlink you want to edit, point to **Hyperlink**, and then click **Open Hyperlink** or **Open in New Window**.

   Your web browser appears, displaying the hyperlink in an existing window or a new window.

3. When you're done, close the browser.

Selected hyperlink

Inserting a Web Browser Control

With the Web Browser control you can display web pages in a frame on a form. You can display a static page or ones that dynamically changes based on fields or controls in your database. For example, you can use address information in a field to display a custom map of the location using a mapping site, such as Google or Bing maps. You can use the Hyperlink Builder to create a relative hyperlink and control how the link opens when you follow it. Hyperlink Builder allows you to specify a base, path, and parameters options. If you want to change the URL based on the data in the form, you can replace URL components with expressions from Expression Builder.

Insert a Web Browser Control

1. Display the form in Layout view.

2. Click the **Design** tab.

3. Click the **Web Browser Control** button.

   - If necessary, click the **More** list arrow or **Controls** button to display the controls.

4. Drag a frame where you want the web page to appear.

5. If necessary, right-click the control frame, and then click **Build Hyperlink**.

6. Click the **Browse the Web** button.

   Your default web browser opens.

7. Navigate to the URL you want, including the results page with the parameters you want.

8. Select the complete URL in the Address bar, copy (Ctrl+C) it, and then close the browser.

9. Click in the Address box in the Insert Hyperlink dialog box, and then paste (Ctrl+X) the URL.

10. Press Tab to fill in the base, paths, and parameters.

11. Click **OK**.

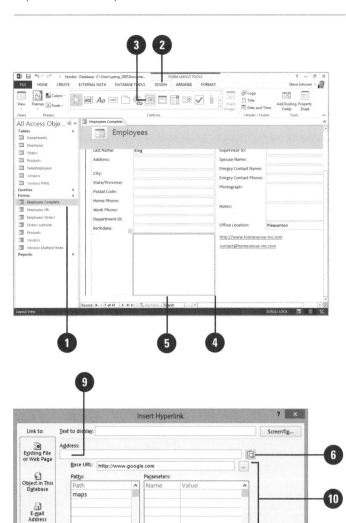

Complete URL

Use Expression Builder with the Web Browser Control

1. Display the form in Layout view.

2. Click the **Design** tab.

3. Right-click the Web Browser control frame, and then click **Build Hyperlink**.

4. Specify an address or use the **Browse the Web** button, and then press Tab to create a base, paths, and parameters.

   See the previous page for details.

5. Click the path or parameter you want to replace, and then click the **Expression Builder** button (...).

6. In the elements list, find the control you want to use, and then double-click it to add it to the expression.

7. Manually enter or select any other operators and expression elements you want to complete the expression.

8. Click **OK**.

9. Click **OK**.

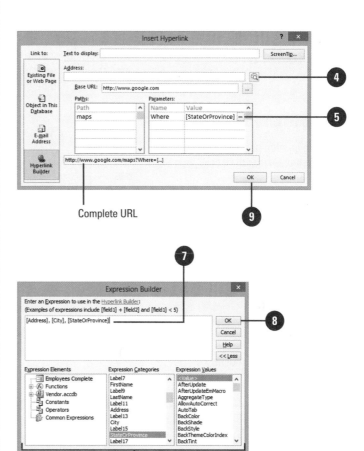

Complete URL

Exporting Database Objects to HTML

In Access, the Export HTML Document command allows you to save a table, query, form, or report as a web page. If the page is saved in HTML format, it represents a snapshot of the data at the time you created the file. If your data changes, you must export it again if you want the web page to be current.

Export to an HTML File

1. In the Navigation pane, select or open a table, query, form, or report.

2. Click the **External Data** tab.

3. If you want to export selected records, select them.

4. Click the **More** button (in the Export group), and then click **HTML Document**.

5. Click **Browse**, select a location, enter a name, and then click **Save**.

6. Select the options you want:

   ◆ **Export data with formatting and layout**.

   ◆ **Open the destination file after the export operation is complete**.

   ◆ **Export only the selected records**.

7. Click **OK**.

8. If you want to use a HTML template, select the **Select a HTML Template** check box, and then specify the template location.

9. Click **OK**, and then click **Close**.

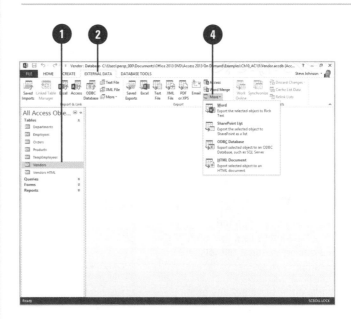

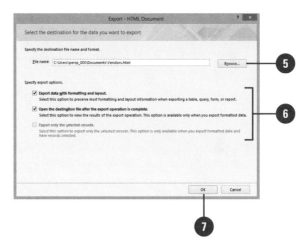

Did You Know?

You can use HTML templates.
Templates are usually stored in the *C:\Program Files\Microsoft Office\Templates\1033\Access* folder. See online Help for more information on creating your own templates.

Importing or Linking to an HTML File

In Access, the Import HTML Document command allows you to import a HTML data into a table. You can import the source data into a new table in the current database, append a copy of imported records to a table, or link to the data source by creating a linked table. Access uses the Import HTML Wizard to help you specify how you want to import the HTML data into your database.

Import or Link to an HTML Document

1. Click the **External Data** tab.

2. Click the **More** button (in the Import group), and then click **HTML Document**.

3. Enter the complete path to the HTML document or click **Browse**, select the HTML document, and then click **OK**.

4. Specify the option how and where you want to store the data in the database:

   ◆ **Import the source data into a new table in the current database.**

   ◆ **Append a copy of the records to the table.**

   ◆ **Link to the data source by creating a linked table.**

5. Click **OK**.

6. Follow the Import HTML wizard instructions to specify how to import the HTML data.

7. When you're done, click **Finish,** and then click **Close**.

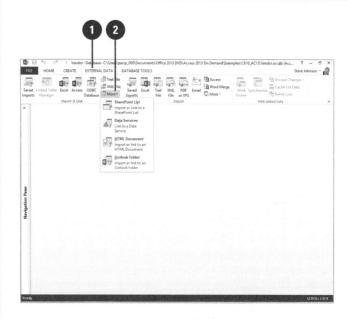

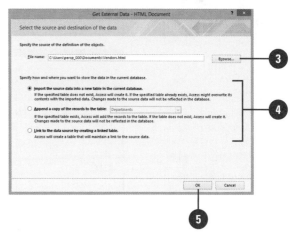

Creating a Table Using SharePoint

If you have access to a Microsoft SharePoint Services site, you can import a SharePoint list into an Access database as a table. A SharePoint Services site is a server application that uses web site templates to create, organize, and share information. To access a SharePoint Services site, you might need access privileges. See your network administrator for a user name and password. Access provides several SharePoint list table templates including: Contacts, Tasks, Issues, Events, Custom, and Existing SharePoint List. After you create a table, you can access it from the Navigation pane, like any other table. It appears with an arrow point to it. When you open it, you can use options on the External Data tab to work with the online linked table.

Create a Table Using a SharePoint List

1. Click the **Create** tab.

2. Click the **SharePoint List** button.

3. Click the SharePoint list template (**Contacts, Tasks, Issues, Events, Custom,** or **Existing SharePoint List**) you want.

4. Enter a SharePoint site address or select an existing one.

5. Type a name and description.

6. To open the list, select the **Open the list when finished** check box.

7. Click **OK**.

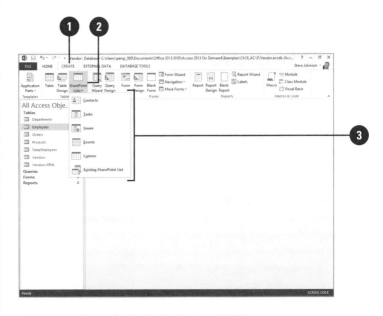

See Also

See "Signing in to SharePoint or SkyDrive" on page 428 for more information on accessing a SharePoint site.

See "Working with Accounts" on page 25 for information on connecting to a Office 365 SharePoint site.

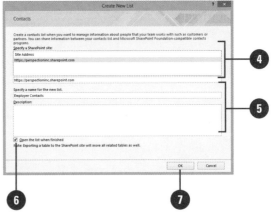

Work with a Table on a SharePoint Site

1. In the Navigation pane, open the table linked to a SharePoint site.

   It appears with an arrow pointing to the table.

2. Click the **External Data** tab.

3. Click the **Datasheet** view.

4. Enter data in the table as desired.

5. To change the table, click the **Design** view, and then make the changes you want just like any other table.

6. To save your changes, click the **Save** button on the Quick Access Toolbar.

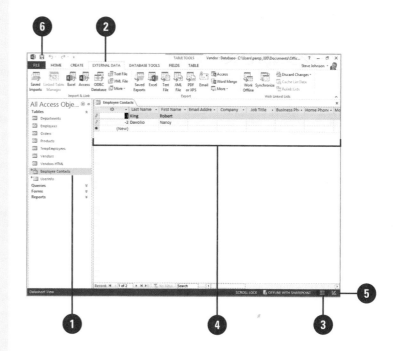

Importing or Linking to SharePoint Data

If you have access to a Microsoft SharePoint Services site, you can import SharePoint data into an Access database as a new or linked table. A wizard takes you step-by-step through the process and asking you to select a SharePoint list and other import options. To access a SharePoint Services site, you might need access privileges. See your network administrator for a user name and password.

Import SharePoint Data

1. Click the **External Data** tab.

2. Click the **More** button (in the Import group), and then click **SharePoint List**.

3. Enter a SharePoint site address or select an existing one.

4. Click the **Import the source data into a new table in the current database** option.

5. Click **Next** to continue.

6. Select the lists you want to import.

7. Select the view you want for each selected list, and then select or clear the **Import display values instead of IDs for fields that look up values stored in another list** check box.

8. Click **OK**, and then complete the rest of the wizard.

See Also

See "Signing in to SharePoint or SkyDrive" on page 428 for more information on accessing a SharePoint site.

See "Working with Accounts" on page 25 for information on connecting to a Office 365 SharePoint site.

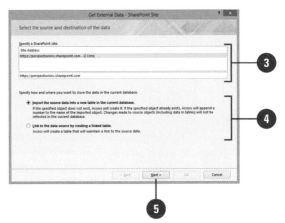

Link to SharePoint Data

① Click the **External Data** tab.

② Click the **More** button (in the Import group), and then click **SharePoint List**.

③ Enter a SharePoint site address or select an existing one.

④ Click the **Link to the data source by creating a linked table** option.

⑤ Click **Next** to continue.

⑥ Select the lists you want to link.

⑦ Click **OK**, and then complete the rest of the wizard.

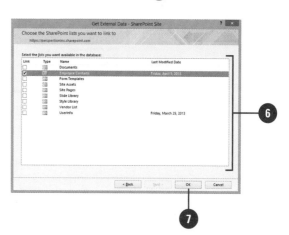

Exporting Data to SharePoint

If you have access to a Microsoft SharePoint Services site, you can export your data to a SharePoint list, which can be shared with others over the web. A wizard takes you step-by-step through the process and creates a SharePoint list for each table and then links each list back to your existing database. To access a SharePoint Services site, you might need access privileges. See your network administrator for a user name and password.

Export Data to a SharePoint Site

1. Open the table you want to move to a SharePoint site.

2. Click the **External Data** tab.

3. Click the **More** button (in the Export group), and then click **SharePoint List**.

4. Enter a SharePoint site address or select an existing one.

5. Type a name and description.

6. To open the list, select the **Open the list when finished** check box.

7. Click **OK**, and then complete the rest of the wizard.

See Also

See "Signing in to SharePoint or SkyDrive" on page 428 for more information on accessing a SharePoint site.

See "Working with Accounts" on page 25 for information on connecting to a Office 365 SharePoint site.

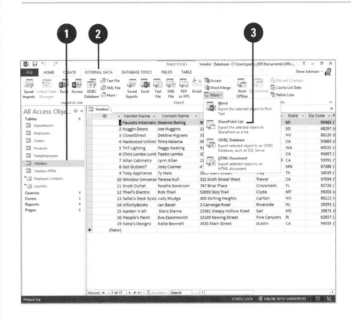

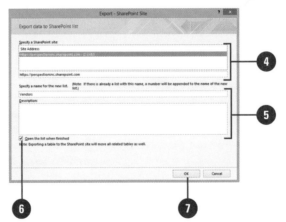

Moving Data to SharePoint

If you have access to a Microsoft SharePoint Services site, you can move your data to a SharePoint list, which can be shared with others over the web. A wizard takes you step-by-step through the process and creates a SharePoint list for each table and then links each list back to your existing database. To access a SharePoint Services site, you might need access privileges. See your network administrator for a user name and password.

Move Data to a SharePoint Site

1. Open the table you want to move to a SharePoint site.

2. Click the **Database Tools** tab.

3. Click the **SharePoint** button.

4. Enter a SharePoint site address or select an existing one from the existing list.

5. Click **Next** to continue.

   The data is moved to the SharePoint site.

6. Select or clear the **Show Details** check box to show or hide information regarding the move.

7. Click **Finish**.

   If issues are encountered, a table appears in the Navigation pane with information.

See Also

See "Working with Accounts" on page 25 for information on connecting to a Office 365 SharePoint site.

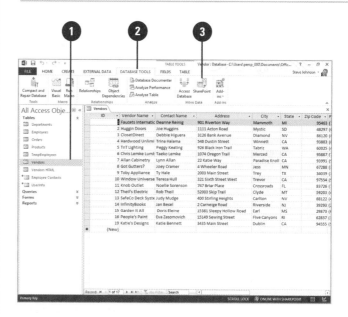

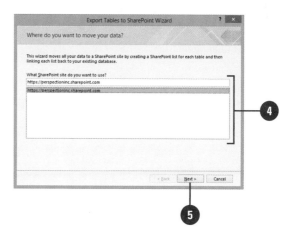

Working with SharePoint Data Offline

After you linked SharePoint data to an Access database, you can work with the data online or offline. If you don't have access to the Internet, you can work with SharePoint data offline on your local computer. When you re-establish a connection, you can synchronize your local changes to the SharePoint site. If you decide not to keep your local changes, you can disregard them. If you ever want to move to another sharePoint site or share your data with another SharePoint site, you can easily relink the data.

Work with SharePoint Data Offline

1. In the Navigation pane, open the table linked to a SharePoint site.

   It appears with an arrow pointing to the table.

2. Click the **External Data** tab.

3. Click the **Datasheet** view.

4. To work offline, click the **Work Offline** button.

5. Enter data in the table as desired.

6. To update lists with data with SharePoint, click the **Synchronize** button.

7. To disregard your offline changes, click the **Discard Changes** button, and then click **Discard All Changes** or **Discard All Changes and Refresh**.

8. To reconnect to the SharePoint site, click the **Work Offline** button again.

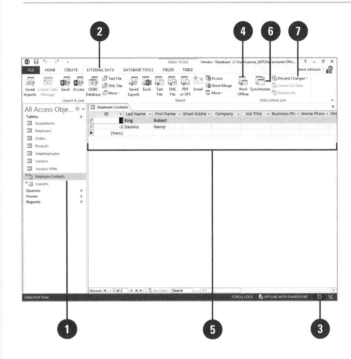

Did You Know?

You can relink a SharePoint list to a different server. Open the database with the SharePoint links, click the External Data tab, click Relink Lists, specify the new site, select the lists to relink, and then click OK.

Publishing a Database to SharePoint

If you want to share a database online, you can save an Access database to a SharePoint site, such as a Document Library on an Office 365 SharePoint site, in a similar way that you save a database on your hard disk. After you save the data for the first time using the SharePoint option on the Save As screen under Save Database As, you can use the Save command on the File tab to republish the database to update the database on the site. If the site stores multiple content types, you might be asked to specify the content type.

Save a Database to a SharePoint Site

1. Open the database you want to save to SharePoint.

2. Click the **File** tab, and then click **Save As**.

3. Click **Save Database As**, and then click **SharePoint**.

4. Click the **Save As** button.

5. Navigate to the network folder location on the SharePoint server where you want to save the file.

6. Type a file name.

7. If necessary, click the **Save as type** list arrow, and then click **Microsoft Access 2007-2013 Database**.

8. Click **Save**.

SharePoint location

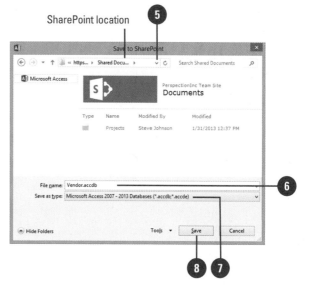

Importing and Exporting Information

Introduction

Microsoft Access allows you to incorporate information from a variety of sources into a database and exchange information from a database into other sources. You can use the Access import and export features to easily move data between your database and other databases and programs.

When you get data from other sources, you have the choice to import the data into a new table or link an existing table of the data to the database. When you import data, Access converts and copies the data into the database file. When you link to the data in another program, the data stays separate from the Access database. You can import data or link to data from several sources, including Microsoft Access, other databases, HTML (a standard web format), Microsoft Excel, Microsoft Exchange, Microsoft Outlook, and SharePoint Services.

If you work with XML (Extensible Markup Language), Access allows you to import and export XML data as well as transform the data to and from other formats using XML related files. XML is a new standard that enables you to move information across the Internet and programs where the data is stored independently of the format so you can use the data more seamlessly in other forms.

The data sharing techniques in Access allow you to exchange data with other Microsoft Office programs. For example, you can merge your Access data with Microsoft Word to create form letters, or you can use Microsoft Excel's analysis tools on your Access data.

If you need to send database objects to others, which cannot be changed, Access provides the option to save a database object as an XPS or PDF file, which are secure fixed-layout formats.

What You'll Do

Import and Link Data

Save Import and Export Settings

Import or Link Data from an Access Database

Import or Link Data from Excel

Import or Link Data from a Mail Program

Get Data from Other Sources

Import and Export XML Data

Export Data to Other Programs

Merge Data with Word

Export Data to Excel

Create a PDF Document

Create an XPS Document

Save a Database Object

Importing and Linking Data

If you have data in other forms, yet need the information in Access, you can import the data into a new table or link the data to the database. When you import data, Access converts and copies the data into the database file. When you link to the data in another program, the data stays separate from the database, yet you can view and edit the data in both the original program and in the Access database.

If you need to use the data in different programs and sources, linking data is the most efficient way to keep the data up-to-date. However, if you plan to use your data only in Access, importing data is the most effective way. Access works faster and more efficiently when you import the data.

In addition to Access databases and projects, you can import or link data using the most common data formats from other programs, such as Microsoft Excel spreadsheets, Microsoft SharePoint Services, Microsoft Exchange, Outlook folders, text files, HTML, XML (Extensible Markup Language), and SQL tables with ODBC (Open Database Connectivity).

When you import data, you cannot append data to an existing table unless you import a spreadsheet or text files. When you link data, you can read and update the external data without altering the external data format in the original data source. Access uses different icons to represent linked tables and nonlinked tables. A diamond shape indicates a linked

Import options

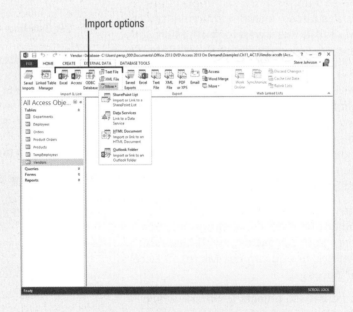

table. If you no longer need a linked table, you can delete the linked table from the Access window. When you delete a linked table, you are deleting only the information that Access uses to open the table. You can re-link to the table again at any time.

You can also import or link data in Access using commands in the Import group on the External Data tab. When you choose one of these commands, the Get External Data dialog box opens, displaying a dialog box similar to a wizard. Use the Browse to select the file you want to import or link, and other options to determine how you want to store the data in the current database.

Get External Data dialog box   Browse button

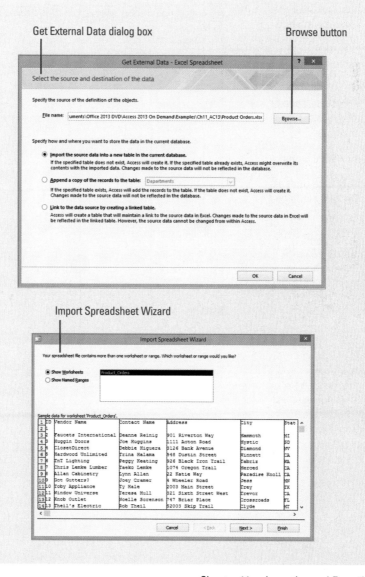

Import Spreadsheet Wizard

Saving Import and Export Settings

When you import or export data in Access, you can save your import and export settings for use again in the future. In the final screen of an import or export wizard, you have the option to save settings. When you select the Save import steps option, additional fields and options appear where you can type a name and description and set specifications to perform the import or export operation at fixed intervals by creating tasks in Outlook. After you save import or export settings, you can use the Manage Data Tasks dialog box to run or delete them, or create an Outlook tasks.

Save Import or Export Settings

1. In the final screen of an import or export wizard, select the **Save import steps** or **Save export steps** check box.

2. Enter a Save as name and a description.

3. To perform this import operation at fixed intervals, select the **Create Outlook Task** check box.

4. Click **Save Import** or **Save Export**.

5. If you selected the Create Outlook Task check box, Outlook starts and creates a task.

   Review and modify the task settings. If you want to make the task recur, click **Recurrence**. When you're done, click **Save and Close**.

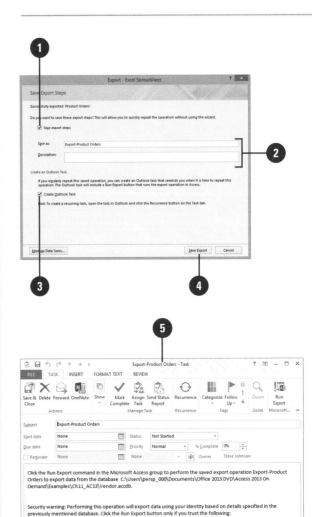

Did You Know?

You can run a saved task from Outlook. In Outlook, click Tasks in the Navigation pane, and then double-click the Access task. Click the Task tab, and then click Run Import. Switch to Access, and then open the imported table in Datasheet view and check the data for errors.

Manage Existing Saved Import and Export Settings

1. Click the **External Data** tab.

2. Click the **Saved Import** or **Saved Export** button.

3. To switch between import and export settings, click the **Saved Imports** or **Saved Exports** tab.

4. Select the saved settings you want to manage.

5. Click the button option you want:

   ◆ **Run.** Executes the saved import or export settings.

   ◆ **Create Outlook Task.** Creates a recurring task to perform the saved import or export settings.

   ◆ **Delete.** Removes the import or export saved settings.

6. Click **Close**.

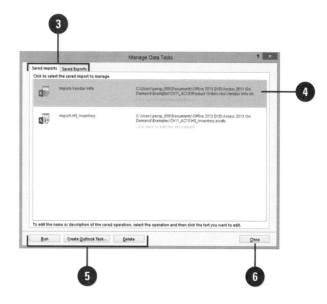

Importing or Linking Data from an Access Database

You can create new tables from other Access databases by importing and linking tables. When you import a table, you copy data from a table in one Access database and place it in a new table in your database. When you link a table, the data stays in its original location, but you can display and access that data from within your database. If data in the original database changes, the changes will appear in your linked database, too. You can also import data from other programs.

Import or Link Data from an Access Database

1. Open the database in which you want to import or link data.

2. Click the **External Data** tab.

3. Click the **Import Access Database** button.

4. Click **Browse**, locate and select the database file that contains the data you want to import, and then click **Open**.

5. Click the import or link option you want.

6. Click **OK**.

7. Click the tab with the database object you want to import or link.

8. Click the objects you want. To deselect an object, click it.

9. Click **OK**.

10. To save import steps, select the **Save import steps** check box, enter a name and description, and then click **Save Import**.

    Otherwise, click **Close**.

Did You Know?

You can delete the link to a linked table. In the Navigation pane, click Tables, click the linked table you want to delete, and then press Delete.

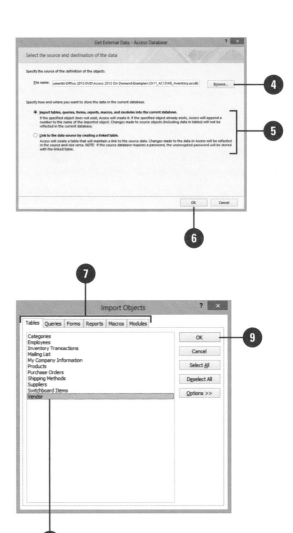

Convert a Linked Table to a Nonlinked Table

1 In the Navigation pane, select the linked table you want to convert.

2 Click the **Home** tab.

3 Click the **Copy** button.

4 Click the **Paste** button.

5 Type a name for the new table.

6 Click the **Structured Only (Local Table)** or **Structure and Data (Local Table)** option.

7 Click **OK**.

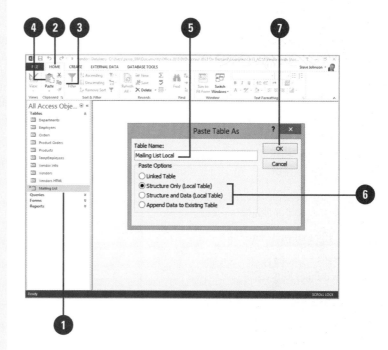

Importing or Linking Data from Excel

If you have data in an Excel spreadsheet, you can use the information in an Access database. You can import or link all the data from a spreadsheet or specific data from a named range. When you import or link data, Access normally creates a new table for the information. For Excel spreadsheet data, you can also append data to an existing table as long as the table field's and spreadsheet column headings match. After you import or link data, you should check to make sure Access assigned the appropriate data type to the imported fields.

Import or Link Data from an Excel Spreadsheet

1. Open the database in which you want to import or link data.

2. Click the **External Data** tab.

3. Click the **Import Excel Spreadsheet** button.

4. Click **Browse**, locate and select the Excel spreadsheet file you want to import or link, and then click **Open**.

5. Click the import, append, or link option you want.

6. Click **OK**.

7. Follow the wizard instructions; some of the requested information includes:

   ◆ A worksheet or named range

   ◆ First row column heading

   ◆ A new or existing table

   ◆ Field information

   ◆ Primary key

   ◆ Table name

8. When you're done, click **Finish**.

9. To save import steps, select the **Save import steps** check box, enter a name and description, and then click **Save Import**.

   Otherwise, click **Close**.

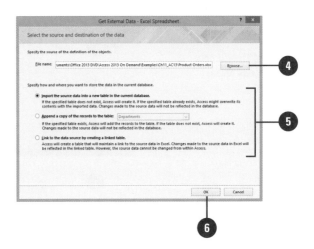

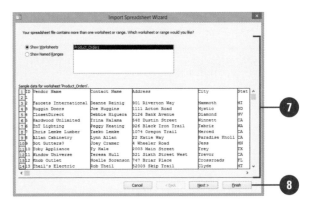

Importing or Linking Data from a Mail Program

If you have data in a mail program, such as Microsoft Exchange or Microsoft Outlook, you can use the Import From Exchange/Outlook Wizard or the Link To Exchange/Outlook Wizard to import or link your Contacts folder. You can use the information from your Contacts folder to create form letters and mailing labels by merging the data using the Microsoft Word Mail Merge Wizard. You need to have Microsoft Outlook, Outlook Express, or Microsoft Exchange installed on your computer to use these wizards to import or link data.

Import or Link Data from Microsoft Exchange or Outlook

1. Open the database in which you want to import or link data.

2. Click the **External Data** tab.

3. Click the **More** button (in the Import & Link group), and then click **Outlook Folder**.

4. Click the import, append, or link option you want.

5. Click **OK**.

   The Import or Link Exchange/Outlook Wizard dialog box opens.

6. Click the **Contacts** folder icon (use the plus and minus signs to display folders), and then click **Next**.

7. Follow the remaining wizard instructions; some of the requested information includes:

   ◆ A worksheet or named range

   ◆ First row column heading

   ◆ A new or existing table

   ◆ Field information

   ◆ Primary key

   ◆ Table name

8. When you're done, click **Finish**.

9. To save import steps, select the **Save import steps** check box, enter a name and description, and then click **Save Import**.

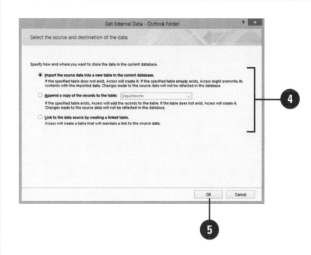

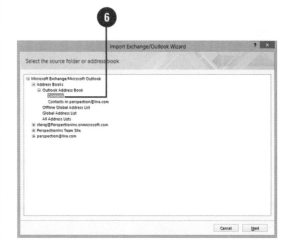

Getting Data from Other Sources

In addition to importing data from Access, Microsoft Excel, Microsoft Exchange, Microsoft Outlook, HTML, SharePoint Services, and text files, you can also import or link data to other sources, such as an ODBC (Open Database Connectivity) Database, such as a SQL Server, or online Data Services. ODBC is a C programming language that allows you to access data from a variety of Database Management Systems (DBMS). For example, you can use Access as a front-end for access data from an Oracle back-end ODBC. If you have data stored on an online Data Service, such as an enterprise Business Data Catalog, you can use Access to connect to the data. Before you get started you need to have Microsoft .NET Framework 4.0 or later installed and get the connection file or information from the Data Service administrator. Access uses a wizard to help you step through the process.

Import or Link to an ODBC Database

1. Open the database into which you want to import data.

2. Click the **External Data** tab.

3. Click the **Import or Link ODBC Database** button.

4. Click the import or link option you want.

5. Click **OK**.

6. Locate and select the file data source.

7. Click **OK**.

8. Follow the instructions in the Import Wizard as needed to set up the data as an Access table.

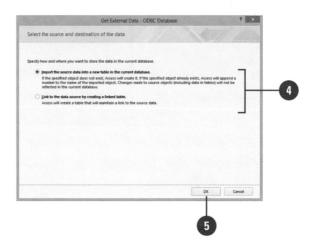

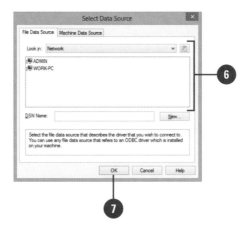

Link Data from Another Source

1. Open the database into which you want to link data.

2. Click the **External Data** tab.

3. Click the **More** button (in the Import & Link group), and then click **Data Services**.

4. Click **Install new connection**.

5. Locate and select the Data Services Connection definition (*.xml) file.

6. Click **OK**.

7. Click **Create Linked Table**.

8. Follow the instructions in the Import Wizard as needed to set up the data as an Access table.

9. Click **Close**.

10. Follow the instructions in the Import Wizard as needed to set up the data as an Access table.

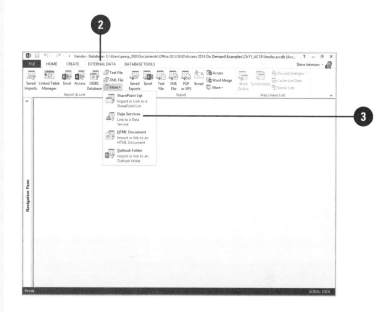

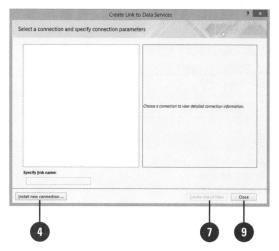

Importing and Exporting XML Data

XML (Extensible Markup Language) is a universal language that enables you to move information across the Internet and programs where the data is stored independently of the format so you can use the data more seamlessly in other forms. XML is fully supported in Office 2007-2013 through Word, Excel, and Access. Access allows you to import and export XML data as well as transform the data to and from other formats using XML related files, such as Extensible Stylesheet Language (XSL). This provides a flexible and consistent way to present your data. When you import and export XML data, you can use an XML Schema (XSD)—a set of rules that defines the elements and content used in an XML file—to ensure the data conforms to a defined structure. XML schemas and XSL transformations are created by developers who understand XML.

Import Data and Schema from XML

1 Open the database in which you want to import.

2 Click the **External Data** tab.

3 Click the **Import XML File** button.

4 Click **Browse**, locate and select the XML data or schema file you want to import, and then click **Open**.

5 Click **OK**.

6 If available, click **Options**, and then click an import option: **Structure Only**, **Structure and Data**, or **Append Data to Existing Table(s)**.

7 To select a transform, click **Transform**, click a transform, and then click **OK**.

8 Click **OK**.

9 Click **OK** again.

10 To save import steps, select the **Save import steps** check box, enter a name and description, and then click **Save Import**.

Otherwise, click **Close**.

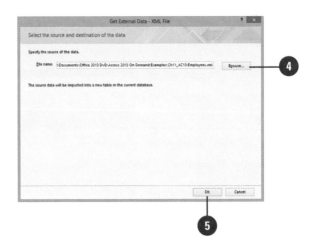

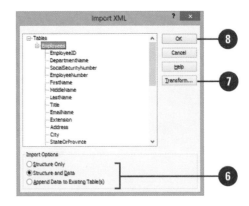

Export XML Data

1. Open the database containing the object you want to export, and then select the database object.

2. Click the **External Data** tab.

3. Click the **Export XML File** button.

4. Click **Browse**, select a location, enter a name, and then click **Save**.

5. Click **OK**.

6. Select the export check boxes you want.

   ◆ **Data (XML).**

   ◆ **Schema of the data (XSD).**

   ◆ **Presentation of your data (XSL)**

7. Click **More Options**.

8. Click the tabs (Data, Schema, and Presentation) with the export type you want, and then select the related options you want.

9. Click **OK**.

10. To save export steps, select the **Save exports step** check box, enter a name and description, and then click **Save Import**.

    Otherwise, click **Close**.

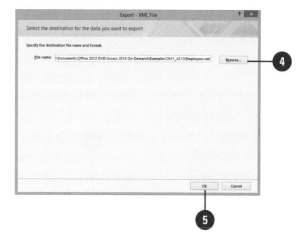

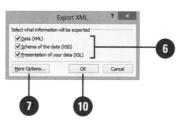

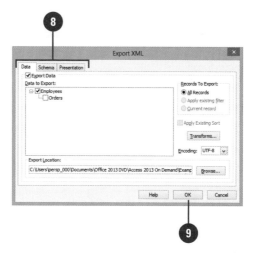

Exporting Data to Other Programs

When you **export** Access data, you save a database object in a new format so that it can be opened in a different program. For example, you might export a table to an Excel worksheet. Or you might want to save your database as an earlier version of Access so someone who hasn't yet upgraded to Access can edit, format, and print it. You can also attach any database object to an e-mail message as an Excel (.xls), Rich Text Format (.rtf), or Hypertext Markup Language (.html) file.

Export an Object to Another Program

1. Open the database containing the object you want to export, and then select the database object.

2. Click the **External Data** tab.

3. Click an export button (in the Export group), or click the **More** button, and then click the command for the type of file you export.

4. Click **Browse**, select a location, enter a name, and then click **Save**.

5. If requested, click the export options you want to use.

6. Click **OK**.

7. If requested, select the options you want, and then click **OK**.

8. To save export steps, select the **Save exports step** check box, enter a name and description, and then click **Save Import**.

   Otherwise, click **Close**.

See Also

See "Exporting Database Objects to HTML" on page 288 for information on exporting data to the web.

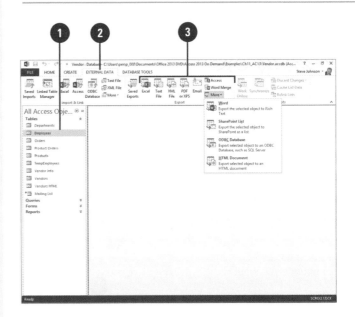

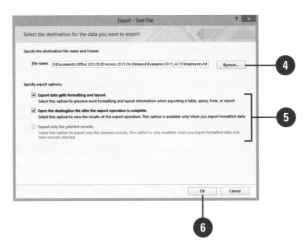

Attach a Database Object to an E-Mail Message

1. In the Navigation pane, select the object you want to attach to an e-mail message.

2. Click the **External Data** tab.

3. Click the **Mail** button.

4. Click the file format you want.

5. Click **OK**.

6. Log on to your e-mail system if necessary, and then type your message.

   Access attaches the object to the message in the format you selected.

Did You Know?

You can copy and paste Access data.
If you want to place only part of an Access object in a file in another program, copy the information you want to insert, and then paste the information in the file where you want it to appear.

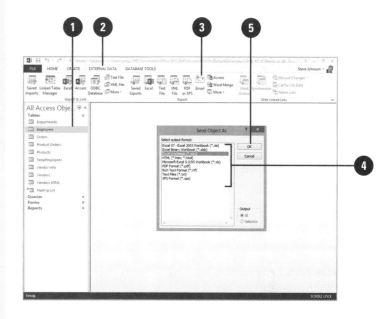

E-mail message

Merging Data with Word

Access is a great program for storing and categorizing large amounts of information. You can combine, or **merge**, database records with Word documents to create tables or produce form letters and envelopes based on names, addresses, and other Access records. For example, you might create a form letter in Word and personalize it with an Access database of names and addresses. Word uses the Mail Merge task pane to step you through the process. Mail merge is the process of combining names and addresses stored in a data file with a main document (usually a form letter) to produce customized documents.

Insert Access Data into a Word Document

1. In the Navigation pane, select the table or query that you want to insert in a Word document.

   IMPORTANT *The database cannot be in exclusive mode.*

2. Click the **External Data** tab.

3. Click the **Word Merge** button.

4. Click the export options you want to use.

5. Click **OK**.

   If you selected the option for linking to an existing Word document, open the document.

6. In Word, follow the step-by-step instructions in the Mail Merge task pane to create a letter or mailing list using the data from Access.

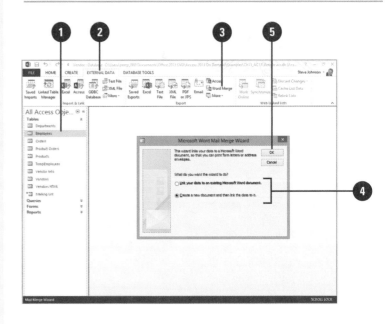

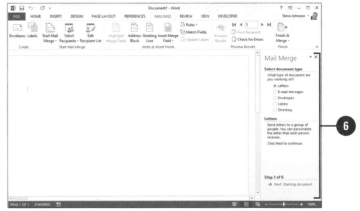

Create a Word Document from an Access Database

1. In the Navigation pane, select the table, query, report, or form that you want to save as a Word document.

2. Click the **External Data** tab.

3. Click the **More** button (in the Export group), and then click **Word**.

4. Click **Browse**, select a location, enter a name, and then click **Save**.

5. Click the export options you want to use.

6. Click **OK**.

   Word opens and displays the document.

7. Edit the document using Word commands and features.

8. To save export steps, select the **Save exports step** check box, enter a name and description, and then click **Save Import**.

   Otherwise, click **Close**.

Did You Know?

You can save in Rich Text Format. A Rich Text Format file (.rtf) retains formatting, such as fonts and styles, and can be opened from Word or other word processing or desktop publishing programs.

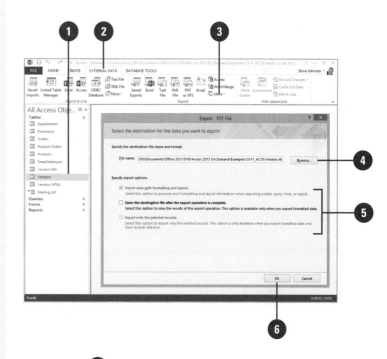

Access data in a Word document

Exporting Data to Excel

Information you want to analyze may not always exist in an Excel workbook; you might have to retrieve it from another Office program, such as Access. Access table data can be easily converted into Excel worksheet data. Before you can analyze Access data in a workbook, you must convert it to an Excel file. You can either use the Excel command in Access to export data as an Excel table file, or use the PivotChart or PivotTable Report option in Excel to use the Access data as a PivotTable, a table you can use to perform calculations with or rearrange large amounts of data.

Export a Table into an Excel Workbook

1 In the Navigation pane, select the table or query that you want to export to Excel.

2 Click the **External Data** tab.

3 Click the **Export to Excel Spreadsheet** button.

4 Click **Browse**, select a location, enter a name, and then click **Save**.

5 Specify the file format.

6 Specify the export options you want.

7 Click **OK**, and then click **Close**.

8 Use Excel tools to edit and analyze the data.

9 To save export steps, select the **Save exports step** check box, enter a name and description, and then click **Save Import**.

Otherwise, click **Close**.

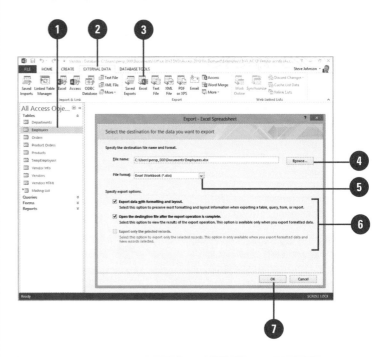

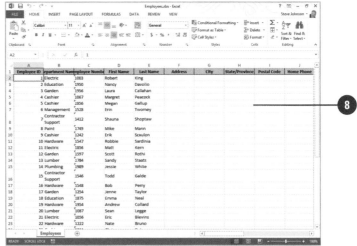

Create an Excel Workbook PivotChart or PivotTable from an Access Database

1. In Excel, click the **Data** tab.

2. Click the **From Access** button.

3. Locate and select the database file, and then click **Open**.

4. Specify the connection options you want for the data link.

5. Click **OK**.

6. Click the table from Access you want to use.

7. Click **OK**.

8. Click the **PivotChart** or **PivotTable Report** option.

9. Click the **Existing worksheet** option, and then specify a cell location, or click the **New worksheet** option. Select or clear the **Add this data to the Data Model** check box (**New!**) to create multiple data tables to a PivotTable.

10. To set refresh, formatting, and layout options for the imported data, click **Properties**, make the changes you want, and then click **OK**.

11. Click **OK**.

12. Use tabs under PivotChart Tools or PivotTable Tools to create and format the Pivotchart or PivotTable report.

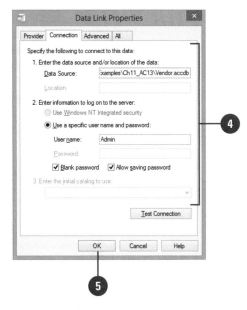

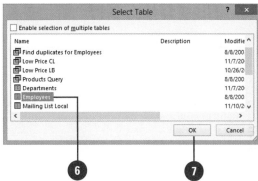

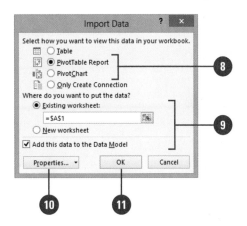

Creating a PDF Document

Portable Document Format (PDF) is a fixed-layout format developed by Adobe Systems that retains the form you intended on a computer monitor or printer. A PDF is useful when you want to create a document primarily intended to be read and printed, not modified. Access allows you to save database objects as a PDF file, which you can send to others for review in an e-mail. To view a PDF file, you need to have Acrobat Reader—free downloadable software from Adobe Systems—installed on your computer.

Save a Database Object as a PDF Document

1 In the Navigation pane, open the object you want to save.

2 Click the **File** tab, click **Save As**, click **Save Object As**, and then click **PDF or XPS**.

3 Click the **Save As** button.

4 Click the **Save as type** list arrow, and then click **PDF**.

5 Click the **Save in** list arrow, and then click the drive or folder where you want to save the file.

6 Type a PDF file name.

7 To open the file in Adobe Reader after saving, select the **Open file after publishing** check box.

8 Click the **Standard** or **Minimize size** option to specify how you want to optimize the file.

9 Click **Options**.

10 Select the publishing options you want, such as what to publish, range to publish, whether to include non-printing information, or PDF options.

11 Click **OK**.

12 Click **Publish**.

13 If necessary, install Adobe Acrobat Reader and related software as directed.

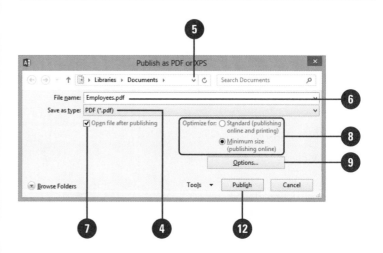

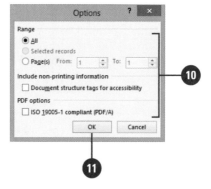

Creating an XPS Document

XML Paper Specification (XPS) is a secure fixed-layout format developed by Microsoft that retains the form you intended on a monitor or printer. An XPS is useful when you want to create a document primarily intended to be read and printed, not modified. Access allows you to save database objects as an XPS file, which you can send to others for review in an e-mail. The XPS format also preserves live links with documents, making files fully functional. To view an XPS file, you need to have a viewer—free downloadable software from Office.com—installed on your computer.

Save a Database Object as an XPS Document

1. In the Navigation pane, open the object you want to save.

2. Click the **File** tab, click **Save As**, click **Save Object As**, and then click **PDF or XPS**.

3. Click the **Save As** button.

4. Click the **Save as type** list arrow, and then click **XPS Document.**

5. Click the **Save in** list arrow, and then click the drive or folder where you want to save the file.

6. Type an XPS file name.

7. To open the file in viewer after saving, select the **Open file after publishing** check box.

8. Click the **Standard** or **Minimize size** option to specify how you want to optimize the file.

9. Click **Options**.

10. Select the publishing options you want, such as what to publish, range to publish, or whether to include non-printing information.

11. Click **OK**.

12. Click **Publish**.

13. If necessary, click **Install** to download and install the Microsoft .NET Framework.

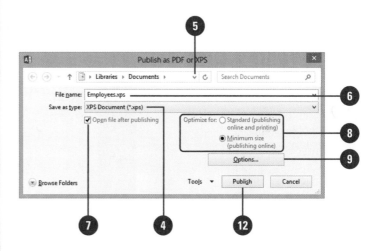

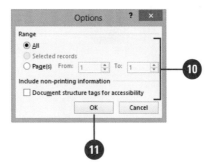

Saving a Database Object

If you have a database object that is similar to a new object you want to create, you can can use the Save Object As command on the Save As submenu on the File tab to create a new one with a different name, and then make the changes you want. You can also convert a database object to a different type. For example, you can convert a form to a report. However, not all objects can be converted to different types of objects. For example, a report can not be converted to another type, or a query can not be converted to a table. If an object can not be converted, the option in the Save As is grayed out or not available.

Save a Database Object as a New Object

1 In the Navigation pane, open the object you want to save.

2 Click the **File** tab, and then click **Save As**.

3 Click **Save Object As**, and then click **Save Object As**.

4 Click the **Save As** button.

5 Type a name for the new object.

6 Click the **As** list arrow, and then select the object type you want: **Table**, **Query**, **Form**, or **Report**.

7 Click **Save**.

Managing a Database

Introduction

Microsoft Access provides tools that help your database operate more efficiently. This includes the ability to compact your database file and to repair it if it is damaged, or split up your database to reduce its size. You can also use Access to analyze the design of your database and tables in order to improve performance and reliability. In addition, Access helps you keep tabs on all the elements in a database with the Documenter utility.

Add-ins are additional programs, designed to run seamlessly within Access. Some add-ins are installed when you run the Access Setup program, while others can be purchased from third-party vendors. The Add-ins Manager makes it easy to add and remove add-ins.

Finally, you can customize your database application by adding a title and an icon that appears in the Windows title bar. You can also specify database application options to display specific elements, such as a certain form on startup or the Status bar, how document windows appear on the screen, either overlapping for tabbed, or allow access with shortcut keys to Access panes and windows, such as the Navigation pane.

What You'll Do

Back Up a Database

Compact and Repair a Database

Change Database Properties

Document a Database

Analyze a Database

Work with Add-Ins

Set Database Application Options

Split a Database

Backing Up a Database

It is vital that you make back up copies of your database on a regular basis so you don't lose valuable data if your computer encounters problems. Access makes it easy to create a back up copy of a database with the Back Up Database option on the Save As screen under Save Database As. When you make a back up copy of your database, save the file to a removable disk or network drive to make sure the file is safe if your computer encounters problems. If you need the back up copy of the database, you can use the Open command on the File tab to restore and view your data.

Back up an Access Database

1. Save and close all objects in a database.

2. Click the **File** tab, and then click **Save As**.

3. Click **Save Database As**, and then click **Back Up Database**.

4. Click the **Save As** button.

5. Click the **Save in** list arrow to select a location for the back up copy.

6. Use the default name or specify a different backup name.

   Access automatically adds the date to the end of the database name.

7. Click **Save**.

See Also

See "Splitting a Database" on page 332 for information on splitting up a database to reduce the size.

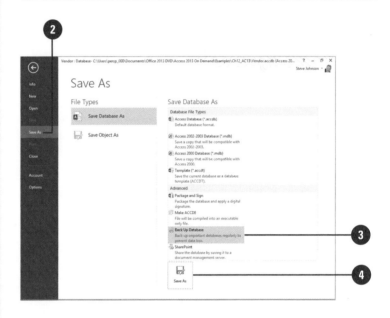

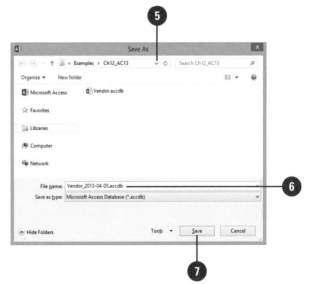

Compacting and Repairing a Database

What do you do when your database starts acting erratically, or when even the simplest tasks cause Access to crash? Problems of this type can occur when a database gets corrupted or when the database file becomes too large. A database can become corrupted when, for example, Access suffers a system crash. Access can repair many of the problems associated with a corrupted database. The size of the database file may also be the trouble. When you delete objects such as forms and reports, Access does not reclaim the space they once occupied. To use this space, you have to **compact** the database, allowing Access to rearrange the data, filling in the space left behind by the deleted objects.

Compact and Repair a Database

1. Make sure all users close the database, and then open the database you want to compact and repair.

2. Click the **File** tab, and then click **Info**.

3. Click the **Compact & Repair Database** button.

   ◆ You can also click the **Compact and Repair Database** button on the Database Tools tab.

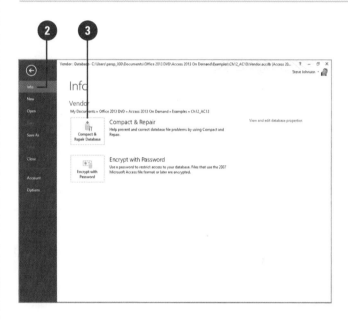

Did You Know?

You can automatically compact and repair a database when you close. Click the File tab, click Options, click Current Database in the left pane, select the Compact on Close check box and then click OK.

See Also

See "Splitting a Database" on page 332 for information on splitting up a database to reduce the size.

Changing Database Properties

You can use document properties—also known as **metadata**—to help you manage and track files. Search tools can use the metadata to find a database using your search criteria, such as title, subject, author, category, keywords, or comments. You can create advanced custom properties to associate more specific criteria for search tools to use. If you associate a database property to an item, the database property updates when you change the item.

Change Database Properties

① Click the **File** tab, click **Info**, and then click **View and edit database properties**.

② Click the tabs to view and add information:

◆ **General.** To find out file location or size.

◆ **Summary.** To add title and author information.

◆ **Statistics.** To display details about the database.

③ Click the **Custom** tab.

④ Type the name for the custom property or select a name from the list.

⑤ Select the data type for the property you want to add.

⑥ Type or specify a value for the property.

⑦ Click **Add** or **Modify**.

⑧ Click **OK**.

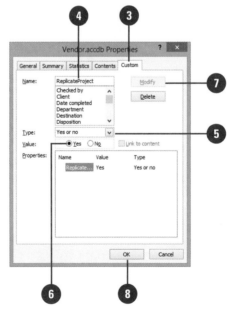

Documenting a Database

Complex databases can include many tables, forms, relationships, and user information. Access helps you keep tabs on all the elements in a database with the **Documenter** utility. You can use Documenter to print all the information about a database in a summary report. After the Documenter creates a report, Access displays it in Print Preview, where you can print the report or export it to another format, such as a PDF or an XPS document, or a Word document.

Document a Database

1. Click the **Database Tools** tab.

2. Click the **Database Documenter** button.

3. Click the **All Object Types** tab.

4. Select the check boxes for the objects you want to document.

5. Click **Options**.

6. Click the definitions you want to print for the selected object(s).

7. Click **OK**.

8. Click **OK**.

9. Check how many pages will print. If necessary, click the **File** tab, click **Print**, click **Print Preview**, and then click the **Print** button to print the pages.

Did You Know?

You can save the Documenter output.
To save the summary report created by the Documenter, click the Word or Text File button on the Print Preview tab. Access will then export the report to a Word or text file. Other export options are available, including PDF or XPS, Snapshot Viewer, HTML Document, XML File, Excel, SharePoint List, or Access Database.

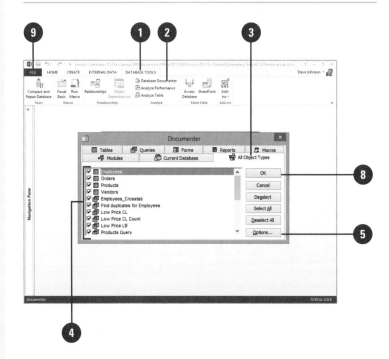

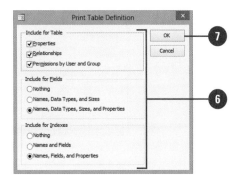

Analyzing a Database

From time to time, you should analyze your database to ensure that it works as efficiently as possible. Begin by running the **Performance Analyzer**, which provides ways to organize your database optimally and helps you make any necessary adjustments. Whenever you determine that several fields in a table store duplicate information, run the **Table Analyzer** to help you split the data into related tables (a process called normalization), but leave the original table intact.

Optimize Database Performance

1. Click the **Database Tools** tab.

2. Click the **Analyze Performance** button.

3. Click the **All Object Types** tab.

4. Select the check boxes for the objects whose performance you want to analyze.

5. Click **OK**.

   If the Performance Analyzer has suggestions for improving the selected object(s), it displays them in its analysis results.

6. Click each item, and then review its analysis notes.

7. Press and hold Ctrl, and then click the suggested optimizations you want Access to perform.

8. Click **Optimize**.

9. Click **Close**.

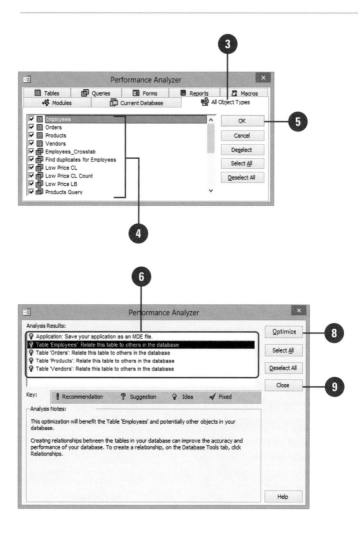

Analyze the Design of Your Tables

1 Click the **Database Tools** tab.

2 Click the **Analyze Table** button.

3 If an explanation screen for the Table Analyzer Wizard opens, read it, click **Next** to continue, and then read the second explanation screen. Click **Next** to continue.

4 Click the table you want to analyze. Click **Next** to continue.

5 Click the option for letting the wizard decide which fields to place in which tables. Click **Next** to continue.

6 Continue following the wizard instructions for naming the new tables, specifying the primary key for the new tables, and so on.

7 Click **Finish**, or click **Cancel** if the wizard recommends not to split the table.

Did You Know?

You can apply performance Analyzer results. The Performance Analyzer returns recommendations, suggestions, and ideas. You should have Access perform the recommended optimizations. Suggested optimizations have potential tradeoffs, and you should review the possible outcomes in the Analysis Notes box before having Access perform them. You can perform idea optimizations manually by following the instructions in the Analysis Notes box.

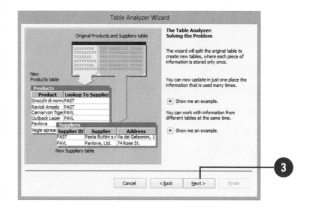

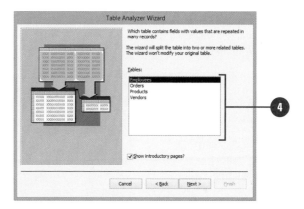

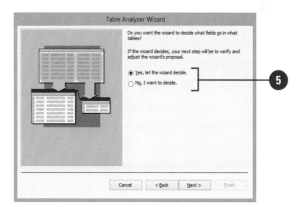

Working with Add-Ins

Add-ins are additional programs, designed to run seamlessly within Access. There are two main types of add-ins: Access and **Component Object Model (COM)**. Access add-ins are custom controls designed specifically for Access, while COM add-ins are designed to run in one or more Office programs and use the file name extension .dll or .exe . To work with Access add-ins, you can use the **Add-In Manager**, a utility to install and remove your add-in files. To view and manage all add-ins (Access, COM, and Disabled), you can use Access Options.

Install and Uninstall Add-Ins

1. Click the **Database Tools** tab.

2. Click the **Add-ins** button, and then **Add-In Manager**.

3. Click **Add New**, locate and select the add-in file (.accda, .accde, .mda, or .mde) you want to install, and then click **Open**.

4. To install an add-in, click the available add-in you want install, and then click **Install**.

5. To remove an add-in, click any installed add-in you want to remove, and then click **Uninstall**.

6. Click **Close**.

See Also

See "Setting Add-in Security Options" on page 346 for more information on setting security options for add-ins to protect your computer.

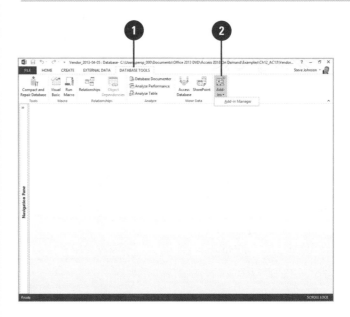

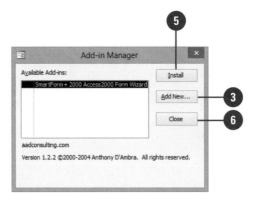

View and Manage Installed Add-ins

① Click the **File** tab, and then click **Options**.

② In the left pane, click **Add-Ins**.

③ View the installed add-ins under the following categories:

◆ **Active Application Add-ins.**

◆ **Inactive Application Add-ins.**

◆ **Document Related Add-ins.**

◆ **Disabled Application Add-ins.**

④ Click the **Manage** list arrow, and then click the add-in list you want to display:

◆ **COM Add-ins.** Opens the COM Add-Ins dialog box and lists the Component Object Model (COM) add-ins.

◆ **Access Add-ins.** Opens the Add-in Manager dialog box with a list of the available Access add-ins.

◆ **Disabled Items.** Opens the Disabled Items dialog box and lists the disabled items that prevent Access from working properly. If you want to try and enable an item, select it, click Enable, click Close, and then restart Access.

⑤ Click **Go**.

The Com Add-Ins, Add-In Manager, or Disabled Items dialog box opens.

⑥ Click **OK** or **Close**.

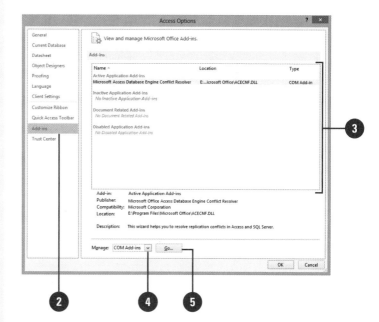

Setting Database Application Options

For each Access database, you can set specific options that don't effect other Access databases. You can customize your database application by adding a title and an icon that appears in the Windows title bar. If you add an icon, you can also enable the Use as Form and Report Icon option to place the icon in the document tabs for forms and reports. You can also specify options to display specific elements, such as a certain form on startup or the Status bar, how document windows appear on the screen, either overlapping for tabbed, or allow access with shortcut keys to Access panes and windows, such as the Navigation pane.

Add a Database Title and Icon

1. Click the **File** tab, and then click **Options**.

2. In the left pane, click **Current Database**.

3. Type an application title for your database.

4. Click **Browse**, locate and select the application icon file, either a bitmap (.bmp) or icon (icon), you want to use.

5. To place the application icon in the tabs atop the forms and reports in the current database, select the **Use as Form and Report Icon** check box.

6. Click **OK**.

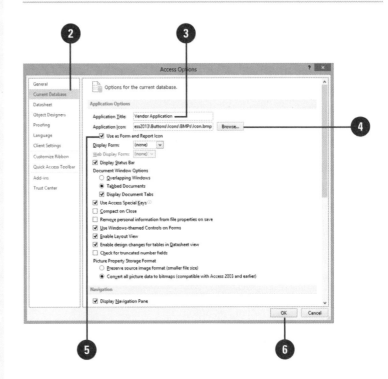

Set Database Application Options

① Click the **File** tab, and then click **Options**.

② In the left pane, click **Current Database**.

③ Select or clear the check boxes or options to change options:

◆ **Display Form.** Select the form to open when you start this database. (Default is none).

◆ **Display Web Form.** Select to allows changes to forms on th web. (Default is none).

◆ **Display Status Bar.** Show or hide the Status bar. (Default on).

◆ **Document Window Options.** Select the Tabbed Documents or Overlapping Windows option. If you select Tabbed Documents, select or clear the Display Document Tabs check box.

◆ **Use Access Special Keys.** Enables or disables shortcut keys. (Default on).

F11 to show or hide the Navigation pane; Ctrl+G to show the Immediate window in the Visual Basic Editor; Alt+F11 to start the Visual Basic Editor; and Ctrl+Break to stop getting records from the server.

◆ **Use Windows-themed Controls on Forms.** Uses your Windows theme on controls in forms and reports. (Default on).

◆ **Enable Layout View for this database.** Show or hides the Layout View button on the Status bar. (Default on).

④ Click **OK**.

⑤ If prompted, click **OK**, and then close and reopen the database for the options to take effect.

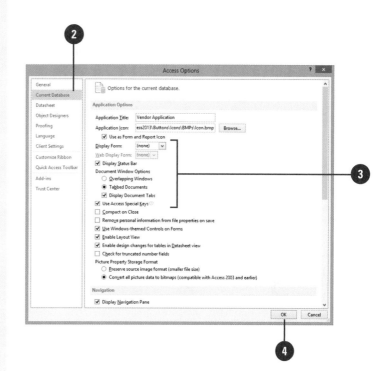

Splitting a Database

You can reduce the size of a database file by splitting the database. When Access **splits** a database, it places the tables in one file, called the **back-end database**, and the other database objects, like forms and reports, in the current database file. This technique stores all of the data in one location, while allowing each user to create his or her own forms and reports in his or her own database files. It is a good idea to back up your database before compacting or splitting it. If an error occurs during either process and data is lost, you can retrieve data from your backup.

Split a Database

1. Make sure all users close the database. Open the database with administrative privileges.

2. Click the **Database Tools** tab.

3. Click the **Access Database** button.

4. Click **Split Database**.

5. Click the **Save in** list arrow, and then specify a location for the split database.

6. Use the default name or specify a different back-end database name.

   Access automatically adds the date along with "_be" to the end of the database name.

7. Click **Split**.

8. Click **OK**.

See Also

See "Backing Up a Database" on page 322 for information on backing up a database.

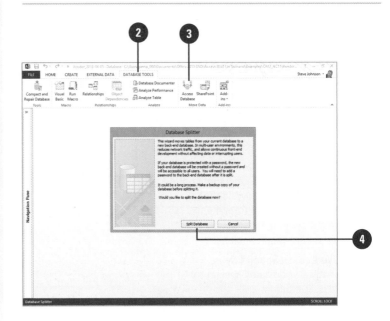

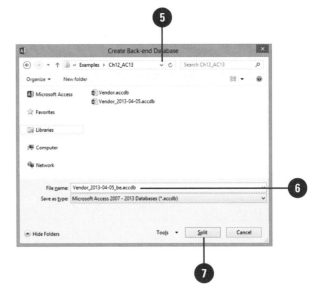

Protecting and Securing a Database

Introduction

Adding a password to protect your database is not only a good idea for security purposes, it's an added feature to make sure that changes to your database aren't made by unauthorized people. When you add database protection, you'll be asked to supply a password, and then enter it again when you want to work on the file. If you need to validate the authenticity of a database, you can package the database in a file and add an invisible digital signature, an electronic secure stamp of authentication on a database.

The Trust Center is a place where you set security options and find the latest technology information as it relates to document privacy, safety, and security from Microsoft. The Trust Center allows you to set security and privacy settings and provides links to Microsoft privacy statements, a customer improvement program, and trustworthy computing practices.

What You'll Do

Add Security Encryption to a Database

Create a Digital Certificate

Add a Digital Signature to a Database

Package and Digitally Sign a Database

Avoid Harmful Attacks

Use the Trust Center

Select Trusted Publishers and Locations

Set Document Related Security Options

Set ActiveX Security Options

Set Add-In Security Options

Set Macro Security Options

Change Message Bar Security Options

Set Privacy Options

Lock a Database

Lock Database Records

Adding Security Encryption to a Database

File encryption is additional security you can apply to a database. File encryption scrambles your password to protect your document from unauthorized people from breaking into the file. You don't have to worry about the encryption, Office handles everything. All you need to do is remember the password. If you forget it, you can't open the file. Password protection takes effect the next time you open the document. Before you can encrypt a database in Access, you need to open the database in Exclusive mode, which allows Access to encrypt the database without any outside connections. You can set the database to Exclusive mode by using the Client Settings pane in Access Options.

Apply File Encryption with a Password

① Click the **File** tab, click **Open**, click **Computer**, and then click **Browse**.

② Locate and select the database you want to encrypt.

③ Click the **Open** button arrow, and then click **Open Exclusive**.

④ Click the **File** tab, and then click **Info**.

⑤ Click the **Encrypt with Password** button.

⑥ Type a password.

⑦ Type the password again.

⑧ Click **OK**.

Did You Know?

You should use strong passwords. Hackers identify passwords as strong or weak. A strong password is a combination of uppercase and lowercase letters, numbers, and symbols, such as Grea8t!, while a weak one doesn't use different character types, such as Hannah1. Be sure to write down your passwords and place them in a secure location.

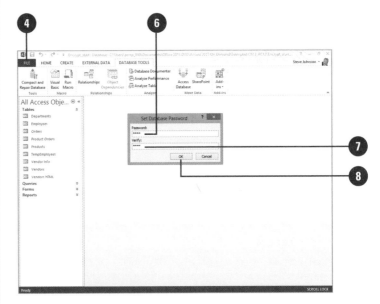

Open a Database with a Password

1. Click the **File** tab, click **Open**, click **Computer**, and then click **Browse**.

2. Locate and select a database with password encryption, and then click **Open**.

3. Type a password.

4. Click **OK**.

Change or Remove the Password Encryption

1. Click the **File** tab, click **Open**, click **Computer**, and then click **Browse**.

2. Locate and select a database with password encryption, click the **Open** button arrow, and then click **Open Exclusive**.

3. Type a password, and then click **OK**.

   The encrypted database opens in exclusive mode.

4. Click the **File** tab, and then click **Info**.

5. Click the **Decrypt Database** button.

6. Type the password.

7. Click **OK**.

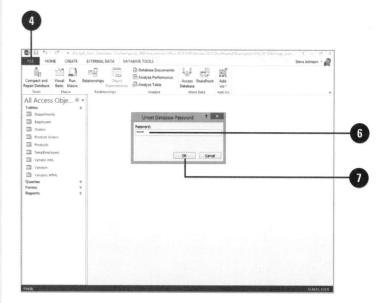

Creating a Digital Certificate

After you've finished a database, you might consider adding an invisible digital signature—an electronic, secure stamp of authentication on a document. Before you can add a digital signature, you need to get a **digital ID**, or **digital certificate**, which provides an electronic way to prove your identity. A digital certificate checks a public key to validate a private key associated with a digital signature. To assure a digital signature is authentic, it must have a valid (non expired or revoked) certificate issued by a reputable certification authority (CA), and the signing person must be from a trusted publisher. If you need a verified authenticate digital certificate, you can obtain one from a trusted Microsoft partner CA. If you don't need a verified digital certificate, you can create one of your own, known as a self-signed certificate. If someone modifies the file, the digital signature is removed and revoked.

Create a Self-signed Certificate

1. Start the **Digital Certificate for VBA Projects** program.

    ◆ From the desktop, double-click the SELFCERT.EXE program.

    ◆ You can locate and download the Microsoft program from the web by searching for SELFCERT.EXE.

2. Enter a name for the self-signed certificate.

3. Click **OK**.

4. Click **OK**.

    Office programs trust a self-signed certificate only on the computer that created it.

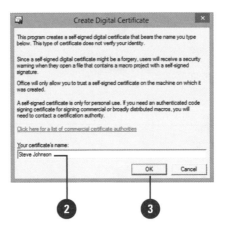

Adding a Digital Signature to a Database

If you want to add a digital signature to a presentation with a macro, you need to add it using the Visual Basic editor. If you open a presentation that contains a signed macro project with a problem, the macro is disabled by default and the Message Bar appears to notify you of the potential problem. You can click Options in the Message Bar to view information about it. For more details, you can click Show Signature Details to view certificate and publisher information. If a digital signature has problems—it's expired, not issued by a trusted publisher, or the presentation has been altered—the certificate information image contains a red X. When there's a problem, contact the signer to have them fix it, or save the presentation to a trusted location, where you can run the macro without security checks.

Sign a Database

1. Open the database you want to sign, and then click the **Database Tools** tab.

2. Click the **Visual Basic** button to open the Visual Basic window.

3. Click the **Tools** menu, and then click **Digital Signature**.

4. Click **Choose**.

5. Select a certificate in the list.

6. To view a certificate, click the **View Certificate** link, and then click **OK**.

7. Click **OK**.

8. Click **OK** again.

9. Click the **Save** and **Close** buttons in the Microsoft Visual Basic window.

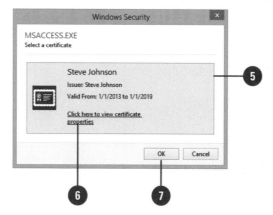

Packaging and Digitally Signing a Database

The Package and Sign command allows you to package, digitally sign, and distribute an Access database. Access saves the database you want in the Access Deployment file format (.accdc), signs the package, and then stores the digitally signed package where you want. Other users can extract the database from the package and work directly in the database.

Create a Signed Package

1. Open the database you want to package and sign.

2. Click the **File** tab, and then click **Save As**.

3. Click **Save Database As**, and then click **Package and Sign**.

4. Click the **Save As** button.

5. Select a digital certificate.

6. Click **OK**.

7. Click the **Save in** list arrow, and then click the drive or folder where you want to save the signed database package.

8. Type a name for the signed database package.

9. Click **Create**.

Extract and Use a Signed Package

① Click the **File** tab, click **Open**, click **Computer**, and then click **Browse**.

② Click the **Files of type** list arrow, and then click **Microsoft Access Signed Packages (*.accdc)**.

③ If the file is located in another folder, click the **Look in** list arrow, and then navigate to the file.

④ Select the .accdc file you want.

⑤ Click **Open**.

⑥ Do one of the following:

◆ If you chose to trust the digital certificate, the Extract Database To dialog box opens. Go to the next step.

◆ If you have not chosen to trust the digital certificate, click **Open** to trust the database, or click **Trust All From Publisher** to trust any certificate from the publisher. The Extract Database To dialog box opens. Go to the next step.

⑦ If necessary, click the **Save in** list arrow, select a location for the extracted database, and then type a different name for the extracted database.

⑧ Click **OK**.

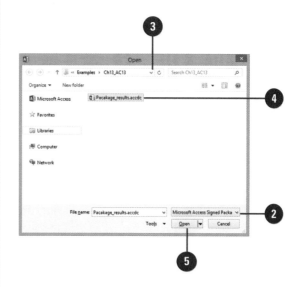

Avoiding Harmful Attacks

Spreading Harmful Infections

Many viruses and other harmful attacks spread through file downloads, attachments in e-mail messages, and data files that have macros, ActiveX controls, add-ins, or Visual Basic for Applications (VBA) code attached to them. Virus writers capitalize on people's curiosity and willingness to accept files from people they know or work with, in order to transmit malicious files disguised as or attached to benign files. When you start downloading files to your computer, you must be aware of the potential for catching a computer virus, worm, or Trojan Horse. Typically, you can't catch one from just reading a mail message or downloading a file, but you can catch one from installing, opening, or running an infected program or attached code.

Understanding Harmful Attacks

Phishing is a scam that tries to steal your identity by sending deceptive e-mail asking you for bank and credit card information online. Phishers spoof the domain names of banks and other companies in order to deceive consumers into thinking that they are visiting a familiar web site.

Phishers create a web address that looks like a familiar web address but is actually altered. This is known as a **homograph**. The domain name is created using alphabet characters from different languages, not just English. For example, the web site address "www.microsoft.com" looks legitimate, but what you can't see is that the "i" is a Cyrillic character from the Russian alphabet.

Don't be fooled by spoofed web sites that looks like the official site. Never respond to requests for personal information via e-mail; most companies have policies that do not ask

for your personal information through e-mail. If you get a suspicious e-mail, call the institution to investigate and report it.

Spam is unsolicited e-mail, which is often annoying and time-consuming to get rid of. Spammers harvest e-mail addresses from web pages and unsolicited e-mail. To avoid spam, use multiple e-mail addresses (one for web forms and another for private e-mail), and opt-out and remove yourself from e-mail lists. See the Microsoft Windows and Microsoft Outlook Help system for specific details.

Spyware is software that collects personal information without your knowledge or permission. Typically, spyware is downloaded and installed on your computer along with free software, such as freeware, games, or music file-sharing programs. Spyware is often associated with **Adware** software that displays advertisements, such as a pop-up ad. Examples of spyware and unauthorized adware include programs that change your home page or search page without your permission. To avoid spyware and adware, read the fine print in license agreements when you install software, scan your computer for spyware and adware with detection and removal software (such as Ad-aware from Lavasoft), and turn on Pop-up Blocker. See the Microsoft Windows Help system for specific details.

Avoiding Harmful Attacks Using Office

There are a few things you can do within any Office program to keep your system safe from the infiltration of harmful attacks.

1) Make sure you activate macro, ActiveX, add-in, and VBA code detection and notification. You can use the Trust Center to help protect you from attached code attacks. The Trust Center checks for trusted publisher and code locations on your computer and provides security options for add-ins, ActiveX controls, and macros to ensure the best possible protection. The Trust Center displays a security alert in the Message Bar when it detects a potentially harmful attack.

2) Make sure you activate web site spoofing detection and notification. You can use the Trust Center to help protect you from homograph attacks. The *Check Office documents that are from or link to suspicious web sites* check box under Privacy Options in the Trust Center is on by default and continually checks for potentially spoofed domain names. The Trust Center displays a security alert in the Message Bar when you have a database open and click a link to a web site with an address that has a potentially spoofed domain name, or you open a file from a web site with an address that has a potentially spoofed domain name.

3) Be very careful of file attachments in e-mail you open. As you receive e-mail, don't open or run an attached file unless you know who sent it and what it contains. If you're not sure, you should delete it. The Attachment Manager provides security information to help you understand more about the file you're opening. See the Microsoft Outlook Help system for specific details.

Avoiding Harmful Attacks Using Windows

There are a few things you can do within Microsoft Windows to keep your system safe from the infiltration of harmful attacks.

1) Make sure Windows Firewall is turned on. Windows Firewall helps block viruses and worms from reaching your computer, but it doesn't detect or disable them if they are already on your computer or come through e-mail. Windows Firewall doesn't block unsolicited e-mail or stop you from opening e-mail with harmful attachments.

2) Make sure Automatic Updates is turned on. Windows Automatic Updates regularly checks the Windows Update web site for important updates that your computer needs, such as security updates, critical updates, and service packs. Each file that you download using Automatic Update has a digital signature from Microsoft to ensure its authenticity and security.

3) Make sure you are using the most up-to-date antivirus software. New viruses and more virulent strains of existing viruses are discovered every day. Unless you update your virus-checking software, new viruses can easily bypass outdated virus checking software. Companies such as McAfee and Symantec offer shareware virus checking programs available for download directly from their web sites. These programs monitor your system, checking each time a file is added to your computer to make sure it's not in some way trying to change or damage valuable system files.

4) Be very careful of the sites from which you download files. Major file repository sites, such as FileZ, Download.com, or TuCows, regularly check the files they receive for viruses before posting them to their web sites. Don't download files from web sites unless you are certain that the sites check their files for viruses. Internet Explorer monitors downloads and warns you about potentially harmful files and gives you the option to block them.

Using the Trust Center

The **Trust Center** is a place where you set security options and find the latest technology information as it relates to document privacy, safety, and security from Microsoft. The Trust Center allows you to set security and privacy settings—Trusted Publishers, Trusted Locations, Add-ins, ActiveX Settings, Macro Settings, Message Bar, and Privacy Options—and provides links to Microsoft privacy statements, a customer improvement program, and trustworthy computing practices.

View the Trust Center

1 Click the **File** tab, and then click **Options**.

2 In the left pane, click **Trust Center**.

3 Click the links in which you want online information at the Microsoft Online web site.

◆ **Show the Microsoft Office privacy statement.** Opens a Microsoft web site detailing privacy practices.

◆ **Office.com privacy statement.** Opens a Microsoft web site detailing privacy practices.

◆ **Customer Experience Improvement Program.** Opens the Microsoft Customer Experience Improvement Program (CEIP) web site.

◆ **Microsoft Trustworthy Computing.** Opens a Microsoft web site detailing security and reliability practices.

4 When you're done, close your web browser or dialog box, and return to Access.

5 Click **OK**.

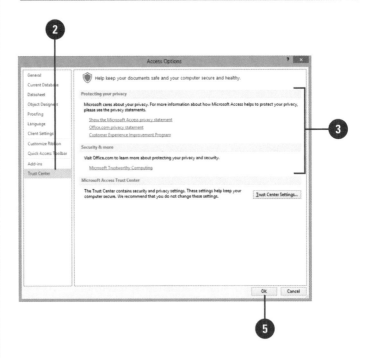

Selecting Trusted Publishers and Locations

The Trust Center security system continually checks for external potentially unsafe content in your documents. Hackers can hide web beacons in external content—images, linked media, data connections and templates—to gather information about you or cause problems. When the Trust Center detects potentially harmful external content, the Message Bar appears with a security alert and options to enable or block the content. Trusted publishers are reputable developers who create application extensions, such as a macro, ActiveX control, or add-in. The Trust Center uses a set of criteria—valid and current digital signature, and reputable certificate—to make sure publishers' code and source locations are safe and secure. If you are sure that the external content is trustworthy, you can add the content publisher and location to your trusted lists, which allows it to run without being checked by the Trust Center.

Modify Trusted Publishers and Locations

1. Click the **File** tab, and then click **Options**.

2. In the left pane, click **Trust Center**.

3. Click **Trust Center Settings**.

4. In the left pane, click **Trusted Publishers**.

5. Select a publisher, and then use the **View** and **Remove** buttons to make the changes you want.

6. In the left pane, click **Trusted Locations**.

7. Select a location, and then use the **Add new location**, **Remove**, and **Modify** buttons to make the changes you want.

8. Select or clear the **Allow Trusted Locations on my network (not recommended)** check box.

9. Select or clear the **Disable all Trusted Locations** check box.

10. Click **OK**.

11. Click **OK**.

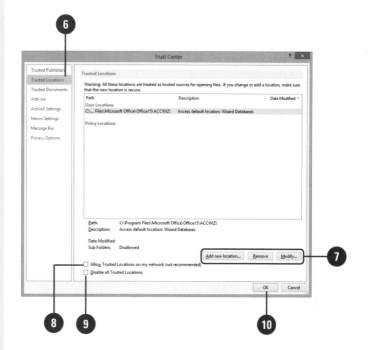

Setting Document Related Security Options

The Trust Center security system allows you to set file-related options to check for potentially unsafe content in your documents. In Trusted Documents, you can set options to open trusted documents without any security prompts for macros, ActiveX controls and other types of active content in the document. For a trusted document, you won't be prompted the next time you open the document even if new active content was added to the document or changes were made to existing active content. You should only trust documents if you trust the source, which you can do by enabling content using the Message bar when you open a database.

Set Options for Trusted Documents

1. Click the **File** tab, and then click **Options**.

2. In the left pane, click **Trust Center**.

3. Click **Trust Center Settings**.

4. In the left pane, click **Trusted Documents**.

5. Select or clear the check boxes you do or don't want.

   ◆ **Allow documents on a network to be trusted.**

   ◆ **Disable Trusted Documents.**

6. To clear all trusted documents so they are no longer trusted, click **Clear**.

7. Click **OK**.

8. Click **OK**.

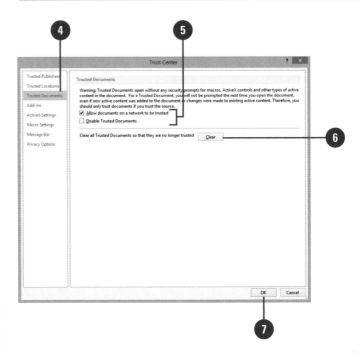

Setting ActiveX Security Options

An ActiveX control provides additional functionality, such as a text box, button, dialog box, or small utility program. ActiveX controls are software code, so hackers can use them to do malicious harm, such as spreading a virus. You can use the Trust Center to prevent ActiveX controls from harming your computer. If the ActiveX security options are not set to the level you want, you can change them in the Trust Center. If you change ActiveX control settings in one Office program, it effects all Microsoft Office programs. The Trust Center uses a set of criteria—checks the kill bit and Safe for Initialization (SFI) settings—to make sure ActiveX controls run safely.

Change ActiveX Security Settings

1. Click the **File** tab, and then click **Options**.

2. In the left pane, click **Trust Center**.

3. Click **Trust Center Settings**.

4. In the left pane, click **ActiveX Settings**.

5. Click the option you want for ActiveX in documents not in a trusted location.

   ◆ Disable all controls without notification.

   ◆ Prompt me before enabling Unsafe for Initialization controls with additional restrictions and Save for Initialization (SFI) controls with minimal restrictions (default).

   ◆ Prompt me before enabling all controls with minimal restrictions.

   ◆ Enable all controls with restrictions and without prompting (not recommended, potentially dangerous controls can run).

6. Click **OK**.

7. Click **OK**.

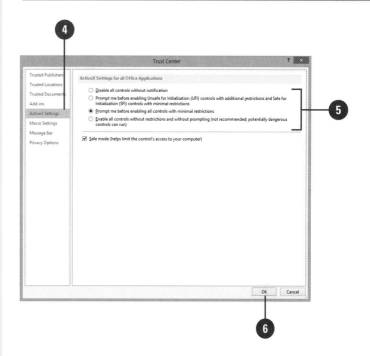

Setting Add-In Security Options

An add-in, such as smart tags, extends functionality to Microsoft Office programs. An add-in can add buttons and custom commands to the Ribbon. Since add-ins are software code added to Microsoft Office programs, hackers can use them to do malicious harm, such as spreading a virus. The Trust Center uses a set of criteria—valid and current digital signature, reputable certificate and a trusted publisher—to make sure add-ins are safe and secure. If it discovers a potentially unsafe add-in, it disables the code and notifies you in the Message Bar. If you're not sure whether an add-in is disabled, you can use the Trust Center to display disabled items and enable them one at a time to help you pin point any problems. If the add-in security options are not set to the level you need, you can change them in the Trust Center.

Set Add-In Security Options

1 Click the **File** tab, and then click **Options**.

2 In the left pane, click **Trust Center**.

3 Click **Trust Center Settings**.

4 In the left pane, click **Add-ins**.

5 Select or clear the check boxes you do or don't want.

- ◆ **Require Application Add-ins to be signed by Trusted Publisher.** Select to check for a digital signature on the .dll file.

- ◆ **Disable notification for unsigned add-ins (code will remain disabled).** Only available if the above check box is selected. Select to disable unsigned add-ins without notification.

- ◆ **Disable all Application Add-ins (may impair functionality).** Select to disable all add-ins without any notifications.

6 Click **OK**.

7 Click **OK**.

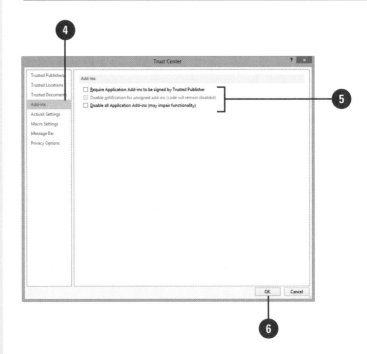

View Disabled Items

① Click the **File** tab, and then click **Options**.

② In the left pane, click **Add-Ins**.

③ Click the **Manage** list arrow, and then click **Disabled Items**.

④ Click **Go**.

⑤ In the dialog box, you can select an item, click **Enable** to activate and reload the add-in, and then click **Close**.

⑥ Click **OK**.

See Also

See "Warnings About Macros and Add-Ins" on page 31 for more information on opening databases with macros and add-ins.

Setting Macro Security Options

A macro allows you to automate frequently used steps or tasks to save time and work more efficiently. Macros are written using VBA (Visual Basic for Applications) code, which opens the door to hackers to do malicious harm, such as spreading a virus. The Trust Center uses a set of criteria—valid and current digital signature, reputable certificate and a trusted publisher—to make sure macros are safe and secure. If the Trust Center discovers a potentially unsafe macro, it disables the code and notifies you in the Message Bar. You can click Options on the Message Bar to enable it or set other security options. If the macro security options are not set to the level you need, you can change them in the Trust Center.

Change Macro Security Settings

1 Click the **File** tab, and then click **Options**.

2 In the left pane, click **Trust Center**.

3 Click **Trust Center Settings**.

4 In the left pane, click **Macro Settings**.

5 Click the option you want for macros in documents not in a trusted location.

- ◆ **Disable all macros without notification.**

- ◆ **Disable all macros with notification.** (default)

- ◆ **Disable all macros except digitally signed macros.**

- ◆ **Enable all macros (not recommended, potentially dangerous code can run).**

6 Click **OK**.

7 Click **OK**.

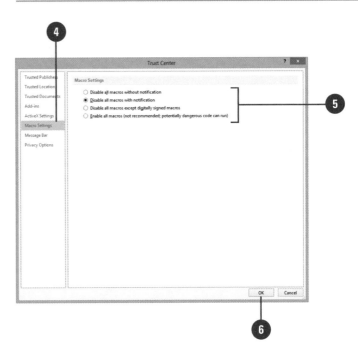

See Also

See "Warnings About Macros and Add-Ins" on page 31 for more information on opening databases with macros and add-ins.

Changing Message Bar Security Options

The Message Bar displays security alerts when Office detects potentially unsafe content in an open document. The Message Bar appears below the Ribbon when a potential problem arises. The Message Bar provides a security warning and options to enable external content or leave it blocked. If you don't want to receive alerts about security issues, you can disable the Message Bar.

Modify Message Bar Security Options

1. Click the **File** tab, and then click **Options**.

2. In the left pane, click **Trust Center**.

3. Click **Trust Center Settings**.

4. In the left pane, click **Message Bar**.

5. Click the option you want for showing the Message bar.

   ◆ **Show the Message Bar in all applications when active content, such as ActiveX controls and macros, has been blocked.** (default)

   This option is not selected if you selected the Disable all macros without notification check box in the Macros pane of the Trust Center.

   ◆ **Never show information about blocked content.**

6. Click **OK**.

7. Click **OK**.

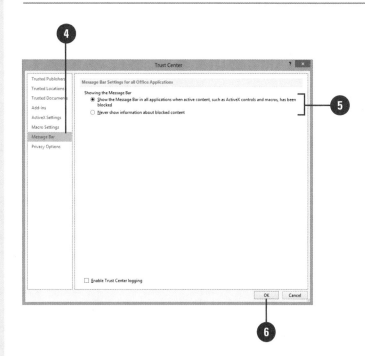

Setting Privacy Options

Privacy options in the Trust Center allow you to set security settings that protect your privacy online. For example, the *Check Microsoft Office documents that are from or link to suspicious web sites* option checks for spoofed web sites and protects you from phishing schemes. You can also set options to help Microsoft troubleshoot your computer or Access for fixes and improvements. If you use the Research task pane, you can enable or disable checking for and installing new services.

Set Privacy Options

1 Click the **File** tab, and then click **Options**.

2 In the left pane, click **Trust Center**.

3 Click **Trust Center Settings**.

4 In the left pane, click **Privacy Options**.

5 Select or clear the check boxes you do or don't want.

◆ **Allow Office to connect to the Internet.** Select to get up-to-date Help content.

◆ **Download a file periodically that helps determine system problems.** Select to have Microsoft request error reports, update trouble-shooting help, and accept downloads from Office.com.

◆ **Sign up for the Customer Experience Improvement Program.** Select to sign-up.

◆ **Check Microsoft Office documents that are from or link to suspicious web sites.** Select to check for spoofed web sites.

◆ **Allow the Research task pane to check for and install new services.** Select to use.

◆ **Turn on the Office Feedback Tool (Send a Smile) so that I can send feedback to help improve Office.** Select to use.

6 Click **OK**.

7 Click **OK**.

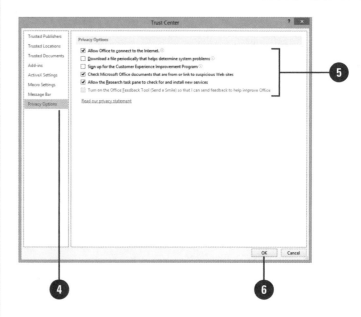

Locking a Database

The Make ACCDE option on the Save As screen under Save Database As allows you to lock a database file, and prevent users from viewing or modifying VBA code and making changes to forms or reports. The command changes the database file extension from .accdb to .accde. If the Access 2007-2013 database .accdb file contains any VBA code, only the compiled (or executable) code is include in the new .accde file. When you open a .accde file, Access creates and opens a temporary locking file with the file extension .laccdb to prevent conflicts. When you close the file, Access automatically deletes the temporary file.

Create a Locked Database

1. Open the Access 2007-2013 .accdb database file you want to save as an .accde file.

2. Click the **File** tab, and then click **Save As**.

3. Click **Save Database As**, and then click **Make ACCDE**.

4. Click the **Save As** button.

5. Click the **Save in** list arrow, and then click the drive or folder where you want to save the .accde file.

6. Type a name for the .accde file.

7. Click **Save**.

Locking Database Records

In a multi-user environment, several users could attempt to edit the same record simultaneously. Access prevents conflicts of this sort using **record locking**, ensuring that only one user at a time can edit data. You can also prevent conflicts by opening the database in **exclusive mode**, preventing all other users from accessing the database while you're using it. This technique is useful for administrators who need sole access to the system while making changes to the database itself.

Set Record Locking

1. Click the **File** tab, and then click **Options**.

2. In the left pane, click **Client Settings**.

3. Click the **Shared** or **Exclusive** option to indicate whether the default strategy for opening the database is shared (allowing simultaneous access by other users) or exclusive (keeping out other users).

4. Click the Default Record Locking strategy option you want to use: **No locks**, **All records**, or **Edited record**.

5. Select the **Open databases by using record-level locking** check box.

6. Click **OK**.

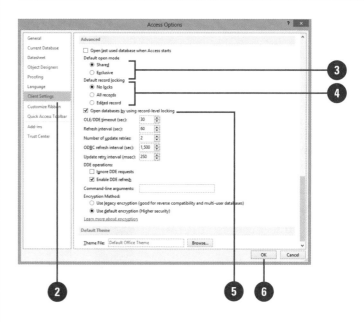

Record Locking Strategies

Locking Type	Description
No Locks	Access does not lock the record you're editing. When you save changes, Access gives you the option to overwrite another user's changes, copy your version to the clipboard, or discard your changes.
All Records	Access locks all records in the table for the entire time you have it open, so no one else can edit or lock the records.
Edited Record	Access locks the record you're currently editing and displays a locked record indicator to other users who may try to edit the record.

Customizing Access

Introduction

There are several ways you can customize Microsoft Access to meet your needs and the needs of those who will use the databases you create. You can use Access Options to set display, editing, and object design options. Some of the other Access customization features allow you to set a default font and related attributes to use when you are typing text or numbers. You can change the location of the Ribbon and the configuration of the Quick Access Toolbar to include commands not available on the Ribbon. To make Access easier to use with touch screens, the program provides Touch/Mouse Mode, which adds or removes more space between commands on the Ribbon.

Access Options also includes some common settings for all Office programs that allow you to customize your work environment to your personal preferences. You can change general options to personalize the appearance of the Access window with an Office Background at the top of the program window or Office Theme color scheme.

In addition to Access, Microsoft Office 2013 also comes with other helpful tools including Upload Center, Lync, Lync Recording Manager, SkyDrive Pro, Language Preferences, Spreadsheet or Database Compare, and Telemetry Log or Dashboard. If you want to add or remove Office features, reinstall Office, or remove it entirely, you can use Office Setup's maintenance feature.

What You'll Do

Set Current Database Options

Set Object Designers Options

Set Database File Options

Set Editing Options

Change Datasheet Options

Set Office Options

Set General Options

Work with Touch Screens

Access Commands Not in the Ribbon

Use Multiple Languages

Work with Office Tools

Maintain and Repair Office

Setting Current Database Options

You can customize the way Access appears when you work on a data-base. If you need more room to view another row of data, you can hide the Status bar or Navigation pane. To customize the way you work with database objects, you can choose to display them as tabbed docu-ments for easy access or overlapping windows for a custom interface. Tabbed documents display one object at a time and uses tabs to allow you to switch between them. You can also display Layout view, which allows you to make design changes while you browse a form or report. You can choose display options you want for the open database on the Current Database pane in Access Options.

Change Display Options

1 Click the **File** tab, and then click **Options**.

2 In the left pane, click **Current Database**.

3 Select or clear the check boxes or options to change display options. Some options include:

◆ **Display Form.** Select the form to open when you start this database. (Default is (none).

◆ **Web Display Form.** Select to set, change or remove forms on the web. (Default is (none).

◆ **Display Status Bar.** Show or hide the Status bar. (Default on).

◆ **Document Window Options.** Select the Overlapping Windows or Tabbed Documents option. If you select Tabbed Documents, select or clear the Display Document Tabs check box. (Default is Tabbed Documents).

◆ **Use Access Special Keys.** Enables or disables shortcut keys. (Default on).

F11 to show or hide the Navigation pane; Ctrl+G to show the Immediate window in the Visual Basic Editor; Alt+F11 to start the Visual Basic Editor; and Ctrl+Break to stop retrieving records.

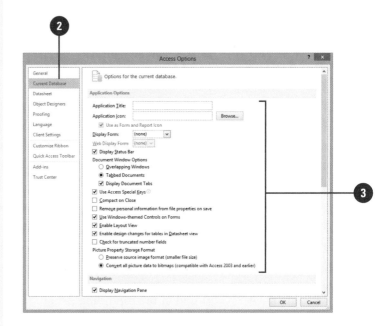

- **Use Windows-themed Controls on Forms.** Uses your Windows theme on controls in forms and reports. (Default on).

- **Enable Layout View.** Show or hides the Layout View button on the Status bar. (Default on).

- **Enable design changes for tables in Datasheet view (for this database).** Allows you to change the design of tables in Datasheet view. (Default on).

- **Display Navigation Pane.** Show or hide the Navigation pane. (Default on).

- **Navigation Options.** Click this button to customize the Navigation pane. You can show or hide objects, group objects, change categories, or show the Search bar.

- **Ribbon Name.** Select the name of a custom Ribbon group. (Default on).

- **Shortcut Full Menus.** Set or change the default menu bar for shortcut menus. (Default is Default).

- **Allow Full Menus.** Enable or disable full menus, instead of frequently-used menus. (Default on).

- **All Default Shortcut Menu.** Enable or disable the shortcut pop-up menu. (Default on).

④ Click **OK**.

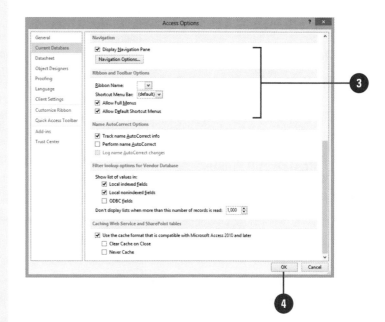

Setting Object Designers Options

Creating and working with tables, queries, forms, and reports are an important part of creating a database. You can change specific options for each database object type to help you customize Access to match the way you work. For example, you can set the default field type, default text field size, or default number field size in new tables. For queries, you can set the default font type and size. For new forms and reports, you can specify selection behavior or templates. Object design options are available on the Object Designers pane in Access Options.

Change Table Object Designer Options

1. Click the **File** tab, and then click **Options**.

2. In the left pane, click **Object Designers**.

3. Specify the Table design options you want. Some options include:

   ◆ **Default field type.** Set the default data type for fields in new tables and fields (Default is Text).

   ◆ **Default text field size.** Set the maximum number of characters for a field. (Default is 255)

   ◆ **Default number field size.** Set the integer type for fields with the Text data type. (Default is Long Integer)

   ◆ **AutoIndex on Import/Create.** Enter beginning or ending characters to match fields for indexing.

   ◆ **Show Property Update Options buttons.** Show or hide the Property Update Options button. (Default on)

4. Click **OK**.

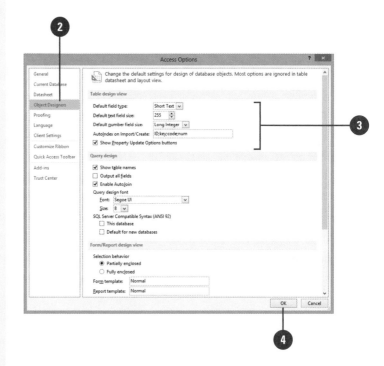

Change Query Object Designer Options

1 Click the **File** tab, and then click **Options**.

2 In the left pane, click **Object Designers**.

3 Specify the Query design options you want. Some options include:

- ◆ **Show table names.** Show or hide the table row in the query design grid. (Default on).

- ◆ **Enable Autojoin.** Select to automatically define a relationship between two tables (Default on).

- ◆ **Query design font.** Select the font style and size for query design.

4 Click **OK**.

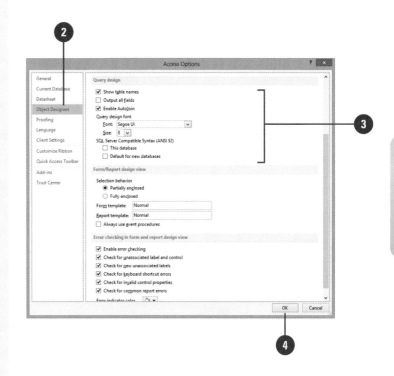

Change Forms/Reports Object Designer Options

1 Click the **File** tab, and then click **Options**.

2 In the left pane, click **Object Designers**.

3 Specify the Forms/Reports design options you want. Some options include:

- ◆ **Selection behavior.** Specify how the selection rectangle selects objects. (Default is Partially enclosed).

- ◆ **Form or Report Template.** Enter the name of an existing form or report. The form or report becomes the template for all new forms or reports. (Default template is "Normal").

4 Click **OK**.

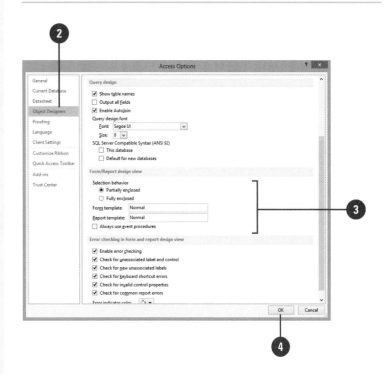

Setting Database File Options

If you always save database in a specific folder, you can change the default location where they are saved. You can change the default local folder locations for opening and saving databases. Access specifies default folder locations based typical places where Microsoft stores things. However, if you want to change them to a location better suited for your needs, you can use the Browse button on the General pane. If you typically create a blank database in earlier versions of Access, you can specify a default file format. If you're working on the same database for a while, you can set an option to automatically open the last used database when Access starts to save some time. If you prefer not to use the Backstage when you open or save files, you can set an option to not show it (**New!**); you go straight to the Open or Save dialog box.

Change Database File Options

1. Click the **File** tab, and then click **Options**.

2. In the left pane, click **General**.

3. Select default file related options for Access you want:

   ◆ **Default file format for Blank Database**. Select an Access file format for creating blank databases.

   ◆ **Default database folder**. Specify a folder location as the default for opening and saving databases.

4. In the left pane, click **Client Settings**.

5. Select any of the following options:

   ◆ **Don't show the Backstage when opening or saving files**. Select to go straight to the Open or Save As dialog box (**New!**).

   ◆ **Open last used database when Access starts**. Select to open the last opened database on start up.

6. Click **OK**.

Setting Editing Options

If you spend a lot of time modifying database fields, you can set editing options in Access to customize the way you work. You can set options to specify the move direction after pressing Enter, the behavior when you enter a field or use the Find or Replace command, the arrow key direction, and whether to ask for confirmation when you make changes for certain types of tasks. Editing options are available on the Client Settings pane in Access Options.

Change Edit Options

① Click the **File** tab, and then click **Options**.

② In the left pane, click **Client Settings**.

③ Select or clear the check boxes or options to change editing options. Some options include:

◆ **Move after enter.** (Default is Next field).

◆ **Behavior entering field.** (Default is Select entire field)

◆ **Arrow key behavior.** (Default is Next field).

◆ **Default find/replace behavior.** (Default is Fast search).

◆ **Confirm.** Confirm record changes, document deletions, or action queries. (Default is all on).

◆ **Default direction.** Display direction for objects. (Default is Left-to-right).

◆ **General alignment.** Display character alignment based on language. (Default is Interface mode).

◆ **Cursor movement.** Language based cursor movement. (Default is Logical).

④ Click **OK**.

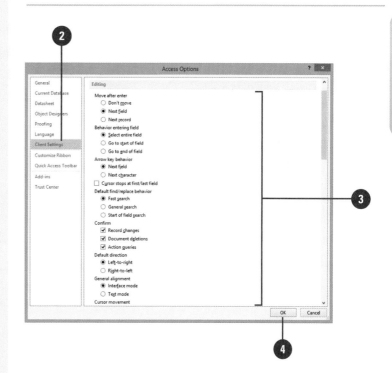

Changing Datasheet Formatting Options

If you want to print a datasheet, you can use formatting tools to make it look better than the standard display. You can specify whether to show or hide either the horizontal or vertical gridlines, or both, or apply formatting special effects—such flat, raised, or sunken—to cells. If you prefer a larger or smaller cell size or specific font, style and size, you specify the default column and font settings you want.

Change Datasheet Default Formatting Options

1. Click the **File** tab, and then click **Options**.

2. In the left pane, click **Datasheet**.

3. Select the default gridlines and cell effects you want, and the default column width you want.

4. Select the default font and style you want.

5. Click **OK**.

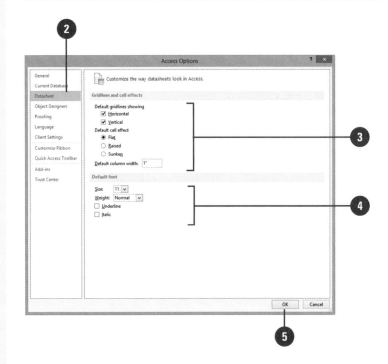

Setting Office Options

Access Options includes some common settings for all Office programs that allow you to customize your work environment to your personal preferences. You can change general options to personalize the appearance of the Access window with an Office Background (**New!**) at the top of the program window or Office Theme (**New!**) color scheme. You can specify if you want to use these settings regardless to whether you are signed in to Office. In addition to signing in to Access with a Microsoft account, you can also personalize Access with your user name and initials, which appear in database properties.

Change Office Options

1. Click the **File** tab, and then click **Options**.

2. In the left pane, click **General**.

3. Type your name and initials as you want them to appear in Properties, and review comments.

4. Select Office related options for Access you want:

   ◆ **Always use these values regardless of sign in to Office**. Select to always use the Office options (**New!**).

   ◆ **Office Background**. Select to apply a background at the top of the program window (**New!**).

   ◆ **Office Theme**. Select to apply a color scheme to the program window (**New!**).

5. Click **OK**.

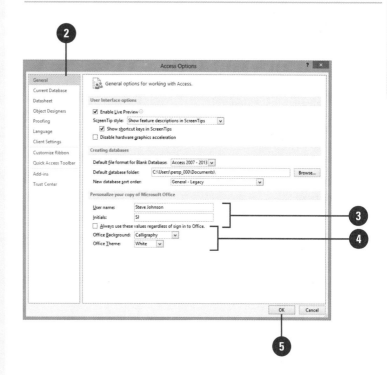

Did You Know?

You can set a default Office theme for databases. Click the File tab, click Options, click Client Settings in the left pane, scroll to the bottom, click Browse, locate and select the Office theme (.thmx), click Open, and then click OK.

Setting General Options

Each person uses Access in a different way. Access Options allows you to change general options to personalize what appears in the Access window. You can set user interface options to enable live preview to show option changes when you point to them, such as themes, specify a display style for ScreenTips, whether to show or hide keyboard short-cuts in ScreenTips, or whether to enable or disable hardware graphics acceleration (**New!**), which can sometimes cause display problems with Office programs. A hardware graphics accelerator is typically used with high performance games.

Change General User Interface Options

1. Click the **File** tab, and then click **Options**.

2. In the left pane, click **General**.

3. Select the User Interface options for Access you want:

   ◆ **Enable Live Preview**. Select to show preview changes in a database.

   ◆ **ScreenTip style**. Click the list arrow to select a screentip option: Show enhanced ScreenTips, Don't show enhanced ScreenTips, or Don't show ScreenTips.

   ◆ **Show shortcut keys in ScreenTips**. Select to show keyboard shortcuts in ScreenTips.

   ◆ **Disable hardware graphics acceleration**. Select to correct display problems (**New!**). Graphic accelerator are typically used for games.

4. Click **OK**.

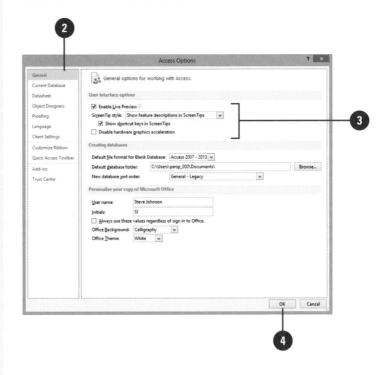

Working with Touch Screens

If you're working with Access on a touch screen device, all you need is your finger to make gestures (**New!**). A gesture is the movement of one or more fingers on a touch screen or pad. For example, touching the screen is called tapping or dragging your finger with a flicking motion at the end of the movement is called swiping. You can swipe, tap, scroll, zoom, and pan within any Access view to navigate between and work in a database. To make Access easier to use with touch screens, the program provides Touch/Mouse Mode (**New!**), which adds or removes more space between commands on the Ribbon.

Use Touch/Mouse Mode

① Click the **Quick Access Toolbar** list arrow, and then click **Touch/Mouse Mode**.

This adds the button to the Quick Access Toolbar.

② Click **Touch/Mouse Mode** button on the Quick Access Toolbar.

③ Click **Mouse** or **Touch**.

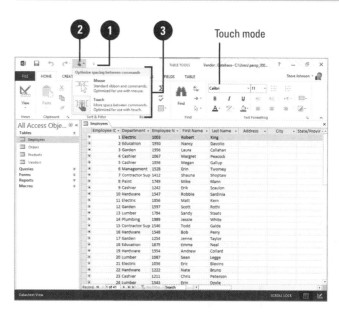

Touch mode

Did You Know?

You can use touch commands. In Office, you can use the following touch commands:

Click - Tap in the file.

Double-click - Double-tap in the file.

Drag - Tap and slide.

Zoom - Pinch or stretch two fingers.

Pan - Pinch or stretch two fingers and drag.

Scroll - Touch and slide up or down.

Swipe - Touch and flick right or left.

Select - Tap an object. For multiple objects, select one (tap and hold), and then tap others. For text, tap and drag.

You can make text and objects bigger. In Windows, open the Control Panel, tap Appearance & Personalization, tap Display, and tap Medium - 125% or Larger - 150%, and then tap Apply.

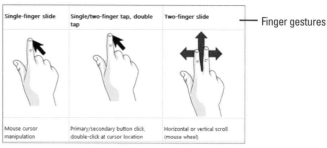

Finger gestures

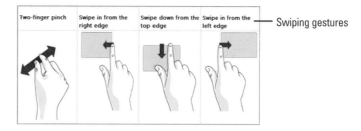

Swiping gestures

Accessing Commands Not in the Ribbon

If you don't see a command in the Ribbon that was available in an earlier version of Access, you might think Microsoft removed it from the product. To see if a command is available, check out the Customize Ribbon or Quick Access section in Access Options. The Quick Access Toolbar and Custom Ribbon gives you access to commands not in the Ribbon, which you can add to the toolbar or ribbon. For example, you can add the following commands: Filter By Selection, Filter Excluding Selection, OLE/DDE Links, Split, Subform, Size to Fit Form, AutoFormat, Switchboard Manager, or Revert.

Add Commands Not in the Ribbon to the Quick Access Toolbar or Ribbon

1. Click the **File** tab, click **Options**, and then click **Quick Access Toolbar** or **Customize Ribbon**.

2. Click the **Choose commands from** list arrow, and then click **Commands Not in the Ribbon**.

3. Click the **Customize Quick Access Toolbar** and then click **For all documents (Default)**, or click the **Customize the Ribbon** list arrow, and then click **For All Tabs**.

4. Click the command you want to add (left column).

   TIMESAVER *For the Quick Access Toolbar, click <Separator>, and then click Add to insert a separator line between buttons.*

5. Click **Add**.

6. Click the **Move Up** and **Move Down** arrow buttons to arrange the commands in the order you want them to appear.

7. To reset the Quick Access Toolbar to its original state, click **Reset**, click **Reset only Quick Access Toolbar** or **Reset only selected Ribbon tab**, and then click **Yes**.

8. Click **OK**.

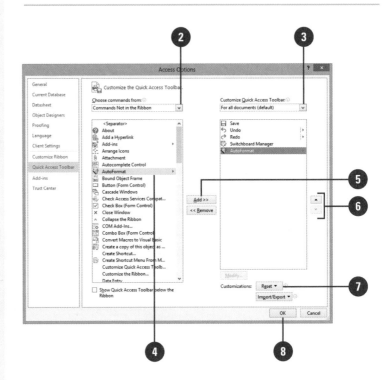

Using Multiple Languages

International Microsoft Office users can change the language that appears on their screens by changing the default language settings. Users around the world can enter, display, and edit text in all supported languages—including European languages, Japanese, Chinese, Korean, Hebrew, and Arabic—to name a few. You'll probably be able to use Office programs in your native language. If the text in your document is written in more than one language, you can automatically detect languages or designate the language of selected text so the spelling checker uses the right dictionary. You can set preferences for editing, display, and Help languages. If you don't have the keyboard layout or related software installed, you can click links to add or enable them.

Add a Language to Office Programs

1. Click the **File** tab, click **Options**, and then click **Language**.

   ◆ You can also click **Microsoft Office 2013 Language Preferences** on the All Apps screen (Win 8) or on the Start menu under Microsoft Office and Microsoft Office Tools (Win 7).

2. Click the **Language** list arrow, and then select the language you want to enable.

3. Click **Add**.

4. To enable the correct keyboard layout for the installed language, click the **Not enabled** link to open the Text Services and Input Language dialog box, where you can select a keyboard layout, and then click **OK**.

5. Set the language priority order for the buttons, tabs, and Help for the Display and Help languages.

6. Click **OK**, and then click **Yes** (if necessary) to quit and restart Office.

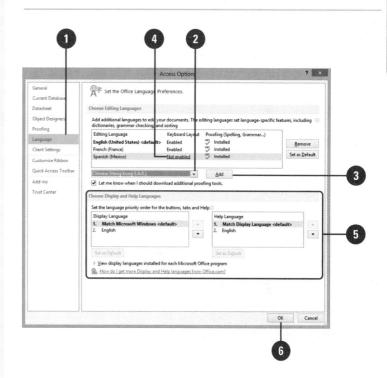

Working with Office Tools

In addition to the main programs, Office 2013 includes some helpful tools including SkyDrive Pro (**New!**), Upload Center, Language Preferences, Database or Spreadsheet Compare (**New!**), and Telemetry Log or Dashboard (**New!**). With SkyDrive Pro, you can connect and synchronize your SkyDrive cloud storage on a SharePoint site with your desktop. As you upload files to a server, like a SharePoint site, you can use the Upload Center to view progress or issues on a transfer. The Upload Center shows you pending uploads, recently uploaded files and all cached files from a server. If you need to compare two Excel spreadsheets, you can use the Spreadsheet Compare tool, a stand-alone app. Telemetry Log records Office events in an Excel spreadsheet to help you troubleshoot problems. Telemetry Dashboard is an Excel spreadsheet that connects to an SQL database to collect client data from other sources in a shared folder.

Compare Databases or Spreadsheets

1. Start **Database Compare 2013** or **Spreadsheet Compare 2013**.

   ◆ **Windows 8.** Click the tile on the All Apps screen.

   ◆ **Windows 7.** Click **Start** on the taskbar, point to **All Programs**, point to **Microsoft Office**, and then point to **Office 2013 Tools**.

2. Click the **Browse** folder, and then select the two files you want to compare.

3. For a database, select or clear option check boxes to specify what you want to compare, and then select the **Full** or **Brief** option.

4. Click **Compare** or **OK**.

5. For a spreadsheet, select or clear option check boxes to show or hide results.

6. Use the Results (database) or Home (spreadsheet) tab to show results.

7. To exit, click the **Close** button.

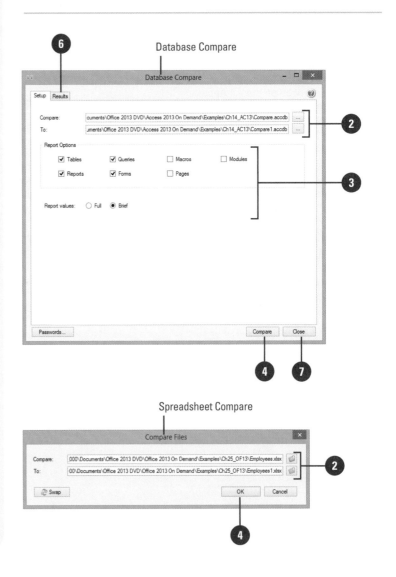

Database Compare

Spreadsheet Compare

Work with the Upload Center

1. Start **Office 2013 Upload Center**.

   - **Windows 8.** Click the tile on the All Apps screen.

   - **Windows 7.** Click **Start** on the taskbar, point to **All Programs**, point to **Microsoft Office**, and then point to **Office 2013 Tools**.

   - **Desktop taskbar.** Click the **Upload Center** icon on the desktop taskbar, and then click **Open Upload Center.**

2. To display pending uploads, click the **View** list arrow, and then click **Pending Uploads**.

3. Use any of the following options:

   - **Actions.** Use options to open the selected file, open site with the file, save a copy, or discard changes.

   - **Upload All.** Use to upload all files.

   - **Pause Uploads.** Use to pause the selected file.

   - **Settings.** Use to open settings dialog box.

   - **Refresh.** Use to refresh the files in the Upload Center.

4. To resolve issues or take actions, click **Resolve** or **Actions**, and then select an option.

5. To display recent uploads, click the **View** list arrow, and then click **Recently Uploaded**.

6. To exit Upload Center, click the **Close** button.

See Also

See "Syncing Documents on SharePoint" on page 434 for information on using SkyDrive Pro.

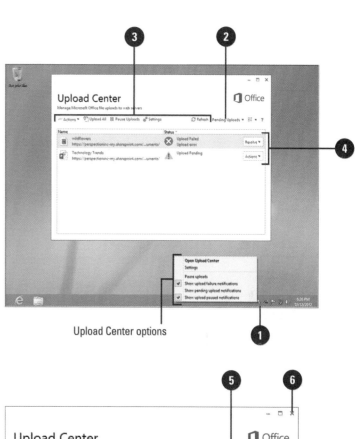

Upload Center options

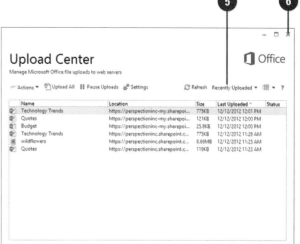

Maintaining and Repairing Office

At times you may determine that an Office program is not working as efficiently as it once did. This sometimes happens when you install new software or move files into new folders. Office does the work for you with the Repair option, which locates, diagnoses, and fixes any errors in the program itself. Note that this feature does not repair personal files like documents, presentations, or workbooks. If the Repair option does not fix the problem, you might have to reinstall Office. If you want to add or remove features, reinstall Office, or remove it entirely, you can use Office Setup's maintenance feature.

Perform Maintenance on Office Programs

1. Insert the Office disc in your drive or navigate to the folder with the setup program.

2. In File or Windows Explorer, double-click the Setup icon.

3. Click one of the following maintenance buttons.

   ◆ **Add or Remove Features** to change which features are installed or remove specific features.

   ◆ **Remove** to uninstall Microsoft Office 2013 from this computer.

   ◆ **Repair** to repair Microsoft Office 2013 to its original state.

   ◆ **Enter a Product Key** to type the product registration key (located in the product packaging) for Office 2013.

4. Click **Continue**, and then follow the wizard instructions to complete the maintenance.

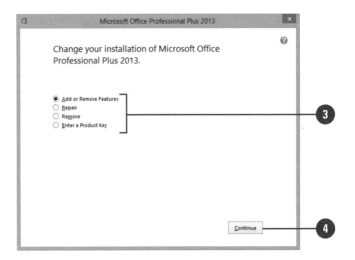

For Your Information

Updating Office 2013 along with Windows 8

Microsoft continually improves Office with updates that include bug fixes and feature improvements. With Windows 8, you can automatically get updates to Office 2013 along with the operating system. To set the update option, open the Desktop app, open the Control Panel, click System and Security, click Windows Update, click Change settings in the left pane, select the Give Me Updates For Other Microsoft Products When I Update Window check box, and then click OK. When Windows 8 scans your system and checks for updates, it also checks for Office 2013 updates (**New!**) as well as other Microsoft products.

Automating and Extending a Database

Introduction

If you find yourself repeating the same sequence of tasks over and over again, you can save time and effort by creating a macro to automate the entire sequence with a single command. Macros allow you to create new commands designed to work with a particular database. With the Macro Designer, you can quickly build a macro by using one or more predefined actions from the Action Catalog pane and specifying any parameters. You can attach macros to button and form controls or the Quick Access Toolbar or create macros that run only if a particular condition is met.

If you want to create customized Microsoft Access applications, you'll need to learn how to work with the Microsoft Office programming language, **Microsoft Visual Basic for Applications**, or **VBA**. VBA is more powerful and more flexible than Access macros, and you can use it in all major Office applications to extend the functionality of the program.

To create a VBA application, you have to learn VBA conventions and syntax. Access provides extensive online Help available to assist you in this task. Office makes VBA more user-friendly by providing the Visual Basic Editor, an application that includes several tools to help you write error-free VBA applications.

With VBA you can create applications that run when the user initially opens a database, or you can link applications to buttons, text boxes, or other controls. You can even use VBA to create your own custom functions, supplementing Access's library of built-in functions. VBA may be a difficult language for the new user, but its benefits make the effort of learning it worthwhile.

What You'll Do

Automating a Database with Macros

A **macro** is a stored collection of **actions** that perform a particular task, such as maximizing the Access program window, opening a specific form and report or printing a group of reports. You can create macros to automate a repetitive or complex task or to automate a series of tasks. Using a macro to automate repetitive tasks guarantees consistency and minimizes errors caused when you forget a step. Using a macro can also protect you from unnecessary complexity. You can perform multiple tasks with a single button or keystroke. For whatever reason you create them, macros can dramatically increase your productivity when working with your database.

Macros consist of actions or commands that are needed to complete the operation you want to automate. Opening, importing, saving, searching, querying, filtering, sorting, printing, and saving are examples of actions.

Parameters, also known as arguments, are additional pieces of information required or optional to carry out an individual action. For example, an OpenTable macro action would require arguments that identify the name of the table you want to open, the view in which to display the table, and the kinds of changes a user would be able to make in this table. Parameters are used in expressions to pass values and references for use in macros.

With the Macro Designer, you can build a macro by selecting one or more predefined actions from the Action Catalog pane or drop-down lists, and specifying any parameters. After building the macro, you need to save it with a meaningful name like any other object in Access. If you want to automatically run a macro when Access starts up, all you need to do is name the macro AutoExec. All macros appear in the Navigation pane under Macros where you can run, edit, or remove them.

Actions that make up the macro   Create a macro

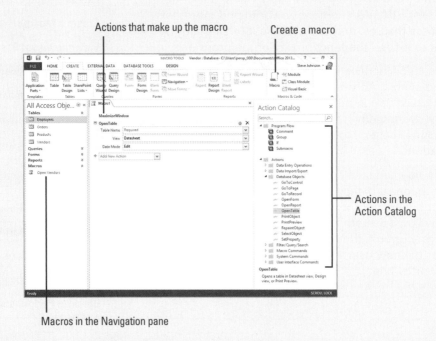

Actions in the Action Catalog

Macros in the Navigation pane

Using the Action Catalog

When you create or edit a macro, you can use the predefined actions in the Action Catalog to help you quickly build the functionality you want. When you open a macro, the Design tab under Macro Tools appears with options to work with actions in a macro along with the Action Catalog pane. You can click the Action Catalog button to show or hide the Action Catalog pane. You can also click the Show All Actions button to display all actions or only the actions allowed in the current database. You can quickly identify an action allowed in the database by the lightning bolt icon next to it. If an action is not allowed, a warning icon appears next to it.

The Action Catalog pane displays a Search box at the top, a folder tree list of *Program Flow* options, predefined *Actions*, and objects *In this Database* with macros in the middle,

and a description of the selected item at the bottom.

If you know what action you want to use, you can use the Search box at the top of the Action Catalog pane to find it. If you're not sure, you can browse a list of predefined actions. The actions are organized into categories: Data Entry Operations, Data Import/Export, Database Options, Filter/Query/Search, Macro Commands, System Commands, User Interface Commands, and Window Management. If you want to use an existing macro within another macro, you can select them from the In this Database category.

The Program Flow category provides options that allow you to add macro comments, create macro groups, create If condition to execute macros, or create submacros to build more advanced macros.

Design tab under Macro Tools   Action Catalog pane

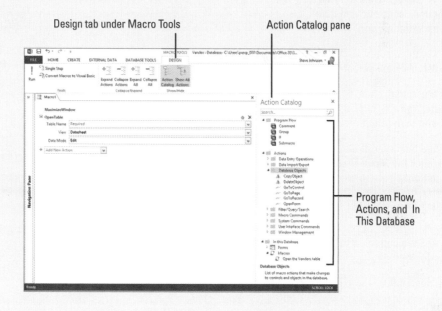

Program Flow, Actions, and In This Database

Creating or Editing a Macro

Before you begin creating a macro, you should plan the actions required to complete the tasks you want to automate. Test each step needed to carry out the operation and write them down as you go. If you want to run a macro to automatically run when you open a database, simply name the macro AutoExec, which is a special name that Access looks for when it starts up. To bypass the AutoExec macro and any other startup options, simply hold down the Shift key while you start the database (including enabling content). If you don't want others to bypass the AutoExec macro, you can set the AllowBypassKey property to False by using VBA code. If you no longer want to use the startup AutoExec macro or any other one, you can delete it like any other object.

Create and Save a Macro

1. Click the **Create** tab.

2. Click the **Macro** button.

3. Click the **Design** tab under Macro Tools.

4. If necessary, click the **Action Catalog** button to show the Action Catalog pane. To show all actions, click the **Show All Actions** button.

5. Locate and drag an action from the Action Catalog pane to the Macro window or click the **Add New Action** list arrow, and then select an action.

6. To work with an action in the macro list, click toe select it.

7. Within the action, enter a parameter value or click a list arrow, and then select a value.

8. To change the order of actions in the list, click the **Move Up** or **Move Down** button.

9. To remove an action from the list, click the **Delete** button.

10. Click the **Save** button on the Quick Access Toolbar.

11. Enter a descriptive macro name.

12. Click **OK**.

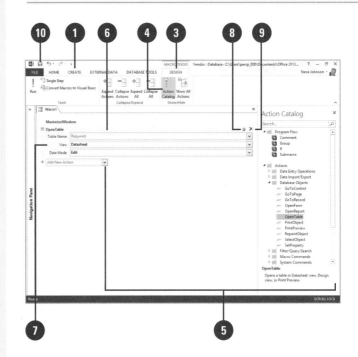

Edit an Existing Macro

1 In the Navigation pane, right-click the macro you want to edit, and then click **Design View**.

2 To show or hide an action, select the action, and then click the **Expand Actions** or **Collapse Actions** button.

 ◆ To show or hide all actions, click the **Expand All** or **Collapse All** button.

3 To work with an action in the macro list, click toe select it.

4 To add an action, drag an action from the Action Catalog pane to the Macro window or click the **Add New Action** list arrow, and then select an action.

 ◆ To show or hide the Action Catalog pane, click the **Action Catalog** button.

5 To change the order of actions in the list, click the **Move Up** or **Move Down** button.

6 To remove an action from the list, click the **Delete** button.

7 Click the **Save** button on the Quick Access Toolbar.

8 Click the **Close** button.

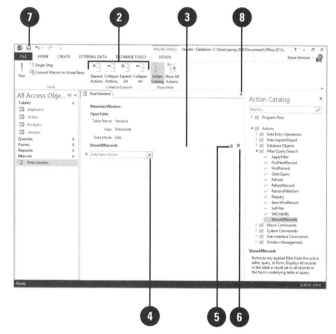

Did You Know?

You can create a new macro based on an existing one. Open the macro in Macro Design view, click the File tab, click Save As, click Save Object As, and then click Save As. Give the macro a new name, and then modify the new macro as needed.

Running and Testing a Macro

To have a macro perform its actions, you must run it, or instruct it to execute its actions. There are two ways to run a macro. You can have the macro perform all the steps in a sequence at once, or you can test a macro by running it to perform one step at a time, allowing you to review the results of each step. By testing your macro, you might discover that it did not perform all its tasks in the way you expected. If so, you can make changes and retest the macro as you continue to make adjustments in Macro Design view. Keep in mind that a macro will perform only the actions that are appropriate in the currently active view, so be sure to display the correct view before you run the macro; you can have the first action in the macro display the view in which you want to run the macro.

Run a Macro in a Sequence

1 Display the macro you want to run in Macro Design view.

◆ In the Navigation pane, right-click the macro, and then click **Design View**.

TIMESAVER *In the Navigation pane, double-click the macro you want to run.*

2 Click the **Design** tab.

If your macro does not automatically switch you to the correct view, switch to the view in which you want to run the macro.

3 Click the **Run** button.

If the macro encounters an action it cannot perform, a message box appears, indicating a problem.

4 If necessary, click **OK** to close the message box.

5 Click **Stop All Macros** to stop the macro.

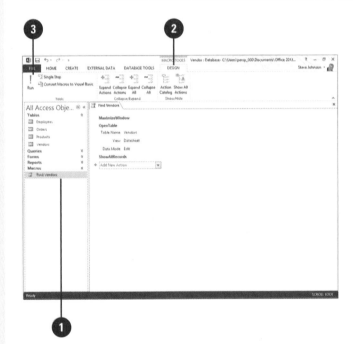

Test a Macro Step-by-Step

1. Display the macro you want to run in Macro Design view.

2. Click the **Design** tab.

3. Click the **Single Step** button.

   If necessary, switch to the view in which you want to run the macro.

4. Click the **Run** button.

5. Click **Step** to perform the first action in the macro.

6. Repeat step 5 until the macro finishes.

   If the macro encounters an action it cannot perform, you see a message box stating the action it could not carry out.

7. Click **OK** to close the message box.

8. Click **Stop All Macros** to stop the macro.

Did You Know?

You can run all steps in a macro. If the Single Step button on the Macro Design tab is active, you can still run all the steps in the macro without stopping. In the Macro Single Step dialog box, click Continue.

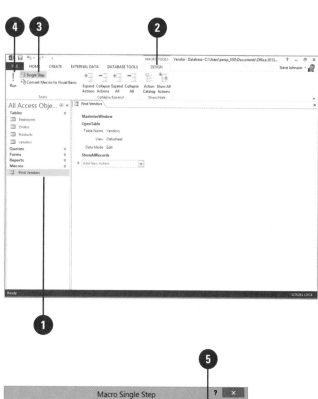

Creating a Macro Group

If you have numerous macros, grouping related macros in macro groups can help you to manage them more easily. When Access runs a macro group, the first macro in the group starts with the first action, continuing until it reaches a new macro name or the last action in the window. To run a macro group, use the macro group name followed by the macro name. For example, you can refer to a macro group named Report1 in the Employees macro as Report1.Employees.

Create a Macro Group

1. Create a new macro or display an existing one in Macro Design view.

2. Click the **Design** tab.

3. To show the Action Catalog pane, click the **Action Catalog** button.

4. Drag the **Group** icon to the Macro window where you want to place it; a position line appears with the placement point.

   ◆ To display options, click the **Expand** icon for Program Flow.

5. Type a name for the macro group.

6. To add a new action to the group, drag an action from the Action Catalog pane to the Macro window or click the **Add New Action** list arrow, and then select an action.

7. To move an existing action into the group, drag the action into the group; a position line appears with the placement point.

8. Click the **Save** button on the Quick Access Toolbar. For a new macro, enter a name, and then click **OK**.

9. Click the **Close** button.

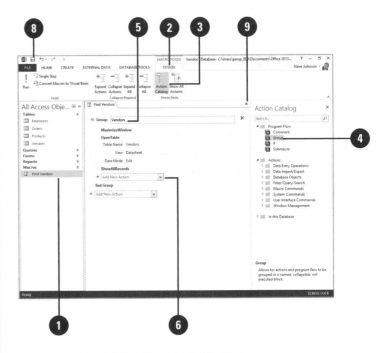

Creating a Macro Condition

Sometimes you may want a macro to run only if some prior condition is met. For example, you could create a macro that prints a report only if the number of records to print is greater than zero. You can do this by creating a **conditional expression**, an expression that Access evaluates as true or false, with Expression Builder. If the condition is true, Access carries out the actions in the macro.

Create a Macro Condition

1. Create a new macro or display an existing one in Macro Design view.

2. Click the **Design** tab.

3. To show the Action Catalog pane, click the **Action Catalog** button.

4. Drag the **If** icon to the Macro window where you want to place it; a position line appears with the placement point.

   ◆ To display options, click the **Expand** icon for Program Flow.

5. Enter an expression, or click the **Expression Builder**.

6. Enter an expression that Access could evaluate as either true or false.

7. Click **OK**.

8. To execute an action for the true condition, add a new action or drag an existing action to the Then area.

9. If you want to execute an action for the false condition, click **Add Else** or **Add Else If**, and then add a new action or drag an existing action to it.

10. Click the **Save** button on the Quick Access Toolbar. For a new macro, enter a name, and then click **OK**.

11. Click the **Close** button.

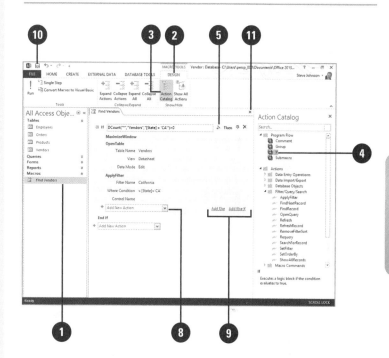

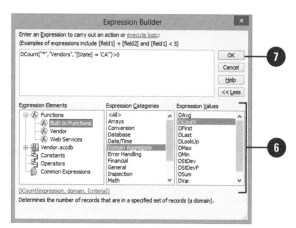

Adding Comments to a Macro

When you create a macro, it's a good practice to add a comment. Especially if the macro is complex. A comment can be very helpful as a guide to what the macro does and how it goes about automating a series of tasks. Adding a comment is quick and easy. Simply drag the Comment icon in the Action catalog pane to the Macro window, and then start typing in the Comment box. You can move the comment around or delete it if you no longer want it just like any other action.

Add a Comments to a Macro

1. Create a new macro or display an existing one in Macro Design view.

2. Click the **Design** tab.

3. To show the Action Catalog pane, click the **Action Catalog** button.

4. Drag the **Comment** icon to the Macro window where you want to place it; a position line appears with the placement point.

   ◆ To display options, click the **Expand** icon for Program Flow.

5. Enter a comment.

6. Click the **Save** button on the Quick Access Toolbar. For a new macro, enter a name, and then click **OK**.

7. Click the **Close** button.

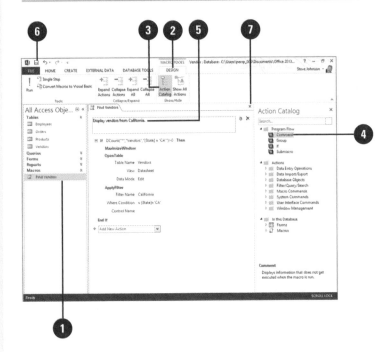

Creating a Message Box

When you create a macro, you may want to give database users information about how the macro works as it runs. You can create message boxes for your macros that, for example, ask the user if he or she wants to proceed. You do this with the MessageBox action. The MessageBox action allows you to specify the text of the message, whether or not a beep sounds when the box is displayed, the type of box that appears, and the box's title. Access supports five different types of message boxes. Each one has a different icon. The icons convey the importance of the message box, ranging from merely being informative to indicating a serious error.

Create a Message Box

1. Create a new macro or display an existing one in Macro Design view.

2. Click the **Design** tab.

3. To show the Action Catalog pane, click the **Action Catalog** button.

4. Drag the **MessageBox** icon to the Macro window where you want to place it; a position line appears with the placement point.

   ◆ To display options, click the **Expand** icon for Actions, and then click the **Expand** icon for User Interface Commands.

5. Enter or specify the following information for the Message box:

   ◆ Specify the text you want contained in the Message box.

   ◆ Indicate whether a beep will accompany the message.

   ◆ Specify the box type: **None**, **Critical**, **Warning?**, **Warning!**, or **Information**.

   ◆ Enter the box title.

6. Click the **Save** button on the Quick Access Toolbar. For a new macro, enter a name, and then click **OK**.

7. Click the **Close** button.

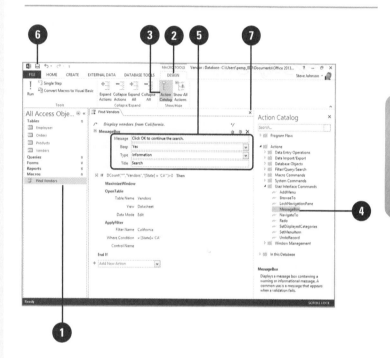

Message box

Assigning a Macro to an Event

An **event** is a specific action that occurs on or with a certain object. Clicking a button is an event, called the Click event. The Click event in this case occurs on the button object. Other events include the Dbl Click event (for double-clicking) and the On Enter event, which occurs, for example, when a user "enters" a field by clicking it. If you want to run a macro in response to an event, you have to work in the object's property sheet. The property sheet lists all of the events applicable to the object. You can choose the event and then specify the macro that will run when it occurs, or create a new macro in the Macro window.

Assign a Macro to an Event

1. In Design view, select the object in which the event will occur.

2. Click the **Design** tab.

3. Click the **Property Sheet** button.

   TIMESAVER *You can double-click an object to open the Property Sheet.*

4. Click the **Event** tab.

5. Click the box for the event you want to use.

6. Click the list arrow, and then click the macro you want to use.

7. Click the **Close** button.

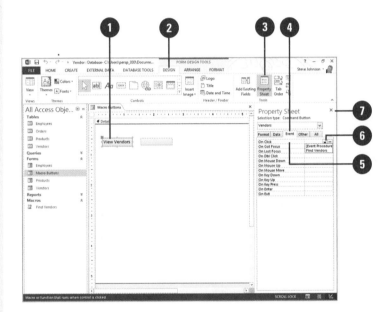

Create a New Macro for an Event

1. In Design view, select the object in you want the event to occur.

2. Click the **Design** tab.

3. Click the **Property Sheet** button.

   TIMESAVER *You can double-click an object to open the Property Sheet.*

4. Click the **Event** tab.

5. Click the specific event to which you want to assign the macro.

6. Click the **Expression Builder** button.

7. Click **Macro Builder**.

8. Click **OK**.

9. Select the actions for the new macro, and then close the Macro window.

10. Click the **Save** button.

11. Enter a name for the new macro, and then click **OK**.

12. Click the **Close** button.

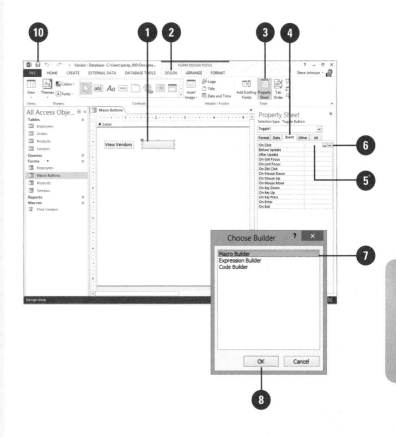

For Your Information

Creating an Embedded Macro

An embedded macro is stored in the event property of a form, report, or control instead of the Navigation pane under Macros. An embedded marco is used when you want to copy, import, or export a form or report object, because the embedded macro stays with the object. An embedded macro runs each time the event property is triggered. To create an embedded macro, right-click the form or report you want to use, click Design View, click the Design tab, click the Property Sheet button, click the control or section that contains the event you want to embed a macro, click the Event tab, click the event property, click the Builder button (...), click Macro Builder, and then click OK. Click the first row of the Action column, click the list arrow, and then click the action you want. You can add other actions as desired. When you're done, click the Save button and then click the Close button.

Assigning a Macro to a Button

Database designers often attach macros to form controls, particularly buttons, so that when a user clicks the button, the macro is activated. If you create a button, you can use the Button control with the Control Wizard to specify the action that will occur when the button is clicked. If you want to assign a macro to a button, you choose the action of running the macro.

Assign a Macro to a Button

1. In Design view for a form, click the **Design** tab under Form Design Tools.

2. Click the **More** list arrow for Controls, and then click **Use Control Wizards** to highlight it.

3. Click the **Button** button.

4. Drag the image onto the form, report, or page.

   The wizard opens, displaying options.

5. Click **Miscellaneous**.

6. Click **Run Macro** and then click **Next** to continue.

7. Choose the macro you want to run, and then click **Next** to continue.

8. Specify the text or image that will appear on the button, and then click **Next** to continue

9. Enter a name for the command button control, and then click **Finish**.

10. Save the form or report, and then test the button to verify that your macro runs when the button is clicked.

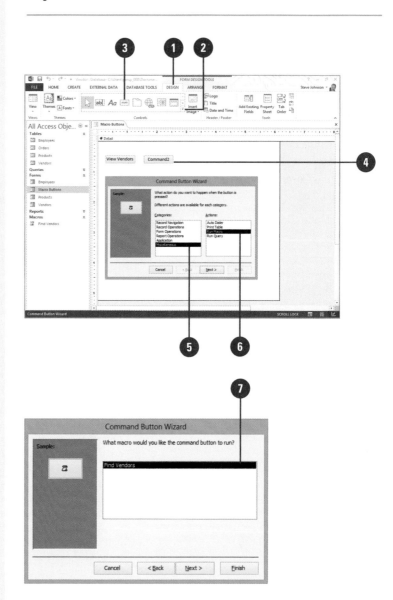

Assigning a Macro to a Toolbar

After you create a macro, you can add the macro to the Quick Access Toolbar for easy access. When you create a macro, the macro name appears in the list of available commands when you customize the Quick Access Toolbar in Access Options. When you point to a macro button on the Quick Access Toolbar, a ScreenTip appears, displaying the macro name.

Assign a Macro to a Toolbar

1. Click the **Customize Quick Access Toolbar** list arrow, and then click **More Commands**.

2. Click the **Choose command from** list arrow, and then click **Macros**.

3. Click the **Customize Quick Access Toolbar** list arrow, and then click **For all documents** (default).

4. Click the macro you want to add (left column).

5. Click **Add**.

6. Click the **Move Up** and **Move Down** arrow buttons to arrange the commands in the order you want them to appear.

7. Click **Modify**.

8. Type a name for the button.

9. Click an icon in the symbol list.

10. Click **OK**.

11. Click **OK**.

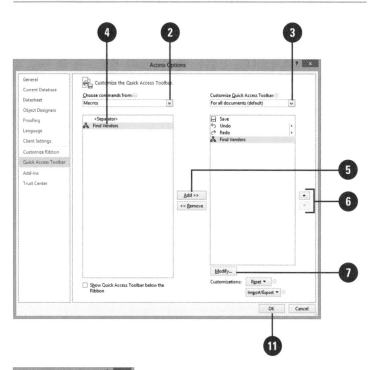

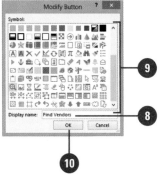

Macro button

Extending a Database with VBA

Microsoft Office applications like Access, Excel, and Word share a common programming language: VBA. With VBA, you can develop applications that combine tools from these Office products, as well as other programs that support VBA. Because of the language's power and flexibility, programmers often prefer to use VBA over Access macros to customize their Access applications.

Introducing the Structure of VBA

VBA is an **object-oriented** programming language because, when you develop a VBA application, you manipulate objects. An object can be anything within your database, such as a table, query, or a database. Even Access itself is considered an object. Objects can have properties that describe the object's characteristics. Text boxes, for example, have the Font property, which describes the font Access uses to display the text. A text box also has properties that indicate whether the text is bold or italic.

Objects also have methods, actions that can be done to the object. Deleting and inserting are examples of methods available with a record object. Closely related to methods are events. An **event** is a specific action that occurs on or with an object. Clicking a form button initiates the Click event for the button object. VBA also refers to an event associated with an object as an event property. The form button, for example, has the Click event property. You can use VBA to either respond to an event or to initiate an event.

Writing VBA Code

Unlike Access macros, which are created in the Macro Design window, the VBA programmer types the statements, or **code**, that make up the VBA program. Those statements follow a set of rules, called **syntax**, that govern how commands are formulated. For example, to change the property of a particular object, the command follows the general form:

> Object.Property = Expression

where **Object** is the name of a VBA object, **Property** is the name of a property that object has, and **Expression** is a value that will be assigned to the property. The following statement sets the Caption property of the Departments form:

> Forms!Departments.Caption="Department Form"

You can use Access's online Help to learn about specific object and property names. If you want to apply a method to an object, the syntax is:

> Object.Method arg1, arg2, ...

where **Object** is the name of a VBA object, **Method** is the name of method that can be applied to that object, and **arg1**, **arg2**, ... are optional **arguments** that provide additional information for the method operation. For example, to move to page 2 of a multipage form, you could use the GoToPage method as follows:

> Forms!Departments.GoToPage 2

Working with Procedures

You don't run VBA commands individually. Instead they are organized into groups of commands called **procedures**. A procedure either performs an action or calculates a value. Procedures that perform actions are called **Sub procedures**. You can run a Sub procedure directly, or Access can run it for you in response to an event, such as clicking a button or opening a form. A Sub procedure initiated by an event is also called an **event procedure**. Access provides event procedure templates to help you easily create procedures for common events. Event procedures are displayed in each object's event properties list.

A procedure that calculates a value is called a **function procedure**. By creating function procedures you can create your own function library, supplementing the Access collection of built-in functions. You can access these functions from within the Expression Builder, making it easy for them to be used over and over again.

Working with Modules

Procedures are collected and organized within **modules**. Modules generally belong to two types: class modules and standard modules. A **class module** is associated with a specific object. For example, each form or report can have its own class module, called a **form module** or **report module**. In more advanced VBA programs, the class module can be associated with an object created by the user.

Standard modules are not associated with specific objects, and they can be run from anywhere within a database. This is usually not the case with class modules. Standard modules are listed in the Navigation pane on the Modules Object list.

Building VBA Projects

A collection of modules is further organized into a **project**. Usually a project has the same name as a database. You can create projects that are not tied into any specific databases, saving them as Access add-ins that provide extra functionality to Access.

Using the Visual Basic Editor

You create VBA commands, procedures, and modules in Office's **Visual Basic Editor**. This is the same editor used by Excel, Word, and other Office applications. Thus, you can apply what you learn about creating programs in Access to these other applications.

The Project Explorer

One of the fundamental tools in the Visual Basic Editor is the Project Explorer. The **Project Explorer** presents a hierarchical view of all of the projects and modules currently open in Access, including standard and class modules.

The Modules Window

You write all of your VBA code in the **Modules** window. The Modules window acts as a basic text editor, but it includes several tools to help you write error-free codes. Access also provides hints as you write your code to help you avoid syntax errors.

The Object Browser

There are hundreds of objects available to you. Each object has a myriad of properties, methods, and events. Trying to keep track of all of them is daunting, but the Visual Basic Editor supplies the **Object Browser**, which helps you examine the complete collection of objects, properties, and methods available for a given object.

Creating a Module

All modules in a database are listed in the Modules section of the Navigation pane. You can open a module for editing or create a new module. When you edit a module or design a new one, Access automatically starts the Visual Basic Editor. You can use the Module or Class Module button on the Create tab to quickly create a new module.

Create a New Standard Module or Class Module

1. Click the **Create** tab.

2. Click **Module** or **Class Module** button.

   Access starts the Visual Basic Editor, opening a new module window.

Did You Know?

You can open the Visual Basic Editor. You can open the Visual Basic Editor directly by pressing and holding Alt while you press F11. You can also toggle back and forth between Access and the Visual Basic Editor by pressing and holding Alt while you press F11.

See Also

See "Extending a Database with VBA" on page 384 for information on modules.

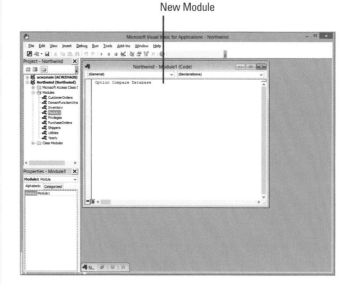

New Module

Viewing the Visual Basic Editor

The Project Explorer displays a hierarchical list of all open projects and modules.

The Modules window allows you to enter VBA commands.

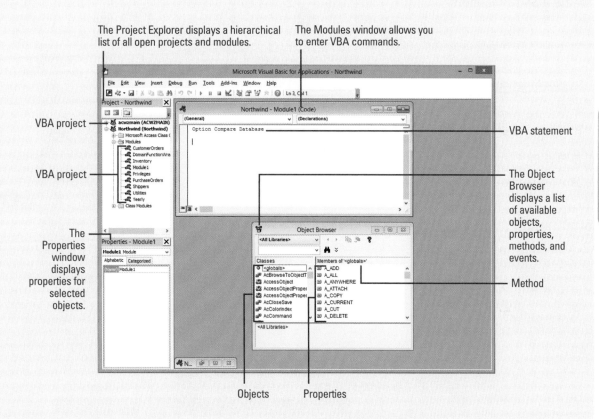

VBA project

VBA project

The Properties window displays properties for selected objects.

VBA statement

The Object Browser displays a list of available objects, properties, methods, and events.

Method

Objects

Properties

Creating a Sub Procedure

You can either type a Sub procedure directly into the Modules window, or the Visual Basic Editor can insert it for you. Sub procedures all begin with the line: Sub ProcedureName( ) where ProcedureName is the name of the Sub procedure. If the Sub procedure includes arguments, enter them between the opening and closing parentheses. Not every Sub procedure requires arguments. After entering the first line, which names the procedure, you can insert the procedure's VBA commands. Each Sub procedure ends with the line: End Sub.

Create a Sub Procedure

1. In the Visual Basic Editor, click the Module window to select it.

2. Click the **Insert** menu, and then click **Procedure**.

3. Enter the procedure's name.

4. Click the **Sub** option, if necessary.

5. Click **OK**.

   The Editor inserts the opening and closing lines of the new Sub procedure.

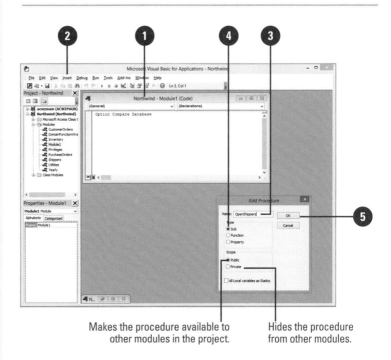

Makes the procedure available to other modules in the project.

Hides the procedure from other modules.

Indicates that Sub procedure is available to other modules.

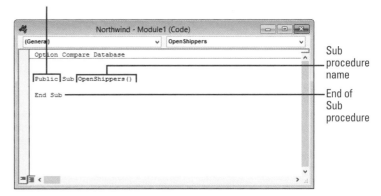

Sub procedure name

End of Sub procedure

Writing VBA Commands

You insert VBA commands by typing them into the appropriate place in the Module window. This, of course, requires some knowledge of VBA. Access provides online Help to assist you in writing VBA code. The Visual Basic Editor also helps you with hints that help you complete a command accurately. If you have entered a command incorrectly, the Editor notifies you of the error and may suggest ways of correcting the problem. One of the most useful VBA objects you'll encounter in writing VBA code is the DoCmd object, which represents Access commands. You can use DoCmd in your commands to perform basic operations, like opening tables, reports, and forms.

Write a VBA Command to Open a Table

1. Click the Modules window to activate it.

2. Click a blank line after the Sub *ProcedureName* command in the Modules window.

3. Type **DoCmd**. Make sure you include the period.

4. Double-click **OpenTable** in the list box that appears, and then press the Spacebar.

5. As indicated by the hints supplied by the Editor, type the name of a table from the current database. Make sure you enclose the name in quotation marks.

6. Type a comma.

7. Double-click **acViewNormal** to open the table in Normal view.

8. Type a comma.

9. Double-click **acReadOnly** to open the table in Read-only mode.

10. Press Enter to add a new blank line below the command.

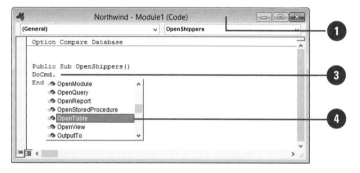

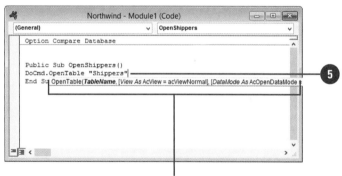

As you type the VBA command, the Editor displays the correct syntax. Optional arguments are enclosed in square brackets [ ].

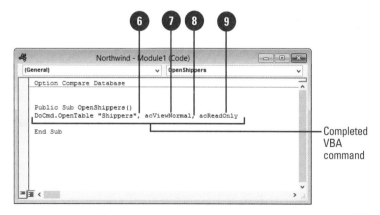

Completed VBA command

Running a Sub Procedure

After writing a Sub procedure, you may want to test it. You can run a Sub procedure from within the Visual Basic Editor, but you might have to return to Access to view the results. If the Sub procedure is a long one, you can also click buttons to pause it or to stop it altogether.

Run a Sub Procedure

1. Click the **Save** button on the toolbar to save changes to the VBA project.

2. Enter a name for your module, if requested, and then click **OK**.

3. Click anywhere within the Sub procedure that you want to run.

4. Click the **Run Sub/User Form** button on the toolbar.

   If the Macros dialog box appears, select the macro you want to run, and then click **Run**.

5. Return to Access, if necessary, to view the results of your Sub procedure.

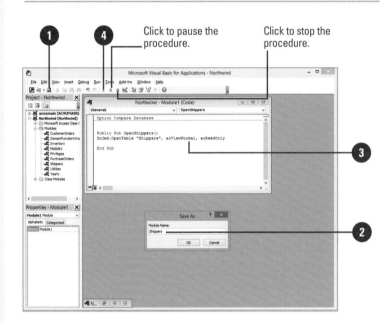

Click to pause the procedure.

Click to stop the procedure.

Copying Commands from the Object Browser

The Object Browser displays a hierarchical list of all of the objects, properties, methods, and events available to VBA procedures. The browser organizes these different objects into libraries. The list of libraries is not limited to those built into Access itself. It also includes libraries from other Access projects and add-ins. You can use the Object Browser as a reference tool, or you can copy and paste commands from the browser directly into your Sub procedures.

Insert an Object from the Object Browser

1. In the Visual Basic Editor, click the **Object Browser** button on the toolbar to display the Object Browser.

2. Click the **Libraries** list arrow, and then select the library that contains your object.

3. Select the object you want to insert.

4. Click the **Copy** button.

5. Return to the Sub procedure in the Modules window.

6. Click the location in the Sub procedure where you want to paste the object name.

7. Click the **Paste** button on the toolbar.

Enter a search string for an object, property, method, or event.

Click to search for an object, property, method, or event.

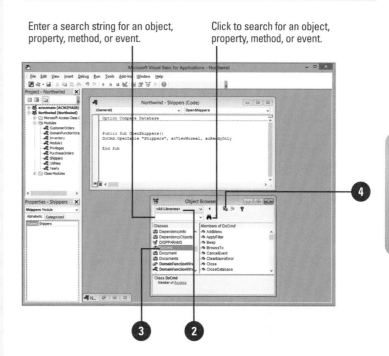

Creating a Custom Function

In addition to Sub procedures, you can also create function procedures that Access uses as custom functions. Each function procedure begins with the line: FunctionName( ) where FunctionName is the name of the function procedure. Within the parentheses, place any variables needed for the calculation of the function. You can learn more about variables from Access's online Help. After statement of the function's name and variables, add VBA commands to calculate the result of the function. The function concludes with the End Function line.

Create a Custom Function

1. In the Visual Basic Editor, open a Modules window.

2. Click the **Insert** menu, and then click **Procedure**.

   ◆ To create a new module, click the **Insert** menu, and then click **Module**.

3. Enter the function's name.

4. Click the **Function** option.

5. Click **OK**.

   The Editor inserts the opening and closing lines of your new custom function.

6. Enter variable names needed for the function.

7. Enter VBA commands required to calculate the function's value.

8. Insert a line assigning the calculated value to a variable with the same name as the function.

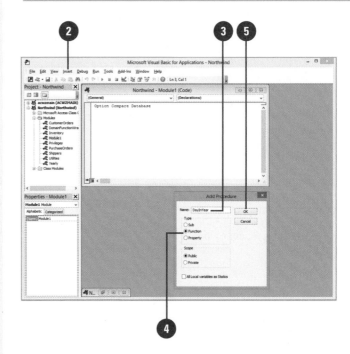

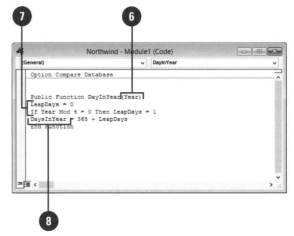

Running a Custom Function

Once you've completed a custom function, you can use it in any Access query, report, or form. The easiest way to access the function is through the Expression Builder. After you open the Expression Builder, you can access the custom function using the Functions folder.

Run a Custom Function

① Open Expression Builder from any query, report, or form.

② Double-click the **Functions** folder.

③ Double-click the name of the project containing your custom function (usually the name of the current database).

④ Click the module containing the custom function.

⑤ Double-click the name of the custom function.

⑥ Edit the function, replacing the variable names within the parentheses with the appropriate field names or constants.

⑦ Click **OK**.

⑧ Test your query, form, or report to verify the values returned by the custom function.

⑥ The variable name is replaced with a reference to the Year field in the Years table.

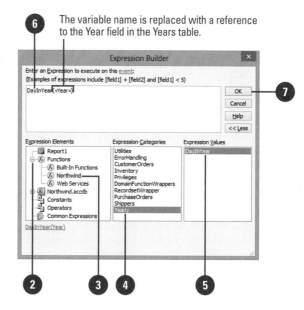

Did You Know?

You can save a module. Save changes to your module before using a customized function. Otherwise, the function will not appear in the Expression Builder.

Creating a Class Module for a Form or Report

Similar to the standard modules that you create, you can also create class modules with Access using the Create tab or the Visual Basic Editor. You usually begin a class module in Design view for a form or report. In most cases, class modules are associated with events such as clicking a form button or opening the form. You can access class modules in the Modules Object list in the Navigation pane or from within the Project Explorer.

Create a Class Module for a Form or Report

1. Display a form or report in Design view.

2. Click the **Design** tab.

3. Click the control or object within the form or report in which you want to create a class module.

4. Click the **Property Sheet** button.

5. Click the **Event** tab.

6. Click the event box that you want to associate with a VBA procedure.

7. Click the **Expression Builder** button.

8. Click **Code Builder**.

9. Click **OK**.

    The Visual Basic Editor opens a Modules window and automatically creates an Event procedure for the control and event you selected.

10. Enter the VBA commands you want.

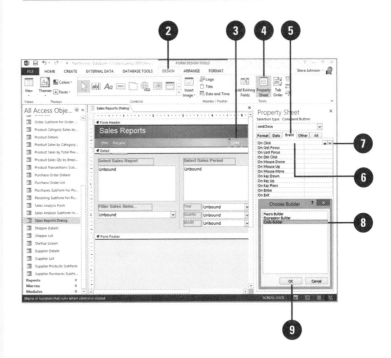

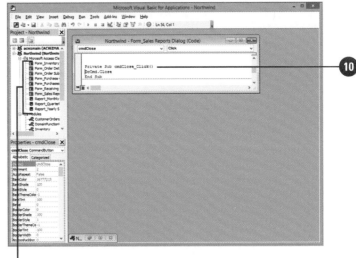

The Project Explorer lists all of the forms and report modules, as well as other class modules.

> **See Also**
>
> *See "Creating a Module" on page 386 for information on creating a class module using the Create tab.*

Setting Project Properties

By default, Access assigns the same name to the project containing your VBA modules and procedures as your database's name. You can change the project's name to make it more descriptive. You can also password-protect your VBA project to keep other users from accessing and changing your procedures.

Set Project Properties

1. Open the Visual Basic Editor by pressing and holding Alt while pressing F11.

2. Select your project from the list of projects in Project Explorer.

3. Click the **Tools** menu, and then click *ProjectName* Properties, where *ProjectName* is the current name of your project.

4. Click the **General** tab.

5. Enter a new name for your project, if necessary.

6. Enter a description of your VBA project.

7. Click the **Protection** tab.

8. Click the **Lock project for viewing** check box if you want to keep others from viewing your project's source code.

9. Enter a password to unlock the project for viewing.

10. Confirm the unlocking password.

11. Click **OK**.

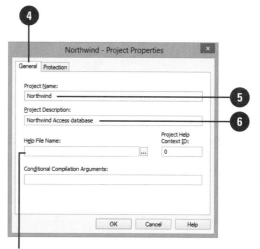

If you've created a Help file for your project, enter the name and location of the file here.

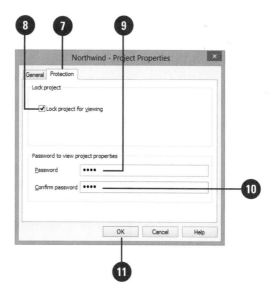

Did You Know?

You need to remember your project password. Save your password. If you lose it, you will not be able to open your code to edit it later.

Debugging a Procedure

The Visual Basic Editor provides several tools to help you write error-free code. However, sometimes a procedure does not act the way you expect it to. To deal with this problem, you can use the Editor's debugging tools to help you locate the source of the trouble. One the most common approaches to debug failed code is to "walk through" the procedure step by step, examining each thing the procedure does. In this way, you can try to locate the exact statement that is causing you trouble.

Stepping Through a Procedure

1 Click the **View** menu, point to **Toolbars**, and then click **Debug**.

2 Click the first line of the procedure you want to debug.

3 Click the **Step Into** button on the Debug toolbar to run the current statement and then to move to the next line in the procedure.

4 Continue clicking the **Step Into** button to move through the procedure one line at a time, examining the results of the procedure as you go.

5 Click the **Stop** button on the Debug toolbar to halt the procedure at a specific line.

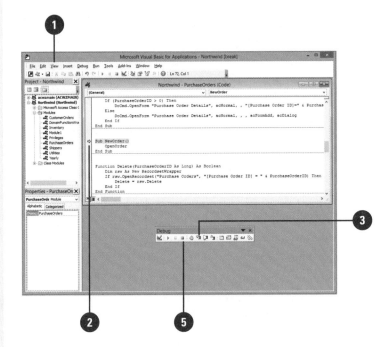

Identifying VBA Debugging Tools

Click to open the Immediate window.

Click to open the Locals window.

Click to Open the Watch window.

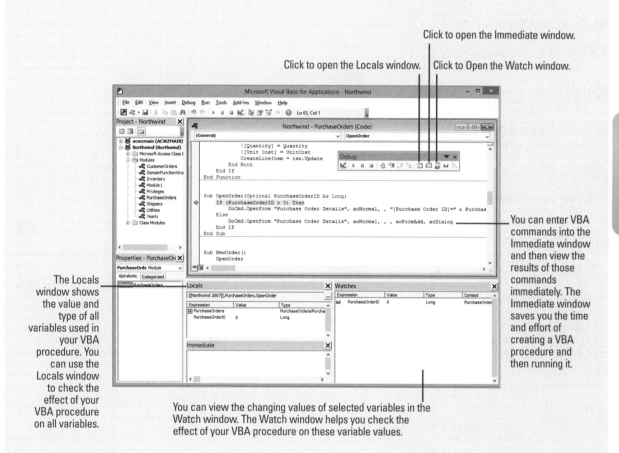

You can enter VBA commands into the Immediate window and then view the results of those commands immediately. The Immediate window saves you the time and effort of creating a VBA procedure and then running it.

The Locals window shows the value and type of all variables used in your VBA procedure. You can use the Locals window to check the effect of your VBA procedure on all variables.

You can view the changing values of selected variables in the Watch window. The Watch window helps you check the effect of your VBA procedure on these variable values.

Optimizing Performance with an ACCDE File

If you share your modules with others, you may want to convert the database file to ACCDE format. In creating an ACCDE file, Access removes the editable source code and then compacts the database. Your VBA programs will continue to run, but others cannot view or edit them. There are several advantages to converting a database to ACCDE format. In ACCDE format, a database is smaller, and its performance will improve as it optimizes memory usage. However, you should create an ACCDE file only after the original database has been thoroughly tested.

Make an ACCDE File

1. Open the database you want to save as an ACCDE database.

2. Click the **File** tab, and then click **Save As**.

3. Click **Save Database As**, and then click **Make ACCDE**.

4. Click the **Save As** button.

5. Specify a location.

6. Enter a name for the ACCDE file.

7. Click **Save**.

Did You Know?

You can save the original database. Make a backup copy of the original database. You'll need it if you have to edit your VBA modules or add new ones.

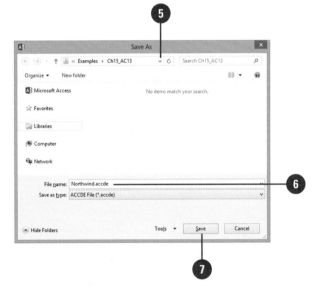

Creating a Web App with Access

16

Introduction

You can create two types of databases with Microsoft Access 2013: desktop or web app. A desktop database provides a traditional database, while a web app database provides a browser-based database app that uses SQL Azure or SQL Server. A desktop database resides on your local system, while a web app resides on a web site equipped with Access Services, such as Microsoft SharePoint Server 2013 or an Office 365 SharePoint site. A SharePoint server is a web hosting application that provides Internet Information Services (IIS). The Office 365 site is a subscription-based site that allows you to share and work with Office apps and documents on the web using SharePoint services. You'll need an Office 365 plan for business, either Small Business or Enterprise to create web apps. You can get a 30-day trial version to try it out.

If you have an Access 2010 web database, you can edit it in Access 2013. Unfortunately, you cannot update it to a web app. Instead, you need to create a new custom web app and then import the tables and recreate the forms.

After you create a web app, you need to add a table to it or use an existing one from a template for storing data. When you're finished creating a web app, it's already to use. All you need to do is click the Launch App button on the Home tab. Now, users can access your web app on the Internet and add information.

If you want to share your web app for others to use, you can create a package file to make it easier to distribute and use on a SharePoint site or as a template for use through an internal corporate site or the Office Store, either for free or a fee. Users can install it and then use Access installed on their computer to customize it. Others can use or modify your web app based on their permissions for the SharePoint site.

Creating a Web App

A web app (**New!**) in Access provides a browser-based database app that uses SQL Azure or SQL Server. A web app resides on a SharePoint server or Office 365 site—a subscription-based Microsoft SharePoint site—(**New!**), unlike a desktop database, which resides on your local system. A web app can be viewed, used and shared on the web. You can use a template to create a web app, or you can create a custom one from scratch. The Access web app templates help you create web app databases suited to your specific needs. Each template provides a complete out-of-the-box database with predefined fields, tables, queries, reports, and forms. If you can't find the template you want, additional templates are available at Office.com. If you need a custom web database, you create a custom web app (**New!**), and then you can add the tables, forms, and reports that make up the inner parts of the web app. When you create a web app database, you need to assign a name and web server location. To add a location for easy access, you can click Accounts (**New!**) on the File tab. As you work on the app, Access automatically saves it to the server periodically.

Create a Custom Web App

1. Start Access, or click the **File** tab and then click **New**.

    The Start or New screen opens, displaying templates and recently opened databases.

2. Click **Custom web app (New!)**.

3. Type in a name for the web app.

4. Select or specify the web server location (**New!**). For Office 365 help, click the help link.

5. Click **Create**.

6. At this point, create the inner parts of the custom web app:

    ◆ **Add Tables and Data.** Add tables and data to the web app.

    ◆ **Modify the Web App.** Select the table, and then click the **Edit** button.

7. To begin using the app in your browser, click the **Home** tab, and then click the **Launch App** button.

8. To close the app, click the **Close** button in the Access window or click the **File** tab, and then click **Close**.

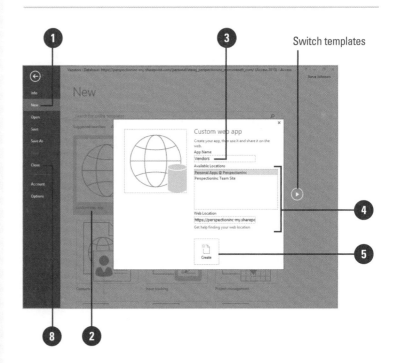

Switch templates

Create a Web App Using a Template

1. Start Access, or click the **File** tab and then click **New**.

    The Start or New screen opens, displaying templates and recently opened databases.

2. Click a suggested search (**New!**) or enter a search, and then select a category (**New!**).

3. Click the web app template you want.

    The icon for the web app includes a globe, while a desktop database doesn't.

4. Type in a name for the web app.

5. Select or specify the web server location (**New!**).

6. Click **Create**.

7. At this point, create the inner parts of the custom web app:

    ◆ **Add Tables and Data.** Add tables and data to the web app.

    ◆ **Modify the Web App.** Select the table, and then click the **Edit** button.

8. To begin using the app in your browser, click the **Home** tab, and then click the **Launch App** button.

9. To close the app, click the **Close** button in the Access window or click the **File** tab, and then click **Close**.

Did You Know?

You can check your server location or database name. If you open a web app and don't know its name or where it's used, click the File tab, and then click Info.

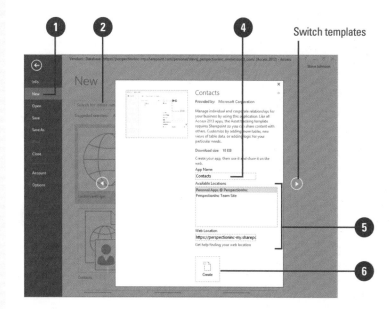

Switch templates

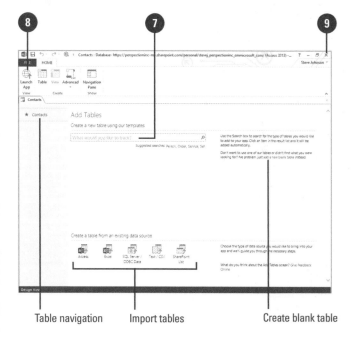

Table navigation   Import tables   Create blank table

Opening a Web App

After you created a web app on a SharePoint server, you can open it directly from the site just like you can open a desktop database. Access, like all Office 2013 programs, is integrated to work with online services (**New!**) to make it easier for you to open and save web apps directly from the File tab. Before you can use these online services, you need to add (connect) them to your Microsoft account. During the process, you'll need to provide a user name and password to establish a connection. With your SharePoint account connected, you can open and save web apps directly to a SharePoint site. If you don't have access to your own SharePoint site, you can subscribe to Office 365, a Microsoft web site with SharePoint services.

Open a Web App from SharePoint

1. Click the **File** tab, and then click **Open**.

2. Click the SharePoint name.

3. Click **Browse** or a recent folder.

4. Navigate to the site location with the web app, and then select the web app.

5. Click **Open**.

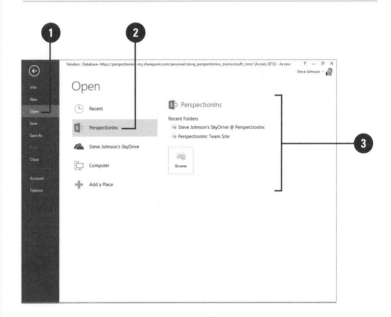

Did You Know?

You can add a place for easy access later. In the Open screen, click Add a Place, click Office 365 SharePoint or SkyDrive, and then follow the on-screen connection instructions.

See Also

See "Working with Accounts" on page 25 for more information on establishing a connection to a Office 365 Share-Point site.

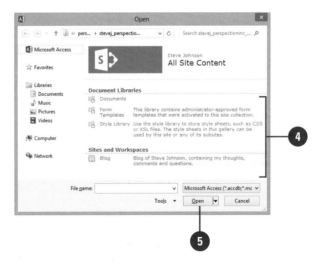

Open a Recently Opened Web App

1. Click the **File** tab, and then click **Open**.

    TIMESAVER *In the Start screen (***New!***), click a recent web app.*

2. Click **Recent** (**New!**).

3. To pin or unpin an Access file (desktop database or web app), point to a file (displays the pin):

    ◆ **Pin an Access file.** Click the **Pin** icon on the Recent list.

    ◆ **Unpin an Access file.** Click the **Unpin** icon to display a pin on the Recent list.

4. Click the web app you want to open.

    A web app appears with a globe icon.

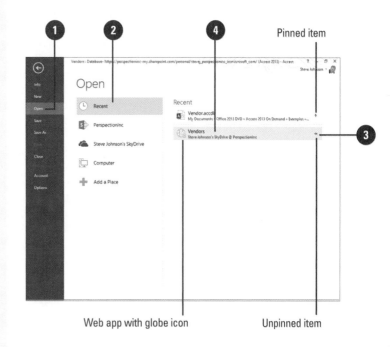

Pinned item

Web app with globe icon   Unpinned item

Open recent Access files on the Start screen

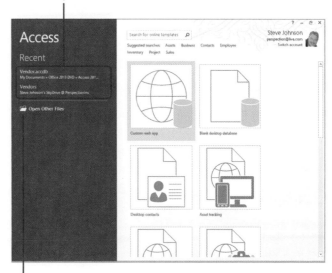

Click to open an Access file from the Open dialog box

Adding Tables and Data to a Web App

After you create a custom web app, you need to add a table to it for storing data. If you created a web app from a template (**New!**), it already contains predefined tables, however, you can always add your own custom tables. You can add a blank table or template table. Some template tables are related, so more than one table will be created. A multi-table icon indicates a table has related tables, which creates a relational database. Access creates views for each table (**New!**) that display data from related tables. After you create a table, you can enter data manually in Access or on the web in your browser. If you have existing data in an external source, such as an Access database, Microsoft Excel file, SQL Server/ODBC source, text files, or SharePoint List, you can import (**New!**) it into a web app. When you import from a SharePoint List, the data is only linked to its original source where the data can only be viewed and not edited. When you import data, Access creates a new table, which is not integrated with other tables, so you'll need to create relationships using a lookup field as desired.

Add a Table to a Web App

① In Access, open the web app, and then click the **Table** button (**New!**) on the Home tab.

◆ If you created a new web app, it automatically opens to this screen to add a table.

② Use any of the following to add a table:

◆ **Template Table.** Click a suggested search (**New!**) or enter a search (**New!**) and press Enter, and then click the template you want to use.

To cancel the search, click the **Close** button in the Search box.

◆ **Blank Table.** Click the **add a new blank table** link.

The new table appears in Design View.

③ To exit tables, click the **Table** button.

④ To add or modify data to tables in Access, select the table, click the **Settings** button (Gear icon), and then click **View Data**. When you're done, click the **Close** button.

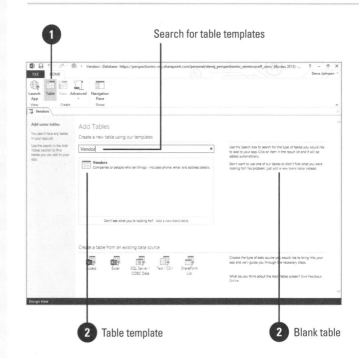

Search for table templates

② Table template   ② Blank table

Import Data into a Table in a Web App

1 In Access, open the web app, and then click the **Table** button (**New!**) on the Home tab.

◆ If you created a new web app, it automatically opens to this screen to add a table.

2 Click the icon for the type of data you want to import.

3 Click the **Browse** button.

4 Navigate to the folder location, select the import file, and then click **Open**.

5 Click **OK**.

6 Follow the on-screen instructions to import the data, and then click **Close**; steps vary depending on the data type.

7 To exit tables, click the **Table** button.

8 To add or modify data to tables in Access, select the table, click the **Settings** button (Gear icon), and then click **View Data**. When you're done, click the **Close** button.

Did You Know?

You can copy and paste data from Microsoft Excel. If you have a spreadsheet open, such as Microsoft Excel, you can also copy data and then paste it directly into one of the datasheet views in your web app.

You can open tables and objects in the Navigation pane. Click the Navigation pane button on the Home tab. It works just like the Navigation pane for a desktop database.

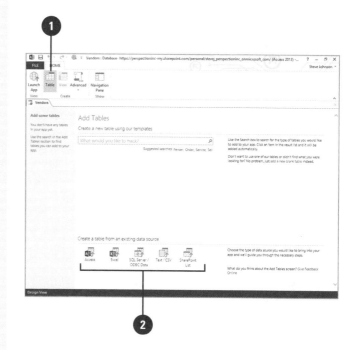

Viewing and Editing Data in a Web App

When you create a web app and add tables, Access automatically creates view, switchboards, and other user interface elements, so you don't have to do it. This provides a consistent way for users to navigate within web apps. With the built-in views, Access includes an Action Bar (**New!**) with buttons for adding, editing, saving, and deleting records. You can open the web app from Access or your browser by using the Launch App View button (**New!**) or within your browser by entering the URL for the SharePoint site. In your browser, you can navigate between tables, display records in List or Datasheet views, and use Action Bar buttons to view, enter, and edit data on the web. As you enter data, AutoComplete (**New!**) looks up data from related tables or drill through links (**New!**) to let you view details about a related item.

View or Edit Data in a Web App from Access

1. In Access, open the web app.

2. Click the **Table** button on the Home tab.

3. In the left pane, click the table you want to use.

4. Click the **Settings** button (Gear icon), and then click **View Data**.

    A table tab with the table data appears in Datasheet view.

5. To edit data, click a data cell, click to place the insertion point, modify the data, and then press Enter or click a different cell.

6. To add a data record, click the **Add** button or enter table data in the (New) row at the bottom of the table.

7. To delete a data record, select a cell in the data record, click the **Delete** button, and then click **Yes**.

8. To sort or filter table data, point to a table heading, click the down arrow, and then select a sort command or filter option.

9. When you're done, click the **Close** button for the table.

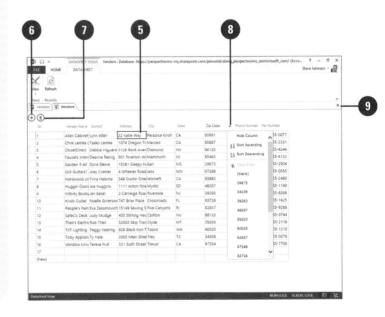

View or Edit Data in a Web App from a Web Browser

1. In Access, open the web app.

2. Click the **Launch App View** button on the Home tab. If prompted, sign-in to your site.

   Your default web browser opens, displaying your web app.

3. In the left pane, click the table you want to use.

4. Click **List**, **Datasheet**, or other custom view.

5. Select the record you want to view or modify.

   - **Search.** In List view, use the Search box to find a record.

6. Use the available buttons on the Action Bar:

   - **Add.** Adds a new record.
   - **Delete.** Deletes the current or selected record.
   - **Edit.** Modifies the current or selected record in List view. In Datasheet view, you can edit directly in the cell.
   - **Save.** Saves the added or edited record in List view.
   - **Close.** Closes the current record in List view.

7. To exit your browser and return to Access, click the **Settings** button (Gear icon), and then click **Customize in Access**.

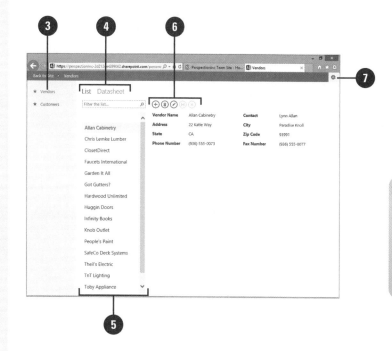

Did You Know?

You can rename or delete a table. Open the web app, click the Table button, select the table, click the Settings button, and then click Rename (then specify a name), or Delete (then confirm).

For Your Information

Hiding a Table in a Web Browser

If you don't want to display a table from a web app in a web browser, you can hide it. To hide a table, open the web app in Access, click the Table button, select the table you want to hide, click the Settings button, and then click Hide. The hidden table is dimmed out in the Tile pane. To show the table, select the table, click the Settings button, and then click Unhide.

Creating a View in a Web App

If the built-in views don't meet all your needs, you can create a customized view (**New!**). When you create a custom view, you specify a view name, select a view type, and the record source. The view types include List Details, Datasheet, Summary, or Blank. Each view includes the standard table navigation and Actions Bar buttons. After you create a custom view, you can open it in a browser, edit, rename, duplicate or delete it. When you delete a view, you are not deleting the data.

Create a Custom View in a Web App

1. In Access, open the web app.

2. Select the table you want to create a custom view.

3. Click the **View** button on the Home tab.

   TIMESAVER *Click the Add New View button (+) next to the current views.*

4. On the menu, specify the following:

   ◆ **View Name.** Provides a name for the view.

   ◆ **View Type.** Select a type.

      ◆ **List Details.** Displays a search list and one record.

      ◆ **Datasheet.** Displays a spreadsheet view.

      ◆ **Summary.** Displays List Details view with columns.

      ◆ **Blank.** Displays a blank page.

   ◆ **Record Source.** Specifies the data to display in the view.

5. Click **Add New View**.

   The custom view appears next to the built-in ones.

6. To edit or remove a view, select the view, click the **Settings** button (Gear icon), and then click an option: **Open in Browser**, **Edit**, **Rename**, **Duplicate**, or **Delete**.

Add New View button

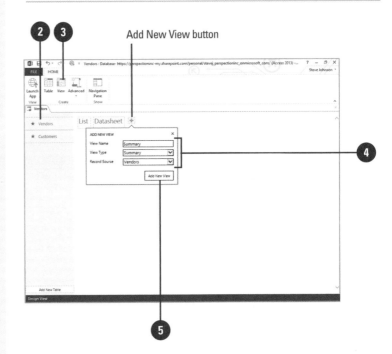

New view

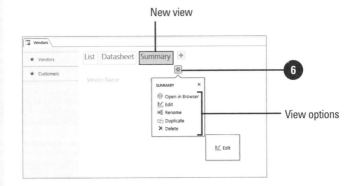

View options

Modify a Custom View in a Web App

① In Access, open the web app.

② Select the table you want to change a custom view.

③ Select the view you want to change.

④ Click the **Settings** button (Gear icon), and then **Edit**.

⑤ To change view properties, select the view (outside edge), and then click a property button next to the item:

◆ Data. Select a data table or query source.

◆ Formatting. Edit the view name.

◆ Actions. Click **On Click** or **After Update**, select one or more actions from the drop-down list or Action Catalog pane.

⑥ To change view controls, select the view control, click the **Data** button, and then specify the data related options you want; options vary depending on the type of control you select.

⑦ When you're done, click the **Close** button for the view.

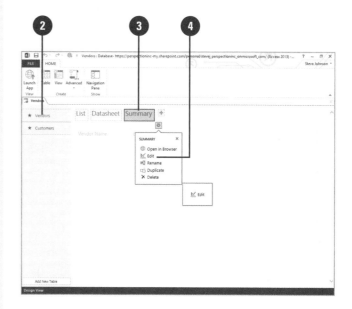

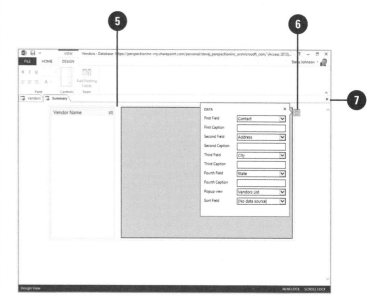

Did You Know?

You can rename, duplicate, or delete a custom view. Open the table with the custom view, select the view, click the Setting button, and then click Rename, Duplicate, or Delete. Specify a name or click Yes to confirm the deletion.

Modifying a Web App

After you create a web app using a template or by adding tables to a blank one, you can make changes to it based on your own needs. As you work with the web app in Access or your web browser, you can identify the changes you want, and then make them in Access. You can add, move, resize, or delete controls (**New!**)—such as a text box, label, button, image, AutoComplete, or hyperlink—as well as change properties. When you select a control or table, you can change property settings in three areas (**New!**): Data, Formatting, and Actions. If you want to add functionality to a control, you can add a macro to it using Actions (**New!**). To customize the web app, you can add buttons to the Action Bar (**New!**) to execute a macro action as well as change properties.

Modify a Web App

1. In Access, open the web app.

2. In the left pane, click the table you want to use.

3. Click **List**, **Datasheet**, or other custom view.

4. Click the **Edit** button in the middle of the view.

   The Design tab under View appears, display design options.

5. To add controls, use either of the following:

   ◆ **Ribbon.** Click a control button on the Design tab.

   ◆ **Field List.** Click the **Add Existing Fields** button, and then double-click or drag a field into the view.

6. To modify the layout, do any of the following:

   ◆ **Move.** Point to a control (cursor changes to a four-headed arrow), and then drag.

   ◆ **Resize.** Point to the end of a control (cursor changes to a two-headed arrow), and then drag.

   ◆ **Delete.** Select a control, and then press Delete. When you delete a control, you are not deleting the data.

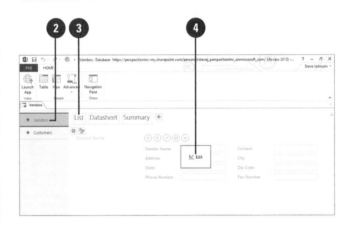

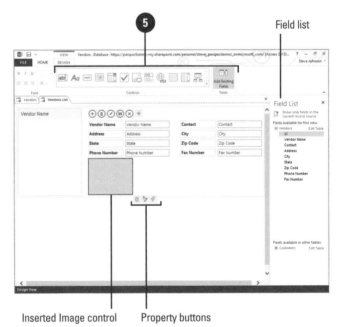

Field list

Inserted Image control   Property buttons

7. To change properties, select the control, and then click a property button next to the item; options vary depending on the control:

- ♦ **Data.** Specify a control name, source, and default value.
- ♦ **Formatting.** Specify a Tooltip, Visible or Hidden, Enable or not, and an Input Hint.
- ♦ **Actions.** Click **On Click** or **After Update**, select one or more actions from the drop-down list or Action Catalog pane.

8. To change table properties, click outside the table to select it, and then click a property button next to the item:

- ♦ **Data.** Select a record source.
- ♦ **Formatting.** Specify ActionBar Visible or Hidden, and a Caption title.
- ♦ **Actions.** Click **On Load** or **On Current Update**, select one or more actions from the drop-down list or Action Catalog pane.

9. To add a custom macro action to the Action Bar, do the following:

- ♦ Click the **Add custom action** button, and then click the **Data** button.
- ♦ Specify a name and Tooltip, and then select a button icon.
- ♦ Click **On Click**, select one or more actions from the drop-down list or Action Catalog pane.
- ♦ Click the **Save** button on the Design tab under Macro Tools, and then click the **Close** button.

10. Click the **Save** button on the Quick Access Toolbar to save the web app.

6   Selected control

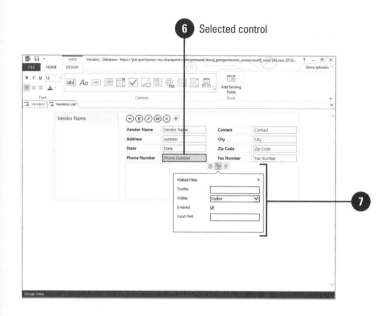

7

Add custom action button

New Action Bar button   Data button

10

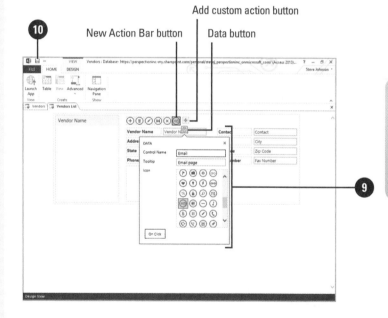

9

Changing Properties in a Web App

When you select a table or control, you can change property settings in three areas (**New!**): Data, Formatting, and Actions. You can access property settings when you select a table or individual control, such as a text box, label, button, Web Browser, combo box, check box, image, AutoComplete, or hyperlink, and then click the Data, Formatting, or Actions button next to the element. The property options vary depending on the selected element, either a table or control. The **Data** button allows you to select a data source for a table or field. The **Formatting** button allows you to specify whether an element is visible or hidden and add a caption or tooltip. The **Actions** button allows you to create a macro to add functionality to your web app.

Change Table Properties in a Web App

1. In Access, open the web app.

2. In the left pane, click the table you want to use.

3. Click **List**, **Datasheet**, or other custom view.

4. Click the **Edit** button in the middle of the view.

   The Design tab under View appears, display design options.

5. Click outside the table to select it.

6. Click a property button next to the selected table:

   ◆ Data. Select a record source.

   ◆ Formatting. Specify ActionBar Visible or Hidden, and a Caption title.

   ◆ Actions. Click **On Load** or **On Current Update**, select one or more actions from the drop-down list or Action Catalog pane.

7. Click the **Save** button on the Quick Access Toolbar to save the web app.

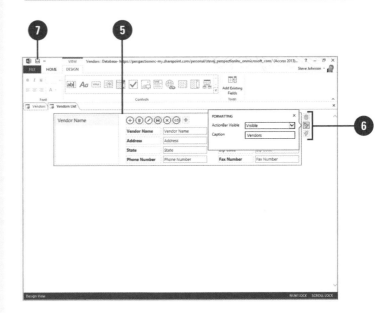

Change Control Properties in a Web App

1. In Access, open the web app.

2. In the left pane, click the table you want to use.

3. Click **List**, **Datasheet**, or other custom view.

4. Click the **Edit** button in the middle of the view.

   The Design tab under View appears, display design options.

5. Select the control you want to change.

6. Click a property button next to the item; options vary depending on the control:

   ◆ Data. Specify a control name, source, and default value.

   ◆ Formatting. Specify a Tooltip, Visible or Hidden, Enable or not, and an Input Hint.

   ◆ Actions. Click **On Click** or **After Update**, select one or more actions from the drop-down list or Action Catalog pane.

7. Click the **Save** button on the Quick Access Toolbar to save the web app.

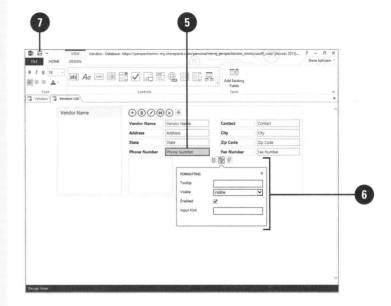

Creating Actions in a Web App

If you want to add functionality to a web app, you can add a macro to it. You can create a macro or data macro using the Advanced button on the Home tab or create a macro and assign it to an Action button using the Add Custom Action button (**New!**). A **macro** is a series of functions to automate a task, such as GoToRecord, MessageBox, SetProperty. A **data macro** is a macro attached to a table of data events, such as add, update, delete, or validate data. Creating a macro may require some knowledge of the SQL language to set criteria and access data in the web app, which is outside the scope of this book and can be found on the web. After you create a macro, you can assign it to an action button on the Action Bar (**New!**) for easy access in the web app.

Create a Macro for a Web App

1. In Access, open the web app.

2. Click the **Advanced** button on the Home tab, and then click **Macro** or **Data Macro**.

   A new macro opens and the Design tab under Macro Tools.

3. To create a parameter to use in a data macro, click **Create Parameter**, enter a name, select a type, and enter a description.

4. Select one or more functions from the **Add New Action** list or drag them from Action Catalog pane.

5. Specify the criteria or conditions you want for the selected function.

6. To manage the items in a macro, do any of the following:

   ◆ **Delete.** Click the **Delete** button (x) next to it.

   ◆ **Collapse or Expand.** Click the **Collapse** (-) or **Expand** (+) icon.

7. Click the **Save** button on the Quick Access Toolbar to save the web app. Specify a name, and then click **OK**.

8. When you're done, click the **Close** button.

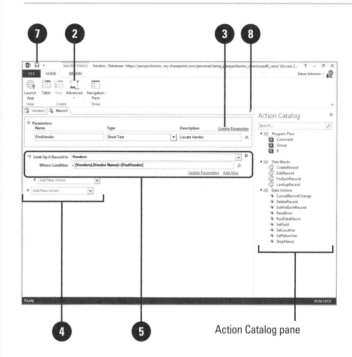

Action Catalog pane

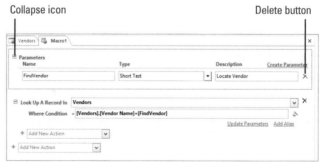

Collapse icon   Delete button

Create an Action Button in a Web App

1. In Access, open the web app.

2. In the left pane, click the table you want to use.

3. Click **List**, **Datasheet**, or other custom view.

4. Click the **Edit** button in the middle of the view.

   The Design tab under View appears, display design options.

5. Click the **Add custom action** button.

   A new Action Bar button appears selected. When the button is selected, a Data button appears.

6. Click the **Data** button.

7. Specify a name and Tooltip, and then select a button icon.

8. Click **On Click**.

   A new macro opens along with the Design tab under Macro Tools.

9. Create a new macro or use an existing one.

   ◆ **Create a New Macro.** From the Add New Action list, select an action or drag one from the Action Catalog pane.

   ◆ **Use an Existing Macro.** From the Add New Action list, select **RunMacro** or **RunDataMacro**.

10. Specify the criteria or conditions you want for the selected action, if needed.

11. Click the **Save** button on the Design tab under Macro Tools.

12. Click the **Close** button on the Design tab under Macro Tools.

13. Click the **Save** button on the Quick Access Toolbar to save the web app.

New Action Bar button

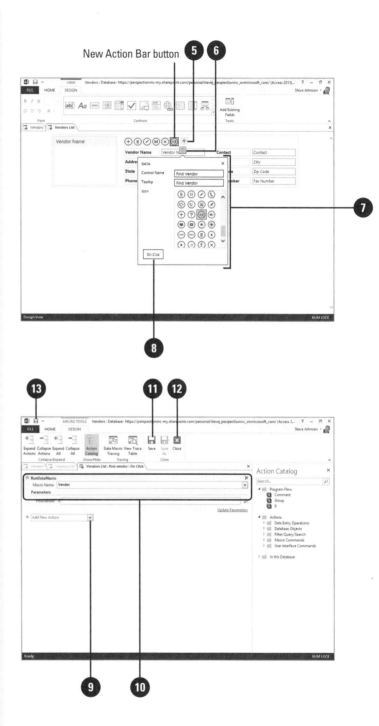

Creating Database Objects in Web Apps

In addition to the custom web related features you can include in a web app, you can also add desktop database objects to a web app (**New!**). You can create a Query, Blank View, List View, Datasheet View, Macro, Data Macro, or On Start Macro. The On Start Macro—similar to the AutoExec macro (for a desktop database)—runs when you open the web app in a web browser. You can create these objects in a web app just like you can in a desktop database. After you access the command in the web app to create the object, the process to complete it is the same in a desktop database.

Create Database Objects and Views in Web Apps

1. In Access, open the web app.

2. Click the **Advanced** button on the Home tab.

3. On the menu, click the type of object you want to create:

   ◆ **Query.** Add the tables/queries you want, and then specify the sort/filter criteria. A query is a criteria-based data search.

   ◆ **Blank View.** Drag the fields you want in the view from the Field List.

   ◆ **List View.** Specify the controls and fields you want in the view.

   ◆ **Datasheet View.** Specify the controls and fields you want in the view.

   ◆ **Macro.** Use the Action Catalog pane to specify the actions you want for the macro. A macro is a series of commands for a task that you can execute to automate it.

   ◆ **Data Macro.** Specify the macro actions you want for table data events.

   ◆ **On Start Macro.** Specify the macro you want to run when you start the web app in a web browser.

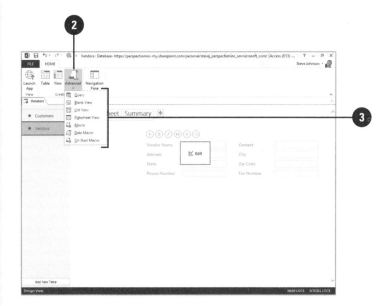

Using the Navigation Pane with Web Apps

The Navigation pane is a central place for accessing all the objects in a web app (**New!**), just like with a desktop database. These objects work together to help you store and manage your data. Objects are organized into categories, such as tables or forms, by object type in the Navigation pane. With the Navigation pane, you can view the objects in a web app, and open objects to view or edit them. You can change the Navigation pane display. You can click Object bars on the Navigation pane to expand or collapse objects in categories or use the Search box to find objects in a long list.

Use the Navigation Pane with Web Apps

1. In Access, open the web app.

2. Click the **Navigation Pane** button on the Home tab to show or hide the Navigation pane.

3. Click the Object bar you want to expand and view objects.

   ◆ When you click an Object bar, the object display expands or collapses.

4. To search for an object, click in the Search box, type the criteria you want.

   As you type, the objects that match the criteria appear in the Navigation pane.

   ◆ To cancel the search, click the **Clear Search String** button.

5. To open an object, double-click the object in the Navigation pane.

   ◆ To close an object, click the **Close** button for the object.

6. To close the Navigation pane, click the **Navigation Pane** button on the Home tab or click the **Shutter Bar Open/Close** button on the Navigation pane.

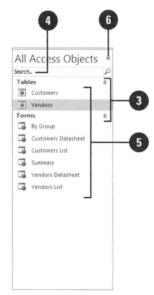

Launching a Web App in a Web Browser

You can open a web app from Access or your browser by using the Launch App View button (**New!**) or within your browser by entering the URL for the SharePoint site. You can find out and view the URL for a web app when you open it in Access. In your browser, you can navigate between tables, display records in List or Datasheet views, and use Action Bar buttons to view, enter, and edit data on the web. As you enter data, AutoComplete (**New!**) looks up data from related tables or drill through links (**New!**) to let you view details about a related item.

Launch a Web App in a Web Browser from Access

1. In Access, open the web app.

2. Click the **Launch App View** button on the Home tab. If prompted, sign-in to your site.

   Your default web browser opens, displaying your web app.

3. In the left pane, click the table you want to use.

4. Click **List**, **Datasheet**, or other custom view.

5. Select the record you want to view or modify.

   ◆ **Search.** In List view, use the Search box to find a record.

6. Use the available buttons on the Action Bar:

   ◆ **Add.** Adds a new record.

   ◆ **Delete.** Deletes the current or selected record.

   ◆ **Edit.** Modifies the current or selected record in List view. In Datasheet view, you can edit directly in the cell.

   ◆ **Save.** Saves the added or edited record in List view.

   ◆ **Close.** Closes the current record in List view.

7. To exit your browser and return to Access, click the **Settings** button (Gear icon), and then click **Customize in Access**.

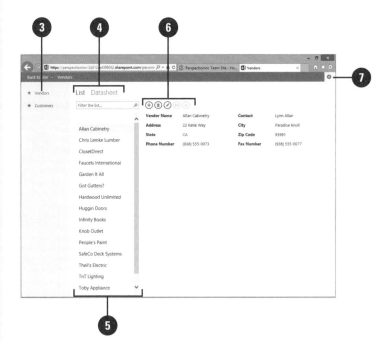

Launch a Web App in a Web Browser

1. Open your web browser.

2. Enter the complete URL to the web app on the SharePoint site, and then sign in.

   Your default web browser opens, displaying your web app.

   ◆ **Get URL.** When you open the web app in Access, the URL appears at the top of the screen or on the Info screen (on the File tab).

   ◆ **Copy URL.** In Access, right-click the web app in the Recent list, and then click **Copy path to clipboard**. You can paste it in the Address bar.

3. In the left pane, click the table you want to use.

4. Click **List**, **Datasheet**, or other custom view.

5. Select the record you want to view or modify.

   ◆ **Search.** In List view, use the Search box to find a record.

6. Use the available buttons on the Action Bar:

   ◆ **Add.** Adds a new record.

   ◆ **Delete.** Deletes the current or selected record.

   ◆ **Edit.** Modifies the current or selected record in List view. In Datasheet view, you can edit directly in the cell.

   ◆ **Save.** Saves the added or edited record in List view.

   ◆ **Close.** Closes the current record in List view.

7. To exit your browser, click the **Close** button.

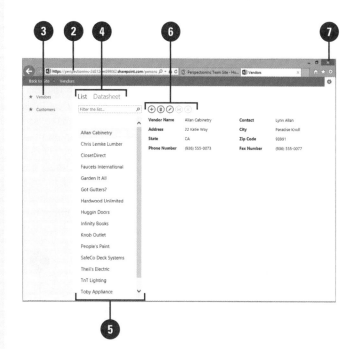

Packaging a Web App

When you're finished creating a web app, you can allow others to use it on a SharePoint or Office 365 site. You can create a package file (**New!**) of your web app to make it easier to distribute and share with others. Access automatically saves your web app periodically, so creating a package is also a good way to create different versions or a backup of your web app. You can create a package with just the design of the app or include any data you have entered in it. After you package the web app, you can make it available on a SharePoint site or as a template for use through an internal site or the Office Store, either for free or a fee. Users can install it and then use Access installed on their computer to customize it. Others can use or modify your web app based on their permissions—Designer, Author, and Reader—on the SharePoint site. Designers can make design changes to views and tables; Authors can change data, but not the design; and Readers can only read data.

Package a Web App

1. In Access, open the web app.

2. Click the **File** tab, and then click **Save As**.

3. Click **Save Database As**.

4. Click **Save as Package**.

   The Create New Package from This App dialog box opens.

5. Enter a name for the web app package.

6. To save the data along with the design, select the **Include Data in Package** check box.

7. Click **OK**.

8. Specify a name and location, and then click **OK**.

   Access saves the file as an App Package with the APP extension.

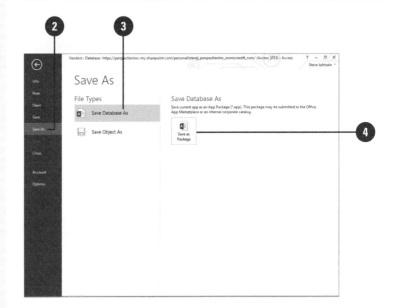

Working with a Web App on SharePoint

In addition to opening a web app from Access or your browser, you can also access and work with web app data (**New!**) from a SharePoint site. You can access a SharePoint site, such as Office 365, and then navigate to the site contents where you can view and work with lists, libraries, and other apps on the site. If you have saved a web app from Access on a SharePoint site, you can view and work with its contents in your web browser.

Work with a Web App on a SharePoint Site

1. Open your web browser, go to SharePoint Team Site web address or *www.office365.com*, and then sign in.

2. Navigate to the SharePoint site. For Office 365 SharePoint, click **Sites**, and then click **Team Site**.

3. Display the site contents.

4. Click the web app from the site contents list.

5. View or edit the contents of the web app.

   ◆ **View contents.** Scroll to view the contents of the web app.

   ◆ **Edit contents.** Click to select a data cell, and then edit it.

   ◆ **More options.** Click the **More Options** button (3 dots) to display a context menu with options.

6. To exit your browser, click the **Close** button.

See Also

See "Signing in to SharePoint or SkyDrive" on page 428 for information on signing in to Office 365 SharePoint.

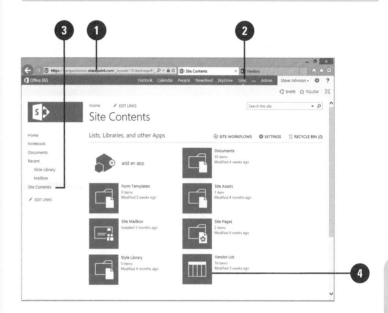

More Options button

Changing Web App Settings on SharePoint

After you save or install a web app on a SharePoint site, such as Office 365, you can change settings on the SharePoint site to customize permissions and management for the web app (**New!**). You can also change a variety of general settings, such as versioning, validation, rating, audience targeting, and forms, as well as the permission and management settings for online use. You can also get the direct web address for the web app that you or others can use to directly access it from a browser.

Change Web App Settings on a SharePoint Site

1. Open your web browser, go to SharePoint Team Site web address or *www.office365.com*, and then sign in.

2. Navigate to the SharePoint site. For Office 365 SharePoint, click **Sites**, and then click **Team Site**.

3. Display the site contents.

4. Point to the web app from the site contents list, and then click the **More Options** button (3 dots).

5. Click **Settings**.

6. Change web app settings or view the web address:

   ◆ **Settings.** Click a link, select the options you want, and then click **OK** or click the **Back** button on your browser.

   ◆ **Web Address.** Use this address to directly access the web app in a browser.

7. To exit your browser, click the **Close** button.

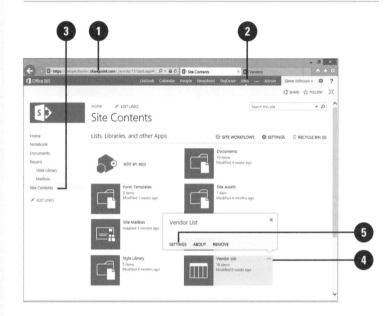

Web address

Did You Know?

You can remove a web app on SharePoint. In your browser, display the site contents, point to the web app, click the More Options button (3 dots), and then click Remove.

Adding a Web App from the SharePoint Store

In addition to creating web apps using templates on the Start or New screen, you can also add and use web apps from the SharePoint Store (**New!**). Some of the web apps charge a fee, while others are free. You can search for web apps by price or category in order to find the ones you want. After you install a web app (which takes almost no time at all) to your SharePoint site from the SharePoint Store, you can use it online as well as customize it back in Access.

Add a Web App from the SharePoint Store

1. Open your web browser, go to SharePoint Team Site web address or *www.office365.com*, and then sign in.

2. Navigate to the SharePoint site. For Office 365 SharePoint, click **Sites**, and then click **Team Site**.

3. Display the site contents.

4. Click **add an app**.

5. Click **SharePoint Store**.

6. Click the app icon you want, and then click **Add It**.

   Your app is installed to your SharePoint site, which you can start using online.

7. To customize the app in Access, click the **Settings** icon (Gear icon), and then click **Customize in Access**.

8. To exit your browser, click the **Close** button.

Working Online with Office Documents

Introduction

Instead of storing and working on Office documents on your desktop, you can store them on the web and work on them with an Office Web App. An Office Web App allows you to work with an Office document in a web browser. The process of using the web instead of a desktop as a base of operation is known as **cloud computing**. SkyDrive and SharePoint are two types of cloud computing sites, where you can store and share information. SkyDrive is a free service provided by Microsoft, which is available at *www.skydrive.com* with a Microsoft account, while SharePoint is web server software created by Microsoft.

When you store an Office document on SkyDrive or on a Microsoft SharePoint server configured with Office Web Apps, such as Office 365 SharePoint, a subscription-based service provided by Microsoft, you can view or edit the document in a web browser using the same look and feel as an Office 2013 program. To make storing files on SkyDrive or SharePoint quick and easy, Office 2013 programs provide command on the Save As screen on the File tab for you to save Office documents directly to a SkyDrive or SharePoint folder.

If you have a Windows Phone, Apple iOS (iPhone and iPad), BlackBerry, or Android, you can use your web browser or Office Web Apps to work with your Office documents from anywhere. You can view and edit Office documents stored on your phone, sent to you as e-mail attachments, or stored on a SkyDrive or SharePoint site. Since the files are synced online, the changes you make on your mobile device are available on your desktop too.

What You'll Do

Work Online with SharePoint and SkyDrive

Sign in to SharePoint or SkyDrive

Save and Open on SharePoint or SkyDrive

Access Documents on SharePoint

Sync Documents on SharePoint

Share Documents on SkyDrive

Access Documents on SkyDrive

Manage Documents on SkyDrive

Download or Upload Documents on SkyDrive

Create Office Documents on SkyDrive

Send Links to Documents on SkyDrive

Compare the Office Desktop App to the Web App

Work with Office Web Apps

Save or Print Documents in Office Web Apps

Co-author Documents with Office Web Apps

Block Co-authoring Documents

Working Online with SharePoint and SkyDrive

Office 2013 is integrated to work with online services (**New!**) to make it easier for you to save and open Office documents on other devices and share Office documents with others. Office provides two main online services: SkyDrive and SharePoint. **SkyDrive** is a personal cloud storage and sharing system on the web provided as a free service by Microsoft at *www.skydrive.com* with a Microsoft account. You can store and share information, such as contacts, e-mail (using hotmail), photos, and files. Microsoft **SharePoint** server is an organizational cloud storage, sharing, and tracking system with customizable apps hosted on the web by an organization. Instead of setting up your own SharePoint site, you can use **Office 365**, a subscription-based Microsoft web site with SharePoint services that allows you to take advantage of expanded cloud capabilities.

Connecting to a SkyDrive or SharePoint Site

You can access and connect to a SkyDrive and SharePoint site by using your web browser or any Office 2013 program. For SkyDrive, you can also use a stand-alone app, such as SkyDrive (Win 8) or SkyDrive for Windows (Win 7 or 8)—an app downloaded from the SkyDrive site that allows you to access files from Windows Explorer.

In order to connect to SkyDrive or SharePoint from Office, you need to sign in and connect with your account. When you set up Office 2013, it requests a Microsoft account to work with SkyDrive and other online services. However, you can add other accounts for Office 365 SharePoint and other online services, such as Facebook, Twitter, Linkedin, and Flickr. To access account settings in Office, click the user name (upper-right corner of any Office program), and then click an account option, or click the File tab, and then click Accounts. You can add, switch, or modify accounts or sign out entirely.

SkyDrive or SkyDrive Pro?

When you install Office 2013, you also get a helpful tool called SkyDrive Pro (**New!**). The name is similar to SkyDrive, however it works with SharePoint, not SkyDrive personal. A SharePoint site includes its own SkyDrive as well as other Document Libraries. With SkyDrive Pro, you can connect to and synchronize the contents of a SkyDrive or Document Library on a SharePoint or Office 365 site with a folder on your desktop. SkyDrive Pro performs the same function for SharePoint sites as the stand-alone SkyDrive apps—SkyDrive (Win 8) or SkyDrive for Windows (Win 7 or 8)—do for a personal SkyDrive.

Using a SkyDrive or SharePoint Site from Office

In Office 2013, you can save and open documents directly to a SkyDrive or SharePoint site. With your Office documents on a SkyDrive or SharePoint site, you can do a lot of things. You can sync the files from the SkyDrive or SharePoint site to your desktop or other devices, such as a tablet or mobile phone for easy access from anywhere. You can view or edit Office documents online from an Office program or Office Web App, and get access to files even when you're offline. You can share a document with other people using e-mail or social networks (**New!**) and even work on the same Office document at the same time with more than one person (**New!**).

Using Office 365

Office 365 is a subscription-based Microsoft web site with SharePoint services that provides cloud-based storage and sync capabilities to keep your Office content up-to-date everywhere. Office 365 provides web-based collaboration and sharing that allows you to work with Outlook mail, calendar, people, newsfeed, SkyDrive, and SharePoint Team sites and public web sites. Newsfeed lets you follow documents, sites and people to track what they are doing. You can also collaborate with instant messaging, video/audio conferencing and online meetings with Lync. In Outlook, you can access Site Mailboxes (**New!**) with e-mail and documents in the same place. You can access Office 365 at *www.office365.com*, where you can sign up for a subscription or trial.

Using Office Web Apps

An Office Web App allows you to work with an Office document in a web browser. When you store an Office document on a SkyDrive or SharePoint site, you can view or edit the document in a web browser using the same look and feel as an Office 2013 program, although some what limited in functionality. Office Web Apps provide a web-based version of Word, Excel, PowerPoint, and OneNote (**New!**). For a SharePoint site, Access and Lync are also available. You can view Office documents in a web browser using a Web App or edit the document in the desktop Office program.

Using Office on Mobile Devices

If you have a Windows Phone, Apple iOS (iPhone and iPad), BlackBerry, or Android, you can use your web browser or Office Web Apps to work with your Office documents from any-where. You can view and edit Office documents stored on your phone, sent to you as e-mail attachments, or stored on a SkyDrive or SharePoint site. Since the files are synced online, the changes you make on your mobile device are available on your desktop too.

Using Office Co-authoring

If you're working on a SharePoint site, you can have multiple authors work on the same Office document from a Document Library at the same time without intruding on one another's work or locking out other users. When multiple authors are working on the same document, you can see who is editing the document and where they are working in the Status bar or on the File tab Info screen. Any changes made by other authors get merged into the main document where you can review and modify them. You can co-author Office documents using Word, Excel, PowerPoint, and Visio Professional (**New!**) as well as Word Web App (**New!**) and PowerPoint App (**New!**), which include support for comments and revision marks (**New!**).

Word Web App in a web browser

Signing in to SharePoint or SkyDrive

Office provides access to two main online services: SkyDrive and SharePoint. SkyDrive personal is a free storage and sharing service provided by Microsoft. SharePoint is a web-hosted server for storage, sharing, and tracking documents. Instead of setting up your own SharePoint site, you can use Office 365 SharePoint, a subscription-based service provided by Microsoft. Before you can work with Office documents on SkyDrive or SharePoint, you need to create a Microsoft account for SkyDrive or a site account for SharePoint. When you set up Office 2013, it requests a Microsoft account to work with online services, such as SkyDrive. If you already have a Hotmail, Messenger, Windows Live, or Xbox Live account, you can use it as your Microsoft account. To get a SharePoint account, you need to contact your site administrator or sign up for Office 365. After you establish accounts, you need to add them to Office in order to work seamlessly with the online services (**New!**).

Sign in to Office 365 SharePoint

1. Open your web browser, and go to *www.office365.com*.

2. If you don't have an account, click the link to get a free trial. Follow the online instructions to create the account.

3. Click the **Sign in** link.

4. Enter your User ID and Password for your Office 365 account.

5. Select the **Remember me** and/or **Keep me signed in** check boxes to speed up sign in process in the future. However, it allows others who have access to your computer to sign in.

6. Click **Sign in**.

   Your Office 365 SharePoint site appears in your web browser.

7. To sign out, click the Account Name on the toolbar, and then click **Sign out**.

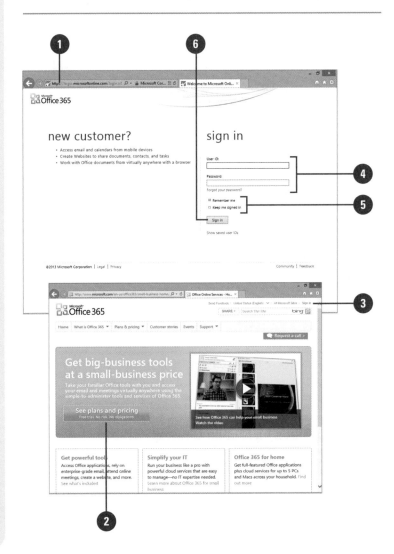

Sign in to SkyDrive

1. Open your web browser, and go to *www.skydrive.com*.

2. If you don't have a Microsoft account, click the link to get a free account. Follow the online instructions to create the account.

3. Enter you Microsoft account user name and password.

4. Select the **Keep me signed in** check box to speed up sign in process in the future. However, it allows others who have access to your computer to sign in.

5. Click **Sign in**.

   Your SkyDrive site appears in your web browser.

6. To sign out, click the Account Name on the toolbar, and then click **Sign out**.

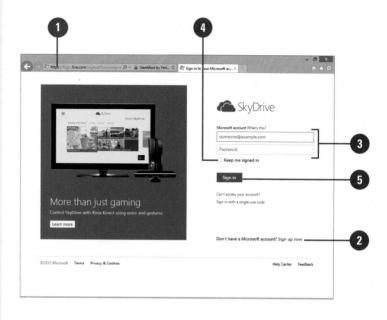

Add Online Storage Services

1. Click the **File** tab, and then click **Account** (**New!**).

2. Click **Add a service** (**New!**), and then point to **Storage**.

3. Click **Office 365 SharePoint** or **SkyDrive**, and then follow the on-screen connection instructions to sign in and add the service.

4. Click the **Back** button to exit the File tab.

Saving and Opening on SharePoint or SkyDrive

Office is integrated to work with online services (**New!**) to make it easier for you to save and open Office documents on other devices and share Office documents with others. With your Microsoft or SharePoint account, you can save Office documents directly to a SkyDrive (**New!**), a cloud-based online storage system, or Office 365, a Microsoft web site with SharePoint services. When you save documents online, you can have multiple authors work on the same Office document from the server at the same time (**New!**). Before you can use these online services, you need to add (connect) them to Office 2013. During the process, you'll need to provide a user name and password to establish a connection.

Save an Office Document to SharePoint or SkyDrive

1. Create or open an Office document.

2. Click the **File** tab, and then click **Save As**.

3. Click the SkyDrive or SharePoint name.

    ◆ **Sign in.** If prompted, sign-in to your account.

4. Click **Browse** or a recent folder.

5. Navigate to the location where you want to save the file.

6. Type a document file name.

7. Click the **Save as type** list arrow, and then click **<Program> <Document>**, such as PowerPoint Presentation, Word Document, or Excel Workbook.

8. Click **Save**.

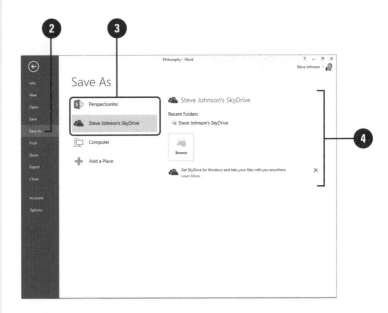

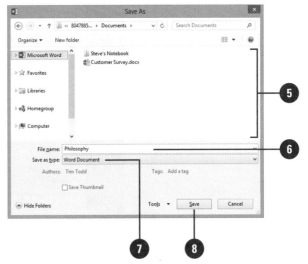

Open an Office Document from SharePoint or SkyDrive

① Click the **File** tab, and then click **Open**.

② Click the SkyDrive or SharePoint name.

③ Click **Browse** or a recent folder.

④ Navigate to the location where you want to open the file, and then select the Office file.

⑤ Click **Open**.

Did You Know?

You can add a place for easy access later. In the Open or Save As screen, click Add a Place, click Office 365 SharePoint or SkyDrive, and then follow the on-screen connection instructions.

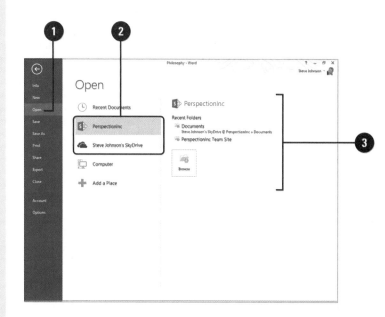

Office 365 SharePoint

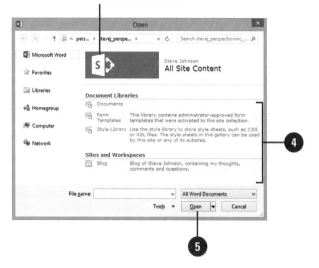

Accessing Documents on SharePoint

Any Office document that resides on SharePoint (**New!**) can be accessed from any computer or device that has an Internet connection. You can access Office documents on SharePoint using your web browser or File Explorer on your desktop. In your web browser, you can navigate to a document and then open it in an Office Web App. An Office Web App provides a subset of the features in the desktop version. In your desktop, you can open File Explorer, navigate to a document in a SharePoint Document Library or SkyDrive Pro (**New!**), and then open it in the Office Desktop App. SkyDrive Pro is SkyDrive on SharePoint, which is separate and different from SkyDrive personal.

Access SharePoint in a Web Browser

1. Open your web browser, go to SharePoint Team Site web address or *www.office365.com*, and then sign in.

2. Navigate to the SharePoint or SkyDrive folders:
   - **SharePoint.** Click **Sites**, click **Team Site**, and then click a library.
   - **SkyDrive.** Click **SkyDrive**.

3. Click a folder icon to navigate to the folder with the Office document.

4. To navigate back to a previous location, click a navigation or Home link, or click the Back button.

5. To manage files, select the files or folders you want to work with, click the **Files** tab, and then use the toolbar buttons, such as Create Folder, Delete, Upload Document, Download Copy, or Share.

6. To open an Office document in the Office Web App, click the document name link.
   - To edit the document, click the **Edit <document>** menu, and then click **Edit in <program>** or **Edit in <program> Web App**.
   - To exit and return, click the **File** tab, and then click **Exit**.

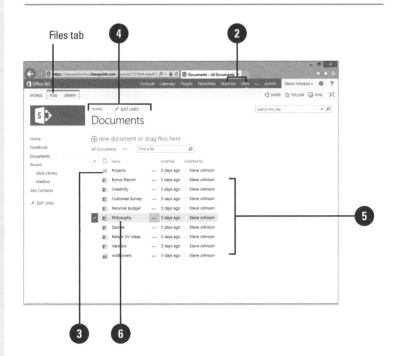

Files tab

Access SharePoint from a Desktop

① In the Start screen, click the Desktop tile (Win 8).

② Click the **File Explorer** icon on the taskbar.

③ In the Navigate pane under Favorites, click either of the following:

   ◆ **SharePoint.** Opens the Document Library folders on the SharePoint Team Site.

   ◆ **SkyDrive Pro.** Opens the Documents folder on the SharePoint SkyDrive.

④ Click a folder icon to navigate to the folder with the Office document.

⑤ To add or remove files, use the following:

   ◆ Add. Copy and paste or drag files to the folder.

   ◆ Remove. Select the files, and then click the **Delete** button on the Home tab.

   The folders are synchronized for both locations, desktop and site.

⑥ To open an Office document in the Office Desktop App, double-click the document icon.

   ◆ To exit, click the **Close** button.

See Also

See "Syncing Documents on SharePoint" on page 434 for information on setting up to use SkyDrive Pro for SharePoint.

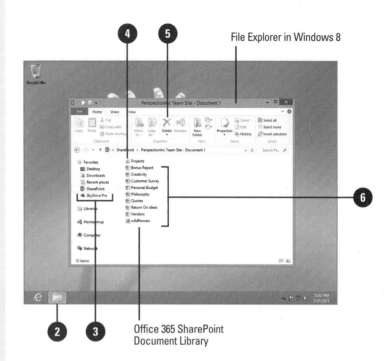

File Explorer in Windows 8

Office 365 SharePoint Document Library

Syncing Documents on SharePoint

With SkyDrive Pro (**New!**), you can connect to and sync the contents of a SkyDrive or Document Library on a SharePoint (Team Site) or Office 365 site with a folder on your desktop. You can set up the sync by entering a site address to the SkyDrive or Document Library or using the SYNC button on the SharePoint or Office 365 site for the open SkyDrive or Document Library. After creating a connection, you'll notice a SkyDrive Pro cloud icon on the notification tray in the taskbar, which you can use to access the desktop folder or modify syncing options. SkyDrive Pro syncs to your user folder by default, though you can change the location. In the Open and Save As dialog boxes in Office programs or in an Explorer window in Windows, you can select the site —SharePoint or SkyDrive Pro—from the Favorites list to access your files.

Set Up or Change SkyDrive Pro for SharePoint

1. Start **SkyDrive Pro 2013**.

    ◆ **Windows 8.** Click the tile on the Start screen.

    ◆ **Windows 7.** Click **Start** on the taskbar, point to **All Programs**, and then point to **Microsoft Office**.

    ◆ **Office 365 Site.** Click **SkyDrive** or **Sites**, display the library to sync, and then click **SYNC** on the toolbar.

    The site is connected to your system or a dialog box opens.

2. Enter the URL address to the SkyDrive or Document library on the SharePoint or Office 365 site.

3. To change the desktop folder, click the **Change** link.

4. Click **Sync Now**.

    After you setup SkyDrive Pro, starting the program opens the folder on your desktop.

Office 365 SharePoint SkyDrive

Click to select a SkyDrive or SharePoint site (Libraries)

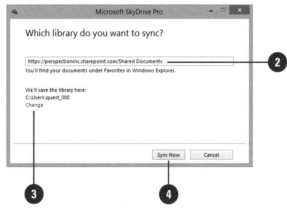

Work with SkyDrive Pro on SharePoint

1 In the desktop, click the **SkyDrive Pro** icon on the desktop taskbar, and then click **Open your SkyDrive Pro folder**.

2 Click **SkyDrive Pro** or **SharePoint** in the Navigate pane under Favorites, and then navigate to the folder you want to use.

3 To add or remove files, use the following:

◆ **Add.** Copy and paste or drag files to the folder.

◆ **Remove.** Select the files, and then click the **Delete** button on the Home tab.

The folders are synchronized for both locations, desktop and site.

4 To change syncing options, click the **SkyDrive Pro** icon on the desktop taskbar, and then click any of the following:

◆ **Sync a new library.** Use to add a new SharePoint site library.

◆ **Sync now.** Use to manually sync files.

◆ **Pause syncing.** Use to pause syncing.

◆ **View sync programs.** Use to open Office Upload Center.

◆ **Stop syncing a folder.** Use to select a folder to stop syncing.

5 To exit SkyDrive Pro, click the **SkyDrive Pro** icon on the desktop taskbar, and then click **Exit**.

See Also

See "Working with Office Tools" on page 366 for information on using Office 2013 Upload Center.

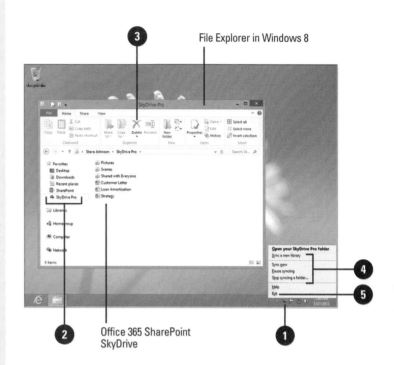

File Explorer in Windows 8

Office 365 SharePoint SkyDrive

Sharing Documents on SkyDrive

After you save an Office document to a SkyDrive (**New!**), you can share it with others. On the Share screen under the File tab, you can use three related options—Invite People (**New!**), Get a Sharing Link (**New!**), and Post to Social Networks (**New!**)—to allow others to access to a SkyDrive document. The Invite People option allows you to send an invitation for other to access the SkyDrive document. The Get a Sharing Link option lets you create links to the document you can share with others. And finally, the Post to Social Networks option lets you make blog posts on your connected social networks, such as Facebook, Linkedin, Twitter, Flickr, or Google.

Invite People to Share a SkyDrive Document

1. Open the Office document you want to share.

2. Click the **File** tab, click **Share**, and then click **Invite People**.

3. If the document is not saved to a SkyDrive, click the **Save To Cloud** button, and then save it to your SkyDrive. If prompted, sign-in to your account.

4. Enter a contact name or click the Address Book button to select a contact.

5. Click the **Access** list arrow, and then click **Can edit** or **Can view**.

6. Enter a message for the invitation.

7. Select or clear the **Require user to sign in before accessing document** check box.

8. Click **Share**.

    An email is sent to the contact with a link to access the SkyDrive document, and contact status appears at the bottom of the Share screen.

    You can click the contacts to send mail or instant messages.

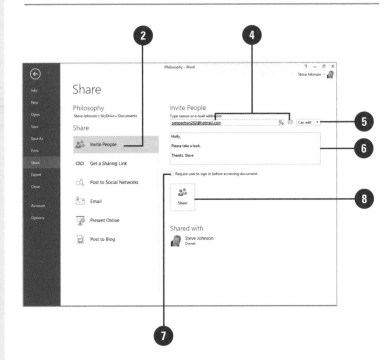

Get a Sharing Link to a SkyDrive Document

1. Open the Office document you want to share.

2. Click the **File** tab, click **Share**, and then click **Get a Sharing Link**.

3. Click the **Create Link** button for View Link or Edit Link.

   A link to the SkyDrive document appears and a status icon appears at the bottom of the Share screen.

4. Select and copy (Ctrl+C) the link, where you can paste it in a place, such as a network, where others can access it.

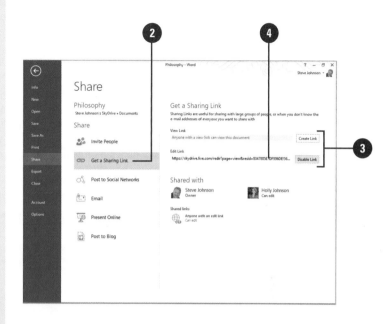

Post a SkyDrive Document Link to a Social Network

1. In Word and Excel, open the Office document you want to share.

2. Click the **File** tab, click **Share**, and then click **Post to Social Networks**.

   If you're not connected to your social networks, click the **Click here to connect social networks** link to make the connections you want, and then click **Refresh** button.

3. Select the check boxes for the connected social networks you want to post.

4. Click the **Access** list arrow, and then click **Can edit** or **Can view**.

5. Enter a message for the post.

6. Click the **Post** button.

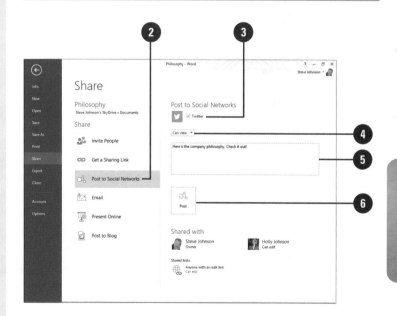

Accessing Documents on SkyDrive

Any Office document that resides on a SkyDrive (**New!**) can be accessed from any computer or device that has an Internet connection. You can access Office documents on SkyDrive using your web browser or a SkyDrive app on your desktop or device, including smartphones and tablets. In your web browser, you can navigate to a document and then open it in an Office Web App. An Office Web App provides a subset of the features in the desktop version. In your desktop or device, you can open the SkyDrive app, navigate to a document, and then open it in the Office Desktop App or Office Web App. If you don't have the app on your desktop or device, you can download it at *http://apps.live.com/skydrive*.

Access a SkyDrive in a Web Browser

1 Open your web browser, go to *www.skydrive.com*, and then sign in.

◆ You can also go to Windows Live, *www.live.com*, and then click the **SkyDrive** link.

2 Click a folder icon to navigate to the folder with the Office document.

3 To navigate back to a previous location, click a navigation link.

4 To change the view in the current folder, click a view button: **List** or **Tiles**.

5 To sort the documents in the current folder, click the **Sort by:** link, and then click **Name**, **Date modified**, **Date created**, or **Size**.

6 To open an Office document in the Office Web App, click the document icon.

◆ To open an Office document in the Office Desktop App, right-click the document, and then click **Open in <program>**.

◆ To exit and return, click the **File** tab, and then click **Exit**.

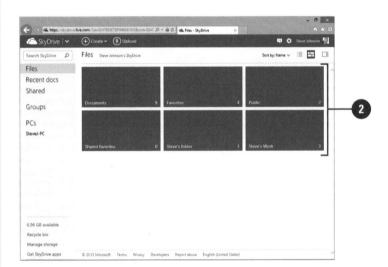

Access a SkyDrive from a Desktop or Device

① In the Start screen, click the **SkyDrive** tile.

   ◆ **Download.** You can download the SkyDrive app for devices at *http://apps.live.com/skydrive*.

② Click a folder icon to navigate to the folder with the Office document.

③ To navigate back to a previous location, click the **Back** button.

④ To change the view in the current folder, click the **Thumbnails** or **Details** button on the App bar.

⑤ To open an Office document in the Office Desktop App (desktop) or Web App (device), click the document icon.

   ◆ To exit, click the **Close** button (Desktop App or click the **File** tab, and then click **Exit** (Web App).

Did You Know?

You can manage storage space on a SkyDrive. SkyDrive comes with 7 GB of free space that you can use with your Microsoft account. You can view your storage usage and purchase more space if you want under options. In the SkyDrive app (Win 8), click Settings on the Charm bar, and then click Options. In your web browser, click the Settings button, and then click Options.

SkyDrive app on Windows 8

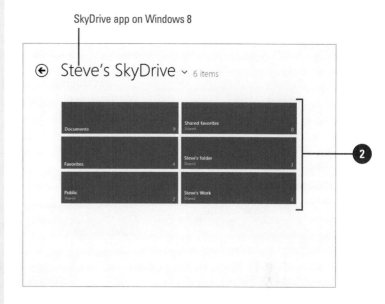

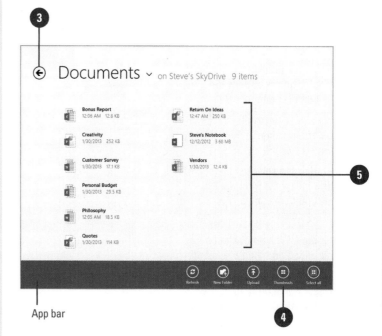

App bar

Managing Documents on SkyDrive

SkyDrive comes with four default folders: Documents, Favorites, Shared Favorites, and Public. The Documents and Favorites folders are private for your eyes only, while the Shared Favorites and Public folders are viewable by everyone in your SkyDrive (Windows Live) network. If you want to share your documents with others, then you need to add, move, or copy them to the Public folder. Instead of using the default folders, you can create and use your own. If you no longer need a file or folder, you can delete it. You cannot rename a default folder, however, you can rename the ones you create.

Work with SkyDrive Files or Folders in a Web browser

1 Open your web browser, go to *www.skydrive.com*, and then sign in.

2 Navigate to the folder where you want to manage files or folders.

3 To create a folder, click the **Create** list arrow, click **Folder**, type a name for the folder, and then press Enter or click outside the box.

4 Point to a file or folder to display a check box, and then click the check box to select it.

- ◆ You can select multiple files or folders to delete, move, or copy them.

5 To manage the selected file(s) or folder(s), click the **Manage** list arrow, and then click any of the following commands:

- ◆ **Rename.** Type a new name for the folder, and then press Enter or click outside the box.

- ◆ **Delete.** Click **Undo** to cancel it or click the **Close** button.

- ◆ **Move to.** Select the destination folder, and then click **Move**.

- ◆ **Copy to.** Select the destination folder, and then click **Copy**.

New folder

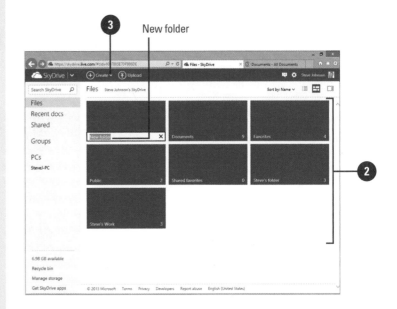

Work with SkyDrive Files or Folders from a Desktop

1 In the Start screen, click the **SkyDrive** tile.

◆ **Download.** You can download the SkyDrive app for devices at *http://apps.live.com/skydrive*.

2 Navigate to the folder where you want to manage files or folders.

3 To create a folder, click the **New Folder** on the App bar, type a name for the folder, and then click **Create folder**.

4 Right-click a file or folder to select it.

◆ You can select multiple files or folders to delete or move them.

5 To manage the selected file(s) or folder(s), click the **Manage** button on the App bar, and then click any of the following commands:

◆ **Rename.** Type a new name for the folder, and then click **Rename**.

◆ **Delete.** Click **Delete** to confirm the deletion.

◆ **Move.** Select the destination folder, and then click **Move here** on the Apps bar.

SkyDrive app on Windows 8

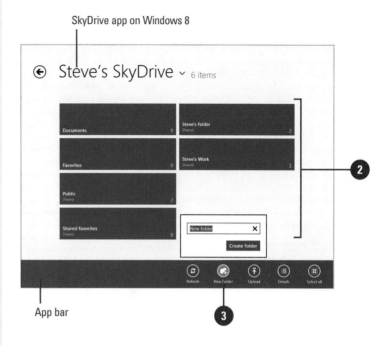

App bar

Downloading or Uploading Documents on SkyDrive

When you no longer want a document or folder of documents on SkyDrive or you want to share them with others, you can download them to your local drive on your computer. You can download individual files one at a time in their native Office file format, such as .docx, or a multiple selection of documents or an entire folder of documents as a zipped file. The .zip file format compresses all the files in the folder into a single file. You can open a zipped file on Microsoft Windows by double-clicking it and then using an Extract button or by using the Winzip.exe software, which you can download for free from the web at one of many download sites, such as *www.download.com*. If you have one or more documents or entire folder of documents on a local drive, and want to include on your SkyDrive, you can upload them to the cloud site, so you can access them from other computers and devices.

Download or Upload a File or Folder on SkyDrive

1. Open your web browser, go to *www.skydrive.com*, and then sign in.

2. Navigate to the folder where you want to download or upload files or folders.

3. To upload files or folders to the SkyDrive, click the **Upload** button, select the files or folders you want, and then click **Open**.

4. Point to a file or folder to display a check box, and then click the check box to select it. You can select multiple files or folders.

5. To download the selected file(s) or folder(s), click the **Download** button.

6. Click **Save**, navigate to the location where you want to download the file, and then click **Save**.

   The document is downloaded to the specified folder.

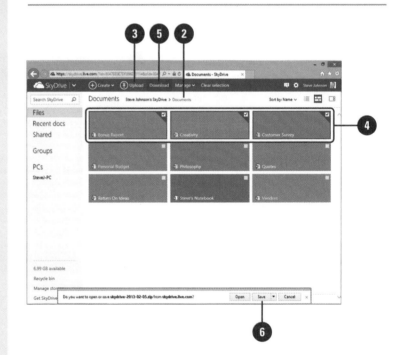

Creating Office Documents on SkyDrive

When you're working on SkyDrive, you create a new Office document. You can create an Excel workbook, a PowerPoint presentation, a Word document, or an OneNote notebook. This option allows you to create a new Office document on a computer that doesn't have the Microsoft Office software. So, if you're working on a different computer while you're on the road that doesn't have the Office programs installed and you need to create a new document to get some work done, you can do it online on SkyDrive.

Create Office Documents on SkyDrive

1. Open your web browser, go to *www.skydrive.com*, and then sign in.

2. Navigate to the folder where you want to create a new Office document.

3. Click the **Create** list arrow, and then click a document option:

   ◆ **Word document.**

   ◆ **Excel workbook.**

   ◆ **PowerPoint presentation.**

   ◆ **OneNote notebook.**

4. Type a name for the document.

5. Click **Create**.

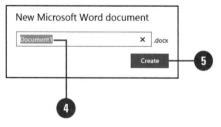

Sending Links to Documents on SkyDrive

After you upload your Office documents to a folder on SkyDrive, you can share access to them with others for review with Office Web Apps. You can share access to individual Office documents or an entire folder on SkyDrive by sending a link in e-mail, posting a link in Twitter, Facebook, LinkedIn or other online services (**New!**), or creating a link (**New!**) and sending it to those you want to access it. In addition, you can also embed a link in a blog or web page, so others can access the folder. The recipients of the link can click it to access the documents on SkyDrive.

Send a Link to a File or Folder

1 Open your web browser, go to *www.skydrive.com*, and then sign in.

2 Navigate to the folder with the documents you want to share.

3 Point to a file or folder to display a check box, and then click the check box to select it. You can select multiple files or folders.

4 Click the **Sharing** button.

5 For a folder, click **Share this folder**. To cancel, click **Don't share this folder**.

6 Click **Send email**, **Post to <service>** (**New!**), or **Get a link** (**New!**) to select a send method.

7 Specify the following for the selected method:

◆ **Send email.** Specify recipients, select or clear options to edit or require sign in, and then click **Share**.

◆ **Post to <service>.** Select the check boxes for the services you want, enter a message, select or clear the option to edit, and then click **Post**.

◆ **Get a Link.** Click **Create** for View only or View and edit, or click **Make public** for everyone to access. Press Ctrl+C to copy the link, and then click **Done**. You can paste the link for others to use.

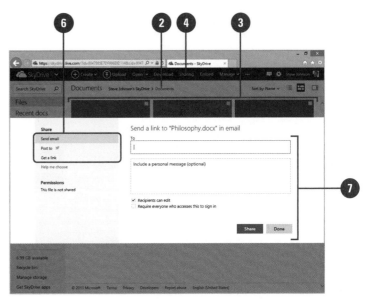

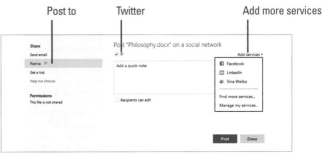

Post to   Twitter   Add more services

Get a link

Embed a Link to a File or Folder in a Blog or Web Page

1. Open your web browser, go to *www.skydrive.com*, and then sign in.

2. Navigate to the folder with the documents you want to share.

3. Point to a file or folder to display a check box, and then click the check box to select it. You can select multiple files or folders.

4. Click the **Embed** button (**New!**).

5. Click **Generate**.

6. Click the **Copy** link to copy the embed code to the Clipboard.

7. Click **Done**.

8. Paste the code into a blog post or web page.

   ◆ **Blog.** Create a blog post in a blogger, such as Windows Live Writer, and then paste the code.

   ◆ **Web Page.** Open a web page in an HTML editor, and then paste the code.

9. Open your web browser, display the blog post or web page, and then click the link to the shared folder or document on SkyDrive.

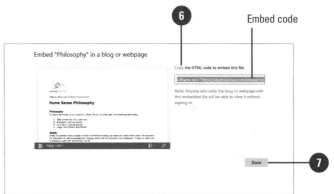

Embed code

Comparing the Office Desktop App to the Web App

An Office Web App provides a subset of the features in the desktop version. Each Office Web App comes with a scaled-down version of the desktop Ribbon and Quick Access Toolbar. The Web Apps Ribbon typically comes with a File tab, Home tab, Insert tab, and View tab. Within each tab, you get a sub- set of commands on the desktop Ribbon. There are no contextual tabs in the Office Web Apps. The Quick Access Toolbar appears above the Ribbon and contains just the Undo and Redo buttons. The content area for each of the Office Web Apps is similar to the desk- top version.

Desktop App

File tab
Click to access file commands.

Quick Access Toolbar
Click to access commands on this customizable toolbar.

Tabs
Click to access tools and commands.

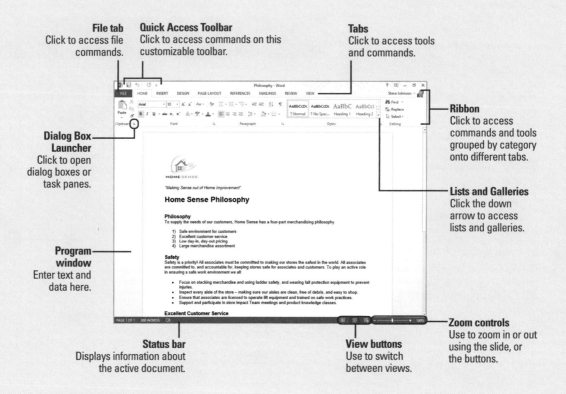

Dialog Box Launcher
Click to open dialog boxes or task panes.

Program window
Enter text and data here.

Ribbon
Click to access commands and tools grouped by category onto different tabs.

Lists and Galleries
Click the down arrow to access lists and galleries.

Zoom controls
Use to zoom in or out using the slide, or the buttons.

Status bar
Displays information about the active document.

View buttons
Use to switch between views.

Web App (Edit in Browser)

Quick Access Toolbar
Click to access commands
on a toolbar.

Tabs
Click to access tools
and commands.

File tab
Click to access
file commands.

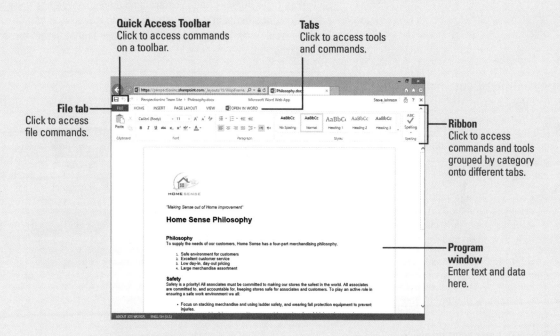

Ribbon
Click to access
commands and tools
grouped by category
onto different tabs.

**Program
window**
Enter text and data
here.

Web App (View in Browser)

File tab
Click to access
file commands.

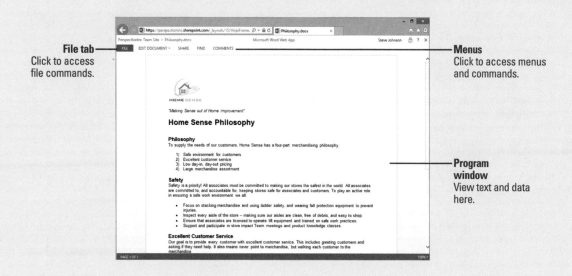

Menus
Click to access menus
and commands.

**Program
window**
View text and data
here.

Working with Office Web Apps

An Office Web App allows you to work with an Office document stored on a SkyDrive (**New!**) or SharePoint site in a web browser and on different mobile devices—such as Windows Phones, Apple iOS (iPhones, and iPads), BlackBerry, and Android. Office Web Apps provide a web-based version of Word, Excel, PowerPoint, and OneNote (**New!**). For a SharePoint site, Access and Lync are also available. You can view or edit Office documents in a web browser using a Web App or in the Desktop App. An Office Web App provides a subset of the features in the desktop version.

View an Office Document Using Office Web Apps

1. Open your web browser, and then go to *www.skydrive.com* or SharePoint Team Site web address.

   ◆ **From E-mail or Posts.** If you received an e-mail or a post with a sharing link, click the link to access the document.

2. Navigate to the folder with the document you want to open.

3. Click the Office document you want to view.

   The Web App opens, displaying the document.

4. Use the menus and tools to navigate and view the document.

   ◆ **File management.** You can use the File tab to edit, save as, print, or share the document.

   ◆ **Edit document.** Click the **Edit \<document\>** menu, and then click **Edit in \<program\>** or **Edit in \<program\> Web App.**

5. To exit, click the **File** tab, and then click **Exit** (Web App) or click the **Close** button (desktop program).

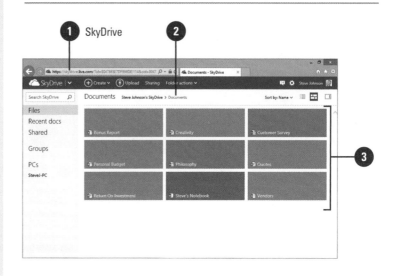

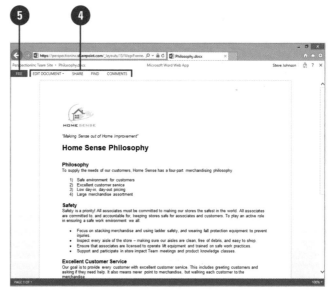

Edit an Office Document Using Office Web Apps

1. Open your web browser, and then go to *www.skydrive.com* or SharePoint Team Site web address.

   ◆ **From E-mail or Posts.** If you received an e-mail or a post with a sharing link, click the link to access the document.

2. Navigate to the folder with the document you want to open.

3. Click the Office document you want to edit.

   The Web App opens, displaying the document.

4. Click the **Edit <document>** menu, and then click **Edit in <program> Web App.**

   ◆ **Edit in Desktop App.** Click the **Edit <document>** menu, and then click **Edit in <program>.**

5. Use the Ribbon tabs to make changes to the Office document; any changes in a Web App are automatically saved.

   ◆ **View Document in Reading View.** To view the document in non editing mode, click the **View** tab, and then click the **Reading View** button.

6. To close the document and switch to work local in the Desktop App, click the **Open in <program>** button.

7. To exit, click the **File** tab, and then click **Exit** (Web App) or click the **Close** button (desktop program).

SkyDrive

Saving or Printing Documents in Office Web Apps

As you work in an Office document in a web browser, an Office Web App automatically saves your work, so you don't have to do it. However, you might want to download a version to your local computer or network location as a backup or save a copy (in the Excel Web App) of a document in the original location with a different name. Besides saving an Office document, you can also print it to a printer (in the Excel Web App) or create a printable PDF (in the Word Web App and PowerPoint Web App).

Save or Download an Office Document in an Office Web App

1. Open your web browser, and then go to *www.skydrive.com* or SharePoint Team Site web address.

2. Navigate to the folder with the document you want to open.

3. Click the Office document you want to edit.

   The Web App opens, displaying the document.

4. Click the **Edit <document>** menu, and then click **Edit in <program> Web App.**

5. Click the **File** tab, click **Save As**, and then click an option (options vary depending on the Office Web App):

   - **Download.** Downloads the entire document to your computer.

   - **Save a Copy.** In Excel, saves a copy of the workbook in the same online folder as the original.

6. Click **Save**.

7. Navigate to the location where you want to download the file, and then click **Save**.

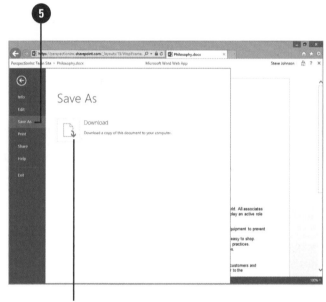

Download button

Print or PDF an Office Document in an Office Web App

1. Open your web browser, and then go to *www.skydrive.com* or SharePoint Team Site web address.

2. Navigate to the folder with the document you want to open.

3. Click the Office document you want to edit.

   The Web App opens, displaying the document.

4. Click the **Edit <document>** menu, and then click **Edit in <program> Web App.**

5. Click the **File** tab, click **Print**, and then click an option (options vary depending on the Office Web App):

   ◆ **Print to PDF.** In Word and PowerPoint, creates saves a copy of the document in the same online folder as the original. Click a link to view the PDF or click **Close.**

   ◆ **Print.** In Excel, select an option to print the current selection or entire sheet, click **Print**, and then click **Print** again in the web browser window.

Print to PDF

Print to a printer in Excel

Co-authoring Documents with Office Web Apps

If you're working with an Office document stored on a SharePoint site, multiple authors can collaborate on the same document at the same time (**New!**), known as co-authoring. Co-authoring allows you to see who is editing the document and where they are working in the Status bar or on the File tab Info screen. With Office Web Apps you can simultaneously edit documents, known as co-authoring. Co-authoring allows two or more people to work on a document at the same time in real-time without the need to save and reject or accept changes. If two people edit the same thing, each Office Web App deals with differently. Before you can co-author a document, you need to send a link in e-mail, online service post, such as Twitter, Facebook, or LinkedIn, to those you want to share the Office document or embed a link in a blog or web page, so others can access it.

Co-author an Office Document on SharePoint

1. Have each author open the Office document from the library on the SharePoint site.

   ◆ **From Office.** Click the **File** tab, click **Open**, click the SharePoint site, click **Browse**, and then open the document.

   ◆ **From Web browser.** Start your web browser, go to the SharePoint site address, and then open the document.

   ◆ **From E-mail or Posts.** If you received an e-mail or a post with a sharing link, click the link to access the document.

2. If prompted, sign in to the SharePoint site.

   The Web App opens, displaying the document.

3. For a Web App, click the **Edit <document>** menu, and then click **Edit in <program>** or **Edit in <program> Web App.**

① Click to display the menu

Use to share a link to the document

Options to send a link to the document

4. To view who is editing the documents, click the **Authors** button on the Status bar or click the **File** tab, and then click **Info**.

- On the Share screen, you can use the **Share with People** button to send a message.

5. Each author can edit the document using the program tools.

- **Comments and Track Changes.** In Word, PowerPoint, and Excel (desktop), each author can insert and show comments and enable track changes during editing so all the authors can see the changes being made.

6. To exit, click the **File** tab, and then click **Exit** (Web App) or click the **Close** button (desktop program).

See Also

See "Working with Office Web Apps" on page 448 for more information on using Office Web Apps.

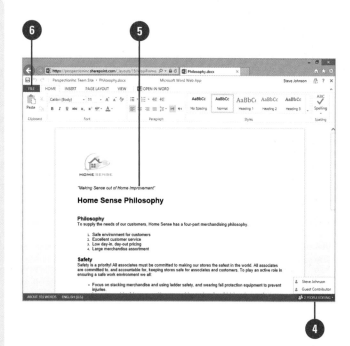

For Your Information

Roundtripping with Office Web Apps

When you edit or view an Office document with an Office Web App, the file format doesn't change or affect the content of the file. In other words, you can upload an Office file to the web, make changes using an Office Web App, download the file back to your desktop, and then make changes to it using your desktop Office App without any problems. This is called **roundtripping**. Any unsupported features in the Office Web App doesn't affect the Office file during a roundtrip.

Blocking Co-authoring Documents

Co-authoring allows multiple people to edit an Office document stored on a SharePoint site. When multiple people open the same Office document from a SharePoint site, the number of authors editing it appears in the Status bar, which you can click to find out who is currently editing it. If the item is not on the Status bar, you can right-click the Status bar to display it. If you don't want to let multiple authors edit all or part of a Word document, all you need to do is select the content in the document and then use the Block Authors button on the Review tab to prevent others from making changes. At any time, you can release all the blocked areas, so others can edit it.

Block Co-authoring of a Document on SharePoint

① In Word, open the document from the SharePoint site.

◆ You can also open a local Word document, and then save it to the SharePoint site.

② Select the text you want to prevent others from changing.

③ Click the **Review** tab.

④ Click the **Block Authors** button, and then click **Block Authors**.

The selected area is marked with an icon and dashed outline to let others know the area is blocked.

⑤ To unlock all blocked areas, click the **Block Authors** button, and then click **Release All of My Blocked Areas**.

⑥ Click the **File** tab, and then click **Save** to apply the changes.

See Also

See "Co-authoring Document with Office Web Apps" on page 454 for more information on co-authoring documents on SharePoint.

Blocked content indicator

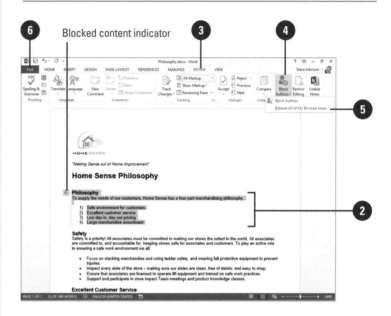

New! Features

Microsoft Access 2013

Microsoft Access 2013 is a powerful database program that enables you to easily compose and edit desktop databases and web apps for local or online use. Access 2013 contains many new tools specifically designed to improve the way you interact with the program, and the way you collaborate with others in organizing and collecting data. With enhancements to the user interface, and the addition of web app development and deployment tools, you can accomplish a variety of business or personal tasks more easily in Access 2013.

Only New Features

If you're already familiar with Microsoft Access 2010, you can access and download all the tasks in this book with Microsoft Access 2013 New Features to help make your transition to the new version simple and smooth. The Microsoft Access 2013 New Features as well as other 2010 to 2013 transition helpers are available on the web at *www.perspection.com.*

What's New

If you're searching for what's new in Access 2013, just look for the icon: New!. The new icon appears in the table of contents and throughout this book so you can quickly and easily identify a new or improved feature in Access 2013. The following is a brief description of each new feature and it's location in this book.

Office 2013

- ◆ **Start Screen (p. 4, 12)** Office programs open to a Start screen where you have options to open an existing document or create a new blank document (database) or one from a template.

- ◆ **Back Button (p. 7)** The File tab provides a Back button that lets you return back to the main screen for the Office program.

- ◆ **New Screen (p. 12)** The New command on the File tab opens to the New screen where you have options to create a new blank document (database) or one from a template.

- **Office 365 and SharePoint (p. 12, 14, 26, 426-434)** SharePoint server is an organizational cloud storage, sharing, and tracking system with customizable apps on the web. Office 365 is a subscription-based Microsoft web site with SharePoint services that allows you to take advantage of expanded cloud and sharing capabilities.

- **SkyDrive (p. 14, 26, 426-431, 436-444)** SkyDrive is a cloud-based online storage system that requires a Microsoft account to access. You can open and save files from a SkyDrive directly from Office, and share them with others. In addition, you can use three related options—Invite People, Get a Sharing Link, and Post to Social Networks—to allow others to access to a SkyDrive document.

- **Pin Recent Files or Folders (p. 14-15)** If you frequently open a specific file or folder, you can pin a recently used file or folder to the Start, Open, or Save As screens. If you frequently use a template, you can pin the template to the Start or New screen.

- **Windows Help (p. 20-21)** The web browser-like Help Viewer allows you to browse a catalog of topics to locate information, use popular searches, or enter your own phrases to search for information.

- **User Account (p. 25)** Office integrates a user account that lets you connect to online services, such as SkyDrive, Office 365 SharePoint, YouTube, Facebook, Linkedin, Twitter, and Flickr. Within any Office 2013 program, you can add, modify or switch accounts or sign out entirely.

- **Online Services (p. 25, 26)** You can connect to and integrate online services into Office programs. The online services include SkyDrive and Office 365 SharePoint for storage, Flickr and YouTube for images and video, and Facebook, LinkedIn, and Twitter for sharing and messaging.

- **Document Windows (p. 28)** Office documents open in their own program window instead of one program window and a collection of individual windows to make it easier to display several windows at once.

- **No Exit Command (p. 28)** Except for Outlook, the File tab doesn't have an Exit command. Since each document opens in its own program window, it's not needed. To exit, you click the Close button on the program window.

- **Templates (p. 50-54)** When you save a template in the default Access template folder, the database template becomes available on the Start or New screen under the Personal tab, and the application part becomes available on the Applications Parts button on the Create tab.

- **Excel Data Model (p. 316-317)** You can add multiple tables in a PivotTable using the Excel Data Model. A Data Model is a collection of tables and their relationship between the data. When you have more than one table and a common column in a Data Model, you can create a relationship between them that lets you build PivotTables and other reports using fields from each table.

- **Save Options (p. 358)** Office adds a new save option, which allows you to use (default) or bypass the Backstage when opening or saving files.

- **Office Background and Theme (p. 361)** You can select an Office program window background and theme in General Options.

- **Hardware Graphics Acceleration (p. 362)**   If your system includes a hardware graphics accelerator for gaming, it may create problems in the Access window. You can disable hardware graphics acceleration to fix the problem.

- **Touch/Mouse Mode (p. 363)**   To make Office easier to use with a touch screen, each Office program provides Touch/Mouse Mode, which adds or removes more space between commands on the Ribbon.

- **Office Web Apps (p. 446-454)**   An Office Web App allows you to work with an Office document stored on a SkyDrive or SharePoint site in a web browser or on different mobile devices. Office Web Apps provide a web-based version of Word, Excel, PowerPoint, and OneNote.

Office Tools

- **Upload Center (p. 366-367)**   The Upload Center shows you pending uploads, recently uploaded files and all cached files from a server in one location.

- **Spreadsheet or Database Compare (p. 366-367)**   If you need to compare two Excel spreadsheets or Access databases, you can use the Spreadsheet Compare or Database Compare tools.

- **Lync Recording Manager (p. 366-367)**   If not everyone is able to attend an online Lync meeting, you can record the session to play it back later. You can manage the recording with the Lync Recording Manager tool.

- **Lync (p. 366-367)**   Microsoft Lync is an instant messaging program that allows you to send and receive instant messages, hold video chats, meetings, and share files.

- **Telemetry Log or Dashboard (p. 366-367)**   Telemetry Log records Office events in an Excel spreadsheet to help you troubleshoot problems. Telemetry Database is an Excel spreadsheet that connects to an SQL database to collect client data from other sources in a shared folder.

- **SkyDrive Pro (p. 366-367)**   With SkyDrive Pro, you can connect and synchronize your SkyDrive cloud storage on a SharePoint site with your desktop.

- **Update Office (p. 368)**   With Windows 8, you can automatically get updates to Office 2013 along with the operating system.

Access 2013

- **Web App Database (p. 12, 400-401)**   A web app is a browser-based database app that uses SQL Azure or SQL server. A web app allows users to enter and work with data from a browser. You can use the Start or New screen to create a custom web app database or one from a template. A web app resides on a SharePoint server or Office 365 SharePoint site.

- **Web App Templates and Table Templates (p. 12-13, 400-401, 404-405)**   When you create a web app from a template, it already contains predefined table templates, however, you can add your own templates and custom tables.

- **Application Part Templates (p. 50-54)** When you save a template in the default Access template folder, the database template becomes available on the Start or New screen under the Personal tab, and the application part becomes available on the Applications Parts button on the Create tab.

- **Text and Memo Data Types (p. 78, 85)** The Text data type has been renamed to Short Text and the Memo data type has been renamed Long Text.

- **Open a Web App (p. 402-403)** You can open the web app in your browser from Access by using the Launch App View button or within your browser by entering the URL for the SharePoint site.

- **Import Data in a Web App (p. 404-405)** If you have existing data in an external source, such as an Access database, Microsoft Excel file, SQL Server/ODBC source, text files, or SharePoint List, you can import it into a web app.

- **View and Edit Data in a Web App (p. 406-407)** With the built-in views, Access includes an Action Bar with buttons for adding, editing, saving, and deleting records. As you enter data, AutoComplete looks up data from related tables or drill through links to let you view details about a related item.

- **Custom Views in Web Apps (p. 408-409)** Instead of using a built-in view, you can create a customized view. When you add a custom view, you specify a view name, select a view type, and the record source. The view types include List Details, Datasheet, Summary, or Blank.

- **Change Properties in a Web App (p. 410-413)** When you select a table or control, you can change property settings in three areas: Data, Formatting, and Actions.

- **Action Bar in Web Apps (p. 410-411, 414-415)** In your browser, you can use Action Bar buttons to view, enter, and edit data on the web. If you want to add functionality, you can add buttons to the Action Bar to execute a macro action as well as change properties.

- **Database Objects in Web Apps (p. 416)** In addition to the custom web related features you can include in a web app, you can also add desktop database objects to a web app. You can create a Query, Blank View, List View, Datasheet View, Macro, Data Macro, or On Start Macro.

- **Navigation Pane in Web Apps (p. 417)** The Navigation pane is a central place for accessing all the objects in a web app, just like with a desktop database.

- **Launch a Web App (p. 418-19)** You can open a web app from Access or your browser by using the Launch App View button or within your browser by entering the URL for the SharePoint site.

- **Enter Data in a Web App (p. 418-419)** As you enter data in a web app, AutoComplete looks up data from related tables or drill through links to let you view details about a related item.

- **Package a Web App (p. 420)** You can create a package file of your web app to make it easier to distribute and share on a SharePoint or Office 365 site.

- **Use a Web App on SharePoint (p. 421-422)** In addition to opening a web app from Access or your browser, you can also access and work with a web app data from a SharePoint site.

◆ **Use a Web App on SharePoint (p. 423)**   You can add web apps from the SharePoint Store to your SharePoint site. After you install a web app to your SharePoint site from the SharePoint Store, you can use it online as well as customize it back in Access.

What Happened To . . .

◆ **Exit Command**   The command has been removed from the File tab. Since each database opens in its own program window, it's not needed. To exit, you click the Close button on the program window.

◆ **Microsoft Office Picture Manager**   Picture Manager has been replaced by Windows Photo Gallery.

◆ **Microsoft Clip Organizer**   Clip Organizer has been replaced by Online Pictures, which allows you to insert content from the Office.com Clip Art collection and other resources, such as Bing Image/Video search, Flickr, and your SkyDrive or Facebook page.

◆ **Access Data Projects (ADP)**   The option to open Access Data Project files has been removed.

◆ **Access support of Jet 3.x IISAM**   The ability to open Access 97 databases has been removed. You need to open an Access 97 database in Access 2007 or 2010, and then save it in the .accdb file format.

◆ **PivotCharts and PivotTables**   The ability to create PivotCharts and PivotTables has been removed with Office Web Components.

◆ **Text and Memo Data Types**   The Text data type has been renamed to Short Text and the Memo data type has been renamed Long Text.

◆ **dBASE Support**   The ability to connect to an external dBASE database has been removed.

◆ **Smart Tags Property**   The Smart Tags (Action Tags) has been removed as a property in table.

◆ **Access Data Collection**   The ability to create new Data Collection forms has been removed. However, you can process data collection forms that were created in earlier versions of Access.

◆ **Access 2003 Toolbar and Menus**   The ability to bypass the Ribbon interface and show Access 2003 toolbars and menus has been removed.

◆ **Access Replication Options**   Replication options for .mdb files in Access 2010 or earlier are no longer available.

◆ **Access Source Code Control**   The Developer Source Code Control has been removed as an add-in.

◆ **Access Three-State Workflow**   The entry point for workflow has been removed. In user interface macros, the Workflow commands are no longer available.

◆ **Access Upsizing Wizard**   The Upsizing Wizard has been removed.

Microsoft Office Specialist

About the MOS Program

The Microsoft Office Specialist (MOS) certification is the globally recognized standard for validating expertise with the Microsoft Office suite of business productivity programs. Earning an MOS certificate acknowledges you have the expertise to work with Microsoft Office programs. To earn the MOS certification, you must pass a certification exam for the Microsoft Office desktop applications of Microsoft Word, Excel, PowerPoint, Outlook, Access, OneNote, SharePoint, or Office 365. (The availability of Microsoft Office Specialist certification exams varies by program, program version, and language. Visit *www.microsoft.com* and search on *MOS* or *Microsoft Office Specialist* for exam availability and more information about the program.) The Microsoft Office Specialist program is the only Microsoft-approved program in the world for certifying proficiency with Microsoft Office programs.

What Does This Logo Mean?

It means this book has been approved by the Microsoft Office Specialist program to be certified courseware for learning Microsoft Access 2013 and preparing for the certification exam. This book will prepare you for the Microsoft Office Specialist exam for Microsoft Access 2013. Each certification level, either Core or Expert, has a set of objectives, which are organized into broader skill sets. Content that pertains to a Microsoft Office Specialist objective is identified with the following objective number and the specific pages throughout this book:

AC13S-1.1
AC13S-2.2

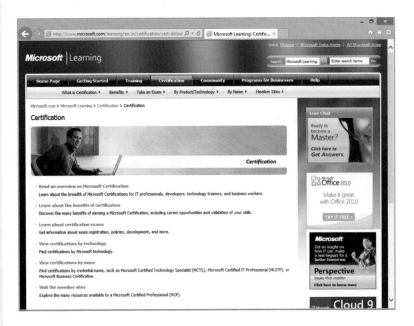

Preparing for a MOS Exam

Every Microsoft Office Specialist certification exam is developed from a list of objectives based on how Microsoft Office programs are actually used in the workplace. The list of objectives determine the scope of each exam, so they provide you with the information you need to prepare for MOS certification. Microsoft Office Specialist Approved Courseware, including the On Demand series, is reviewed and approved on the basis of its coverage of the objectives. To prepare for the certification exam, you

should review and perform each task identified with a MOS objective to confirm that you can meet the requirements for the exam.

Taking a MOS Exam

The Microsoft Office Specialist certification exams are not written exams. Instead, the exams are performance-based examinations that allow you to interact with a "live"

Office program as you complete a series of objective-based tasks. All the standard ribbons, tabs, toolbars, and keyboard shortcuts are available during the exam. Microsoft Office Specialist exams for Office 2013 programs consist of 25 to 35 questions, each of which requires you to complete one or more tasks using the Office program for which you are seeking certification. A typical exam takes from 45 to 60 minutes. Passing percentages range from 70 to 80 percent correct.

The Exam Experience

After you fill out a series of information screens, the testing software starts the exam and the Office program. The test questions appear in the exam dialog box in the lower right corner of the screen.

- The timer starts when the first question appears and displays the remaining exam time at the top of the exam dialog box. If the timer and the counter are distracting, you can click the timer to remove the display.

- The counter at the top of the exam dialog box tracks how many questions you have completed and how many remain.

- If you think you have made a mistake, you can click the Reset button to restart the question. The Reset button does not restart the entire exam or extend the exam time limit.

- When you complete a question, click the Next button to move to the next question. It is not possible to move back to a previous question on the exam.

- If the exam dialog box gets in your way, you can click the Minimize button in the upper right corner of the exam dialog box to hide it, or you can drag the title bar to another part of the screen to move it.

Tips for Taking an Exam

- Carefully read and follow all instructions provided in each question.

- Make sure all steps in a task are completed before proceeding to the next exam question.

- Enter requested information as it appears in the instructions without formatting unless you are explicitly requested otherwise.

- Close all dialog boxes before proceeding to the next exam question unless you are specifically instructed otherwise.

- Do not leave tables, boxes, or cells "active" unless instructed otherwise.

- Do not cut and paste information from the exam interface into the program.

- When you print a document from an Office program during the exam, nothing actually gets printed.

- Errant keystrokes or mouse clicks do not count against your score as long as you achieve the correct end result. You are scored based on the end result, not the method you use to achieve it. However, if a specific method is explicitly requested, you need to use it to get credit for the results.

- The overall exam is timed, so taking too long on individual questions may leave you without enough time to complete the entire exam.

- If you experience computer problems during the exam, immediately notify a testing center administrator to restart your exam where you were interrupted.

Exam Results

At the end of the exam, a score report appears indicating whether you passed or failed the exam. An official certificate is mailed to successful candidates in approximately two to three weeks.

Getting More Information

To learn more about the Microsoft Office Specialist program, read a list of frequently asked questions, and locate the nearest testing center, visit:

www.microsoft.com

For a more detailed list of Microsoft Office Specialist program objectives, visit:

www.perspection.com

Index

i

A